SHAKESPEARE
MATTERS

SHAKESPEARE MATTERS

History, Teaching, Performance

Edited by
Lloyd Davis

DELAWARE

Newark: University of Delaware Press
London: Associated University Presses

Associated University Presses
2010 Eastpark Boulevard
Cranbury, NJ 08512

Associated University Presses
Unit 304, The Chandlery
50 Westminster Bridge Road
London SE1 7QY, England

Associated University Presses
P.O. Box 338, Port Credit
Mississauga, Ontario
Canada L5G 4L8

The paper used in this publication meets the requirements of the American National Standard for Permanence of Paper for Printed Library Materials Z39.48-1984.

Library of Congress Cataloging-in-Publication Data

Shakespeare matters : history, teaching, performance / edited by Lloyd Davis.
    p.   cm.
Includes bibliographical references and index.
ISBN 0-87413-790-X (alk. paper)
    1. Shakespeare, William, 1564–1616—Criticism and interpretation—History.   2. Shakespeare, William, 1564–1616—Study and teaching.   3. Shakespeare, William, 1564–1616—Stage history.   I. Davis, Lloyd, 1959–
PR2965 .S43   2003
822.3'3—dc21   2002151283

Contents

Acknowledgments

A GREAT DEBT OF THANKS IS DUE TO ALL THE PEOPLE WHO ATTENDED the 1998 Australian and New Zealand Shakespeare Association Conference at the University of Queensland and made it a memorable event. This volume represents some of the dialogue and debate that took place at the conference over Shakespeare's diverse roles and value in historical and contemporary cultures. I am especially grateful to all the contributors to this collection for their support and interest in the project, and also to Richard Fotheringham for helping me organize the 1998 conference.

Donald C. Mell, at the University of Delaware Press, and Julien Yoseloff and Christine Retz, at Associated University Presses, have offered much help and advice on putting the collection together. Kim Wilkins provided indispensable research assistance.

My greatest support and encouragement come from Julia, Charlotte, and Joseph.

*　　*　　*

SHAKESPEARE
MATTERS

Introduction: Shakespearean Cultures

Lloyd Davis

AT THE BEGINNING OF THE TWENTY-FIRST CENTURY, INTERNATIONAL interest in Shakespeare's work has never been greater. Numerous films, proliferating websites and CD-ROM packages, significant new publishing series of the plays, poems, and critical studies abound. Shakespeare's name continues to feature in numerous culture industries both in- and outside the academy. The essays in this volume exemplify the range and energy of these interests. They span literary and dramatic criticism, theater and textual studies, teaching and pedagogy—in short, a microcosm of the wide-ranging concerns and approaches that are the hallmark of contemporary Shakespeare studies. The authors teach, research, and perform in different countries and contexts: Australia, New Zealand, Canada, Korea, Singapore, the United States and the United Kingdom. Their varied backgrounds afford challenging and innovative viewpoints on the way that Shakespeare and his plays continue to be understood and reproduced in many cultural contexts.[1]

The collected essays address three significant areas in current Shakespeare studies: the complex effects of social and historical meanings in the plays; the notable function of Shakespeare's work in educational practices and traditions; and the plays' pivotal role, as performance and literary texts, in conceptualizing theatricality, textuality, and authorship from the sixteenth century to the present. In each area, the authors discuss numerous issues by applying and debating key approaches to Shakespeare's work, including new historicism, cultural materialism, feminism, and postcolonialism. Linking the three areas is a recurring set of critical concepts and positions. Whether the immediate issues in question are the effects of the market in the early modern period (Lindley), the impacts of class and ethnicity in education (O'Malley), or the tensions among editing, authorship, and subjectivity (Bedford), these chapters display a collective intent to explore the

13

historical and cultural weight of Shakespeare's work. In doing so, the authors range across such topics as rhetoric, memory, and subjectivity (Cohen, Beehler); sexuality and status (Walker, Blake, Davis); technology and pedagogy (Mullin, Estok, Steen); and postcolonialism and late-twentieth-century politics (Kelly, Maclennan). A recurrent focus on the cultural implications of Shakespeare's work—those dimensions that on the one hand motivate his continued popularity but on the other risk being effaced by its naturalizing force—integrates all authors' work across these areas. It takes us to the heart of why Shakespeare continues to *matter* in the multiple cultures and subcultures of both the critical, educational, and theatrical spheres, and the wider community to which they contribute significantly.

The essays examine the values and uses assumed by Shakespeare's work, in particular historical contexts and institutions, in relation to distinct cultural practices from acting to editing to teaching. All the authors consider the reciprocal impacts between the plays and the multiple settings around them, which include the many differing circumstances in which they were first written and performed, and have since been repeatedly reproduced. The volume identifies these contexts in three interacting ways—the historical, the pedagogical, and the performative—and each is treated through a distinct section: "History: Materialism, Gender, and Language;" "Teaching: Technology, Pedagogy, and Ideology;" and "Performance: Texts and Productions." At the same time, there are many lines of analysis that continue across these sections. For example, ideologies of gender and class are crucial educational issues as much as they are key elements in representations of the early modern period (hence Walker's, O'Malley's, and Bowen's essays reiterate and adapt interpretive positions raised by Howard, Davis, and Blake). Market forces and materialist concerns drive the histories of Shakespeare editing and performance as much as they shape Elizabethan and Jacobean social formations (as Day's, Maclennan's, and Kelly's chapters show by applying the kinds of historicized accounts offered by Lindley and Madelaine to more recent contexts and productions).

Each section of the volume opens with an essay that addresses significant themes in its own right but also serves to initiate dialogue for and among the ensuing chapters. Jean Howard analyzes key issues and possible problems in materialist and historicist criticism of Shakespeare. Michael Mullin discusses the ways in which Shakespeare and modern interactive technologies can combine in teaching, along with their potential effects for faculty and students. Richard Madelaine considers various complications within historical understandings of the social and theatrical conditions in which the plays of Shakespeare and his contemporaries were performed. The essays that follow the opening chapters expand on issues under each section's topic. Those in the first section discuss early modern conceptions of history, materialism, language, and sexuality in relation to the plays. The chapters in the second section examine the pedagogical functions that Shakespeare fulfills in various institutions, including community colleges, universities, and prisons. The potential role of Shakespearean drama in gender and environmentally aware pedagogies is also examined, as are the educational effects of focusing on Shakespeare to the exclusion of his contemporaries, especially female writers from the sixteenth and seventeenth centuries. The third and final section studies a number of performance and textual issues: the role of theatricality in Elizabethan culture, the infrastructure of early modern acting companies, debates over the editing of Shakespeare's plays, and reproductions of Shakespeare in modern ideological contexts in Britain and in Australia. Throughout, the volume addresses and expands our understanding of the cultural politics and poetics of Shakespeare's work in literary, theatrical, and educational history.[2]

The first section is "History: Materialism, Gender, and Language," and Jean E. Howard's essay "Material Shakespeare/ Materialist Shakespeare" opens the collection by contending that Marxist modes of analysis are still relevant—in fact are crucial—to the exploration of early modern culture. Howard argues that the current fetishization of material culture as an object of investigation is often confused with materialist analyses of cultural productions. At the same time she discusses the ways in which Marxist modes of analysis have to be transformed—through dialogue and interaction with other critical discourses, including feminism, postcolonialism, and queer studies—if they are to remain adequate to current conditions. In discussing these issues, the essay maps out many of the critical terms and debates that explain Shakespeare's continued significance—his "mattering," in terms of the volume's title—and that are developed in subsequent chapters.

Derek Cohen's essay, "The Past of *Macbeth*" focuses on the complex interactions and contradictions between personal and cultural history that are staged in Shakespeare's tragedy. Cohen begins by identifying something singular about historical representation in the play: the characters of *Macbeth* are almost entirely without evident personal history. Only scattered mention is made of the events and time that precede the beginning of the drama. Indeed, Lady Macbeth's memory of having given suck is one of few specific memories of a world that existed before the play began. The implications of such selective and limited temporal focus supply subtle insight into the workings of drama as history and history as drama. On the dramatic level, the action is made more intense by the lack of personal pasts. On the historical level, the past cannot be measured or invoked as a molding force in the lives of the characters with anything like the depth or power that operates in Shakespeare's other plays. *Macbeth* explores with great intensity the costs of the breakdown between the historical past and the cultural, personal present.

Arthur Lindley also explores the impacts of historical and material forces on subjective experience in his reading of *Antony and Cleopatra*. In "Antony, Cleopatra, the Market, and the End(s) of History," he argues that commerce remains the play's dirty secret. Its world is one of barter in which relationships are transactional, profit motivated, and temporary. The difference between Rome and Egypt is not, as is often assumed, between business and pleasure, but between two different kinds of business and, for that matter, two kinds of pleasure. One society trades in honor and hoarded treasure, the other "trade[s] in love." Caesar, "the universal landlord," as Pompey says of him, "gets money where / He loses hearts." One culture saves, the other lavishes. One culture thrives in the fluidity of endless transaction, the other longs for stasis. Rome is also associated with the newly and increasingly centralized state of Shakespeare's England, with its business culture of purchased monopolies and enclosure; Egypt, with the traditional marketplace of independent small traders, is also, for Shakespeare as well as Bakhtin, the place of carnival. Octavius is proleptically identified with corporate ruthlessness, just as the bountiful Antony, Egyptian carnival's reluctant patron, is identified with a dying tradition of aristocratic largesse.

Shakespeare's dramatic adaptations of historical tensions between classical and early modern beliefs and discourses are explored in further detail in Sharon A. Beehler's essay, " 'Confederate Season': Shakespeare and the Elizabethan Understanding of *Kairos*." For Shakespeare's contemporaries the idea of *Kairos* was familiar from such sources as Gorgias and the Sophists, as well as from discussions of time in theological treatises by Reformation writers. For rhetoricians, interest in *Kairos* lies in the circumstances (moral, ethical, physical, political) that contextualize logos, the "word" as used in suasive discourse. For theologians, interest resides in the conditions that produce a gap in temporal existence, which might permit encounters with the eternal. In both, there is a sense of suspension, a moment of possibility in which human decision making must occur. Beehler examines these theories and then focuses on *Hamlet*, demonstrating Shakespeare's thematic and dramaturgic interest in the principles of rhetorical and theological *Kairos* as a topos through which fateful personal and social events are played out.

The following two essays focus on Shakespeare's representation of sexual relations, institutions, and practices. In " 'Sick Desires': *All's Well That Ends Well* and the Civilizing Process," I explore connections between the rhetoric of manners and characters' sexual relations. Many of the characters appear caught at points of contradiction in prevailing codes of knowledge and behavior. The effects of such contradictions are widespread, threatening courtly careers, social and sexual reputation, family harmony, and honor. These intricacies of action and relationship are most sharply concentrated on the young count, Bertram. The contradictions in his behavior exemplify breakdowns in gender norms and practices that troubled many commentators in the late sixteenth and early seventeenth centuries. The essay examines *All's Well* as a particularly vivid illustration of social pressures that strongly impinge upon male identity and desire in the period. Shakespeare dramatizes shifting codes of manners and social meaning as they affect notions of shame, privacy, public control, and demeanor.

In her essay "Breaking Rank in Shakespearean Marriage Plots," Ann Blake continues to explore the links between sexuality and social status. Blake focuses on Shakespeare's use of marital arrangements and relationships to dramatize class differences among characters. She notes that there is abundant evidence that Shakespeare's age saw itself, sometimes anxiously, as one of great social mobility. One of the most obvious means of moving up the social ladder was by marriage; yet the proverbial prescription for happiness in marriage was to marry within one's rank, and most people did in fact do so. Nonetheless, theater audiences seem to have enjoyed plays in which marriages across class boundaries were presented in a positive light—a smart move by an impoverished young gentleman, repairing the family fortunes by marrying a rich farmer's daughter; or, more romantically, when a young woman of humble rank is wooed for her beauty and marries into the ranks of the gentry. Blake contends that Shakespeare's plays do not fit simply into this pattern, for they do not concern themselves with love across ranks within a single society. They stage instead the complex limits and pressures in marriage as a romantic, sexual, social, and economic relationship.

The essays in the opening section map some of the complex cultural and personal relations represented in Shakespeare's text in materialist, subjective, and historical terms. Those in the following section maintain this cultural-personal focus but switch perspective to more contemporary settings and practices—those of classrooms and teaching, where Shakespeare's work remains central. The effects of gender, tradition, self-identity, resources, and technology are crucial to educational programs, and the cultural status of the Shakespearean canon (not to mention its adaptability) ensures its significance for debates over pedagogical principles and outcomes in the humanities.

Michael Mullin's essay "Shakespeare on the Web" opens the section, which is titled "Teaching: Technology, Pedagogy, and Ideology." Like all the chapters in this part, it presents a range of informative examples and viewpoints on teaching that invite readers to reflect on their own pedagogical ideas and practices. The chapter assesses the numerous Shakespearean resources now available on the World Wide Web, which can be used for teaching and research, and for general interest. Mullin discusses the Shakespeare Globe USA Website, which he himself founded, and other links to a wide variety of materials on the Web, such as tours of the Globe Theater in London, and excerpts of Shakespeare in performance. Mullin also discusses *CyberShakespeare: Shakespeare Courses on the Web*, the development of modules for asynchronous, interactive, multimedia distance learning over the Internet. The essay outlines and examines the pedagogical advantages and implications of adopting such approaches in teaching Shakespeare to college and university students.

The following group of essays considers the teaching of Shakespeare in specific institutional contexts. In "Cultural Appropriations of Shakespeare in the Classroom," Susan Gushee O'Malley discusses a course she taught at the Center for Worker Education at City College of the City University of New York. O'Malley sought to counter a recurrent cultural effect where students are so busy genuflecting in front of official constructions of Shakespeare that they often engage superficially with the text. By examining how several writers rewrote Shakespearean plays in order to fulfill different cultural and ideological needs, the course positioned the students to interact with the plays more authentically. They read *The Tempest* and George Lamming's *The Plea-*

sure of Exile, Aime Cesaire's *The Tempest*, Michelle Cliff's *No Telephone to Heaven*, and poems by Edward Brathwaite and Lemuel Johnson; *Othello* and Sudanese novelist Tayib Salih's *Season of Migration to the North*; and *King Lear* and Jane Smiley's *A Thousand Acres*. Students also viewed parts of many films, some of which were appropriations, such as Spencer Tracy's *Broken Lance*, a rewrite of *King Lear*, and *Forbidden Planet*, a rewrite of *The Tempest*. Although the aim was to have the students analyze the cultural work achieved by each text, what many of the students wanted to do was to write their own appropriations: Prospero became a drug lord in a Queens housing project; *Othello* was moved to Nicaragua where Iago became Irene, a black woman in love with a transformed Othello; Lear became an aged mother of three daughters transplanted to Staten Island, the play now a short story entitled "O'Leary's Trash and Treasures." Many of these rewritings were culturally effective in their own right, and the experience of producing them caused the students to read the plays more courageously and creatively. The essay thus discusses the importance of enabling self-reflexivity in students, opening up spaces for them to think about what and how they are learning as they are doing it.

In the next essay Laura Raidonis Bates discusses such questions of reflexivity for both the instructor and a particularly striking group of students. She analyzes the intense experience of teaching Shakespeare in a number of prison settings. Bates begins "The Uses of Shakespeare in Criminal Rehabilitation" by asking whether there is a limit to Shakespeare's alleged universality: can his works reach even hard-core inner-city semi-literate criminal offenders, and, if so, in what ways does it reach them? Initially, she suggests, working with Shakespeare's texts offers inmates an especially valuable vehicle by which to improve their basic reading skills. A high school dropout or an adult who reads at a child's level feels a sense of accomplishment in mastering the "paragon" of the English language. Then, workshopping the scenes as a group (often involving real-life members of rival gangs, who would not hesitate to kill each other if they met on the outside) provides inmates with desperately needed training in collaborative skills. Finally, and perhaps most significantly, Shakespeare's unbiased treatment of issues such as violence and social responsibility allows inmates to view their own situations from others' perspectives. From teaching a number of plays in different prisons and to quite different groups of inmates, Bates concludes that in many ways Shakespeare's work can be as relevant to these groups as to other, more traditional audiences. Her essay provokes all teachers of Shakespeare to reconsider the stakes that their own work may carry.

Sara Jayne Steen's essay, "Whose Will, or Who's Will? Teaching Shakespeare Him-Self," relocates Shakespeare in a university context and examines ways in which recent critical and theoretical issues can be integrated with undergraduate teaching. Steen notes that one of the few difficulties of teaching Shakespeare is that undergraduate students often have little cultural or literary context for the works. In order to relocate Shakespeare within his cultural context, and at the same time lead students to ask of themselves the kinds of useful questions that current scholars are asking, Shakespeare's works can be juxtaposed with thematically related texts by other early modern male and female writers. Recently Steen taught an undergraduate course entitled "In Search of the Self." In this course, which includes Shakespeare's sonnets and *Twelfth Night*, clusters of works allow students to make multiple connections among Shakespeare and other sixteenth- and seventeenth-century writers as seemingly diverse as Anne Askew, Edmund Spenser, Arabella Stuart, John Webster, and Margaret Cavendish. The essay goes on to discuss three approaches that proved to be particularly fruitful in teaching Shakespeare's sonnets and *Twelfth Night* within a larger context: subjectivity, narrativity, and gender. Taken together, these three approaches invite students to debate not only the works themselves but also material book culture, gender ideology, and the making of history and literature.

In his essay "Teaching the Environment of *The Winter's Tale*: Ecocritical Theory and Pedagogy for Shakespeare," Simon C. Estok turns to one current critical movement, ecocriticism, and considers its pertinence for teaching the play. He begins by noting that sustained ecocritical readings of *The Winter's Tale* are not part of the play's interpretive history. Part of the reason is simply that the relevant critical and pedagogical terms are only now becoming available. Estok maintains that one of the tasks of ecocriticism is to look at how "ecophobia" overlaps and interlocks with other structures of fear and domination, and he goes on to discuss the general receptivity toward green issues in Shakespeare criticism, with particular focus on *The Winter's Tale*. For a play such as this one—that foregrounds the pastoral tradition, stresses the relationship between nature and art, and is deeply rooted in conceptual dividedness—an ecocritical approach can help not only to give students an understanding of the literary traditions at work in the text. It can also give insights about *inter-connectedness*, that is, about ways in which nonliterary texts and assumptions about nature come to bear on the play; of ways that the division between men and women in the play might be viewed as part of a larger dynamic through which difference is designated; and of ways that the play might be seen to participate in our own relationship with the natural world.

The essay by Kim Walker, "Wrangling Pedantry: Education in *The Taming of the Shrew*," begins by focusing on educational history in the sixteenth century, especially its gender implications. Walker notes that it is now commonplace to read back from Bianca's refusal of her husband's summons in the final scene to argue that her earlier docility is a deliberate pose. Similarly, Bianca's courting by the two false tutors (in act 3, scene 1) has often been interpreted as the moment when her "whiteness" is tainted by means of witty, flirtatious behaviour, which reveals that her modesty is feminine posturing. Yet such notions of Bianca's duplicity construct her character in dichotomous terms, much as Hortensio does when the woman he first describes as "my treasure . . . the jewel of my life" later becomes whorelike for him, a woman who casts her "wandering eyes on every stale." The essay re-examines these scenes in a different way, relating them to the numerous patriarchal anxieties attendant on women's education in the early modern period. Walker then discusses the representation of education in the play in broader transhistorical terms, reading the scene against other versions of the *Shrew*: the earlier *The Taming of a Shrew*, Gascoigne's *Supposes*, John Lacey's *Sauny the Scot*, the film *Kiss Me Kate*, and Charles Marowitz's *Shrew*.

One of the notable features in the preceding essays is that they often consider the academic benefits of placing Shakespeare in comparative contexts, contrasting and paralleling his work to that of contemporaries and later writers. The critical and pedagogical implications of comparative approaches to reading and teaching Shakespeare's plays are debated by Barbara Bowen in her essay "Beyond Shakespearean Exceptionalism," which closes the section. Bowen poses two significant questions: how can we shake off the traces of a critical practice based in the belief that Shakespeare is like no one else—an exception? And, what are the consequences of this epistemological legacy for teaching, performing, and reading his works? She argues that we are at a crossroads in Shakespeare studies, where it is possible but still difficult to move beyond exceptionalism as a critical framework.

Much of the scholarship of the past twenty years has disturbed
the notion of Shakespeare's singularity, relocating his work
within an early modern culture that seems both richer and more
heterogeneous than it did to an earlier generation of critics. But
women writers have largely eluded the Shakespearean critical
gaze, while works by male writers have often been inadequately
theorized in accounts of early women's writing. The paper explores what it would mean to read Shakespeare as if women writers mattered. It considers his *Rape of Lucrece* and Aemilia
Lanyer's *Salve Deus* as parallel treatments of foundational cultural myths, both rooted in sexualized and gendered acts of violence. In closing, it turns to the question of whether the
contestatory model of culture offered by some postcolonial critics—in which the dominant languages, literacies, and memories
are always assumed to be in competition with other, less visible
ones—might be useful for rethinking the relation between Shakespeare and women writers. Like the other chapters in this section, Bowen's essay raises numerous questions and provides
some important responses about the ways in which Shakespeare's work will be conceptualized and taught in coming years.

The third and final section of the volume, "Performance: Texts
and Productions," shifts the focus on Shakespeare's cultural significance from educational contexts to those in publishing and
theater. In doing so, it continues to underscore the importance of
locating Shakespeare's work in specific historical and social settings. Thus the section opens with Richard Madelaine's reexamination of the conditions in which boy actors worked in early
modern theater. His essay "Material Boys: Apprenticeship and
the Boy Actors' Shakespearean Roles" develops a nuanced cultural and historical view of the boys' careers. If in performance
an actor's status is always, in a sense, suspended, for the boys this
meant partial liberation from being gender-specific adolescents or
lowly apprentices. But though they might conceal their position,
they couldn't actually change it, and the most challenging Shakespearean roles for boys exploit the tension—palpable to male apprentices expected to play female or minor parts—between
established codes of behavior and an impetus in the socially dis-
advantaged to subvert. Since in the public theater the boys' apprenticeship was designed to produce a competent adult actor,
Madelaine suggests that we should assume it involved performing a variety of roles, not only female ones, and that the convention of female characters in male disguise has its origin in the
apprenticeship system. That convention always allowed the actor

to expand his repertoire with male roles, however small; and for an experienced actor a more demanding male role might be created, perhaps as an "apprentice-piece," for example Portia, disguised as Balthazar, delivering one of the drama's most famous set speeches. Madelaine concludes that the significance of the boy actors can only be fully gauged by a synthesis of historical, social, and theatrical analysis. It is very much this kind of integrated approach to textual and performative issues that the following chapters in the section adopt.

In his essay titled " 'Betwixt' and 'between': Variant Readings in the Folio and First Quarto Versions of *Richard III* and W. W. Greg's Concept of Memorial Reconstruction," Adrian Kiernander develops a multifaceted perspective in order to reassess traditional editorial judgments about the relative provenance of the two versions of *Richard III*. The essay is the result of Kiernander's ongoing editorial work on the text of *Richard III* for the Australian Bell Shakespeare series, where he decided to use the first quarto as a base. By focusing on the quarto and folio texts of *Richard III*, the essay reexamines the evidence for the idea that some texts of Shakespeare's plays are based on memorial reconstructions by actors. While this explanation has been seriously challenged, it continues to retain a strong hold on editorial practice. In the case of *Richard III* the idea has been used to privilege the folio text over the first quarto, through scholarly logic that Kiernander maintains is circular ("The folio text is the better text, therefore the readings in the folio are the better readings, therefore the folio text with the better readings is the better text . . ."). Using observations about textual practices in recent studies, such as E. A. J. Honigmann's work on *Othello*, the essay attempts to explore and challenge the orthodoxy about the memorial reconstruction of the quarto *Richard III*, and perhaps some other plays as well. Kiernander suggests a number of alternative explanations for the patterns of variation between or betwixt the two versions and assesses the implications of the variants for stage performance of the play.

The following chapter considers the implications of recent debates about textual theory and editorial practice for notions of literary and cultural history. In "The Case of the Rouged Corpse: Shakespeare, Malone, and the Modern Subject," Ron Bedford inquires into some of the contentious issues that circulate around Edmond Malone's Shakespeare enterprise and the 1790 edition of the plays. He starts by contrasting Margreta de Grazia's provocative *Shakespeare Verbatim* (1991) with Peter Martin's *Ed-*

mond Malone, Shakespearean Scholar (1995); both focus on Malone's achievements but with very different emphases. De Grazia sees Malone's textual and critical imperatives as a now-redundant construct of late-eighteenth-century England, while Martin defends them as those that mainstream scholars have always assented to and that form the basis of an incontrovertible tradition. In light of this critical contrast, Bedford reconsiders many of the links between editorial and ideological practices that have been recently proclaimed. Among the key issues that emerge in considering Malone's enterprise are questions of editorial protocol, of historicizer versus idealist (or archivist versus transcendentalist, Malone versus Coleridge), and also appeals to larger cultural arguments about the eighteenth-century emergence of the "bourgeois" or "modern" subject and the nature of the "individual."

In her essay "Determination and Proof: Colley Cibber and the Materialization of Shakespeare's *Richard III* in the Twentieth Century," Gillian M. Day also traces the influence of eighteenth-century reproductions of Shakespeare into the contemporary world, but does so by focusing on theatrical and performance traditions rather than textual history. In the light of recent British stage and film responses to *Richard III*'s metadramatic dimension, Day examines the rationalist ethic underpinning Colley Cibber's adaptation and the lingering influence of its structure on major twentieth-century productions of Shakespeare's play. Initially, the essay considers the impact on the play of Cibber's textual revision and staging choices. It asks whether the popularity of Cibber's structure in productions of Shakespeare's *Richard III* since 1877 can be attributed in part to the fading frame of reference for Shakespeare's dramatic allusions and historical detail. Cibberesque influences on psycho-social interpretations from Henry Irving onward have defined Richard in humanist terms, presenting him, as do Shakespeare's sources, as victim or product of a materialist-rationalist world rather than as ironic manipulator of this rationale. A complicating consequence of the popularity of Cibber's Richard has been the play's own incorporation into the mythical history that it ironizes. Olivier's acknowledgment of this paradox in his 1955 film of *Richard III* heralded the last half-century's recognition of the play's thematic ambiguity. An analogous irony was foregrounded in the 1991 (English) National Theater production, which identified the influence of *Richard III*'s own theatrical past with its historiographical debate. The clichéd comparison between Richard and Hitler was granted a critical dimension, focusing attention on the cliché itself in a manner comparable to those elements of contemporary theatrical and historical allusion in Shakespeare's text that are now more or less inaccessible to many modern audiences.

The changing connections between Shakespeare's works and audiences across radically different times and places is the subject of Philippa Kelly's "New Faces for Shakespeare in Contemporary Australia." Kelly begins by examining what is at stake in the remarks of a nineteenth-century reviewer, indignantly horrified by an actor playing Cordelia who burst out laughing as Lear carries her onstage in the final scene. Kelly suggests that by guffawing in Lear's face the actor breaks with convention in two ways. In refusing to "stay dead," she takes Cordelia's disobedience to new levels of metadramatic self-parody. The actor also adds her own disruption of nineteenth-century performance conventions, which generally sought to tame the play into a vision of moral redemption. While her laughter is seen by the reviewer as the last gasp in an appalling production, it could also be seen to mock the idea that the chaotic world of *King Lear* can be healed. Perhaps it irreverently reaffirms Edmund's vision of unyielding "nature," oblivious to the forces of human love and longing. Kelly uses "the laughing Cordelia" as a springboard to explore critical complexity and diversity that are necessarily at work in an endlessly renegotiated "Shakespeare." She examines some of the material conditions that pertain to such reconfigurations, discussing Australian versions and revisions of Shakespeare in contrast to some British and North American ones.

The last essay in this section, Ian Maclennan's "Materialist Shakespeare and Ideological Performance: Michael Bogdanov and Shakespeare in Production," examines Bogdanov's radical interpretations of the plays of Shakespeare in the context of the conservative British government of the 1980s. Bogdanov's productions often included vividly contemporary costumes, manners, and allusions—spiked Mohawk cuts of the punk subculture of the late 1970s, or a drunk from the audience attacking the theater staff and attempting to destroy the set. In removing traditional accretions and elitism that have attended many Shakespearean productions, and by alienating audience members who object to portrayals of contemporary culture within the plays, Bogdanov's goal seems to be to indoctrinate the rest of the audience and to assist it in accessing the plays in his terms. With Michael Pennington and others, he founded the ESC, the English Shakespeare Company, during the 1980s and created productions

of Shakespearean plays, particularly the *Henry* plays, which allowed the audience to experience a political agenda within an artistic framework. Maclennan examines Bogdanov's production
history, drawing upon the director's explicit remarks and implicit
intentions, in order to analyze these productions in terms of an
anticonservative ideological agenda.

The final chapter in the collection is an epilogue by R. S. White,
which maps the major changes in Shakespearean criticism that
occurred over the twentieth century. By using the metaphor of
the London underground, White attempts to conceptualize the
network of Shakespeare studies in the last one hundred years,
providing a working model of the relationship between the past
and the present and raising theoretical questions on their links
and connections. White's critical survey reveals the varied ways
in which Shakespeare's work has been understood to *matter* and
to *mean* to readers and audiences, teachers and students, from its
own time to the present. He examines the multiple "Shakespearean cultures"—historical, national, and critical—that have
shaped receptions and reproductions of his work.

The thesis that runs through *Shakespeare Matters* is that
Shakespeare's plays are remarkable for the numerous ways in
which they have been involved not only in critical and historical
debates but also in touching the lives of vast numbers of people
in many different ways and situations. As a whole, the collection
focuses on the diverse uses to which Shakespeare and his work
have been put, from the Elizabethan period through the late
twentieth century. Together the authors contend that "Shakespeare" continues to play a significant role in all kinds of places,
locations, and ways of producing knowledge. The ongoing importance of Shakespeare's work lies in its complex implication in
popular, intellectual, and ideological spheres of social and cultural life.

NOTES

1. The essays in this volume were originally presented as papers at the Material Shakespeare Conference that was held in Brisbane, Australia, in July 1998.
The conference was organized by the Australian and New Zealand Shakespeare
Association (ANZSA) and attracted a wide range of scholars, teachers, theater
practitioners, and students from throughout Australasia and further afield.

2. Unless otherwise noted, all references to Shakespeare's work throughout
the volume are to *The Norton Shakespeare*, ed. Stephen Greenblatt, Jean E.
Howard, Walter Cohen, and Katharine Eisaman Maus (New York: Norton,
1997).

I

History: Materialism, Gender, and Language

Material Shakespeare/Materialist Shakespeare

Jean E. Howard

SUDDENLY, "THINGS" ARE IN FASHION IN EARLY MODERN STUDIES. Steven Mullaney was a critical pioneer among new historicists when in 1988 he focused attention upon early modern English "wundercabinets" and upon the habits of collection and systems of classification they revealed.[1] But by now, the year 2000, the historical study of early modern literature and culture is sailing through a veritable sea of material objects salvaged from the deep abyss of time. Pride of place is perhaps claimed by the material book itself. Not only engaged in reading the stories and poems contained in early modern texts, a number of critics are assiduously examining the typefaces, bindings, printers' devices, and the title-pages of successive editions of these texts to learn something about the material forms in which they circulated in the world, who oversaw their production, and who sold and read them.[2] In addition, presses and journals are publishing essays and books that foreground accounts of early modern textiles and clothing, foodstuffs, cooking utensils, furniture, decorative arts, house design, bodies, and conveyances for travel.[3]

But if the field is increasingly interested in "materiality," it is less clear what the relationship of this work is to the modes of analysis connected with historical materialism. "Material Shakespeare"—the title of the conference that spawned this volume—provokes meditation on this very point, however. Is there anything important to say about the relationship among the material forms Shakespeare or his contemporaries took on the stage and on the page in the early modern period, the material world represented in these same texts, and the modes of production characteristic of the complex transition to capitalism?

In the United States academy, at least, this kind of question has not been asked very often in the last two decades of early modern studies. Analyses of Shakespeare explicitly drawing upon

Marxist modes of analysis have been fairly infrequent for a number of reasons, some fairly straightforward and some more convoluted.[4] At the simplest level, Marxism has never taken strong root in America's political and cultural soil. In fact, to many people its European origins and overtly partisan qualities have seemed to situate Marxism uniquely athwart the pragmatic, ostentatiously nonideological mainstream of much of America's public life. Within the American academy, the McCarthy era produced what amounted to a purge of the Marxist Left from the university system,[5] and in the United States the student radicalism of the 1960s and 1970s, though to some extent sympathetic with Communist regimes in Vietnam and China, was hardly an activism that primarily grew out of a Marxist analysis of the nation's economic or political policies.

In the particular arena of literary studies, when "theory" overtook the United States academy in the late 1970s and the 1980s, it was non-Marxist aspects of poststructuralist and psychoanalytic thought that achieved the greatest cachet. In the case of early modern studies, it has become something of a truism to note that while in Britain a Marxist-inflected cultural materialism became the dominant form of historicist practice in the 1980s, in the United States a Foucauldian new historicism or cultural poetics achieved ascendancy and eschewed the grand narratives and causal determinations of traditional Marxist accounts of culture.[6]

Of course, there are some compelling intellectual reasons to be wary of an unthoughtful relationship to Marxist modes of analysis. The Eurocentrism of its historical account of the development of capitalism, its relative indifference to nonclass-based modes of exploitation, and some of its more deterministic formulations of the relationship of base and superstructure can compromise its adequacy as a flexible and comprehensive analytic tool. But in the American academy, at least, discussion of Marxism so often remains at the level of caricature that sophisticated accounts of its strengths and weaknesses are relatively rare, as is an understanding of the diversity of thought contained within the Marxist tradition and of the many ways in which contemporary Marxists have queried and transformed aspects of Marxism's nineteenth-century conceptual apparatus. Cornel West has eloquently lamented the poverty of reductive accounts of Marxism that obscure a clear-eyed assessment of its usefulness: "in these days of Marxist-bashing, it is often assumed that vulgar Marxist thought exhausts the Marxist tradition—as if monocausal accounts of history, essentialist conceptions of society, or reductionist readings

of culture are all Marxist thought has to offer." Assessing the resources and the inadequacies of this tradition, he goes on to add:

> The high intellectual moments of Marxist theory—Marx's own his-
> torical and economic analyses, Georg Lukacs' theory of reification,
> and Antonio Gramsci's conceptions of hegemony—are those that
> bring together explanatory power, analytical flexibility, and a passion
> for social freedom. Yet certain crucial phenomena of the modern
> world—nationalism, racism, gender oppression, homophobia, ecologi-
> cal devastation—have not been adequately understood by Marxist
> theorists. My rejoinder simply is that these complex phenomena can-
> not be grasped, or changed, without the insights of Marxist theory,
> although we do need other theories to account for them fully.[7]

West's remarks suggest several important points: first, that
Marxism comprises a long, complex, and varied tradition of
thought not reducible to a set of clichés; second, that part of its
uniqueness lies in a dual commitment to explanatory analysis
and transformative action; third, that there can be a productive
synergy between Marxist inquiry and affiliated knowledge-making projects such as feminist, queer, race, and environmental
studies.

The interarticulation of critical paradigms is a crucial aspect
of contemporary progressive scholarship. Critics are now rightly
impatient with the idea of a grand theory that will subordinate
all forms of political criticism to its own foundational conceptualizations, as if to say, "Let no dogs bark but me." I lived through
a moment in the early 1980s when—as I see it now—those of us
interested in doing Marxist work on gender got diverted into the
attempt to create a single master theory that would explain both
patriarchal and class-based oppressions and modes of exploitation, a kind of Casaubonesque *Key to All Mythologies*, or at least
to all oppressions.[8] That project foundered in part because many
of the feminists involved had *too much* reverence for Marx. We
were trying to make feminism fit inside Marxist categories, rather
than remaking and expanding those categories. But since then,
those doing materialist feminist work have breathed freer air,
allying themselves with Marxism, employing many of its methodologies and categories of analysis, but also creating new ones and
modifying the received tradition, insisting on the particularity of
modes of oppression and exploitation affecting gendered subjects.
Materialist feminism denotes a strongly demarcated arena within
feminism. Unlike radical feminism it does not assume an essential feminist difference, but sees all difference as historically pro-

duced; unlike psychoanalytical feminism, it locates the origins of difference less in intrafamiliar experiences or even in language acquisition, but more within the historically produced divisions of labor (both productive and reproductive), the differential access to cultural capital, and the different histories of the relationship between family and state. This interarticulation of Marxism and feminism has altered both to produce genuinely new understandings of the role of gender and class in particular histories of oppression.[9]

As a leading African-American scholar and activist, as a socialist who also embraces an antihomophobic and profeminist politics, Cornel West certainly knows something about the need for complex approaches to social and cultural analysis and about the necessity of interarticulating knowledge-making paradigms. Yet his point is *also* that one cannot afford to leave Marx out. Especially at the present moment, when late capitalism goes largely unfettered and unchallenged, creating new forms of superexploitation and new forms of ecological disequilibrium in the pursuit of profit—at this moment Marxism is needed not only for its sophisticated critique of capital and the modes of subjectification and stratification that accompany it, but also for its articulation of alternative visions of social possibility.

Critics who question my own Marxist commitments often ask what a literary scholar can contribute to either the analytic or the transformative agendas of Marxism. Literature teachers, as others persistently remind me, do not make most kinds of social policy, do not manage the economy, and do not fight for social justice through the legal system. Is it therefore not a naive form of romanticism to affiliate oneself with a Marxist project? In part, as a literary scholar, participation in that project means finding the mode of intervention appropriate to the sphere in which I work. What I do is read and analyze the texts of culture, but those acts of reading and analysis are never natural or uncontested activities. Rather, they are places of struggle and debate in which the common sense that upholds the status quo can either be affirmed or challenged. Over time, Marxism has developed traditions of ideology critique and symptomatic reading that pose a persistent and necessary challenge to bourgeois assertions of the universality of art and its autonomy from ideology.[10] These strategies of reading need to continue to be taught, certainly, and along with them a commitment to reading beyond the fragments of culture toward a more coherent account of the interconnections between different spheres of the social formation.

Let me be more specific. In early modern studies at this moment, especially in the United States, one legacy of poststructuralism has been a certain fragmentation of knowledge, a hesitation to move beyond the anecdote or local sites to make wider claims about early modern culture. An almost obsessive fear of falling prey to a reductive "master narrative" has severely inhibited the range and character of the narratives being written about the period. The time is ripe to put Humpty-Dumpty together again, that is, to reclaim the resources of Marxism to offer wide-ranging accounts of the interconnections between the local, the national, and the global, between the past and the present, or between the economic and the political and cultural. This need not mean a return to deterministic narratives in which capitalism has an inevitable and universal teleology or in which the economic mode of production determines everything else about a social formation. The widespread recognition of the multiple histories of capitalism in different parts of the globe, the development of theories of relative autonomy, and the powerful cases that have been made for the effects of culture and politics on economic development all give the lie to caricatured accounts of the predictability of Marxist cultural analysis.[11] Moreover, a narrative of interconnections is not necessarily a "master narrative" in the sense of aspiring to universal truth claims of the sort discredited by critiques of Enlightenment epistemologies. Rather, narratives of interconnection can be offered as alternatives to local and topical analyses, but alternatives whose usefulness lies in their greater explanatory power and fidelity to the facts as they are known, rather than in some impossible claim to absolute, suprahistorical truth.[12]

My proposal shares much with what Nancy Fraser and Linda Nicholson, in their critique of the fragmentation of knowledge in postmodernity, demand: namely, the construction of "large narratives" that attempt to articulate interconnections between different spheres. They use the term as an alternative, on the one hand, to "master narratives," and on the other to "local narratives." The former they associate with Enlightenment aspirations to true, scientific, and totalizing explanations of society; the latter with a postmodern distrust of overarching explanatory schema. In their conception, large narratives attempt connections between spheres of consumption and production, culture and the state, and the economy and divisions of labor along lines of sex, class, and race. But for Fraser and Nicholson these large narratives are admittedly partial, provisional, and historically situated, rather than scientific and all-encompassing. Nonetheless, they find such narratives essential if one is to formulate adequate analyses of such complex social problems as the oppression of women.[13] It seems to me one needs to reclaim the potential within Marxism for creating—in, with, and against other paradigms and traditions—just such narratives of interconnection. Marxism is useful now if, as a situated and highly developed knowledge-making project, it can offer readings of texts and of society that are more powerful, persuasive, and illuminating than others can offer, and if it can address questions that seem urgent. It goes without saying, also, that Marxist modes of analysis are useful only when they do more than confirm or retell a preknown story. They have to speak to the particulars of the object being read, its pleasure and surprises and incoherencies, and they have to retain the capacity to alter received critical narratives. This is to say no more than that they must be good criticism as well as Marxist criticism.

So let us return to where I began this paper, namely, with the observation that early modern studies is suddenly awash with artifacts, and that the lexicon of favored critical terms has been expanded to include *matter*, *materialist*, and *materiality*. As scholars busily examine the properties of books, bodies, houses, clothing, maps, products, and objects, we are experiencing the marked "thingafication" of the critical scene.[14] This trend is partly a reaction to poststructuralism's hypertextuality. After more than a decade's fascination with langue, parole, discourse, and ideology, there is something reassuringly solid about turning to the study of woodcuts, joint stools, and ruffs. Yet a concern with material things also chimes with the postmodern zeitgeist and the contemporary fascination in many arenas of culture with style, fashion, surfaces, and objects of consumer culture. As is true with many aspects of postmodernity, it is not always clear what the political valence of such scholarship is. Sometimes the emphasis on the material aspects of early modern culture has a positivist and curatorial cast: this is what was in the early modern gentry home; here is what people sat on and here is what they ate.[15] Some of the attention to changes in material life is, of course, more political and looks at the way material goods, such as clothing, were manipulated by early modern subjects in struggles over social place, or functioned as not-uncomplicated indexes of the class positions of their owners or of the emerging global market in which England was to play an increasingly important part in the seventeenth century.[16]

But what might be gained if the study of early modern material culture were to engage in a more complex and systematic fashion with historical materialism, to which it at present bears at best a tangential relationship? What kinds of interconnections and large narratives might ensue from such an encounter? And perhaps more fundamentally, how might commonsense assumptions about the status of material "things" be disrupted?[17] As an historical materialist, Marx himself gave primacy to economic forces in the development of human history and so to the forces and relations of production dominant and in conflict in any historical era. But his aggressive anti-idealist view of history did not imply a reductive, naive, or celebratory understanding of things or of matter. Rather, it enabled him to analyze with enormous acuity the ways in which, first, human labor transforms raw matter into useful objects, and then the social processes by which such objects can come to accrue exchange value, be transformed into commodities, and achieve the allure and seeming autonomy that obscure the human labor accompanying their making and in part giving them their value. In writing of things that have become commodities, Marx is fully alive to the mystery and glamor of the commodity and to the complexity of the sociopsychic processes eventuating in its fetishization. Recall, for example, his dazzling account in the opening sections of *Capital* of the strangeness of that "material" thing, the commodity:

A commodity appears, at first sight, a very trivial thing, and easily understood. Its analysis shows that it is, in reality, a very queer thing, abounding in metaphysical subtleties and theological niceties. So far as it is a value in use, there is nothing mysterious about it. . . . But so soon as it steps forth as a commodity, it is changed into something transcendent. . . . A commodity is therefore a mysterious thing, simply because in it the social character of men's labour appears to them as an objective character stamped upon the product of that labour; because the relation of the producers to the sum total of their own labour is presented to them as a social relation, existing not between themselves, but between the products of their labour. This is the reason why the products of labour become commodities, social things whose qualities are at the same time perceptible and imperceptible to the senses. . . . The existence of the things *qua* commodities, and the value relation between the products of labour which stamps them as commodities, have absolutely no connection with their physical properties and with the material relations arising therefore. There is a definite social relation between men, that assumes, in their eyes, the fantastic form of a relation between things.[18]

This dense but crucial passage reveals the fallacy of believing that within capitalist culture the phenomenal world reveals its meanings directly and openly, that "things" are transparent, that the real is what one can see and touch. For Marx there is something eerily unreal about the commodity. It is a thing, certainly, but a thing that, under capitalist conditions of production and consumption, hides and effaces the labor that produced it and the labor that allows surplus value to be extracted from it. Marx stresses that in looking at a commodity, one can easily make the mistake of believing that value resides in the thing itself, in its physical properties. What is lost from sight in the dead matter of the commodity is the living labor of its maker; what is occluded in the exchange of commodities is the social relation between the makers of those commodities, leaving us in a world where social relations take the "fantastic form of a relation between things."

Marx was aware of the seductiveness of the commodity, and his work is a salutary reminder that in examining aspects of the material life of early modern England one should be careful not simply to grow enamored of "things" or succumb to the Whiggish view that life simply grew materially better for more and more people during this period without considering at whose cost and accompanied by what profound changes in the means of production and in social relations of every type. Shakespeare's *The Taming of the Shrew*, for example, has long been studied for its depiction of the violence underlying the transformation of early modern women, here the women of the urban merchant class, into wives.[19] What has more recently been noticed is the play's unusual attention to the dense material texture of the households in which these women will live, work, and reproduce.[20] When Petruchio proclaims that Kate (the "commodity" fretting on her father's hands) is "my goods, my chattels. She is my house, / My household-stuff, my field, my barn, / My horse, my ox, my ass, my anything,"[21] he is not only delineating her lack of rights as a *feme covert*; he is also making her equivalent to his other possessions and situating her, rhetorically, among them. Furthermore, as Natasha Korda has brilliantly argued, Kate's "taming" involves disciplining her into a proper housewife whose principal duty will be the discreet and modest management and display of household goods. Firmly located in the ever-proliferating domain of "things" over which, as a gentry housewife, she will now be expected to preside, Kate's agency will be limited to creative compliance with the will of the master of this domestic domain.[22] In the case of *The Taming of the Shrew* the proliferation of commodities is associated not only with a marriage between rural gentry and urban merchant classes, but also with a changing sex-gender system in which a new subject position for the "wife" is being negotiated, one in which a woman of Kate's class will be disciplined into managerial housewifery and reproductive labor. What is unusual about *The Taming of the Shrew* is the degree to which it reveals, albeit in the form of farce, the violence that supplements and underlies discursive injunctions from pulpit and from conduct books concerning wifely obedience and diligence in household matters. Read from a certain angle, Shakespeare's comedy reveals connections between a violent reconfiguration of the gender system and the not-so-innocent material transformation of gentry and merchant households in the course of the sixteenth century.

Perhaps of all the early modern stage genres, however, city comedy is the one in which the artifacts of early modern material life are mostly fully explored. Many appear as props; many more are referred to in dialogue. Analyzing these objects can reveal something about what Marx identified as the emerging allure of the commodity; it also permits the construction of dense narratives of interconnection in which one can discern contradictions in the evolving gender and class systems of the early modern period and their relationship to changes in the mode of production. *The Shoemaker's Holiday* (1599) is one of the earliest city comedies and one that places artisanal work and the products of artisanal labor at stage center. To work with one's hands in craft production is straightforwardly valorized as the essence of English manly virtue. An aristocratic figure, Lacy, for example, can only prove himself a worthy suitor of Rose, the daughter of a former lord mayor, by temporarily assuming the clothes and doing the work of a shoemaker. Labor and the production of craft commodities, rather than his inherited rank, ennoble him.

However, there is a contradiction at the heart of this text. While the play puts actual shoes and those who make them in the forefront of our attention, what actually makes the shoemaker Simon Eyre a wealthy man is not the shoes his men produce, but the vast profits he secretly and somewhat questionably accrues from acquiring the contents of a great merchant ship bearing sugar, civet, almonds, and other luxury items. Paradoxically, the play exalts artisanal life and the commodities produced by artisan hands while wittingly or unwittingly acknowledging the increasing obsolescence of such work as a path to wealth. In actuality, it was the great trading companies, such as the Levant Company, that by the end of the sixteenth century were bringing foreign luxury goods into England, the truly dazzling commodities that are not actually glimpsed on the stage but which magically catapult Eyre into the position of lord mayor and interlocutor with the king.[23] Shoes, the object whose manufacture is highlighted on stage, reveal the handicraft skills of the men who make them. Eyre's journeyman, Rafe, has a wife, Jane, whose identity can be known, for example, by the distinctiveness of the shoes made for her in Eyre's shop. But in actuality, it is the commodities we never see on stage (almonds and civet, for example), derived from the labor of unseen workmen in foreign lands, which actually produce truly astounding new levels of wealth. The labor of Eyre's men, while lauded, does not make either them or the master rich, though despite Eyre's surface joviality, he imposes a fairly strict labor regime on his crew. Enjoined to work hard, and to fight hard in England's wars in France, these shoemakers will soon be the proletarianized wage labor group of the future.

At the same time, the representation of the women in the play delineates the several fates awaiting women under emerging capitalism. Jane, the poor woman attached to Rafe, the workman who is impressed into service for the wars in France, always works, first in Eyre's shop and, after her husband goes to war, in a shop elsewhere in London. Poverty and low social status keep her in the workforce despite marriage. Margery Eyre and her maidservants also work in Eyre's shop, but unlike the men they are constantly subject to denigration and bodily slurs. Eyre, for example, calls maidservants "powder-beef queans" and "fat midriff-swag-belly whores" and his wife "Dame Clapperdudgeon" and "soused conger."[24] Clearly, though some women are involved in productive labor, they are satirized in the crudest terms, their laboring bodies represented as low and disgusting.[25] Upon Eyre's elevation, Margery, moreover, is the one upon whom negative judgments about his rise are displaced. While he insists on maintaining his bluff ways, she assumes mock-elegant speech and turns consumer, angling to buy a fashionable farthingale, a French hood, a wig, a fan, and a mask, proclaiming that "I must enlarge my bum" (10.37–38). Ironically, while consumers like Margery are necessary to fuel the commodity market in which everyone is increasingly involved, she is satirized for it nonetheless, becoming the locus for anxieties about what the dominance of the placeless market and the influx of foreign commodities will do to traditional society. If Kate in *Taming of the Shrew* is fashioned into a modest consumer and manager of goods, Margery represents the feminized specter of the consumer out of control.

The ideal woman in Dekker's text, by contrast, is Rose, the daughter of a former lord mayor, who now resides outside the city in a country house and is magically removed from the world of shops, productive labor, and also from any overt preoccupation with consumption. Though she clearly has many luxury items at her disposal, which we know about because she tries to bribe her maid with some of them (a cambric apron, gloves, purple stockings, and a stomacher [2.59–60]), all that she herself is shown consuming is a pair of handcrafted English shoes, taken to her by the very workman who made them.

Simultaneously nostalgic for a particular social world and set of social relations, *The Shoemaker's Holiday* nonetheless presciently anticipates many elements of the fully capitalist world that is to come: the imposition of a work discipline on an increasingly wage-oriented labor force, the sequestering of middle-class women in the home where they will preside over the domain of things, the decline of the traditional guilds, and the transformation of the aristocracy from a military, landowning class to one that must accommodate itself to the realities of the fortunes to be made in trade. If ever a play participates in the ideological management of the consequences of emerging capitalism, Dekker's is it.

I would argue, moreover, that to account adequately for the material objects and properties of this text within the framework of historical materialism—I mean the shoe by which Jane's identity is traced, the articles of apparel purchased by Margery Eyre, the commodities in the hold of the ship Simon acquires, the clothes the aristocrat Lacy wears before he supposedly sets off to war, the articles Rose gives her maid to insure her aid in tracking Lacy, the instruments of production in Simon's workshop, the household items used by Margery—adequately to account for these things requires telling an ambitious narrative about the transitional nature of early modern economic, social, and cultural life. It means reading these objects symptomatically, not simply as signifiers of status or objects of psychic investments, though that is necessary, but for their role in a particular dramatic narrative masking the contradictions of a changing mode of production. In short, one has to risk big explanatory schema of the sort Fraser and Nicholson have invoked, schema dependent on the interarticulation of feminist and Marxist paradigms.

This particular conjunction of Marxist and feminist modes of inquiry seems to me to have particular promise in producing innovative work in the early modern and other fields. Right now, in my own university and elsewhere, the conjunction of Marxist and feminist work is finding a new impetus in the emergence of global and transnational feminist courses and research agendas. Of course, in tamer forms global feminism can mean a pallid multiculturalism that examines the ways African, Asian, and Western women differ; promotes tolerance; and often mystifies economic inequality as cultural difference. Marxist feminism proves a powerful irritant and challenge to this kind of liberal feminism. In its Marxist-inflected forms, global feminism attends to the power, the global reach, and history-making capacities of capital to explain women's places in global divisions of labor, the connections and divisions among women across national boundaries and across the North-South divide.[26] Recognizing that globally women are divided by "race," class, and geopolitical locations, the goal is not to reify differences but to unpack the economic, political, and cultural conditions that produce difference and hold it in place and to produce nuanced narratives that explore the interaction between global forces and local conditions and histories, between economic and political factors and cultural ones. One cannot do this work without a sophisticated understanding of the infinite malleability of capitalism and of its particular, postindustrial manifestions. But the large narratives produced by global feminists also alter the Marxist paradigm by making gender and racialization key aspects of the analysis.

Though much of global feminism focuses on the present conditions of late capital, its techniques are now beginning to inform work on the early modern period as well. While there has been a great deal of scholarship on early modern "explorations" of the globe, it is feminists working within a materialist global paradigm who are leading the way in the production of "large narratives" that are reshaping our understanding of that moment.[27] I take as exemplary here work such as Kim Hall's on the interconnections between certain commodities, such as sugar, which flowed into England in the seventeenth century and the development, on the one hand, of English men's involvement in the slave trade, and on the other, of English women's role in purchasing these commodities and incorporating them into the English diet.[28] In moves clearly indebted to the techniques of a materialist global feminism, Hall is less interested in a product, sugar, in and of itself, and more in the slave labor congealed in the commodity, in the surplus value extracted from its sale, and in the role of white women as consumers and household managers in creating the market for this product. Her work forges connections between domains of knowledge that for some time have been investigated in isolation: namely, the lives and cultural productions of early modern English women, the growth of commodity culture, the development of England's commercial and territorial empires, and the emergence of modern ideas of race at a particular moment in the development of empire. It is precisely as race and gender become part of the narrative being told that the familiar Marxist story of the transition to capitalism is recast.

Not all the arenas where Marxist paradigms might provide a useful challenge and resource are quite so obvious as this one. But even the considerable interest right now in the material history of the early modern book, theaters, and acting companies is amenable to a sophisticated Marxist analysis. We know, for example, so much more than we did only ten years ago about what Terry Eagleton would call the literary and dramatic modes of production in the early modern period.[29] We know about typefaces and their significations, margins, marginalia, title pages, red ink and black ink, booksellers, compositors, press runs, costs of production, location of bookstalls, location of theaters, size of theaters, repertories of different theaters, stability and instability of companies, and so forth. There is a whole stockpile of new knowledge waiting to be integrated into "large narratives" that link this empirical scholarship to the concerns of historical materialism, joining, as Eagleton suggested, the dramatic and literary modes of production to the economic mode of production, the verbal ideologies of the text to its material embodiment, and both to larger patterns of subjectification and discipline, social stratification and commodification.

After the fall of the Berlin wall and the collapse of Communist states in Eastern Europe, there was a great deal of talk about the death of Marxism. That seems premature. As an intellectual paradigm, Marxism cannot be equated with, for example, Soviet totalitarianism, though it can not be entirely extricated from it either. But for exploring certain kinds of questions, Marxism has not yet been superseded. The role of Marxism in early modern studies is to make trouble and offer help, that is, to pressure adjacent knowledge-making projects and to offer tools for reconceptualizing the period we study. Political criticism as a whole cannot, I feel, do without the pressure exerted by Marxism's traditional questions about class; without its structural analysis of the interrelationships of different aspects of the social formation; without the tools of analysis developed by its long, diverse, and rigorous traditions of thought; and without the habits of self-reflection and autocritique embedded in Marxist practice, without which any political criticism becomes sclerotic and self-confirming. "Material Shakespeare" ought in part to be about the Shakespeare that can be produced with the help of historical materialism.

NOTES

1. See Steven Mullaney, "The Rehearsal of Cultures," chapter 3 of *The Place of the Stage: License, Play, and Power in Renaissance England* (Chicago: Univ. of Chicago Press, 1988), 60–87.

2. The bibliography on the new material history of the book is by now too vast to cite in a single footnote, but notable contributors include Peter Blayney, whose "The Publication of Playbooks" appears in *A New History of Early English Drama*, ed. John D. Cox and David Scott Kastan (New York: Columbia Univ. Press, 1997), 383–422, as does Heidi Brayman's " 'Rowme of Its Own': Printed Drama in Early Libraries," 113–30. See also Margreta de Grazia's *Shakespeare Verbatim: The Reproduction of Authenticity and the 1790 Apparatus* (Oxford: Clarendon Press, 1991) for the effect of an edition's material features on the institutionalization of Shakespeare as author; and a range of excellent new work on the material status of the early printed editions of his plays: Laurie Maguire, *Shakespearean Suspect Texts: The "Bad" Quartos and Their Contexts* (New York: Cambridge Univ. Press, 1996); Laurie Maguire and Thomas Berger, eds., *Textual Formations and Reformations* (Newark, Del.: Univ. of Delaware Press, 1998); Michael Warren and Gary Taylor, *The Division of the Kingdoms: Shakespeare's Two Versions of "King Lear"* (Oxford: Oxford Univ. Press, 1983); Steven Urkowitz, *Shakespeare's Revision of "King Lear"* (Princeton: Princeton Univ. Press, 1980); and Randall McLeod, *Crisis in Editing: Texts of the English Renaissance* (New York: AMS Press, 1994).

3. An example of this range of interests was evident in the 1995 conference at the Folger Library entitled "Material London Circa 1600," the proceedings of which are now published as *Material London, ca. 1600*, ed. Lena Orlin (Philadelphia: Univ. of Pennsylvania Press, 2000). See also a number of the essays in *Renaissance Culture and the Everyday*, ed. Patricia Fumerton and Simon Hunt (Philadelphia: Univ. of Pennsylvania Press, 1999), and for sophisticated approaches to the materiality of the early modern body see *The Body in Parts: Fantasies of Corporeality in Early Modern England*, ed. David Hillman and Carla Mazzio (New York: Routledge, 1997).

4. Among the explicitly Marxist work produced during this period from within the United States academy, I would count the following books as especially significant: Walter Cohen, *Drama of a Nation: Public Theater in Renaissance England and Spain* (Ithaca, N.Y.: Cornell Univ. Press, 1985); Michael Bristol, *Carnival and Theater: Plebeian Culture and the Structure of Authority in Renaissance England* (London: Methuen, 1985); Jean E. Howard, *The Stage and Social Struggle in Early Modern England* (London: Routledge, 1994); Richard Halpern, *The Poetics of Primitive Accumulation* (Ithaca, N.Y.: Cornell Univ.

Press, 1991) and *Shakespeare among the Moderns* (Ithaca, N.Y.: Cornell Univ. Press, 1997); Hugh Grady, *The Modernist Shakespeare: Critical Texts in a Material World* (Oxford: Clarendon, 1991) and *Shakespeare's Universal Wolf: Studies in Early Modern Reification* (Oxford: Clarendon, 1996).

5. For a harrowing account of the material consequences of McCarthyism for the American university system, see Ellen Schrecker, *No Ivory Tower: McCarthyism and the Universities* (New York: Oxford Univ. Press, 1986).

6. See, for example, Walter Cohen's account of British and American historical criticism in the 1980s in "Political Criticism of Shakespeare," in *Shakespeare Reproduced: The Text in History and Ideology*, ed. Jean E. Howard and Marion F. O'Connor (London: Methuen, 1987), 18–46.

7. Cornel West, *The Ethical Dimensions of Marxist Thought* (New York: Monthly Review Press, 1991), xxiii.

8. For an account of some aspects of this endeavor, see the essays in *Women and Revolution: A Discussion of the Unhappy Marriage of Marxism and Feminism*, ed. Lydia Sargent (Boston: South End Press, 1981).

9. For useful accounts of materialist feminism and its difference from other forms of non-Marxist feminism see Donna Landry and Gerald MacLean's *Materialist Feminisms* (Oxford: Basil Blackwell, 1993) and Rosemary Hennessy, *Materialist Feminism and the Politics of Discourse* (London: Routledge, 1993).

10. For a striking account of the historicity of the idea of aesthetic autonomy, see Terry Eagleton, *The Ideology of the Aesthetic* (Oxford: Basil Blackwell, 1990).

11. Louis Althusser's theories of the relative autonomy of the cultural and political spheres from the economic, as developed in *Reading Capital*, coauthored with Etienne Balibar (London: Verso, 1979), have been widely influential. In *The Poetics of Primitive Accumulation* (Ithaca, N.Y.: Cornell Univ. Press, 1991), especially 1–15, Richard Halpern demonstrates how, in the early modern moment, certain aspects of bourgeois culture and subjectification occurred in advance of, and as a necessary precondition for, the full-fledged emergence of capitalism.

12. On this point, see my "Towards a Postmodern, Politically Committed, Historical Practice," in *Uses of History: Marxism, Postmodernism, and the Renaissance*, ed. Francis Barker, Peter Hulme, and Margaret Iversen (Manchester: Manchester Univ. Press, 1991), pp. 101–22, especially 115–20.

13. Nancy Fraser and Linda Nicholson, "Social Criticism without Philosophy," in *Universal Abandon? The Politics of Postmodernism*, ed. Andrew Ross (Minneapolis: University of Minnesota Press, 1988), 83–104, especially 100–102.

14. Alan Sinfield has wittily commented on the way, in a concern with "things," scholars are losing the political implications of materialist analysis undertaken in a Marxist framework. He sees scholars increasingly attending to "clothes, pots and pans, needles and pins, and to books and manuscripts *as objects*" and ironically comments: "They are, after all, *stuff*, they are *made of* material, let's *touch* them, you can't get more material than that." See his *"Poetaster*, the Author, and Cultural Production," in *Material London, ca. 1600*, ed. Lena Orlin (Philadelphia: Univ. of Pennsylvania Press, 2000), 75–76.

15. In this category, for example, I would put the very useful work of Joan Thirsk. See especially *Economic Policy and Projects: The Development of a Consumer Society in Early Modern England* (Oxford: Clarendon, 1978).

16. An early example of such work was Chandra Mukerji, *From Graven Im-*

ages: Patterns of Modern Materialism (New York: Columbia Univ. Press, 1983). For an exciting examination of the role of clothing and cloth in the social life of sixteenth- and seventeenth-century England, see Ann Rosalind Jones and Peter Stallybrass's *Renaissance Clothing and the Materials of Memory* (Cambridge: Cambridge Univ. Press, 2000).

17. Recently the postmodern feminist philosopher Judith Butler has attempted to complicate commonsense understandings of matter and materiality. In *Bodies That Matter: On the Discursive Limits of "Sex"* (New York: Routledge, 1993), especially 1–23, she argues that matter has no self-evident status. Even something as seemingly "solid" as the body *has to be brought into being* through a complex process of "materialization," the iterative operations by which discourse and matter are made culturally coextensive one with the other. Discourse does not "create" matter, but neither does it simply name a preexistent material entity as some social constructionists have argued when they talk of culture transforming the raw material provided by nature. Rather, eschewing nature-culture, matter-language binaries, Butler argues that the process of materialization inextricably links discourse and matter. I introduce Butler at this point to suggest that within contemporary philosophy *matter* and *materiality* remain problematic and complex categories, just as they do in Marxist thought. They certainly do not have the self-evident status accorded them in much literary criticism exploring the early modern period.

18. Karl Marx, *Capital*, vol. 1, from *Karl Marx: Selected Writings*, ed. David McLellan (Oxford: Oxford Univ. Press, 1977), 435–36.

19. Lynda Boose, "Scolding Brides and Bridling Scolds: Taming the Woman's Unruly Member," *Shakespeare Quarterly* 42 (1991): 179–213.

20. Lena Orlin, "The Performance of Things in *The Taming of the Shrew*," *The Yearbook of English Studies* 23 (1993): 167–88.

21. *The Taming of the Shrew*, in *The Norton Shakespeare*, ed. Stephen Greenblatt, Jean Howard, Walter Cohen, and Katharine Maus (New York: Norton, 1997). This passage is taken from 3.3.101–3. All other passages from Shakespeare will be taken from this edition of the plays.

22. Natasha Korda, "Household Kates: Domesticating Commodities in *The Taming of the Shrew*," *Shakespeare Quarterly* 47 (1996): 109–31.

23. For a masterful account of the development of the great trading companies in late-sixteenth- and seventeenth-century England, see Robert Brenner, *Merchants and Revolution* (Princeton: Princeton Univ. Press, 1993).

24. Thomas Dekker, *The Shoemaker's Holiday*, ed. R. L. Smallwood and Stanley Wells (Manchester: Manchester Univ. Press, 1979), 4.4–6, 127–29. All other quotations from the play will be taken from this edition.

25. Ronda Arab, "Work, Bodies, and Gender in *The Shoemaker's Holiday*," *Medieval and Renaissance Drama in England* 13 (2001): 182–212.

26. An early example of such work is Maria Mies's *Patriarchy and Accumulation on a World Scale: Women in the International Division of Labour* (London: Zed Books, 1986). See also many of the essays in Chandra Mohanty and Jacqui Alexander's edited collection, *Feminist Genealogies, Colonial Legacies, Democratic Futures* (New York: Routledge, 1997) and, for its dazzling sophistication about North-South interchanges, see Gayatri Spivak's work, especially her *In Other Worlds: Essays in Cultural Politics* (New York: Methuen, 1987) and *A Critique of Postcolonial Reason: Toward a History of the Vanishing Present* (Cambridge: Harvard Univ. Press, 1999).

27. See, for example, Kim Hall's *Things of Darkness: Economies of Race and*

Gender in Early Modern England (Ithaca, N.Y.: Cornell Univ. Press, 1995); Ania Loomba's *Gender, Race, Renaissance Drama* (New York: Oxford Univ. Press, 1992); and Jyotsna Singh's *Colonial Narratives/Cultural Dialogues: "Discoveries" of India in the Language of Colonialism* (London: Routledge, 1996).

28. For a representative essay from this work-in-progress, tentatively entitled *The Taste of Empire: Sugar, Gender, and Material Culture in the Seventeenth Century*, see Kim Hall, "Culinary Spaces / Colonial Spaces: The Gendering of Sugar in the Seventeenth Century," in *Feminist Readings of Early Modern Culture*, ed. Lindsay Kaplan, Valerie Traub, and Dympna Callaghan (Cambridge: Cambridge Univ. Press, 1996), 168–90.

29. Terry Eagleton, *Criticism and Ideology: A Study in Marxist Literary Theory* (London: Verso, 1976), especially chapter 2, "Categories for a Materialist Criticism," 44–63.

The Past of *Macbeth*

Derek Cohen

> What is true of endings is also true of beginnings. Lady Macbeth's mysteriously missing children present an ominous, unknown, but undeniable time before the beginning. Doubtful beginnings are also incidentally inherent in such details of the play as Macduff's non-birth. Indeed the beginnings, sources, causes of almost everything in the play are at best nebulous.
> —Steven Booth, *"King Lear," "Macbeth," Indefinition, and Tragedy*

LADY MACBETH'S CHILDREN, PRESENT EITHER IN HER MIND AS A FIGment, or in her memory as a piece of her history, allude to something singular and usually unnoticed about the play. The characters of Macbeth are almost entirely without evident personal history. There is only the most sparse and scattered mention of the events and the time that precede the beginning of the drama. For a play that centers vividly and painfully on the effects of remorse—a feeling that by definition is possible only by the exercise of memory—this is an astonishing fact. Indeed, Lady Macbeth's memory of having suckled her infant is one of remarkably few specific memories of a time earlier than the events of the play. Memories such as these lend sensory focus to the present; they fill it suddenly and disquietingly with remembered feelings. More usually in *Macbeth* those feelings are of fear and danger and produce the sensation and threat of panic in the actors in the tragedy.

Tragedy is, I think, a response to the human urge to panic in the face of dread. The fear of disintegration is constructed as a means of warding off, controlling, or mastering the panic impulse. Tragedy is panic with circumference and form. The deconstructionist notion of immanent displacement, where the wholeness of the work is illusionary, is well exemplified in the constructions of tragedy. The genre's success is contingent on disaster and the danger of the narrative emotionally overwhelming the boundaries of completeness, which are only ostensible. What lingers beyond these boundaries is the power of the tragic—and the panic—experience of calamity endured. Macbeth, carrying two bloodstained daggers, confronting his wife minutes after the great murder of the play, asks, "Didst thou not hear a noise?" (2.2.14). He has heard the stamping of the hoof of Pan; the abyss yawns and he must act to avoid it. Evident here is a clear link between tragedy and memory: the memory that produces the impulse to panic is amongst the most powerful stimuli of the dread by which tragedy is animated and that, at the same time, it seeks to contain.

The characters of the play make only about a dozen direct references in the whole of *Macbeth* to personal experiences before the action of the drama begins.[1] These references themselves fall into two categories: specific memories of particular events or people, and vague allusions to possible and probable memories of feelings and sensations that seem to have preceded the action. The categories themselves are capable of resolution into subcategories and types—such as, in the first instances, the difference between persons actually known and remembered and those known by report. In short, the world that existed before the first line of the play is presented as nebulous and curiously disconnected from the present action. The play exists solidly in the present; its protagonists lean hopefully and desperately toward the future. This tendency away from the present and toward a better time is appropriate for a play so specific in its complimentary references to James, the reigning monarch, and one that, John Turner argues, explores "the language, metaphor and myth of a society which we are encouraged to identify as the prehistory of the present."[2]

The implications of such selective and limited temporal focuses offer subtle insights into the workings of the drama as drama, and drama as history. On the dramatic level, the excitement of the play is made more intense by this absence of the personal. On the historical level, the past cannot be measured or invoked as a molding force in the lives of the characters with anything like the depth or power with which it operates in other dramas. In *Othello*, for example, every crucial action is almost literally informed by specified preplay experiences and remembered actual events, and registered, if not distorted, by history. This presence of the past richly informs and determines the play's character and direction. *Othello*'s past is replete with remembered detail and is a source of energy in the present, while *Macbeth*'s is poor and random. The difference in each case is a strong determinant of action.

Now, this is not to say that the twelve references to the past are the only evidence of past life. Clearly, other ways of presenting history and the merely personal past in *Macbeth* do exist. Certain historical realities are vivid. A multiplicity of facts, allusions, practices, habits of address, modes of discourse and of speech, and customs of verbal and physical behavior indicate the reality of the past and the groundedness of the play in a vital history. And indeed the drama insistently implies continuity with the history it enacts and with which it continuously becomes a part. For example, his title alone tells a great deal about Macbeth the individual subject and Macbeth the social and political personage. The title, thane of Glamis, indicates a locus in a social order that is itself imbricated in an established political and historical tradition. Of Macbeth's history within this context, we learn much within minutes of hearing his name: he is a valued and loyal soldier of his monarch; he has wealth and friends; he is married; he is, more simply, a man of a certain age—young enough to be a vigorous warrior and old enough to command men; he inhabits an old country; his nation possesses evidence of a stable and long-established political system.

In other words, Macbeth, like every other character in the play, is making and participating in the making of history. These are material facts about Macbeth that the audience absorbs spontaneously because they are based upon justly unquestioned assumptions about drama, culture, and social living. They help preserve the illusion that this play, like all other plays, is a complete slice out of the past. The illusion is the more ambiguous in the case of *Macbeth* since the play is so specifically concerned with the monarch for whom it was to be performed and with the issue of treason, which remained so close to his own experience. As Steven Mullaney has written:

> at the heart of *Macbeth*'s dramaturgical concerns lies the developing absolutism of the Jacobean state. If sixteenth-century political cosmology precluded the possibility of a fully intentional treason . . . that same cosmology radically restricted the power of authority to control or contain treason's amphibology. . . . James was endeavoring to extend the threshold, to redefine the boundaries of rule, and his claims for absolutism were . . . grounded in the figure of a king who could, from his quasi-divine perspective, spy into the mystery of things, including the indecipherable countenance and amphibolic tongue of treason.[3]

The actual treason of the earl of Gowrie and the strange correlatives of the story of that treason—such as the refusal of the traitor's corpse to bleed until the written evidence of its treachery was discovered on the body in the form of allegedly magical writings—made of *Macbeth* an uncanny, bordered mirror into which the king must have gazed with mixed but mainly satisfied feelings.[4]

But the facts are, nevertheless, the mere givens of the drama. Its discursive constructions of the history or story it tells and enacts are generally silent on, or only allusive to, those features of the past that imply its own history. Indeed, my point largely is that one of the singular aspects of the various discourses of *Macbeth* is the force of that very silence and the heavy emphasis on present and future that displaces it. The impetus of *Macbeth*, its energies and motives of violently gaining and keeping power, is *felt* and carried by a relentless tension between the present tense and the unremittingly hopeful anticipation of security supplied by the future. Part of the mystery of the witches of *Macbeth*, and of preternatural characters generally, is precisely that they are not subject to time or the constructions of history, or, for that matter, to the changes that history and the past enforce. Paradoxically, however, just because they are old it follows that they must be subject, in some usually undefined fashion, to the temporal workings of nature, even if not in a normal or recognizable human sense. The witches crucially define the drama: their presence in the first scene establishes the commanding authority of the uncanny as the new and essential realm of habitation and action. From the moment he sees them, Macbeth is made aware that he has ceased to live in a world of rational matters. This being the case, the irrational becomes valorized, and the unthinkable and unmanageable suddenly acquire realizable possibility. This has become a world where the abnormal and the absurd have the power to speak and to predict—all earlier bets are off. The witches are terrible evidence of the contamination that adheres to "the warrior returning to his homeland, still tainted with the slaughter of war," according to René Girard, who goes on to explain that the "returning warrior risks carrying the seed of violence into the very heart of the city" or among his people.[5] Macbeth moves forward from his encounter with the witches without having cleansed himself of the blood that clings to him after the battle. His plunge into murder is an almost logical progression by which he seals his connection to the present and his distance from the past.

The first direct reference to any life experience prior to the beginning of the play comes in the fourth scene. Malcolm is report-
ing a version of the thane of Cawdor's death by "one that saw him
die" (1.4.4). The speech alludes to the trust, faith, and friendship
that existed before Cawdor's earlier treachery:

> That very frankly he confessed his treasons,
> Implored your highness' pardon, and set forth
> A deep repentance. Nothing in his life
> Became him like the leaving it. He died
> As one that had been studied in his death
> To throw away the dearest thing he owed
> As 'twere a careless trifle.

> (1.4.5–11)

It is not clear that Cawdor is already dead at the start of the
play—but it is possible. This secondhand report, however, strikes
a peculiar note. The strangeness and violence of language and action of the first three scenes are given a kind of respite here: it is
a still moment of reflection that interrupts and thus momentarily
transforms the process of history-in-the-making that the play so
egregiously is. Duncan's response to the speech, filled with yearning and disappointment, is deeply ironic:

> There's no art
> To find the mind's construction in the face.
> He was a gentleman on whom I built
> An absolute trust.

> (1.4.11–14)

The past, in Duncan's words quoted earlier, was a good place with
good men in it. We see here the beginning of the process of unrav-
eling the present. The lines imply an impulse of reflection, which
is a necessary precondition of the making of history. The speaker
seems to reconstruct himself in the immediate present as a being
outside of his present self, as someone whose earlier self—
unenlightened, unknowing, and innocent, but whole and compre-
hending—is being contrasted with the present self. This clash of
selves, first heard in Duncan's sorrowful recollection, is the
source of Macbeth's manic energy. As the Elizabethan theater
was forced to explore its own contradictory and anomalous place
because of its marginal location in the city Liberties,[6] so the characters it created were often found enacting that marginality by a
compulsive retrospectivity driven by the need to bring the past

into the present view. The dividedness of Macbeth's selves is not, however, contingent upon time, upon the past's habit of ambushing the present, as might be said to be the case with Othello. Rather, it is the clash of interior with exterior realities that becomes tragically irreconcilable in him. The division of consciousness and experience in Macbeth himself, and in the play more generally, is remarked on by Graham Holderness, who writes of a "central historical contradiction" at its heart: "Ambition in this society is not some eccentric personality disorder, but a central historical contradiction: a natural extension of the militaristic violence which is both liberated and restrained by the feudal pattern of authority."[7]

Even Lady Macbeth, in the play's second allusion to the preplay past, recalls a time when virtue held sway and contrasts it with the present from which the past needs must become detached for her ambitions to achieve fulfillment. To her, Macbeth's formerly evident goodness has become an impediment to the present endeavor; it is old-fashioned. As we shall see, this is not the first time that life before the play impinges on the urgent demands of the present. In act 1, scene 4, she recalls her husband's potential insufficiency for evil deeds:

> Yet do I fear thy nature.
> It is too full o' th' milk of human kindness
> To catch the nearest way. Thou wouldst be great,
> Art not without ambition, but without
> The illness should attend it.
>
> (1.5.14–18)

This passage too is only indirectly about what was. It refers to a wife's old knowledge of her husband. Thus, while the passage allusively incorporates the past, its use of the historic present contributes to the senses of urgency and immediacy that characterize the greater part of the drama. The "wouldst" stands as an obstacle to the "should" and generates a tension within the wife as she attempts to correct the contradiction between the selves of her husband.

Without doubt, the memory—specific, precise, tactile—of a preplay experience that has prompted the greatest, deepest, most extensive speculation is that of Lady Macbeth in act 1, scene 7, when she recalls the experience of nursing her own baby: "I have given suck" (1.7.54). The reference to mothering her own child, and the warm, loving feelings and physical memories of being sucked on and releasing milk from her breast in a timeless rhythm, seems to be grounded in felt recollections that evince the sensory memory of "how tender 'tis to love the babe that milks me" (1.7.55). This is not mere rhetoric: the line's monosyllabism is a typical Shakespearean means of representing authentic emotion. Robert Weimann notes that it is the contrast between the elevated metaphor and simple everyday speech that sharpens the effect of both. Within the range of expressive modes, the "everyday syntax and diction" can carry the force of tragic experience as powerfully as the elevated.[8] That Lady Macbeth should use the memory of that experience to drive home and recover her capacity for violence is her way of suppressing the gentle and "natural" in favor of the possible—the Crown.

It is surely no accident that Lady Macbeth's next memory of her life before the play links her with equal force and solidity to other familial and tender realities. In act 2, scene 2, yet another specifically defined and grounded memory gives the action a terrible and transforming jolt. Lady Macbeth has looked at the sleeping king:

> Had he not resembled
> My father as he slept, I had done't.
> *(Enter Macbeth below)*
>> My husband! (2.2.12–13)

This is one of those Shakespearean moments when the stated obvious merges with the unspoken in a complicated knot of connected linguistic and psychological implication. The primary force here is memory, but it is memory animated and transformed by nostalgia. The image of her sleeping father reproduced in the sleeping form of the king arouses remorse and conscience in this unlikely woman. Though we may be surprised that she has children, the moment brings to reality the obvious and unsurprising fact that Lady Macbeth is the daughter of a father. We must not, however, let what is obvious obscure what is true and strange; the sudden paralyzing recognition of her father's face in her victim's is a chilling return to the reality of psychological motive and scruple.

The moment radically reverses the movement of the drama. The past lives of these characters, only nervously present up to now, are shown to have a violently transformative power and, in being thus shown, reveal a powerful reason for the absence of the past or, more sinisterly, a reason why these characters may be avoiding it. Through the spontaneous exercise of memory, the past leaps unbidden and unwelcomed into Lady Macbeth's conscious mind from that place in the subconscious where it is kept, only to be prompted to life by familiar images and likenesses. The drama is made fearfully intense here by the momentary possibility that Duncan's life, whose loss is signified by the bloody hands and daggers of Macbeth, might have been saved by the single coincidence of his resemblance to Lady Macbeth's father. Terrible nostalgia is contained in these words; it enforces upon Lady Macbeth a crippling coalescence of memory and feeling that forbids her to act out her desire. Our eyes, filled with the sight of Macbeth covered in blood, tell us that Duncan is already dead; our ears tell us that he might have been spared. The moment is suffused with tragic helplessness; the verge of going back has been traversed. From now on the idea of what might have been springs into awful life, only to be crushed by what is.

The scruple—Lady Macbeth would not have killed her father—adds something to the moment as it interrupts the rapid pace of the plunge to achievement and destruction. The moment is also pregnant with a sign of the weakness of the whole enterprise: that weakness, as the play intermittently and vaguely shows (and conceals), is the continuous presence of the buried and subterranean past. The moment is punctuated by the recognition, made visible, of Macbeth's bloody appearance. Images and signs coalesce with the dominant words of the short speech giving way to the short parade of significant male figures: the king—the "he"—becomes "my father," and "my father" becomes "my husband!" Male identities merge in the powerful image of Macbeth, who stands bloodily before his wife, as the two other male figures, father and king, are reconsigned to memory.

And yet, the past as constructed here, is not separate from the present. It is shown to be a crucial part of it. The fifth example of the use of the preplay past is more purely and conventionally historical. In act 2, scene 4, the Old Man looks back to a less confused and turbulent time. He recalls:

> Threescore and ten I can remember well,
> Within the volume of which time I have seen
> Hours dreadful and things strange, but this sore night
> Hath trifled former knowings.

> (2.4.1–4)

The human habit of trying to make sense of the present by comparing it with the past is a way of supplying a comforting perspec-

tive to present events. It is a familiar cry, perhaps more justifiable
here than usual. The old days were innocent compared to these.
The past gives authority to this grim evaluation of the present
horrors. The Old Man and Ross proceed to catalog the recent
eruptions and deformations of nature as prognostications.

In Macbeth's second reference to the past—and only the sixth
in the play—he uses the idea of history, the authority that the
past is supposed to carry, to manipulate the present. Macbeth
tells the two murderers hired to kill Banquo that

> it was he in the times past which held you
> So under fortune, which you thought had been
> Our innocent self.

(3.1.78–80)

And he asks them,

> Are you so gospelled,
> To pray for this good man and for his issue,
> Whose heavy hand hath bowed you to the grave
> And beggared yours for ever?

(3.1.89–92)

With the murderers, we become ensnared by a possibly falsified
version of the past. There is, of course, no way of confirming this
version of the events before the play. What signifies, however, is
Macbeth's perceived need to use or invent history to advance his
purpose. Thus while he strains to determine the future by the intense and violent perversion of the present, inevitably the past
becomes corrupted and compromised, a thing of use and a means
of stabilizing Macbeth's uncertain rule. The murderers represent
themselves as qualified for their task by virtue of their personal
histories, their preplay lives. The Second Murderer has been
made "reckless" by "vile blows and buffets" (3.1.110) while the
First is "weary with disasters" (3.1.113) and ill luck. Both are
ready for labor, however criminal or violent. Private history has
molded present disposition—an allusion to the social roots of
crime.

The banquet scene supplies yet another occasion for the fusion
of lies and truth; the past is pressed into the service of the present. Macbeth's access of conscience is explained by his lady as a
manifestation of an old condition. When the ghost of Banquo
prompts the plea (or threat), "never shake / Thy gory locks at
me" (3.4.49–50), Lady Macbeth attempts an explanation whose

feebleness adverts to the schism between truth and falsehood that the Macbeth enterprise has caused: "Sit, worthy friends. My lord is often thus, / And hath been from his youth" (3.4.52–53). The excuse is palpable and unconvincing; the hallucination is clearly fired by the recently suborned murder. The history that Lady Macbeth here invents becomes an inadequate buttress of the present. It is invoked in order to give Macbeth's present behavior a link to an innocent, preregal, preplay self. Furthermore, it argues the existence of a youthful, innocent Macbeth, possessed, even as a child, by private demons. The haunted, raving monarch is thus connected to a haunted, raving boy, untrammeled by the responsibilities of power and official authority. It is, of course, doubtful that such a youth ever existed. However, the effect of Lady Macbeth's invention is the creation of a parallel past, one that never existed in reality but one that has acquired discursive existence in the present drama. The deformed and poisoned present of the play thus stands on the shifting sands of real and of invented history. The effect of such simultaneous histories—one true, one false—is to drive the infinitely unstable present further into the wild, strange, and violent realms that Macbeth has carved out for himself.

Macbeth himself, partly raving, partly lucid, harks back over the ages to a long and terrible history of murder in which he has become an infamous actor:

> Blood hath been shed ere now, i' th' olden time
> Ere human statute purged the gentle weal;
> Ay, and since too, murders have been performed
> Too terrible for the ear. The times has been
> That, when the brains were out, the man would die,
> And there an end. But now they rise again
> With twenty mortal murders on their crowns,
> And push us from our stools. This is more strange
> Than such murder is.
>
> (3.4.74–82)

This is the clearest attempt so far in the play to locate the present in a sequential historical pattern. The "olden time" is prehistorical, a period before the existence of law; it was, by Macbeth's desperate reckoning, a time of terrible violence. But even then the laws of nature were in effect: human life is linked through time by murder and violent death and a string of victims who, unlike the present victim, remained dead. The past, in other words, was a stable place, one in which cause and effect—violent killing and sequent death—supplied the safety of predictability: a man whose brains were bashed out was a dead man. In this moment in which Macbeth recognizes Banquo, the play realizes its own temporal indeterminacy. Only a ragged and uncertain future can emerge from a present that is impervious to the laws of certainty, themselves another construction of the laws of nature. Macbeth's terror derives from the unforeseen reign of the unnatural, where nothing is but what is not. In *Macbeth* the laws of nature are in a constant state of transgression.

Macbeth's sense of history is shadowy and sweeping. He is troubled by a past that threatens to engulf his entire being. His response is largely to avoid that past and to immerse himself in the tides of the present time that are sweeping him to the future. The present in the play seems driven by a historic force, famously encapsulated in the repeated word "tomorrow." He constructs history as a terrible and overwhelming force as he faces tomorrow: "all our yesterdays have lighted fools / The way to dusty death"(5.5.21–22).

By contrast, Macduff invokes, in his English scene with Malcolm, a different sense and kind of history. He recalls stable and sure values embodied in the deceased persons of Duncan and his queen:

> Thy royal father
> Was a most sainted king. The queen that bore thee,
> Oft'ner on her knees than on her feet,
> Died every day she lived.
>
> (4.3.109–12)

The past, as remembered here, acquires the sharp edges of persons, behaviors, actions, and precise Christian values. Macduff is both telling and showing it: he remembers king and queen in order to shape and comprehend the present. Macduff harks back to an apparently better time, to a sure and firm-set history that includes national myths and moral touchstones by which the nation has been directed, from which it takes its heroes and villains. From these myths and stories of Scotland's past he draws a moral perspective on the present; he remembers and reminds Malcolm of what Scotland was and may be again.

By contrast, Macbeth's last memory of the world he once occupied and has now lost is contained in the dreadful and dread-filled speech in which he recollects his capacity for ordinary human fear:

I have almost forgot the taste of fears.
The time has been my senses would have cooled
To hear a night shriek, and my fell of hair
Would at a dismal treatise rouse and stir
As life were in't. I have supped full with horrors.
Direness, familiar to my slaughterous thoughts,
Cannot once start me.

                                                  (5.5.9–15)

The past merges with the present in a virtually undiscernible shift. For four-and-a-half lines Macbeth recalls a time gone by in his recollection of the person he once was; the time when he, like others, was susceptible to the feelings of fear; when he, like others, responded to a night shriek in normal terror; when his physical being—his reflexive instincts—responded involuntarily and naturally to the world of sensation. Gary Wills comments that this evident desire of Macbeth to overcome his own fears and, thus, to triumph over his own memories is part of a process set in motion after the murder of the king: "Macbeth engages in a self-refashioning that amounts to sabotage committed upon himself. He systematically disconnects the systems of reflection."[9] Systems of reflection are, of course, entirely dependent upon memory. Macbeth refashions a self almost without memory; his vain mission is to distance himself from the source of his pain. But his memory is, in the end, inescapable. It manifests itself in a myriad of ways and no evasions can put it outside the pulsating interior self that gradually consumes everything it touches.

The final direct and specific reference in *Macbeth* to the world that existed before the play is Macduff's, as he brings into life the nightmare curse: "And let the angel whom thou still hast serv'd / Tell thee, Macduff was from his mother's womb / Untimely ripped" (5.10.14–16). The violent language here produces a curious and mixed effect. Nemesis in this play is necessarily a figure of violence; every dramatic detail has conspired to deny Macbeth a peaceful or a solitary death. The violence of Macduff's birth seems here to be evidence that the ordained mission of his life is to kill Macbeth. Mother and motherhood in this play are themselves ambiguous states in which suckling and giving birth are surrounded by images and details of violence and death. Macduff's invocation of his birth is a discursive and active means of realizing the hideous dream. Of course, the whole is predicated upon a sleight of hand: certainly Macduff was born of woman, unless the word "born" is given an entirely original, etymologically unprecedented meaning. But there has been a rent in nature's design in a world of long ago; it is this detail that convinces Macbeth that Macduff's is the hand that will slay him. The past, that world of which Macbeth is an inevitable part but which he has sought assiduously to deny, is what defeats him in the end. A small tatter in nature's plan from a world he has almost successfully avoided is the blow that crushes the tyrant.

The paucity of references to the preplay past lends immediacy to the dramaturgical discourses of *Macbeth*. From a devastated present, the outlook for most of the play is more devastation, violence, and loneliness. The presentness of the action leaves, as the play's most powerful impression, a sense of dislocation—a dislocation heightened by the nearly ubiquitous imagery of disturbance. The great rush that the Macbeths are making toward the future gives a sense of panic to the enterprise, a sense that is intensified by the apparent absence of a world of past certainties upon which the present can safely rest or depend. Panic is the dominant mood of the early scenes of the play. It is a feeling that hardens into recklessness as the play progresses; but recklessness built on panic is itself fragile. The early scenes of the play are in a constant state of anticipation of disaster. Action is the antidote to panic in this play, but it is not always efficacious. For here the panic born of the possibility of success leads to action, which only produces more panic.

The play in large measure is about what it feels like to have killed the king, in the same way that *Hamlet* is about what it feels like to have to or to want to kill the king. The two plays depend for their terror very largely on nostalgia. As Hamlet hankers for the days of innocence before his father was dead, so Macbeth, more intensely, hankers for the moment, the second, the instant before he took the fatal step. Thus, while the speech "Had I but died an hour before this chance / I had lived a blessèd time, for from this instant / There's nothing serious in mortality" (2.3.87–89) can look like cynical pragmatism, many will see in it nothing but the purest and most fraught expression of remorse in the language. Macbeth is trying with these words to surround and contain the invasion of panic terror. This moment bites back at Macbeth for the rest of his life as though it were the moment he came into being; what alters as he ages in the course of the play is his manner of recollecting it.

The history of Macbeth's life loses meaning in the presence of the great murder. What matters is the present: to deal with, to cope, to do. These needs, after the crisis of murdering the king, are matters of great urgency that belong to the here and the now. The history of Macbeth is absorbed into shadows that the present and future throw over the world he strives to hold onto. Macbeth's life as an outlaw starts after the play has started. His criminality is a feature of that present reality, one that appears to resist historicization; a resistance that is self-consciously centered in the hero himself, who possesses a defiantly individualistic, somewhat ahistorical and apolitical viewpoint upon his own plight. Although his own present life strews evidence of a past everywhere, in his conscious mind, in the words he speaks, Macbeth cannot linger in that old place. And yet, of course, Macbeth, like Lady Macbeth, had both father and mother. His father, Sinell, is remembered only because his death authorizes Macbeth's thanehood; but his mother has no existence in the play. No word in the drama adverts or alludes to a place or time in which the parents of Macbeth possessed relevance or existence, except, of course, in the probably fabricated history that his wife provides to explain his hallucination at the banquet. Where are they, Macbeth's mother, children, brothers, sisters, nurses, teachers? It is not that they are forgotten but that Shakespeare has contrived a means of representing formidable and alarming dramatic pace through the agency of panic and a discourse that maintains its pace by notionally jettisoning the past.

By not providing Macbeth with a fleshed out, substantial past, Shakespeare creates an impression of alienation. Macbeth seems not to belong to anyone; he is alienated even from the roots that personal history provides. He is a prime exemplar of Girard's "surrogate victim," the victim or scapegoat who comes from inside the community.[10] Macbeth is the scapegoat who is guilty of the crimes with which he is charged and for which he is sacrificed. The violence of Scotland and its raging, bloody mayhem achieve apparent resolution in his death by the massive exercise of communal violence that, typically, seeks to extirpate the seeds of its own self-destruction by locating them in the person of the nation's most visible villain. His dependency upon his wife is broken at the moment when he kills Duncan. Lady Macbeth, who remembers her father at an utterly crucial time, is weakened by the memory, but she is also, in a small way, redeemed by it. Her appalling intentional cruelty is momentarily interrupted by a sudden access of human feeling brought on by a potent and literally transforming memory. Her role as a murderess is changed to that of a woman with a conscience. Her inability to kill the king connects with the terrible expressions of remorse and regret of her mad scene where her subconscious mind reveals the existence of a latent humanity and moral instinct. Macbeth's tribulation is that the agon between moral instinct and evil ambition is played out on the stage of his *conscious* mind: he knows, sees, and confronts the horror and evil within himself. The range and extent of his crime are manifested in the intensely present mood of his struggle. Macbeth's reflection is moral and emotional rather than historical. He doesn't yearn for an easier or more innocent time; rather, he longs to recover an easier and more innocent feeling.

Feeling is no less contingent upon memory than upon moral and historical knowledge. The play is filled with evidence of ancient historical memory. Notwithstanding the characters' almost pathological inadvertence to their own past lives, there are intricate layers of historical memory and detail everywhere evident in the discourses of the drama. All of the characters, obviously, exist in a historical context that each persistently and consciously recognizes. Those contexts include the linear history to which each sees himself connected: Macbeth locates himself in a line of Scottish kings; Lady Macbeth in a line of Scottish queens. Fleance is destined to continue an established line, while Malcolm's position is to succeed to it. In short, the past is systematized through the forms of living that the present takes. King James himself is one of the more vivid, if unacknowledged, presences of the play. And Gary Wills offers a multiplicity of details describing the play's homages to the monarch. He includes references to the ways, for example, James—a Scottish Monarch, after all—was *not* to be confused with Duncan; for James possessed a much-touted ability to find, almost magically, the mind's construction in the face: "He was like an angel looking through appearances, according to Coke."[11] Moral certainty itself is measured by its deviation from or its adherence to established norms. In addition to the laws of the land there are the uncodified but ironbound laws of custom—notoriously that of hospitality—that reify the presence of that past.

There are, as well, the mythological pasts that bring into being the ancient Scottish, pagan, and Christian "history" in simplified moral form to add weight and authority to the discourses of disaster with which the present is informed. Golgotha, Bellona, Saint Colm, Hecate, and Tarquin are among those references whose shadowy presence in the drama help support a metaphorical structure by which history and metaphor are intertwined. The past becomes, in references such as these, a nonmaterial but substantial locus of precedent for the present. The past, in other

words, looms ubiquitously in the play: it is large and it determines events, behaviors, and attitudes to a considerable extent.
It possesses chiefly a kind of abstract precision. It is a touchstone
and a referent; but it seems, almost contradictorily, to have little
materiality. Such materiality or literalness as the past does possess in *Macbeth* is limited and discrete, confined to remarkably
few moments.

NOTES

1. As will become evident, it is hard to be specific as to number, some of the
"experiences" being rather vague and allusive while others are quite precisely
remembered events.

2. Graham Holderness, Nick Potter, and John Turner, *Shakespeare: The
Play of History* (London: Macmillan, 1988), 144.

3. Steven Mullaney, *The Place of the Stage: License, Play, and Power in Renaissance England* (Chicago: Univ. of Chicago Press, 1988), 133.

4. Mullaney comments on this episode that it sets the traitor at an uncertain threshold of Renaissance society, athwart a line that sets off the human
from the demonic, the natural from the natural (116).

5. René Girard, *Violence and the Sacred* (Baltimore: Johns Hopkins Univ.
Press, 1977), 41. John Turner addresses the issue of Macbeth's contamination
via Girard in *Shakespeare: The Play of History* (137).

6. Mullaney, *The Place of the Stage*, 31.

7. Graham Holderness, "From Radical Potentiality and Institutional Closure: Shakespeare in Film and Television," in *Shakespeare, "Macbeth": A Case-
book*, ed. John Wain (London: Macmillan, 1994), 259–60.

8. Robert Weimann, *Shakespeare and the Popular Tradition in the Theater*
(Baltimore: Johns Hopkins Univ. Press, 1978), 217.

9. Gary Wills, *Witches and Jesuits: Shakespeare's "Macbeth"* (New York:
Oxford Univ. Press and the New York Public Library, 1995), 128.

10. Girard, *Violence and the Sacred*, 102.

11. Wills, *Witches and Jesuits*, 30.

Antony, Cleopatra, the Market, and the End(s) of History

Arthur Lindley

COMMERCE IS THE DIRTY SECRET OF BAKHTIN'S THEORY OF CARNIVAL. Throughout his definitive (if fictive) account in the first chapter of *Rabelais and His World* and elsewhere, he marginalizes what in practice is as inescapably central to carnival as is its hostility to outsiders: the normal activities of the marketplace and its inhabitants. Carnival is the festivity of the market, after all, and its celebration of change, its projection of values as negotiable and identities as reversible, as well as its reduction of life to appetite and everything spiritual or abstract to the material bodily level, all reflect its origins. A ruthlessly successful character, who happens to run a gaudy restaurant described as a "carnival," in the 1996 film *Big Night* puts these shared principles simply when he says, "I'm a businessman. I'm anything I need to be at any time." Octavius—or Rabelais—could not have put it better. A process of ironic marginalization of embarrassingly monetary valves takes place in *Antony and Cleopatra*, as it does in Bakhtin. Business is Rome's and Egypt's dirty secret. An important part of the business of Shakespeare's play is to publish that secret.[1]

The world of *Antony and Cleopatra* is a world of barter in which relations are customarily transactional and temporary. That fundamental but seldom acknowledged point shapes the presentation of time in a time-obsessed text. The difference between Rome and Egypt is not simply between business and pleasure, as is often assumed, but between two different kinds of business (and, for that matter, two different kinds of pleasure). One society trades in honor and hoarded treasure, the other "trade[s] in love," as Egypt says of herself (2.5.2). Caesar, as Pompey notes, "gets money where / He loses hearts" (2.1.13–14). One culture saves, the other lavishes. Rome is associated with the newly emergent, increasingly centralized state of Shakespeare's England and with its business culture of purchased monopolies and joint-stock companies; Egypt with the traditional marketplace of independent small traders that is also, for Shakespeare as well as Bakhtin, the place of carnival. Octavius is proleptically identified with corporate ruthlessness, just as the bountiful Antony, Egypt's reluctant patron, is identified with a dying tradition of aristocratic largesse. What kills Enobarbus, of course, is Antony's sending of his treasure after him, a gift that reminds its victim of the difference between the two systems.

The train of Roman history runs on the clock-time of bureaucratic order and speeds toward an illusory millennium of monopoly and stasis, Caesar's "time of universal peace" (4.6.4). Egypt embodies and survives in the fluid time of a world of constant transaction that resists closure—the freedom of a market whose purpose is, after all, the indefinite perpetuation of trade—and for which Octavius's peace is death. One order hates flux; the other celebrates it. That means that the Roman order of Octavius is at war with the very nature of time in the fallen, mutable world and tries, like Bakhtin's official order, to defeat it by imposing the illusion of changeless stability. Octavius, an early version of Francis Fukuyama, aims at nothing less than the end of history. Egypt is immersed in mutability, in the ever-vanishing present that it can transcend only by rejecting the source of its vitality to become marble-cold and constant. Both orders attempt to escape the flux of fallen time in ways whose religious and metaphysical dimensions are often noted, but whose commercial bases have been largely ignored. Cleopatra embodies the vitality of the open market, Octavius the principle of monopoly and its agricultural extension, enclosure, which threatens that vitality in the name of order and an aristocratic superiority to trade.

As *The Merchant of Venice* reminds us, there is nothing anachronistic about referring to Shakespeare's interest in the market. The opposition of Rome and Egypt in this play is deeply rooted in the economic and social context of Shakespeare's time. Sixty years ago, L. C. Knights taught us the cultural and literary importance of the proliferation of monopolies in Elizabethan and Jacobean England.[2] One particular form those monopolies took, of course, were joint-stock companies for exploration and trade such as the East India Company and the Levant Company, those precursors of empire. In his recent, magisterial study of the economic history of the period, *Merchants and Revolution*, Robert Brenner traces the rise to commercial and political power of these new merchants, their displacement of the older merchant adventurers, and the pervasive restraints of trade that accompanied the process, since "a free and open trade posed real dangers" for these merchants.[3] The new monopolists were consistently supported by the monarchy since, as Brenner says, "a prosperous merchant community could offer an unrivaled source of financial support."[4] The monopolies—the commercial version of agricultural enclosure—were widely and correctly seen as threats both to free trade and what we would call consumer rights. They were also linked to two other prominent features of the period: the centralization and expansion of the state's revenue operations under Thomas Gresham and the proliferation of spies—who provided commercial information as much as or more than military information—under Francis Walsingham.[5] Overseas ventures and spying, both internal and external, are, as we know, defining features of Octavius's Rome. Shakespeare thus represents the opposition between Rome and Egypt as one between independent traders, in either the marketplace or the exchange, and the archmonopolist and encloser Octavius, whom Thidias calls the "universal landlord" (3.13.72). That conflict, as one might expect, is represented as one between carnival and Lent.

One need not, of course, assume that all these references are equally explicit, let alone that Shakespeare would have expected his audience to look at Cleopatra and think, "Ah, yes, free enterprise!" The closing of markets and fields, however, was very much a live issue at the time of the play: enclosure at the hands of local versions of Octavius produced riots in Kent in 1596 and a "rising" in the Midlands in 1607, close to the date of *Antony and Cleopatra*.[6] Brenner further notes that the expansion of the Levant Company's monopoly in 1589 and 1590 "provoked substantial protests from merchant outsiders," an old order fighting a losing battle against its successor.[7] It does seem, in this regard, that the identification of the aging Antony with a myth of old-aristocratic generosity and the boy Caesar with the cost-accounting "new men," like those of the East India and Levant Companies as well as their friends in government, is quite explicit and is spelled out in such parallel scenes as act 4, scenes 1 and 2, in which the two leaders—one coldly calculating, the other (at least in manner) generous—deal with their troops before battle.[8] As is usually noted, Antony contrasts his old-fashioned mode of fighting with the strategic-planning style of Octavius, who "dealt on lieutenantry, and no practice had / In the brave squares of war" (3.2.39–40). That contrast has a commercial analogue, however, as well as a carnivalesque one.

Cleopatra's association with the carnivalesque is similarly explicit. In a sense, her association with the free market is the implicit product of imagining an opposite to Caesar's quite explicit drive toward global monopoly. The language of commerce in the play, however, is subversive and marginal, since it demystifies the processes of power. It emerges explicitly in the language of losers, such as Pompey, and subordinates, such as Enobarbus and Agrippa; it emerges only inadvertently in the language of the leaders. Its importance is thus registered by its very suppression, as when Octavius denies being a merchant, a charge no one has made (5.2.178–79). In the world of this play the leaders, such as Antony, talk reason of state while stealing another's house. In such a case, it is the man (such as Pompey) whose house has been stolen who is most likely to say what is really going on.

Cleopatra's carnival nature is directly related to the marketplace, the traditional site of carnival, where Antony sits "enthroned" (2.2.221), waiting for his first meeting with her, and where—arrayed in the colors of money—they proclaim their (nominally her) empire:

> I' th' marketplace on a tribunal silvered,
> Cleopatra and himself in chairs of gold
> Were publicly enthroned.
>
> (3.6.3–5)

From their first pageantlike entrance, Antony and Cleopatra's affair is played out as public spectacle, available for promiscuous observation and participation, both royal and common. Enobarbus "saw her once / Hop forty paces through the public street" (2.2.234–35). When the lovers abandon Caesar's ambassadors to "wander through the streets, and note / The qualities of people" (1.1.55–56), they also make themselves available to be noted, both spectators and spectacle, as participants in carnival are supposed to be. As Julian Markels writes, "Cleopatra and the public street are ornaments to each other, and they measure each other's value."[9]

Carnivalesque Cleopatra is linked to the earth and the time-sense appropriate to it. Identified with birth and decay, the cycles of the Nile, "she represents," as Andrew Fichter puts it, "the unbroken circle of appetitive nature."[10] She is also what Philo sees as "a tawny front" (1.1.6), and what she herself describes, a woman "with Phoebus' amorous pinches black, / And wrinkled deep in time" (1.5.28–29)—in Elizabethan eyes at least, a grotesque.[11] A figure of such extreme and pervasive sexual voracity that Romans habitually regard her as debilitating, she figures, like the Wife of Bath, as sexual appetite abnormally prolonged as well as heightened, a summer with no winter in it or to it. She is also, at various times, a shrew, a virago, an ostentatious and self-glorifying liar, a beater of servants and browbeater of lovers, in short, a crowned version of the husband-tormenting wife at whom skimmington rituals were directed: "Shakespeare has represented her in much the same terms Bakhtin uses to identify the grotesque—or popular—body in Renaissance culture. Shakespeare clearly endows her with all the features of carnival."[12]

While she may be "stigmatized" by this identification, as Tennenhouse argues, she is also glorified by it. "In this tradition," Bakhtin says, "woman is essentially related to the material bodily lower stratum; she . . . degrades and regenerates simultaneously."[13] Cleopatra, of course, gives birth to a new, sexualized Antony in the process of subverting the military, Roman one. "Egypt," moreover, rules and is metonymically associated with a country defined by carnival festivity and carnivalesque inversion, a national expression of what Marilyn French calls the "outlaw feminine principle."[14] Egypt everywhere acts out that basic trope of carnivalesque subversion, women on top. Cleopatra "angles," Antony is the fish (2.5.10–14); she drinks him to bed and wears his "sword Philippan" (2.5.21–23). In the most fundamental dynamic of the play, carnivalesque femininity confronts masculine officialdom in the person of Octavius or his various lieutenants. That much is obvious; the entrepreneurial basis of the confrontation, to judge from the criticism, is less so.

If Cleopatra is carnival, then crabbed, parsimonious Caesar, who typically regards feasting his victorious army as "waste" (4.1.16), is a Lenten representative of the plutocratic new lords of Jacobean England.[15] She is, of course, everywhere identified with feasting, a trope Clare Kinney neatly calls "Cleopatra the Comestible."[16] It is her "lascivious wassails" from which Caesar pretends to call Antony back to business (1.4.55–56). She is, at various times "a morsel for a monarch" (1.5.31), an "Egyptian dish" (2.6.123), "a morsel cold upon / Dead Caesar's trencher" (3.13.117–18), even (in her youth) a green salad, and finally, of course, "a dish for the gods" (5.2.265–66). She is not only the purveyor of feasts, but also Feast itself, the literary descendent of Rabelais's Gargamelle as much as Venus. Breakfast at her house is "eight wild boars, roasted whole" (2.2.186) for twelve people. By contrast, when Octavius wants to praise the former Antony, he seizes on the most antifestive kind of feasting: drinking "the

stale of horses" and eating "strange flesh, / Which some did die
to look on" (1.4.61–68). The tyrant, not surprisingly, regards the
proper relation of will to body as tyrannical, an attitude also expressed in his desire to "possess" the time rather than enjoy it
(2.7.95). For Caesar, privation is virtue; bodies, like kingdoms
and moments, exist to be conquered. Lenten in his youth, by contrast, Antony has become carnivalesque in middle age, a testament to Cleopatra's powers of regeneration.

Cleopatra's liquidity is also that of the market as well as the
Nile. When Enobarbus says that "custom" cannot "stale / Her
infinite variety" (2.2.240–41), he clearly means the business
sense of "patronage" as well as the familiar sense of "habit."
After "gipsy," "strumpet" is the first and most frequent term of
Roman abuse thrown at her (see 1.1.13), women who sell themselves being, of course, a threat to men such as Octavius, who
wish to sell them.[17] She "trade[s] in love" (2.5.2), and not merely
by getting armies in return for her favors. (Sleeping with generals
is, after all, Egypt's defense policy.) At their first meeting, as Enobarbus describes it, Antony "for his ordinary"—that is, his
board—"pays his heart / For what his eyes eat only" (2.2.231–
32). Their moment-to-moment relationship is a constant extor-
tion of tribute, whether in the form of pearls, protestations, or
empires. "If it be love, tell me how much" (1.1.14): from her first
words Cleopatra makes it clear that love is a measurable commodity and subject to fluctuation. That commodity is obtained by
what we might call the negotiability of her character. Her moods
are determined by the market: "If you find him sad, / Say I am
dancing" (1.3.3–4). The principle may be that the customer is always wrong, but the transaction nonetheless makes Cleopatra
vulnerable as the purveyor of a product always subject to rejection. The "morsel for a monarch" can easily become the "morsel
cold" on the dead monarch's trencher and despised by the next
customer.

At the same time, however, Cleopatra is the restaurateur as
well as the meal. Octavia is only a commodity, however mystified,
traded by males; Cleopatra is an entrepreneur. This agency con-
jures up the possibility of a world, outside Rome, where women
operate independently. It also makes Cleopatra and carnival the
embodiments of a free market of private traders. As his rivals
find, Octavius aims for monopoly. In his new world order, values
will be fixed because there will be only one purchaser: the sole
surviving "factor for the gods" (2.6.10).[18] His empire is a vast enclosure movement, driven, like enclosure, to maximize profit and

control by eliminating subdivision until there is only a single "universal landlord." By the end of the play, he can assert that "Caesar's no merchant, to make prize with [Cleopatra] / Of things that merchants sold" (5.2.179–80): an assertion of aristocratic superiority to the market that actually declares the market closed. His snobbery is directed not at commerce but at competition. The "sole sir o' th' world," as she calls him (5.2.116), no longer needs to bargain. In effect, the plutocrat retires to his mansion and, like Ben Jonson's usurer in "The Praises of a Countrie-Life," curses trade. Throughout the play, Caesar plays to end "play," in both the carnival and market senses. Cleopatra gives Charmian leave to "play till doomsday" (5.2.227), but Caesar's advancing troops guarantee that doomsday comes a few moments later. Cleopatra bids, Octavius forecloses.

Cleopatra assumes that all relationships are functions of desire; Octavius assumes that they are functions of control. Her appetitive world is comic because it asserts that all desires (hence, all relationships) are renewable. Nothing really ends, nothing dies. One of the play's most startling moves is to equate that comic renegotiability and deferral of closure with the market: "play" of body and feeling with "play" of commercial value. What else does it mean to "trade in love"? What is not sold today can be sold tomorrow. (Always selling the image of gratification and the promise of ownership, Cleopatra is an opportunity for venture capitalism, making promises not unlike those Drake made to his investors: vague but immense profits for a moment's investment. As with Antonio in *The Merchant of Venice*, the risks involved are associated with the uncertainties of the sea.) No value is fixed, nothing truly limited. Any emotional deal can be restructured. He who is sunk today can be refloated tomorrow, as the dead Antony rises in her imagination, bestriding the ocean, kissing Iras in a meadow in Hades. By contrast, Caesar insists on finality because his drive for control can only be fulfilled in universal stasis, to which both Cleopatra and the free market represent vitality and resistance. Cleopatra maintains a comic world in which consequences are perpetually suspended. She no more expects her flight from the battle to cause Antony's retreat than she expects her feigned death to cause his real one. Death in the carnivalesque, of course, only exists to occasion renewal, as bankruptcy is an aberration of the market, not its norm. Cleopatra's vision of a perpetually festive afterlife with Antony and the suicide it facilitates are the ultimate extensions of this comedic principle of escape. Her theatrical multiplicity functions throughout

the play, of course, as a means of resisting possession and control—and eternity is, after all, the ultimate form of deferral. The
play's notorious generic instability is a direct function of Cleopatra's insistence—beyond death—on the commercial, comic, and
carnivalesque.[19]

The Roman sense of time, by contrast, is defined, like the
Roman sense of identity, by both purpose and closure. Romans
deal with mutability by organizing it into a single big, necessarily
Roman, story, whose outline is the progressive emergence of
order out of chaos.[20] Time, as Octavius sees it (and his view prevails by the elimination of other views), hastens toward its end in
"the time of universal peace."[21] That process he, of course, con-
strues as a kind of manifest destiny, characteristically impersonal. "I must perforce / Have shown to thee such a declining
day, / Or look on thine," he says to the deceased Antony, "we
could not stall together" (5.1.37–39). History or nature or market
forces did it, not him. This (cover) story confers not only the retrospective sense of inevitability that stories customarily provide
but a prospective one, since the story is known before it is completed. Time is mapped, plotted, foreknown. Since Shakespeare
shows us the construction of this myth, it will appear to us rather
as public relations: the version Octavius will tell to his followers
in his tent after act 5, scene 1: not destiny but the calculated illusion of it. Like all of Rome's claims to solidity and dignity, this
one is ludicrously false.

Even Romans who see that story as a mystification (such as the
skeptical soldiers who watch Caesar's reaction to Antony's death)
accede to it because it imposes a form on the chaos of experience.
As Janet Adelman and others have shown, Roman rulers habitually equate flux with decay and death, and both with the shifty,
unorganized populace they rule: "this common body, / Like to a
vagabond flag upon the stream, / Goes to, and back . . . / To rot
itself with motion" (1.4.44–47).[22] That is Octavius's view but it
echoes Antony's earlier references to "our slippery people"
(1.2.169–79). In the mythology of both leaders there is an essential Rome that coexists with the real one: the Rome of fortune,
accident, and politic schemes. Octavius will rescue this ideal from
the real. Rome, like the dying Cleopatra, will become marble-cold
and constant. It will become its own monument, its own tomb.

Roman identity is centrally a matter of earning "a place i' [this]
story" (3.13.45), as Enobarbus puts it before losing *his* place.
Having a place in the story does indeed give one an identity, but
only one, and it is necessarily built on denial. When one admits

other possibilities, as Antony has done, one begins to wander into the other potential stories that surround him, the comedies of an- gling and cross-dressing that are Cleopatra's chosen narratives. One will eventually, if unknowingly, find oneself in the much greater dream-narrative of Cleopatra's "Emperor Antony" and one's afterlife together. Enobarbus's barge speech both describes this temptation (Antony being drawn into Cleopatra's perform- ance), but enacts it (in the narrator's bemused fascination), and creates it (in the salacious dreaminess of Agrippa's and Maece- nas's response). The speech, of course, describes the dissolution of the Roman general into the gawking tourist on his way to be- coming the lover, heroic and besotted, of what is—whether he likes it or not—his defining other. To wander from one's single, self-defined story is to re-enter the flux from which the story was supposed to rescue him. It is to re-enter time and become the "cloud that's dragonish" (4.15.2).[23] In commercial terms, it is to be renegotiated.

As we all know, when Antony advises Caesar to "be a child o' th' time," Octavius gives the perfect Roman answer, "Possess it" (2.7.94–95). Here, Caesar is treating time not merely as a com- modity to be owned, as is usually noted, but as space to be colo- nized. "Time" roughly equals "Egypt," the nation or the person. If Octavius ever did decide to seize the day, he would send in the army first and then appoint a governor. To possess the time, in his sense, is to control it from a viewpoint outside it in a kind of virtual timelessness and thus to achieve a kind of imaginary immortality. He who possesses time is not subject to it. Ruling over his (also imaginary) time of universal peace, why should Oc- tavius ever die? (What doesn't change, doesn't die.) On the other hand, children of the time, as Antony will soon demonstrate, have much celerity in dying. To possess the time, however, is inher- ently alienating: an attempt to live outside the medium in which one exists, dolphinlike. Caesar is to life what the chair of the Fed- eral Reserve is to the American stock market: he stands outside the play, cautioning against irrational exuberance. Romans typi- cally view time as history, as extension and therefore as conquer- able space. Concentrating on the past and the future—which is necessarily where stories exist, since the present instant can never itself be a story—they are always inclined to miss the now. Antony, whistling in the marketplace, misses the show Cleopatra has prepared for him and which has to be expended on Enobarbus and his future audience. When at the start of the play Antony wishes to let "Rome in Tiber melt" (1.1.35), he is seeking escape from just this historical, longitudinal sense. The stones of Roman tradition will melt in some apocalyptic future, taking all Roman stories with them, and leaving Antony in the "space" of the present moment where he embraces Cleopatra (1.1.36). Egyptian time, which Antony is attempting to enter, is immersive: one swims in it like the dolphin to which Cleopatra will compare Antony (5.2.88). One possesses it by letting it possess oneself. Gaining the present, one tends to lose past and future. In the mercantile terms with which we started, the past too is constantly renegotiable—Julius Caesar's memory can be displaced by Antony's; both can, nay will, be endlessly rewritten—and the future can be deferred indefinitely. Of course, since Antony remains a Roman, the present moment of act 1, scene 1 must also be conquerable space and a rival empire. But it is an empire whose extension can be no more than the moment required to announce it; in the next instant the "nobleness of life" (1.1.38) turns to wrangling or wandering the streets.

Antony, Octavius, Cleopatra, and Enobarbus share a common purpose: to rescue an identity from the flux, especially by creating a heroic other—Antony as past hero or defeated rival or godlike lover or master—against which to define the heroic self. The Roman sense of identity requires complete control in order to impose complete fixity. Thus it can only be fulfilled in suicide, the ultimate self-defining and self-terminating act, which "shackles accident and bolts up change" (5.2.6), and which is the logical end of the Roman myth of the single defining act, like Enobarbus's betrayal, which defines one's place in the story. Antony makes his wars for Cleopatra, but makes his suicide to fix his own identity as a "Roman by a Roman / Valiantly vanquished" (4.16.59–60). That Roman is himself, of course; he has written even Cleopatra's agency out of his death to create a closed circle of self-definition in which he is killer, victim, and historian. And, of course, it doesn't work. Antony's memory goes on being rewritten into Cleopatra's myth and appropriated by Caesar, who will bury Antony as a lover—thus erasing the political rival—and as a further proof of "his glory which / Brought them to be lamented" (5.2.352–53). Linda Charnes appropriately refers to Caesar in this final role as "the venture capitalist of notorious identity, the Merchant of Legend."[24]

In this play, all roads lead to death. The choice is to melt like an Egyptian or freeze like a Roman. The Egyptian way has, of course, the advantage of not being at war with the condition of life in time, the continuously fluctuating market of desire. It is also not inherently absurd as the Roman attempt to put a stop to mutability is. As "our terrene moon" (3.13.156), Cleopatra, the goddess and not the mere emperor of this world, possesses time more effectively than Caesar: it will slow down, speed up, even pause with her desires. But it won't stay; Egypt loses the present as surely as Rome does. The Egyptian road offers the joy of play and the wealth of protean multiplicity, but it declares its own inadequacy by Cleopatra's attempts to become marble-cold and constant. The inadequacy of Caesar's way is registered not only by the cold knowing in apartness with which he attempts to rule the sublunary world, but also by the vast joke that enfolds his enterprises. He is, after all, God's fool as well as Fortune's knave, building his empire as the necessary stage for that great birth adumbrated by the play's many foreshadowings and biblical echoes. The next "Eastern star"—or "star in the east"—will announce the only agency capable of offering a way out of the deathward flux of the play's Augustinian world: the only love capable of defeating time and closing the market of desire.

NOTES

1. See M. M. Bakhtin, *Rabelais and His World*, trans. Helene Iswolsky (Bloomington, Ind.: Indiana Univ. Press, 1984), 1–58. *Big Night*. Directed by Campbell Scott and Stanley Tucci. 104 min. Columbia/Tristan, 1996.

2. L. C. Knights, *Drama and Society in the Age of Shakespeare* (Cambridge: Cambridge Univ. Press, 1936), 1–173.

3. Robert Brenner, *Merchants and Revolution: Commercial Change, Political Conflict, and London's Overseas Traders, 1550–1653* (Cambridge and New York: Cambridge Univ. Press, 1993), 64. For an outline of the basic process, see pp. 3–23. Without trying to force allegory on the play, I would suggest that the contention between old and new monopolists is eerily suggestive of the contention of the world sharers in *Antony and Cleopatra*, with Pompey and the Egyptians filling the role of the outside traders. However, if Shakespeare needed a model for the power struggle in Rome, he had a very public, important one available in the commercial life of London in his time.

4. Brenner, *Merchants and Revolution*, 54.

5. For a particularly vivid account of Walsingham, the employer of (among others) Christopher Marlowe, see Charles Nicholl, *The Reckoning: The Murder of Christopher Marlowe* (London: Jonathan Cape, 1992), especially 102–13; on Gresham, see Knights, *Drama and Society*, 42–45.

6. See Alan G. R. Smith, *The Emergence of a Nation State: The Commonwealth of England, 1529–1660* (London and New York: Longmans, 1984), 192–93.

7. Brenner, *Merchants and Revolution*, 64.

8. On Antony's and Pompey's association with feudal nobility, see Paul

Yachnin, "'Courtiers of Beauteous Freedom': *Antony and Cleopatra* in Its Time," *Renaissance and Reformation* 15 (1981): 1–20.

9. Julian Markels, *The Pillar of the World: "Antony and Cleopatra" in Shakespeare's Development* (Columbus, Ohio: Ohio State Univ. Press, 1968), 45. I discuss Egypt's carnivalization of Rome in chapter 6 of my book *Hyperion and the Hobbyhorse* (Newark, Del., and London: Univ. of Delaware Press, 1996).

10. Andrew Fichter, *"Antony and Cleopatra:* 'The Time of Universal Peace,'" *Shakespeare Survey* 33 (1980): 103.

11. "A brow of Egypt" is, of course, Theseus's antithesis to "Helen's beauty" in *A Midsummer Night's Dream* (5.1.11).

12. Leonard Tennenhouse, *Power on Display: The Politics of Shakespeare's Genres* (New York and London: Methuen, 1986), 143.

13. Bakhtin, *Rabelais and His World,* 274.

14. See Marilyn French, *Shakespeare's Division of Experience* (London: Cape, 1982), especially chapter 1, 21–31.

15. Shakespeare has heightened the contrast by omitting Plutarch's testimony to the historical Octavius's affability and fondness for plays and women. For a summary of the changes made to Caesar's character, see Vivian Thomas, *Shakespeare's Roman World* (London: Routledge, 1989), 102–3.

16. Clare Kinney, "The Queen's Two Bodies and the Divided Emperor," in *The Renaissance Englishwoman in Print: Counterbalancing the Canon,* ed. Anne M. Haselkorn and Betty S. Travitsky (Amherst, Mass.: Univ. of Massachusetts Press, 1990), 177.

17. The correct term would be "huckster," the Middle English word, surviving in its gendered form at least into the late sixteenth century, for a female retailer of food and drink. See Eileen Power, *Medieval Women,* ed. by M. M. Postan (Cambridge: Cambridge Univ. Press, 1995), 54. The type survived, of course, in the form of Cleopatra's Henrician counterpart, Mrs. Quickly.

18. Pompey's "Factors" clearly means "purchasing agents," its common seventeenth-century meaning, not just "agents," as the word is often glossed.

19. For an excellent discussion of the conflict between Egyptian comedy and Roman tragedy, see Barbara Vincent, "Shakespeare's *Antony and Cleopatra* and the Rise of Comedy," *English Literary Renaissance* 12 (1982): 53–86. Vincent is not concerned, however, with market or carnival.

20. On the Roman devotion to linear narrative, see Linda Charnes, *Notorious Identity: Materializing the Subject in Shakespeare* (Cambridge: Harvard Univ. Press, 1993), 103–47, especially pp. 106–8. On Rome and the play's reaction to a world of "universal mutability," see Geoffrey Miles, *Shakespeare and the Constant Romans* (Oxford: Clarendon, 1996), 169–88.

21. Roman references to the speed of events and the pressure of the times are, of course, innumerable, like the rush of messengers bringing news. On messengers and their significance, see Charnes, *Notorious Identity.*

22. See Janet Adelman, *The Common Liar: An Essay on "Antony and Cleopatra"* (New Haven and London: Yale Univ. Press, 1973), especially 151–57 and Susan Snyder, "Patterns of Motion in *Antony and Cleopatra,*" *Shakespeare Survey* 33 (1980): 113–22.

23. Allyson Newton, "'At the Very Heart of Loss': Shakespeare's Enobarbus and the Rhetoric of Remembering," in *Renaissance Papers 1995,* ed. George Walton Williams and Barbara J. Baines (Raleigh, N.C.: Southeastern Renaissance Conference, 1995), 81–91, remarks on how Enobarbus, like Antony, "feels the pull of his attraction to Cleopatra drawing him from 'firm security' toward the fearful 'gaps' in time and nature that she inhabits" (85).

24. Charnes, *Notorious Identity,* 146.

"Confederate Season": Shakespeare and the Elizabethan Understanding of *Kairos*

Sharon A. Beehler

Aᴸᴛᴇʀ PERSONAL PRONOUNS AND PREPOSITIONS, THE WORD "NOW" stands as the forty-third most frequently used word in the Shakespearean canon. In *Hamlet* it appears seventy-two times, often in passages of considerable import. This word calls attention to the immediate moment, to the present circumstance, and thereby puts the audience more intimately in contact with the situations of the characters. For Elizabethans, awareness of the present moment, especially the "right" moment for action, was a concept deriving from two sources—both classical and both revered by Renaissance society. The first comes from Greek mythology, subsequently finding its way into Hebraic and Christian theology; the second originates with the Sophists, in particular Gorgias, and their theories of rhetoric. Both sources designate the concept as *Kairos*.

In an age of ceremony, timing was everything. When we hear of people participating in holy sacrament, observing royal pageantry, engaging in folk ritual, or practicing legal protocol, we also see that patterns of preparation and culmination abound.[1] But this sense of ceremonial moment is also clearly theatrical, and in the late sixteenth century, England's appetite for the dramatic was at its height. Playwrights and politicians, clergymen and lawyers all recognized the power of drama, especially its emphasis on timing. Shakespearean scholars have written at length about the subject of time as it appears in the playwright's works, and a few have even treated individual plays by investigating the idea of *Kairos*.[2] However, I want to pay more attention to the complexities of that concept as known to Shakespeare's contemporaries.

Kairos has its foundations in both the philosophical and rhetorical principles of opportunity and appropriateness. The former of these principles—the philosophical principle of opportunity—

74

became represented in Greek mythology as a god, *Kairos,* usually figured by a young athletic man, whose most prominent feature was a full lock of hair growing at the front of his head. According to one source, this lock "is the symbol that one must take the favorable opportunity by the forelock."[3] This figure also carried the "scales of decision balanced on the edge of a shaving knife, and [his] momentary or fleeting character was portrayed by the wings on his heels and shoulders."[4] During the medieval period this god began to be represented by a female figure that eventually merged with Fortune, bringing the idea of timeliness face-to-face with the whimsicality associated with the sequent deity. The latter principle—the rhetorical principle of appropriateness— became a significant component of sophistic practice, which saw rhetoric as the art of creating knowledge through the use of language and of structures appropriate to the audience, subject, and occasion.[5] As Renaissance thinkers rediscovered these concepts, contemporary interpretations were added to them, and the notion of timing found a strong foothold in the day-to-day practices of the Elizabethans.

Historical accounts about the beliefs surrounding time in the Renaissance have invariably claimed that this period was transitional in its attitude toward it. The age marked a shift from attention on eternal or God's time to an emphasis on historic, human, or earthly time. This shift in attitude was encouraged by the scientific discoveries that regularized the marking of time through mechanical means: clocks took the place of church bells as the means by which life's events were ordered.[6] Among writers of the period we can see this dichotomy reflected in issues of permanence and mutability, eternal salvation and earthly decay, and Constancy and Fortune's wheel. Hamlet's dilemma, whether "to be or not to be," itself suggests the irreconcilable nature of these contrary conceptions of being in time.

But there is another view as well, one that *does* combine the eternal and the temporal. It can be represented by a child in a playground who wants to hop on a spinning merry-go-round but must wait for precisely the right moment to do so. When the rhythms and spaces align between child and moving platform, then they can come together. The separate continuity of the child's existence temporarily matches and accedes to the movement of the merry-go-round. In order for this to occur, a gap must be opened to allow passage from one state of being to another, and yet we glimpse both simultaneously. For Shakespeare's contemporaries, this phenomenon was familiar as a matter of religious conviction, the moment of revelation when God intervenes in human history. But it was also familiar among students of rhetoric as a persuasive skill: recognition of the proper moment when appropriately chosen words can have power to influence.

Shakespeare's plays have been discussed in light of the former religious notion but not sufficiently with regard to the latter rhetorical one. What matters is that the two principles interrelate and that the playwright sought to make the theatrical experience one that was itself a *Kairotic* moment in the sense of a rhetorical structure that leads to a transcendent experience between players and audience. So structured, Shakespeare's plays (like the merry-go-round) move according to their own rhythms, as does the audience (like the child). As the play progresses, alignment of spectators and play becomes more intimate until finally, at a precisely chosen moment, the two meet for a (usually) single instant of shared experience. Aristotle's views of theater, with the emphasis upon audience reaction, reflect both the classical Greek idea of a *Kairotic* moment and anticipate the Elizabethan adherence to that element of dramatic composition. Consequently, scenes such as Richard II's deposition, Henry V's St. Crispin's Day speech, the murder of Julius Caesar, Macbeth's regicide, the condemnation of Hero, Cleopatra's suicide, Lear's howling at the storm, and the animation of Hermione's statue all remain fixed in audience's memories because of the powerful effect they present, the overwhelming instant when the audience can glimpse something beyond theatrical production.

Many critics who have written about the experience of theater speak of it as a stepping out of normal time into the special conventions of theater time (thus, creating a "double-time" effect). The blending of these two ideas of time enables audiences to observe the *construction* of the play at the same time as they observe the *story* of the play.[7] This helps us to see plays as rhetorical compositions, as Marion Trousdale and others have noted, and therefore as subject to the principles of rhetoric pervasive in the late Renaissance world of Elizabethan and Jacobean England. I will return to such rhetorical issues momentarily.

The religious concept of *Kairos* was developed by early Christians who saw similarities between Greek philosophical beliefs in the "right time"—the proper occasion or *occasio* when circumstances are propitious for accomplishment of a task or goal—and their own awareness of heavenly ordained events. The early Christian church adopted *Kairos* to refer to the spiritual, God-appointed instant when God's (eternal) time breaks through into human (temporal) time. These moments of intersection are variously described as "the fullness of time" and "due season" by the New Testament writers, with special reference to the incarnation of Christ, his baptism by John, the Transfiguration, the miracles, the Last Supper, Christ's Passion and Crucifixion, and the Resurrection. In short, the entire life of Christ (the Word become flesh) is characterized by the Gospel writers and by Paul as a *Kairotic* moment of divine intervention by God in human time.

The secular idea of *Kairos* appears in the Old Testament in the Hebraic word *eth,* which is used to describe the time of natural events, such as evening or harvest; of social events, such as mealtime and marriage; or of human life, such as birth and death. The Book of Ecclesiastes refers to this concept most elegantly when it says, "to everything there is a season, and a time to every purpose under heaven" (3:1). Although Old Testament writers acknowledge the divine influence on human life patterns, their thinking about *Kairos* does not include, as does New Testament writers' thinking, the sense of a direct contact between God and humankind. Moses and the prophets record visits of angels and of God himself to specially selected humans, but such visits do not carry with them the sense of an opportune moment. That idea for them remains connected to human affairs. What is significant in both the religious and rhetorical traditions concerning *Kairotic* moments is the double sense of opportunity presented and of appropriate human response to that opportunity. In the religious context what counts, though, is God's role in providing the opportunity: in terms of Christian theology, with the resurrection of Christ, God's most significant opportunity presents itself to humans.

Throughout the first four centuries of the early Church, until the time of Augustine and the Christianizing of Britain, periods of growth and persecution were marked by momentous activities of individuals (including the Gnostics, Constantine, Jerome, Pope Gregory I, and Augustine) and by crucial events (for example, the establishment of the Holy Roman Empire). To view history in this fashion—as a sequence of significant happenings—calls attention to the tendency we still have to regard time as marked by instances when great occasions occur. So deeply ingrained is the notion of *Kairos*, then, that it is not surprising to discover its firm entrenchment within the Middle Ages nor its influence on the Protestant Reformation. For Martin Luther, history was the place of God's action, much of it mysterious and inexplicable.[8] For Protestants and Catholics alike, though, the practice of the holy sacraments was the most personally significant manifestation of *Kairotic* intercession by God in human life.[9] As mentioned earlier, although religion was certainly the dominant philosophic influence during the sixteenth century (as indicated most strongly by the intensity of debate over religious doctrine and practice), all of Europe was gradually making the change from a mystical sense of time as a sign of God's workings in the world (through seasons and daily cycles) to a mechanical, practical system regulated by clocks. Historian Arno Borst describes the degree to which this change influenced Renaissance life in these terms: "The newly discovered regularity of the planetary movements in God's *machina mundi* surpassed all the medieval chronologists' conjectures. . . . Mathematics supplied them with laws that uniformly obtained everywhere in the open universe, in heaven as well as earth, promising to make them into masters of their world and their time."[10] Clearly, in Shakespeare's day, the senses of sacred and secular time created serious issues.[11] Simultaneously, attitudes toward history were changing as a desire to recapture the past led religious and secular scholars to regard prior events as the source of great lessons for human behavior. Such study also led to the assumption that history provided evidence of God's involvement in human affairs. This emphasis on historical chronicles as a reexamination of God's workings in human events—a search, in other words, for God's opportunities and humankind's responses seen as lessons for contemporary life—was an indication of how firmly *Kairotic* principles were established.

The other contributing influence to this idea of opportune times grew from a renewal of interest in classical rhetoric. In many ways the recovery of this knowledge, coupled with new understandings of history and with the overwhelming sense that England was poised on the brink of extraordinary world influence and cultural achievement, helped make England a site of intellectual and artistic activity unique in its existence. Education was highly esteemed, and the value of rhetoric and oratory were paramount in that system of learning. Although Elizabethan rhetoricians do not speak of *Kairos* by name very often, it is evident from their work that the concept held great weight and was taught to young scholars.

To grasp the understanding of *Kairos* most clearly represented in Shakespeare's plays, we must go back to the writings of Pythagoras and Gorgias. These writers, as leaders of the Sophists, did not share all the concepts of rhetoric advocated by the mainstream writers, such as Cicero and Quintilian, and were consequently less admired by the schoolmasters of Shakespeare's day.[12] Nevertheless, the Sophists were known to sixteenth-century England, and even exercised, as Stephen Greenblatt has claimed, a profound influence on the epistemology of Christopher Marlowe's plays.[13] From Mario Untersteiner's discussion of this movement and of Gorgias, in particular, we can glean the complex ideas that underlie the Sophists' dependence upon *Kairos* in creating their system of rhetoric.

Most significant is the Pythagorean belief that *Kairos* (as a limited, definable moment) offers humans a "polarity of opposites." That is, the *Kairotic* moment itself is free of determined value, requiring human effort to "make the same thing, *according to circumstances*, appear either beautiful or ugly, just or unjust."[14] This radical idea denied any possibility of inherent "goodness" in *Kairos*, a prospect that offended Plato and Aristotle, who believed that the very notion of a moment being "appropriate" implied its purpose of revealing the ideal good. Because Pythagoras made the ethics of *Kairos* ambivalent and subject to the will of the speaker, he was partly responsible for the bad press given to the Sophists who were accused by Plato and Aristotle of simply manipulating language and words for effect, with no righteous goal necessarily in mind.

That the Sophists asked for payment for their teaching only intensified the impression that they were without any moral grounding. But for Gorgias, this ambivalent quality of language was at the heart of knowledge (and, in fact, of being) and simply put greater responsibility upon the speaker to exercise good judgment and "make good use of this art."[15] Determining the "good" depends, for Gorgias, upon "the right and proper moment" when a decision between alternatives must be made.[16] Similarly, "'truth' is determined by [human choice exercised within an instance of] *Kairos*."[17] But even as such determination occurs, the antithesis inherent in classical dialectic cannot be avoided or ignored. Because *Kairos* requires the random choosing of one alternative, it necessarily results in annihilating the other, a profoundly irrational and also tragic action. It is irrational because the decision-making process does not rely upon systematic calculation. And it is tragic because such a choice inevitably involves loss, the loss of the alternative. Untersteiner translates Gorgias's claim as follows, "'I know the irreconcilable conflicts and yet I act': this is tragic action." These seemingly negative qualities make possible a more positive outcome because, according to Gorgian thought, *Kairos* permits "the breaking up of the cycle of the antitheses [a state of skepticism] and [the] creating [of] something new." Nevertheless, this creation will be deceptive (in the sense of partial) because it disallows the radical alternative. For human beings, then, the potential for influence—both good and evil—exists within the *Kairotic* moment. As Gorgias claims, "Power lies in the imposition of one of the two alternatives," a belief that leads Untersteiner to conclude that "the ethic, aesthetic, and rhetoric of Gorgias are all based on *Kairos*."[18]

For Gorgias, then, knowledge, reality, or truth "reached by the dialectic" of *logos* "expresses only *aporiai* [a moment of undecidability; a gap]." The "continual clash and counter-clash of the extremes, into which every attempt to arrest the mobility of *physis* [that is, nature] is resolved" sums up the *Kairotic* endeavor.[19] Such attempts or choices create a dilemma "not soluble by reason," but only by the "persuasive force of *logos* which is released in the instant of the decision (*Kairos*) which has as its object . . . 'the right thing at the right moment,'" and that is itself consistent with "divine and universal law," both of which are only irrationally "known."[20] Therefore, Gorgias concludes, in art "there is something mysterious, which is presupposed by this very concept of 'deception': there is something hidden . . . something which neither the tongue can express nor the eye perceive" and which raises art "to the status of the universal meaning of life."[21] And, as rhetoric is an art, it "seeks, not to falsify truth in opposition to morality, but to impose by means of 'deception' *that which is possible*."[22] In short, then, the rhetorical understanding of *Kairos*, as described by Gorgias and interpreted by Untersteiner, involves (1) the irreducible antithesis of being, (2) an irrational and tragic decision between the alternatives of this antithesis, (3) a necessarily deceptive proposition based on that decision, and (4) a reliance for that decision upon the appropriateness of place, circumstance, language, speaker, and hearer within a "fitting" moment.

It is not difficult to see that the rhetorical concept of *Kairos* as understood by the Sophists shares similar assumptions with the theological concept as used by the early Christians. For the latter, God offers opportunities that humans must accept or decline—both actions are possible—but once a choice has been made, its alternative ceases to be viable. The choice, then, requires following through on the necessary action in spite of awareness that there is no certainty of its being the "right" choice. Consequently, to an extent the action is "deceptive"; that is, it operates as if it were a certainty, even though that certainty is necessarily undermined by the lingering potential of its opposite: the certainty is "constructed," not discovered, within the *aporiai* provided by *Kairos*. The only guidance offered to humans is through the sense of *Kairos* as a moment when a leap of faith seems appropriate despite its irrationality. For Gorgias's rhetoric, though, either choice is "tragic" because it annihilates the other; for the Christian, only the choice that disregards God's time would be considered tragic in the grand scheme of things. Both ideas—the rhetorical and the theological—were known and fundamentally accepted during the Elizabethan era.

In Shakespeare's *Hamlet* we can see these concepts prominently displayed. The characteristic skepticism so often blamed for Hamlet's delay calls attention to his sense of "the clash and counter-clash of extremes," Pythagoras's inherent "polarity of opposites." So he wonders, "Be thou a spirit of health *or* goblin damned" (1.4.21) and whether it is better "to be *or* not to be" (3.1.58). These two questions torment him throughout the play and cause him to hesitate in his action. Too well, he realizes that "there is nothing either good *or* bad but thinking makes it so" (2.2.244–45; emphasis added throughout),[23] an idea that allows him to see the waywardness of public opinion, both with regard to the child actors who have displaced the popularity of the adult players and with regard to his uncle:

> mine uncle is King of Denmark, and those that would make mows at him while my father lived give twenty, forty, an hundred ducats apiece for his picture in little.
>
> (2.2.347–50)

Only through deception can a determination of the real be made, and hence, Hamlet relies upon the players to "catch the conscience of the King" (2.2.582). The players are the supreme examples of rhetorical deception—they can weep "for Hecuba" (2.2.535) in spite of having no connection to her. Polonius also acknowledges the value of this strategy when seeking to spy on Laertes:

> Your bait of falsehood takes this carp of truth;
> And thus do we of wisdom and of reach
> With windlasses and with assays of bias,
> By indirections find directions out.
>
> (2.1.62–65)

Hamlet himself takes on the antic disposition, being "mad in craft" (3.4.73) in order to confuse and mislead Claudius regarding his intentions. And then, of course, Claudius is himself a master deceiver, playing the wise and upright ruler while agonizing over his "rank" offense (3.3.36). Yet even he is caught by the antithesis of penitent and sinner, saying

> My stronger guilt defeats my strong intent,
> And like a man to double business bound
> I stand in pause where I shall first begin,
> And both neglect.
>
> (3.3.40–43)

How similar this sounds to Hamlet's own observation:

> Thus conscience does make cowards of us all,
> And thus the native hue of resolution
> Is sicklied o'er with the pale cast of thought,
> And enterprises of great pith and moment
> With this regard their currents turn awry,
> And lose the name of action.
>
> (3.1.85–90)

Action requires the "right moment" as well as the willingness to choose. And this notion can be seen in the play-within-the play when Luciano, the murderer, approaches his victim,

> Thoughts black, hands apt, drugs fit, and time agreeing,
> Confederate season, else no creature seeing . . .
> On wholesome life usurp immediately.
>
> (3.2.233–38)

His words demonstrate the dual nature of the opportune moment—an evil action depends upon what's "apt," "fit," and "agreeing," making the time a "confederate [that is, suitable] season."[24]

As a scholar, Hamlet senses the need for appropriateness in a rhetorical context, especially when he tells the players to "Suit the action to the word, the word to the action" (3.2.16–17) in order to provide the best display of human nature. What counts, he implies, is the alignment of style and circumstance to the greatest advantage for the benefit of spectators. Hamlet brings in the element of timing when he laments, "How all occasions do inform against me / And spur my dull revenge"(4.4.9.22–23);[25]

"dull" here means "laggardly" or delayed, suggesting that "occasions" (or events, such as Fortinbras's march to Poland) present themselves as reminders, but he fails to take heed of those opportunities that do occur. Action and right timing must go together, but for Hamlet, there is an uncertainty about both. He must overcome his distrust of that uncertainty (the doubled possibility) and act, which is precisely what he comes to realize and what finally enables his revenge.

Hamlet's challenge throughout the play is to find the appropriate time for his revenge. He pulls together his evidence and proceeds with caution, taking on the antic disposition and trying to think rationally about his decisions. It is this last point that causes him trouble because, as we have seen, such action must necessarily be irrational. He illustrates this mode of thought when he observes Claudius at prayer, mistakenly assuming that he needs to seek a "more horrid hint" (terrible opportunity) (3.4.88) and not realizing that eventually such analyzing will not be helpful. When he kills Polonius, he does so without analyzing his choices; so we hear him acknowledging that "heaven hath pleased it so, / To punish me with this, and this with me" (3.4.157–58), a discovery that subsequently enables him to relinquish all control and succumb to the moment itself. Later, in act 5 he makes this attitude even more apparent as he tells Horatio of the inexplicable (and, hence, seemingly irrational) events that saved his life and sent Rosencrantz and Guildenstern to their deaths,

> Rashly—
> And praised be rashness for it: let us know
> Our indiscretion sometime serves us well
> When our deep plots do pall, and that should teach us
> There's a divinity that shapes our ends,
> Rough-hew them how we will.
>
> (5.2.6–11)

This follows immediately on his description of "a kind of fighting" in his heart "That would not let [him] sleep" (5.2.4–5), which suggests the quarreling of opposing feelings or thoughts (that irreducible antithesis inherent in the search for knowledge). "Rashly" (or irrationally), then, he learns of the plot on his life, alters the commission, and seals the document with his father's signet, the having of which he also attributes to heavenly ordinance. Clearly, by this point, the religious sense of *Kairos* is operating in Hamlet's thinking.

When Hamlet receives the challenge to duel with Laertes, he replies to Horatio's anxious warnings with lines that, notwithstanding Waller's dismissal of their religious tenor,[26] speak directly to the understanding of *Kairos* described in this paper:

> We defy augury. There's a special providence in the fall of a sparrow. If it be now, 'tis not to come. If it be not to come, it will be now; if it be not now, yet it will come. The readiness is all.
>
> (5.2.157–60)

Here all the components of *Kairos* come together—an openness to opportunity and what is "fit," an expression of "readiness" to respond, to take advantage of that opportunity when it comes, and a willingness to relinquish reason in favor of acting spontaneously and irrationally, without regard for consequences. Once more Hamlet avers, "thou wouldst not think how all here about my heart—but it is no matter" (5.2.149–51), suggesting again the "fighting" he is experiencing even as he deliberately chooses one course of action—to engage in the contest with Laertes. As God's "scourge and minister" (3.4.159), Hamlet makes restitution for Polonius's treachery, for Rosencrantz and Guildenstern's betrayal, and for Claudius's crime, and in each case he does so by acting spontaneously, in response to circumstances that seem to be beyond his control, to create a new situation. In Hamlet's mind (if not in that of all critics), his revenge comes at an opportune moment when all conditions are appropriate, not according to his own lights but according to a divinely inspired *Kairos*. He calls attention to this condition most noticeably just before the duel: "I am constant to my purposes; they follow the King's pleasure. If his fitness speaks, mine is ready; now or whensoever, provided I be so able as now" (5.2.146.6–8). Appropriately, it is Fortinbras, the man of action whom Hamlet so admires for taking arms over a "straw" (4.4.9.16), who concludes the play by giving orders and claiming his "vantage" (or seizing his opportune moment) in Denmark (5.2.334).

Kairotic moments of profoundest insight in *Hamlet* occur at least three times: first, when Hamlet converses with the Ghost; second, in the "to be or not to be" soliloquy; and third, in the discovery of Yorick's skull. Not surprisingly, these also tend to be the most memorable scenes from the play—the ones artists and scholars have focused on as being most significant. In each of these cases, there is a brief glimpse of that which is normally hidden, a gap that permits contact with an unknown. The Ghost is a

manifestation of life after death. In the "to be or not to be" soliloquy, Hamlet probes deeply into the conditions of life and death
(acknowledging the enigma of the latter). And in the graveyard
scene, Hamlet confronts the physical condition of death, its permanence that paradoxically keeps the body in natural circulation
within the world. Each of these moments involves a mystery:
"the secrets of the prison house" (1.5.14), the "undiscovered
country from whose bourn no traveler returns" (3.1.81–82), and
"Where be your gibes now?" (5.1.175). *Kairos* also involves a
mystery because it forces a crisis of uncertainty; for Hamlet, that
crisis demands choices—whether to act, what action to take, and
what consequences will ensue. It is the last of these—the consequences—that causes him the most anguish because, following
the Ghost's tale of woe, he fears the probability of his own death
should he act in any particular fashion. Only when he can overcome this fear and decide to act will the "right" opportunity be
recognized and seized.

For Hamlet, the matter of response to a right moment, as well
as its consequent action, is paramount. He knows that he *must*
respond, but he cannot make that response because he maintains
too strong a hold upon his own rational ability to choose a course
of action and to identify a proper moment. Thus, when he decides
not to kill Claudius at prayer and then violently slays Polonius,
he relies upon his sense that "The time is out of joint. O cursèd
spite / That ever *I* was born to set it right" (1.5.189–90; emphasis
added). He seems convinced that the matter rests entirely in his
own hands; only later does he come to accept the idea that Providence has a hand in the outcome. He eventually comes to believe
that once he is in sync with heavenly ordinance, he can accomplish his goal.

The conclusion of the play leaves the audience with a question
concerning this belief, however. Hamlet does accomplish his revenge, but the cost is high and suggests a vindictive rather than
a benevolent God who oversees the fall of a sparrow. For the audience, the duel scene invites a momentary suspension of judgment
as good and evil seem balanced. Our sense of the play as a tragedy, with the loss of Hamlet as the revenge hero, leaves us uncertain about the deity who has ordered these events. A sort of
Kairotic moment occurs as we are faced with the opportunity to
choose. Shakespeare is not a preacher, nor does he seem particularly eager to encourage a strongly religious response, but what
he does present is a universal circumstance—the death of an admired figure under avoidable conditions—and he places us in a

position of having to deal with two contrary beliefs simultaneously: first, God is cruel or indifferent to the affairs of humans; and second, God works entirely for the good of humankind. (That God does not exist at all is not an option directly posited by this play.)

Kairos requires recognition, irrational choice, and action. The orator seeks the proper style and the proper occasion to move the audience. The believer seeks the propitious moment of divine intervention. Shakespeare and Hamlet achieve both. Shakespeare moves us by requiring us irrationally to suspend our disbelief and engage with the moment of performance. Hamlet relinquishes his hold on the process of rational decision making and allows Providence to direct the outcome.

As we experience the new millennium, we are reminded that *Hamlet*, probably first performed in 1600, was also a product of a crisis time. Humans have regarded such culminating occasions as times of anticipation when unusual events will occur, including everything from a miraculous birth to Armageddon. The prospect of a *Kairotic* moment causes people to be more alert, more cautious, more anxious than at other times, and those emotions build as the crucial instant approaches. A similar phenomenon of heightened anticipation and suspense occurs for the characters in *Hamlet* and, consequently, for us, the spectators of *Hamlet*, as we breathlessly await the fulfillment of a *Kairotic* moment. A crucial component of the ethos of *Hamlet* is a consequence of a turn-of-the-century mentality deeply informed by religious and rhetorical principles of *Kairos*.

NOTES

1. See Linda Woodbridge and Edward Berry, *True Rites and Maimed Rites: Ritual and Anti-ritual in Shakespeare and His Age* (Urbana, Ill., and Chicago: Univ. of Illinois Press, 1992).

2. Kent Burnside, "Time and Doubletime in *Hamlet*," *Notes and Queries* 43 (June 1996): 159–60; Ernest Schanzer, "Shakespeare and the Doctrine of Time," *Shakespeare Survey* 28 (1975): 7–61; and Zdenek Stríbrny, "The Genesis of Doubletime in Pre-Shakespearean Drama," in *Shakespeare and His Contemporaries: Eastern and Central European Studies*, ed. Jerzy Limon and Jay L. Halio (Newark, Del.: University of Delaware Press, 1993): 108–27 have all focused on "double time" and Aristotle's unities. G. F. Waller's study, *The Strong Necessity of Time* (The Hague: Mouton, 1976), lays out most fully the Elizabethan concepts of time, including *Kairos*, that influenced Shakespeare; see also Frank Kermode, *The Sense of an Ending* (New York: Oxford University Press, 1967). Peter Cummings, "The Alchemical Storm: Etymology, Wordplay,

and the New World *Kairos* in Shakespeare's *The Tempest*," *The Upstart Crow* 12 (1992): 127–40; Donn Ervin Taylor, "'Try in time in despite of a fall': Time and Occasion in *As You Like It*," *Texas Studies in Literature and Language* 24 (1982): 121–36; and Maurice Hunt, "*Kairos* and the Ripeness of Time in *As You Like It*," *Modern Language Quarterly* 52 (1991): 113–35 have each focused on individual plays, bringing to bear much of Waller's work.

3. James L. Kinneavy (citing G. Delling), "*Kairos*: A Neglected Concept in Classical Rhetoric," in *Rhetoric and Praxis: The Contribution of Classical Rhetoric to Practical Reasoning*, ed. Jean Dietz Moss (Washington, D.C.: Catholic Univ. of America Press, 1986), 93.

4. See Taylor, "Time and Occasion," 123.

5. The Latin word for *Kairos* is *occasio*.

6. See Bernard Beckerman, "Historic and Iconic Time in Late Tudor Drama," in *Shakespeare, Man of the Theater: Proceedings of the Second Congress of the ISA, 1981*, ed. Kenneth Muir (Newark, Del.: Univ. of Delaware Press, 1983), 47–54; Arno Borst, *The Ordering of Time*, trans. Andrew Winnard (Chicago: Univ. of Chicago Press, 1993); and Inga Stina Ewbank, "The Triumph of Time in *The Winter's Tale*," in "*The Winter's Tale*": *Critical Essays*, ed. Maurice Hunt (New York: Garland, 1995), 139–55.

7. Marion Trousdale, *Shakespeare and the Rhetoricians* (Chapel Hill, N.C.: Univ. of North Carolina Press, 1982), 26.

8. See Paul Tillich, *The Protestant Era*, trans. James Luther Adams (Chicago: Univ. of Chicago Press, 1922), 38. For Tillich's comprehensive views on the importance of *Kairos* in Christian theology, see also *The Interpretation of History* (New York: Scribners', 1936), especially 123–75, and *Systematic Theology* (Chicago: Univ. of Chicago Press, 1967), especially 369–72.

9. The question of transubstantiation was not essential to *Kairos* because the "presence" of God in the sacramental act provided the underpinnings of both doctrines.

10. Borst, *Ordering of Time*, 101.

11. The popularity of the *carpe diem* motif among Elizabethan poets is a further sign of this interest.

12. According to Miriam Joseph, for instance, the chief sources on rhetoric used in the schools included Aristotle's *Rhetoric*, the *Ad Herennium*, and various works by Cicero and Quintillian; see *Rhetoric in Shakespeare's Time* (1947; reprint, New York: Harbinger, 1962), 20.

13. Stephen Greenblatt, *Renaissance Self-Fashioning: From More to Shakespeare* (Chicago: Univ. of Chicago Press, 1980), 215.

14. Mario Untersteiner, *The Sophists*, trans. Kathleen Freeman (Oxford: Basil Blackwell, 1954), 119–20.

15. Ibid., 199.

16. Ibid., 121.

17. Ibid., 137.

18. Ibid., 159–61.

19. Ibid., 159.

20. Ibid., 177–78.

21. Ibid., 187. This notion proves especially important below in the discussion of *Hamlet*.

22. Ibid., 198; emphasis added.

23. Note too how Hamlet teases Polonius about the interpretation of cloud shapes: the prince implies that the possibilities are endless.

24. That *Kairos* can be used for evil as well as good has biblical precedence. For instance, after the devil tempts Jesus in the wilderness three times, we are told that he "departed from him until a more opportune time" (Luke 4:13). This, of course, implies that divine *Kairos* differs in essence from satanic moments of opportunity and that the latter, because of its deceptive nature, is more thoroughly aligned with the secular, rhetorical sense of *Kairos*.

25. The citation refers to lines included from the second quarto of *Hamlet*, beginning at 4.4.9 of the folio version in *The Norton Shakespeare*. Similar citations are also used later in the essay.

26. In *The Strong Necessity of Time*, Waller observes that "there is an essential difference in tone between such traditional religious exhortations and Hamlet's resigned and weary 'the readiness is all'" (128).

"Sick Desires": *All's Well That Ends Well* and the Civilizing Process

Lloyd Davis

> from seventeen to seven-and-twenty (the most dangerous time of all a man's life, and most slippery to stay well in) they have commonly the rein of all licence in their own hand, and specially such as do live in the court.
>
> —Roger Ascham, *The Schoolmaster* (1570)

Roger Ascham's concern with the fate of upper-class males focuses on self-control and "licence" as crucial issues for masculine identity.[1] Echoing a trope that poets such as Wyatt use in a number of lyrics, and that Sidney would adapt in *Astrophil and Stella*, Ascham identifies the court as a particularly dangerous place, which poses risks and temptations at a time when young men are required to exercise self-control. Just as they are learning how to develop and monitor their behavior independently, young men encounter a situation where they must pay great attention to their actions and where prizes and penalties for conduct can determine the future course of their lives. They may lack the skills to act appropriately in different contexts, let alone be able to exercise the self-observation and reflection necessary to evaluate and adjust their ways. Ascham is less critical of the court itself (at least not the court of his former pupil, Queen Elizabeth) than concerned that young men will be unable to recognize the good models that are there, and so their social education will founder: "The best and worthiest men indeed be sometimes seen [at court], but seldom talked withal. A young gentleman may sometimes kneel to their person, but smally use their company for their better instruction" (47). The idea of "using" someone's company for instruction conveys a reciprocal view of education as valued social experience and of social interaction as an important educational exercise.

Instead of learning from interactions with such figures,

Ascham fears that a young man is more likely to foster naively egocentric conceptions or to model himself on the wrong characters. He will "lie lustily . . . think well of himself . . . bear a brave look to be warlike, though he never looked enemy in the face in war" (48–49). Ascham reiterates Thomas Elyot's worry that the "natures" of the young "be not so much or soon advanced by things well done or spoken, as they be hindered and corrupted by that which in acts or words is wantonly expressed."[2] At court this can often mean for Ascham that the young man is captivated by "the subtle enticement of some lewd servant," since "some serving men do but ill service to their young masters" (50). Underlying these concerns is Ascham's key pedagogical premise that he "ever thought examples to be the best kind of teaching" (120). Here "best" is used primarily in the sense of *most effective*; the ethical sense—the best teaching is that which teaches young men to be morally superior—must remain contingent on the kinds of cases that are presented. Despite the schoolmaster's most earnest efforts, these examples can never be completely guaranteed. Ascham considers that Athens was the perfect commonwealth, "using such discipline and order for youth" (57), but he laments England's current decline, "disobedience doth overflow the banks of good order almost in every place, almost in every degree of man" (51). The French court, often held to be exemplary, as in Antonio's report in the opening scene of *The Duchess of Malfi*, has also lapsed (57–58), while Italy has long had disastrous effects on visitors, producing monstrously hybrid "Italian Englishmen" (81). No matter where he goes, the young man is far more likely to encounter bad examples than good ones.

Ascham considers that education occurs in many contexts, not merely in classrooms. It is intertwined with social and personal experience and therefore always has multiple dimensions and effects, from acting out immediate relations, consolidating or challenging existing traits and knowledge, to preparing participants more or less effectively for future situations. His notion that education is central to character and self-formation exemplifies many sixteenth-century views of schooling as a mode of cultural reproduction that aims to realize the "schooled subject."[3] Such a figure is produced through imitative learning, following examples and learning their implicit modes of conduct rather than memorizing explicit rules in rote manner. Richard Halpern notes that whereas rote learning is a coercive pedagogy, "Humanist rhetorical education tried to evolve a mode of indoctrination based on hegemony and consent rather than force and coercion."[4] Ascham begins *The Schoolmaster* by underscoring the effectiveness of the master's praise in helping "to sharpen a good wit and encourage a will to learning" (13): "chide not hastily . . . but monish him gently, which shall make him both willing to amend, and glad to go forward in love and hope of learning" (19). He later sums up that "learning should be taught rather by love than fear" (41). Elyot also emphasizes that the tutor must ensure the pupil is not dulled by overteaching and should include "pleasant learning and exercise" (20), which follows the child's "own natural disposition, and not by coercion" (25). In his widely read *De Civilitate* (1530), which went through twelve editions in the first year it was published, Erasmus begins with a similar point: "give instruction in manners appropriate to boys . . . to encourage all boys to learn the rules more willingly."[5] The goal of these practices is to produce a student who wants to be taught because he has internalized the values and aims of a social-educational system, which include, in Ascham's words, "good perfectness in learning . . . honesty in manners . . . all faults rightly amended . . . every vice severely corrected" (19–20). Ethical outcomes clearly outnumber what might be thought of as purely academic objectives.

The ratio of ethical to academic goals suggests that at the heart of the educational system lies a concern with identity rather than intellect, character rather than knowledge, or at least a preoccupation with the ways that developing knowledge and intellect are central to acquiring identity, forming character, and succeeding socially. As Halpern concludes, though in more specifically materialist terms than I am using here, Elizabethan grammar schools "helped to create an ideological climate in which economic success and failure were understood through the categories of diligence and laziness, self-discipline and excess, talent and the lack of it."[6] The focus on selfhood is, Elyot notes, the primary duty of the teacher, and hence of the teaching: "The office of a tutor is first to know the nature of his pupil . . . whereto he is most inclined or disposed" (20). Once this nature is known and properly cultivated, it is regarded as the basis for involvement in all kinds of social interaction, or as Erasmus puts it, "external decorum of the body proceeds from a well-ordered mind" and is "very conducive to winning good will" (273). The link from education to conduct to social prosperity is relatively direct and provides the greatest incentive for a young man to assume a taught, trained, and approved individuality, one that is "created within the confines of a governing system."[7] Ascham presents its potential in a reverential tone that underlines its worldly social value, "excellency in learning . . . joined with a comely personage, is a marvelous jewel in the world" (29).

For authors such as Elyot, Erasmus, and Ascham—whose influential works were frequently republished and cited decades after their first appearance—education achieves the multiple benefit of producing young men who not only fit and succeed in their community but who also accept and display its practices. The system that produces them thus effects its own reproduction: the smoother the fit, the greater the success, the stronger the belief its subjects have in its intrinsic value and propriety. Underlying advocacy and praise of this kind of educational practice, however, is Ascham's acknowledgment that other modes of social learning and training are widely used, including more blatantly coercive practices involving rote learning and "ill handling by . . . schoolmasters" (37). Even where an imitative system is predominantly in place, there are risks that the pupil will copy the wrong models or will fail to imitate successfully. Accordingly, throughout the sixteenth century the development of humanist educational paradigms was accompanied by the release of numerous manuals in prose and verse recommending self-surveillance and monitoring by the pupils themselves. It is no longer enough that masters scrutinize and encourage their charges. As Erasmus notes, the students must internalize a teacherly perspective on their own behavior to check and correct habits and demeanor constantly: "when necessity compels such action, it should none the less be done with decency and modesty even if there is no observer present" (277). There appears a sharp sense that one's body and conduct are to be managed and examined by oneself and that they are open to interpretation and misinterpretation by others. De Civilitate is famous for the way it explains a long list of mannerisms, gestures, and actions that are crucial to the way the character of young men will be read. Erasmus demonstrates a highly rhetorical and textual sense of the significance of manners: the cheeks should have "natural and wholesome modesty, not false or artificial coloring"; coughing when one talks is "a gesture of bias and of those who deceitfully contrive their words"; in contrast, discreet yawning or restrained laughing "neither distorts the appearance of the mouth nor evinces a dissolute mind" (275–76). A physical action or condition always seems to hold a moral meaning.

Numerous other texts from the late 1400s through to the 1600s contain similar kinds of precepts and advice. Their effects for the young are to instruct them how to act, how to interpret their own actions, and perhaps also how to conceive of the way others might understand their actions. The probable impact of these works on other readers is to reinforce the importance of perceiving and judging behavior, especially that of one's subordinates (a status young men tended to hold in their customary roles as servants or attendants), in addition to one's own. Sensitivity to and monitoring of manners are clearly ways of exercising power and reinforcing hierarchies of age and class in particular. For example, *The Babees Book* of 1475 counsels children to seek "a name . . . Off gentylnesse [and] of good governaunce," that is, self-control and submission before others.[8] Advice is given on how to carry out single actions such as kneeling, but also for more extended sequences, including entering a room, "komme Inne an esy pace"; being spoken to, "caste nouhte your syhte / Aboute the hous"; or sitting at table, "Youre heede, youre hande, your feete, holde yee in reste" (252–53). In *The Book of Demeanor* (1619), Richard Neste reiterates many points from Erasmus in simple verse for schoolboys to memorize; rote learning and humanist principle draw close together:

> Let not thy privy members be
> Layd open to be view'd,
> It is most shamefull and abhord,
> Detestable and rude. . . .
>
> Retaine not urine nor the winde,
> Which doth thy body vex,
> So it be done with secresie,
> Let that not thee perplex.[9]

A wide range of actions must be regularly monitored by the self and others: "in the morning make water in an vrinal: that by looking on it, you may ghesse some what of the state of your body."[10] The subject can only guess at his physical state, suggesting an awareness that a degree of uncertainty tends to accompany even close, private self-inspection.

Such detailed discussion and attention intimate that the codes of manners and conduct are multiple and changing. The manuals attempt to define what is correct and proper, but in so doing they acknowledge the variety of behaviors and an even greater diversity of responses. Erasmus concludes *De Civilitate* by conceding that "Nor should what I have said be taken to imply that no one can be a good person without good manners" (289). He more or less admits that the detailed system he has established is not always applicable and could be contradictory. The meanings of manners might have no ethical reference. In this kind of complex situation, conduct, training, and education, especially for young men, are held to be of the greatest significance. But it is a significance whose ethical basis cannot be completely established. Rather than suggesting that the system is internally flawed, this uncertainty can reinforce the pressure for self-surveillance on young men: if it is not clear which actions are crucial and what they might signify, then perhaps all need to be rigorously and constantly monitored. Such pressure for ethical self-regard, coupled with anxiety over its effects and even its very possibility, is staged with particular sharpness by Shakespeare in *All's Well That Ends Well.* Many of the play's characters are caught at points of contradiction among and within cultural codes of knowledge and behavior. These codes range from the medical to the fashionable, the martial to the romantic, the familial to the personal. The effects of contradictions are widespread, threatening courtly careers and moral reputation, domestic harmony and honor.

One chief reason for the extent of disruption within the play is that all aspects of the characters' lives and interactions are shown to be involved in more than one code. No piece of behavior or speech is separate from various social consequences, sexuality in particular often being intertwined with other domains. Another reason is that the codes themselves are not entirely consistent or constant—they change over time and according to location and situation, from provincial Rossillion, to the royal court at Paris, to military camps in Florence. What is suitable at the family household or court may be unacceptable elsewhere. Young men are depicted as a socially and geographically mobile group, and their mobility complicates and multiplies the standards they might adopt.[11] Further, in any given context each code is interpreted somewhat differently by observers and participants, who have diverse motives and levels of expertise and experience. There is often little immediate consensus about the impacts and implications of what has occurred, yet all characters continuously observe, overhear, and spy on each other. *All's Well* thus stages a complex of personal and social actions that are informed by preexisting codes but rarely proceed in conformity with them. Despite the elaborate protocols that regulate courtly and military performance, uncertainty about the meanings and results of action is anxiously felt by all characters, from the clown

Lavatch's disappointment when he realizes that his *bon mot*, "O Lord, sir!" "may serve long, but not serve ever" (2.2.4849), to the king's beggarly appeal for audience "content" in the epilogue. The pedagogical logic of imitation, praise, instruction, and unequivocal interpretation rarely prevails in this complicated and inconsistent world.

The play's intricacies of action and relationship are most sharply focused upon the social-sexual fate of the youthful count Bertram, a young man who seems to exemplify the vulnerability that Ascham identifies in that "most dangerous time of all a man's life, and most slippery to stay *well* in" (emphasis added). He, rather than the virginal Helena, is the telos of the action, and for most of the play he remains the elusive object of her desire. The culmination of her efforts is only to win from him a pledge of love, on condition that she can alter his understanding of their relationship by making him "know . . . clearly" how she has "won" him (5.3.311–12). As has often been noted, the finale does not resound romantically but presents an "anticlimax of desire attained" rather than fulfilled.[12] The contrast with Shakespeare's source in Boccaccio is marked. There, Beltrano acknowledges Giletta "for his lawefull wyfe . . . [and] from that time forth hee loved and honoured her as his dere spouse and wyfe."[13] Even Helena's ardor seems to alter as she plans and effects the bed trick. She speeds through the final scenes, desperate to win Bertram to prove the truth of her love, even though the means used may undermine it. For by making herself another's substitute, the bed trick consummates her desire by displacing her own identity with the virginal Diana's, "so lust doth play / With what it loathes, for that which is away" (4.4.24–25). Bertram's defective ethos is intertwined with such deferred and deceived pleasure.

Bertram's elusiveness as sexual object is in part a sign of the high value placed on his status and position by himself and many of the other characters. Helena's fixation is not that dissimilar to either the interest that various colleagues, superiors, and subordinates take in him throughout the play, or, for that matter, the more general concern that Elyot, Ascham, Erasmus, and others hold for the well-being of their male subjects. The young count concentrates a range of preoccupations about the formation of character, as if he is felt to be a kind of test case for the successful operation of pedagogical, socializing processes that construct identity. He is, however, a problematic case in a number of ways. He is unable personally to reconcile the different codes with which he must deal, as he simultaneously practices and learns their conventions. More alarmingly, his repeated failures may suggest that the codes are irreconcilable and that the system they would organize and reproduce is profoundly flawed. If Helena's curing of the king was integral to "ordering the social and political aspects of the state" in the first part of the play,[14] then much social faith depends on the knowledge and love that must finally be instilled in Bertram through the dramatic denouement.

The development of male identity and character is a major and recurrent interest throughout Shakespeare's plays, from *Two Gentlemen of Verona* to *1 Henry IV, Hamlet,* and *Cymbeline.* As discussed earlier, it was also addressed in many sixteenth- and seventeenth-century texts, especially in light of critical changes to traditional aristocratic roles and duties that were then occurring. The young man is the subject of pedagogical and ethical discourses expected to mold an intrinsically prodigal nature into one of respectful enterprise. Ascham's concern with "the rein of all licence" hints at the challenge that sexuality and desire can pose to this training. It is a topic that some of the better-known Italian humanists in the period tended to raise more directly than their northern counterparts. When translated or "Englished," these works can be seen as underscoring the important role of sensuality in self-formation for the very sorts of upper-class readers that a play like *All's Well* represents onstage. Further, it is in Italy that Bertram attempts to prove his masculinity in war and in love. Like many of his contemporaries, Shakespeare identifies continental settings and traditions as riskily integral to masculine self-fashioning.

Castiglione, for example, remarks that the young courtier tends "to love sensually" whereas the older man can use reason to curb passion.[15] More detailed observations are passed by Stefano Guazzo in *The Civil Conversation* (translated in the 1580s). Guazzo and his companion Anniball affirm the necessity of young men seeking the company and advice of their elders. They should be silent before them even though "it is for the most part hatefull to them, by reason of the diversities of complexions, fancies, and conditions. . . . [T]hose young men which eschue the companie of old, hyde their woundes, and make them to fester inwardly. . . . There is no doubt of it, but that young folke learne of old, by reason of their authoritie and wisedome, to moderate their burning desires, to acknowledge their wavering inconstancie, and to correct their other naturall imperfections."[16] Anniball approvingly cites Roman precedents where a young man might be prosecuted for not displaying adequate respect toward elders, before commending "suche a modest shamefastnesse" in him, "that his cheekes may nowe and then bee dyed with a Vermilion, whiche will become him, and is a token of a good nature, and a signe that he wil come to goodnesse."[17] The disgust for innate degeneracy is here imaged as a kind of ulcerous disease. It is recalled in *All's Well* in the king's fistula, the ultimate cause of which is unclear though it seems to be aggravated by the corrupting effects of young men's behavior (he is cured after they leave the court). Anniball's erotic attraction to chaste humility also recalls the intense, equivocal attitudes toward women displayed in plays, poems, and treatises throughout the Renaissance period. Like women, young males were expected to curb and channel incessant desire into deferential subordination to older men, the "framework of death-haunted and nostalgic elders,"[18] who constantly monitor and appraise Bertram's actions. Male self-restraint, however, was to be accompanied by unself-conscious courtly and military performance. A difficult synthesis of subservience and assertiveness is constantly sought but never attained by Bertram.

All's Well is a vivid illustration of the social pressures that strongly impinge upon male identity and desire. Shakespeare stages shifting codes of manners and social meaning as they affect notions of shame, privacy, public control, and demeanor that structure masculinity and femininity. Bertram is unable to adapt to the breakdowns and changes in codes of self-regulation, presentation, and interaction as he moves among familial, courtly, and military contexts. He flounders between conforming to these ethical systems and following the urgings of social-military ambition and sexual desire. Repeatedly he unleashes frustration at being reprimanded or negatively received in attacks against women whom he blames for ruining his status. Misogyny appears to be intertwined with efforts at realizing successful homosocial identity and position.

Gender difference is thus ambiguously implicated in early modern techniques of self-formation. These ethical discourses are aimed chiefly at males. In the main, women are slotted into relatively subordinate roles, "suited to limited purposes, the offices of wife, mother, and mistress of a household."[19] Nonetheless, on certain occasions they are condemned for flaws in the social system, when suddenly they seem to be granted primary responsibility for the way cultural and personal relations are conducted. Helena plays the major role in remedying men's physical and moral ills. However, the result of her efforts is to restore men's authority and virility and to subject herself and other female characters such as Diana to them.[20] In some respects the practices and structures that she consolidates can be compared to the classical ones delineated by Foucault in the later volumes of *The History of Sexuality*. Indeed, the tension between "Bertram's desire to engage in unfettered sexual liaisons and his social obligation to father legitimate heirs,"[21] which he strives to reconcile, condenses the shift Foucault describes from Greek codes of ethical virility, based on the importance of maintaining power over oneself and others, to the emergence of marriage in the late-Roman period as site of the "most active focus for defining a stylistics of moral life."[22] In the earlier system, the onus is on the young male to shape his identity through martial-political "rule of the self over the self," and a key element remains physical control, with sex conceived, in Foucault's account, as a "privileged domain for the ethical formation of the subject."[23] In the later system, conjugal and familial relations provide major criteria for self-knowledge and regulation. *All's Well* juxtaposes two such systems and distinguishes between them in terms of ethical implications rather than historical contrasts. The French court has a definite location in the *longue durée* of the "civilizing process."[24] Awareness of the features of this position and of the changes being wrought by ongoing historical process exemplifies Shakespeare's intuitive cultural intelligence—a consciousness of both the relativity of a particular context and the rich complexity of its mores. He dramatizes the court, in its early modern moment, as continuing to alternate between promoting first one and then the other system for regulating identity. Bertram experiences the contradictions between them as, in Foucault's words, two "different way[s] of constituting oneself as the ethical subject of one's sexual behavior."[25]

The impact of these contradictions can be further detailed by referring to Norbert Elias's analysis of changes in "feelings of shame and delicacy," in behaviors that "society demands and prohibits," in "the threshold of socially instilled displeasure and fear," and in the "distance in behavior and whole psychical structure between children and adults." Elias contends that Erasmus's *De Civilitate* and similar texts articulate an intensified concern with demeanor. Explicit links are made between outward conduct and inner qualities, involving an "increased tendency of people to observe themselves and others," whereby "people mold themselves and others more deliberately than in the Middle Ages," "the social imperative not to offend others becomes more

binding," and the pressure people exert on each other becomes
"much more compelling as a means of social control." The results
are to be seen in wide-ranging and rigorous internalized habits of
"self-control." Constant monitoring of conduct becomes an important instrument in drawing social distinctions, such as those
between provincial and courtly nobility (the very tension that
Bertram experiences when he first comes to Paris). The "embarrassment threshold is raised," and "the distasteful"—including
activities related to sleeping and sex—"is *removed behind the
scenes of social life.*" Elias stresses that these developments are
not only repressive but also productive. They cultivate feelings of
shame and anxiety that produce new forms of behavior and new
ways of thinking about it. They place limits on subordinates
(class or age), inculcate restraint on the instincts, first in the
presence of others and then, when alone, as "automatic self-
restraint," and they create socially and historically specific neu-
roses. Finally, Elias proposes that it is only when the "drives and
impulses come under firmer and stricter control" that marriage
can assume its "strict form as a social institution binding on both
sexes."[26]

All's Well explores these consequences both in the oscillations
between imposing and ignoring changed standards and in characters' anxiety and uncertainty over efforts at self-restraint and
feelings of shame and embarrassment. The opening lines juxtapose contending emotional pressures between family and political
bonds, with Bertram to leave the ancestral house to become a
royal ward. The old courtier Lafew maintains that the two sets of
bonds are united, "You shall find of the King a husband, madam;
you, sir, a father," he says to the son and mother (1.1.6–7). Yet
Bertram's comment on this new subservience, imposed at the
moment he might have expected to succeed his father, sounds
notes of uneasy frustration: "I must attend his majesty's command, to whom I am now in ward, evermore in subjection"
(1.1.3–4). From his youthful perspective, he seems destined to
eternal submission, not only to the king but to the memory of his
father, repeatedly invoked by his mother and the king as a model
of "blood and virtue" (1.1.55). Bertram must try to emulate him
even though, it is made clear to him, he will fall short. The nostalgia of the countess, the king, and Lafew is a means of enjoining
ethical, military, and sexual standards unattainable by the young
males. Its hegemonic impact is manifest as the king compels Bertram to accept Helena. The point is not that Bertram acts at all
acceptably toward Helena, for his desire is molded by an egotisti-

cal, immature knowledge of social relations and values: "A poor physician's daughter my wife! Disdain / Rather corrupt me ever" (2.3.111–12).[27] What is more centrally at stake is the relative lack of restraint over social and sexual desires exercised by a youthful provincial aristocrat, unaware of the degree to which conduct is tightly prescribed at the royal court. Bertram's overt refusal of the king's offers, his obliviousness to the need not to offend but to exercise self-control, contrasts markedly to the other young lords, whose ambiguous replies to Helena allow them to accept or reject her, according to their sense of the weight of her response and their sovereign's will. It is only when the king reverts to a putatively outmoded, hostile register that Bertram understands what is happening and is willing to see himself and his desire as the king sees them: "Pardon, my gracious lord; for I submit / My fancy to your eyes" (2.3.163–64).

In his flight from the court to the Tuscan wars, Bertram seeks a less tightly constrained arena for self-formation, where physical and sexual aggression might remain praiseworthy. Show the Italians, the same king urges the young lords, "that you come / Not to woo honour, but to wed it" (2.1.14–15). Bertram's attempt to seduce the virginal Diana is an opportunity to enact an identity over and against the ethical pressures of familial and sovereign authority, forging "a necessary break with his paternal past."[28] He exults in abjuring his family heritage; abjection makes the sex all the sweeter: "take my ring. / My house, mine honour, yea my life be thine" (4.2.52–53). The well-known irony of Bertram's transgression is that it consummates his marriage and fulfills the seemingly impossible conditions for union that he had previously set before Helena. The bedroom scene is not staged, suggesting in accord with Elias's observation that sex—the means of rebellious self-assertion that Bertram eagerly seeks—has already been institutionalized as a socializing practice. In this respect, "the whole play has endeavored to show how private desire is a consequence of social shaping."[29] The bed trick changes the reality and significance of Bertram's adulterous yearning: transgression is ironically normative.

The final scene completes Bertram's relocation in social and familial order. The keenness of the king, the countess, and Lafew to overlook his "rash faults" (5.3.61) underlines a sensed urgency to celebrate his restored status as metonymic of the civilizing process itself. Before that can be accomplished, all of Bertram's misdemeanors need to be revisited—his rejection of Helena and flight from the king, his seduction of Diana, and his renunciation of lineage. The scene concentrates the phases of the civilizing process from social imperative to self-restraint. Bertram symbolically recommits his offenses as he nervously denies them, but then experiences increasing shame and anxiety before confessing and begging pardon. His conditional acceptance of Helena is mediated by submission to the king: "If she, my liege, can make me know this clearly / I'll love her dearly, ever, ever dearly" (5.3.312–13). Marriage functions as the final step in becoming an acceptable ethical subject, and Bertram's slowly repeated "ever ever dearly" registers the lifelong effects it will carry.

In staging this movement, *All's Well* illuminates the role of gender difference in early modern education and formation of the self in a way not clearly acknowledged in the accounts of Elyot, Erasmus, and Ascham or, perhaps, for that matter by Elias and Foucault. Helena's pursuit of marriage to Bertram is a means of realizing the civilizing process as developed and imposed by the ruling generation of the king, the countess, and Lafew. Her actions rather than theirs become the focus of Bertram's deepest antipathy and fear, inspiring both his futile efforts to assuage discontent through martial and sexual exploits and his misogynist attitudes toward the women whom he encounters. He can thus attack Helena for the repression of "his important blood" (3.7.21), while later beseeching Diana to cure his "sick desires" (4.2.36). So women are positioned as the object of a desire whose restraint it is their role to compel. This is the "sweet use" men "make of what they hate" to which Helena sadly alludes (4.4.22), blaming women for discontent at their own civilized mastery.

NOTES

1. Roger Ascham, *The Scholemaster* (London: Cassell, 1888), 45.

2. Sir Thomas Elyot, *The Book Named the Governor*, ed. S. E. Lehmberg (1531; reprint, Dent: London, 1970), 26–27.

3. Cf. Richard Halpern, *The Poetics of Private Accumulation: English Renaissance Culture and the Genealogy of Capital* (Ithaca, N.Y.: Cornell Univ. Press, 1991), 30; see also 22. For a thorough, recent analysis of humanist educational principles, see Rebecca W. Bushnell, *A Culture of Teaching: Early Modern Humanism in Theory and Practice* (Ithaca, N.Y.: Cornell Univ. Press, 1996).

4. Halpern, *Poetics of Private Accumulation*, 28.

5. Erasmus, *De Civilitate, or On Good Manners for Boys*, in *Collected Works of Erasmus: Literary and Educational Writings*, ed. J. K. Sowards (Toronto: Univ. of Toronto Press, 1974), 3: 273.

6. Halpern, *Poetics of Private Accumulation*, 94.

7. Ibid., 43.

8. *The Babees Book* (1475), in *Early English Meals and Manners*, ed. Frederick J. Furnivall, (London: Kegan Paul, Trench, Trübner, 1868), 257.

9. Richard Neste, *The Book of Demeanor*, in *The School of Vertue*, in *Early English Meals*, 213–14.

10. William Vaughan, *Fifteen Directions to Preserve Health*, in *Naturall and Artificial Directions for Health* (1602), in ibid., 137.

11. Erasmus notes that variations in custom, place, and time will affect what is thought of as good manners; but he also affirms that a criterion of "naturally good or bad taste does exist" (279).

12. Susan Snyder, " 'The King's not here': Displacement and Deferral in *All's Well That Ends Well*," *Shakespeare Quarterly* 43 (1992): 30.

13. Quoted from William Painter's translation in *The Palace of Pleasure* (1575), in *Narrative and Dramatic Sources of Shakespeare*, ed. Geoffrey Bullough (London: Routledge and Kegan Paul, 1968), 2:396.

14. Barbara Hogdon, "The Making of Virgins and Mothers: Sexual Signs, Substitute Scenes and Doubled Presences in *All's Well That Ends Well*," *Philological Quarterly* 66 (1987): 54.

15. Baldassare Castiglione, *The Courtier*, trans. Thomas Hoby (1561; reprint, London: Dent, 1948), 312.

16. Stefano Guazzo, *The Civil Conversation*, trans. George Pettie and Barth Young (1581 and 1586; reprint, New York: AMS Press, 1967), 1:169.

17. Guazzo, *Civil Conversation*, 1:170.

18. R. B. Parker, "War and Sex in *All's Well That Ends Well*," *Shakespeare Survey* 37 (1984): 99.

19. Ruth Kelso, *Doctrine for the Lady of the Renaissance* (Urbana. Ill.: Univ. of Illinois Press, 1956), 42. Kelso's view probably underestimates the complex social activities that these roles could entail, which have started to be examined since her book was written.

20. Cf. Julie Robin Solomon, "Mortality as a Matter of Mind: Toward a Politics of Problems in *All's Well That Ends Well*," *English Literary Renaissance* 23 (1993): 164.

21. Michael D. Friedman, " 'Service is no heritage': Bertram and the Ideology of Procreation," *Studies in Philology* 92 (1995): 81.

22. Michel Foucault, *The Care of the Self*, vol. 3 of *The History of Sexuality*, trans. Robert Hurley (New York: Vintage, 1988), 192.

23. Michel Foucault, *The Use of Pleasure*, vol. 2 of *The History of Sexuality*, trans. Robert Hurley (New York: Vintage, 1990), 70, 139.

24. Norbert Elias, *The Civilizing Process: The History of Manners and State Formation and Civilization*, trans. Edmund Jephcott (Oxford: Blackwell, 1994).

25. Foucault, *Care of the Self*, 240. For a detailed adaptation of Foucault's later position to Renaissance literature, see Michael Schoenfeldt, *Bodies and Selves in Early Modern England: Physiology and Inwardness in Spenser, Shakespeare, Herbert, and Milton* (Cambridge: Cambridge Univ. Press, 2000).

26. Elias, *Civilizing Process*, xii–xiii, 63–65, 79, 82, 86, 94, 99, 110, 112–13, 122–23, 150.

27. See Solomon, "Politics of Problems," 166–67.

28. Lynne M. Simpson, "The Failure to Mourn in *All's Well That Ends Well*," *Shakespeare Studies* 22 (1994): 183.

29. Solomon, "Politics of Problems," 168.

Breaking Rank in Shakespearean Marriage Plots

Ann Blake

IN HIS *HAMLET: A USER'S GUIDE* MICHAEL PENNINGTON, REMARKING on Hamlet's snobbishness, and on Shakespeare's being "damnably vague about distinctions of rank," wishes more were known about "who [in Shakespeare] is socially superior to whom."[1] Anyone interested in the society and culture of early modern England will share this feeling. The concept of rank is central in that world and at the heart of our sense of its strangeness. Penetrating its now-unfamiliar patterns of allegiance and deference is a daunting task but one that must be taken up, for class is as powerful a determining force as gender or race. Investigations into Renaissance notions of class or (less controversially) of *rank*, as into homosexuality or subjectivity, raise the issue of whether the concepts we are trying to investigate may even have existed in forms that we can now readily recognize. By focusing on plays that deal with unequal marriages, one may at least hope to avoid making one historically inappropriate judgment. For these are plays that identify themselves as clearly addressing what were perceived to be, in the contemporary context, discrepancies of rank.

Expressions of anxiety about social mobility that provide evidence of awareness of these discrepancies are often echoed on the stage: "Since every jack became a gentleman, / There's many a gentle person made a jack."[2] A stable hierarchy may have been early modern England's ideal social model, but it was recognized to be under threat from political volatility and new wealth. Ulysses' famous speech in *Troilus and Cressida* insists on respect for degree as the foundation of a harmonious social structure. Without observance of rank there is "discord" or, as it is put in *Timon of Athens*, "confusion":

> Degrees, observances, customs, and laws,
> Decline to your confounding contraries,
> And let confusion live!

> (4.1.19–21)

103

Timon's curse implies a definition of social chaos or anarchy as the obliteration of the principles of order by their mingling with their opposites, a "confounding" of "contraries."

Ulysses' speech, however, does not imply that the distinctions on which the hierarchy is built are either intrinsic or inviolable. Rank is rather the degree to which one is assigned. One occupies a certain rung in the ladder not because of what one is essentially, nor on grounds of merit, but by the accident of birth: by being so placed, and not above or below. Only the monarch might legitimately rearrange the order on the ladder, when he ennobled his subjects. The point of the old question, When Adam delved and Eve span who was then the gentleman? was to draw attention to an essential equality among men if not men and women. We do not need to offer Shakespeare lessons about this matter, any more than about injustice in the distribution of honors. He lived to see a time when titles were for sale, but to comment on this, as some of his contemporaries discovered, was dangerous.[3] Social cohesion, the desired product of the smooth running of that particular model of the social order, is based on a hierarchy, and on the fulfilling of obligations to those above and those below. Such fulfillment of the obligations of rank is a pervasive theme in Shakespeare's historical and political plays. In *Coriolanus* Shakespeare builds a play around the friction produced between various degrees and conditions of men when obligations are believed to be neglected.

In plays that dramatize cross-class marriages, the examination of issues of rank has a narrower, domestic focus. Such plays provide literary evidence of complex and conflicting attitudes to rank. As G. K. Hunter has pointed out, "sexual relations are, of course, the most obvious means by which traditional class boundaries can be transgressed,"[4] and it is when those relationships proceed to the formal status of marriage that the most serious challenge to social conventions arises.[5] The varied dramatic presentations of unequal marriages reveal a range of attitudes in the onstage figures and also in the responses that the plays' structures seem to count on eliciting from their audience. Plays on this theme offered warnings as well as fantasies of fulfilling social aspirations. Moreover, they provided a means of contemplating contradictory feelings and beliefs, setting individual ambition against the desire for social stability, for instance, or the assumption that members of the nobility will be noble against the recognition that virtue is not the prerogative of the nobility.

Marriage plots in English drama of this period appear most frequently in romantic comedies of wooing, where marriage provides an optimistic conclusion; in tragedy they take the form of intrigues driven by adultery or the miseries of enforced marriage and end in death.[6] Tales of Cinderella or of the princess and the third woodcutter's son may shape our expectations of romantic happiness for a worthy low-born spouse, but in the drama of early modern England such endings are rare. Happy marriages occur within one rank, while the results of unequal marriages are usually unhappy, especially in seventeenth-century plays. But this does not mean they are always condemned or presented only as homilies or warnings.

Shakespeare offers various versions of marriages that break the barriers of rank. The following investigation of them is shaped to answer a question suggested by an essay of Harriett Hawkins in which she argued that Shakespeare's plays manifest a "radical romanticism."[7] This phrase refers to her view that the plays demonstrate that love is able to bridge the chasms of "tribal differences" between clans, races, or creeds. Through romantic relationships, love offers the only effective means of combating the intertribal hatreds promoted by "militant national and religious tribalism."[8] The question to be posed here is whether this radical romantic tendency in Shakespeare's work—so remarkable in an age when the writings of educated thinkers were often antiromantic—also extends to reaching across the barriers of rank.

When it comes to marriage in the romantic and predominantly aristocratic settings of Shakespearean comedy or love tragedy, neither rank nor money—the latter the means of constituting rank in less-elevated persons—is a matter of much importance. The merchant class milieu of *The Taming of the Shrew* pays them most attention, but otherwise, apart from the brief moment in *Much Ado about Nothing* when Claudio checks up on Hero's financial situation, only in *The Merchant of Venice* does a concern with money impinge on the romantic plot. "Tribal" differences are, of course, much in evidence in the alliance between Jessica and Lorenzo. Twentieth-century audiences may not be easy with the ramifications for Shylock of the play's romantic transcendence of these differences, any more than they applaud Jessica's theft of Shylock's money. Rank, however, presents no obstacles because it is clearly divorced from money. Antonio's generosity and then Portia's almost mythically abundant wealth—pointed to in the allusions associating her with the golden fleece (1.1.169–71)—are able to resolve Bassanio's financial problems. This comfortable situation is in strong contrast to the concern with wealth and social advancement evident in the families of young lovers of "the middling-sort" in the plays of Shakespeare's contemporaries, whether domestic tragedies or city comedies. *The Merry Wives of Windsor* is, as so often, a Shakespearean exception here. Anne Page finally marries young Fenton, making a small move up the social scale and across the boundary between the upper yeomanry and the lower gentry, and throughout the play the status of her successful suitor is a source of dramatic tension. The most significant and complicated instance of unequal marriage in Shakespeare appears of course in *All's Well That Ends Well*. Critical debate about that "uneasy" play,[9] and especially its ending, has a long history. As a preface to considering the question of rank in the marriage of Bertram and Helena, it is helpful to survey more straightforward instances of cross-class or unequal marriages in Shakespeare, and in particular the (only apparent) unequal matching of Florizel and Perdita in *The Winter's Tale*.

Unequal marriages, often also "enforced," though rarely so in Shakespeare, were a prolific source of dramatic conflict in the plays of his contemporaries. The possible consequences of enforced marriage, at worst, adultery and murder, readily lent themselves to theatrical use. Equality in marriage was the conventional goal, as the term "match," the usual word for marriage at the time, implies. Wise people took the path that, according to Sir Toby Belch, Olivia in *Twelfth Night* proposed to follow: "She'll not match above her degree, neither in estate, years, nor wit."[10] Marriage of equals was seen as natural. Iago, a cunning purveyor of conventional wisdom, suggests to Othello that Desdemona has offended in this respect:

> Not to affect many proposèd matches
> Of her own clime, complexion, and degree,
> Whereto we see in all things nature tends.[11]

Unequal marriage, especially when forced, was recognized as a social evil, proverbially warned against and condemned,[12] as in the last lines of *The Merry Wives of Windsor* where Fenton, speaking of his runaway marriage with Anne Page, says:

> You would have married her, most shamefully,
> Where there was no proportion held in love. . . .
> Th'offence is holy that she hath committed, . . .
> Since therein she doth evitate and shun

A thousand irreligious cursèd hours
Which forcèd marriage would have brought upon her.

(5.5.198–207)

Kings of course might marry as they wished, but at such heights marriage was a political matter, and a king who insisted on marrying a woman thought beneath him risked provoking potential opposition.

In dramatizing the unequal marriages of princes, playwrights appear to have felt free to pull the audience's sympathies in any possible direction, as far as the question of rank is concerned. In *Henry VIII* (*All Is True*) it is snobbery that is condemned. Wolsey, himself the son of a butcher, is enraged when the king's passion for Anne Boleyn, "a Knight's daughter" (3.2.95), threatens to thwart his own dynastic plans for the king's second marriage. The subsequent conflict leads to his fall, while the king's marriage moves beyond criticism when Anne becomes the mother of Elizabeth I. Henry VI is a less sympathetic figure when he marries Margaret of Anjou, the daughter of a king, but a poor one, as Suffolk admits: "yet is he poor / And our nobility will scorn the match."[13] Duped in the matter of marriage by Suffolk, the king incurs the wrath of his nobles and increases the divisions in his kingdom. Less sympathetic still is Edward IV when he marries the lowly Elizabeth Woodville. He shows himself self-indulgent and also politically inept by providing his ambitious brother, Richard, with an opportunity to present him to his own people as irresponsible and lascivious. Richard himself enjoys insulting the lowborn queen and her sons, newly elevated in rank. After Edward's death Richard is soon questioning the queen's virtue and the legitimacy of her royal children. Throughout *Richard III* and in contrast to his brother, the Machiavellian Richard seeks to use marriage for strategic advantage, first marrying Anne and then, after the royal princes are murdered, taking care of another threat, Clarence's daughter, by "meanly" matching her "in marriage" (4.3.37). As he careers to his death, he is finally outmatched in the political marriage game by Elizabeth, who rejects his suit to her daughter in favor of Richmond, the national savior.

In the more politically innocent romantic comedies, matters of degree in marriage are, as already suggested, typically set aside or minimized. For instance, in *As You Like It*, as Ann Jennalie Cook observes in her study of marriage in Shakespeare, the alliance of Orlando with the daughter (and presumably heir) of the rightful duke is allowed to proceed without anxiety about his suitability in rank.[14] He is the son of a gentleman who supported the duke, and that is apparently sufficient to silence any queries in this romantic context. Equally in *Twelfth Night*, once Olivia has confirmed her impression that Cesario's degree is above his "fortunes" and been assured that he is "a gentleman" (1.5.260–61), she is able to give her feelings full rein. In such a romantic context Malvolio stands out. As a pompous upper servant he is readily paralleled in the more satirical plays of Shakespeare's contemporaries, such as Chapman's *The Gentleman Usher* and *Monsieur D'Olive*, but he is also a wooer who seeks to marry above him. He fails, of course. Though he may cite instances of upper servants who have succeed in marrying the ladies they serve, "The Lady of the Strachey married the yeoman of the wardrobe" (2.3.37–38), only he seriously entertains the idea that his lady loves him. Quite how poignant and consequently socially disruptive his ambitions are must be decided by the individual critic or member of the audience. Other unsuccessful suitors appear briefly in Shakespearean comedy, but they are, however ridiculous, always of an ostensibly appropriate rank: Hortensio in *The Taming of the Shrew*, Sir Andrew Aguecheek in *Twelfth Night*, or Roderigo in *Othello*. All fail most obviously because of their inability to match the lady in wit. Apart from Helena in *All's Well That Ends Well*, the Jailer's Daughter in the tragicomedy *The Two Noble Kinsmen* is (possibly) the only Shakespearean woman who falls in love with someone above her.[15] The play gives full attention to her plight and uses her love for Palamon to permit his escape from prison. But it is a lover of her own rank, known simply as the Wooer, who finally cures the forlorn, mad maid when he pretends to be the Palamon she desires. This play makes no move toward a prince and the showgirl resolution.

In Shakespeare's noncollaborative late plays, the romances, lost royal children are a recurrent motif. And in each play it proves impossible to hide their "sparks of nature," as it is phrased in *Cymbeline* (3.3.79). Here we are in a region of romantic superstition about the presence of royalty that, with very different effect, Falstaff invokes to escape from his predicament after the Gadshill robbery in *1 Henry IV*: "The lion will not touch the true prince—instinct is a great matter" (2.5.249–50). The three lost princesses in the romances all manage, though disguised, to impress noble or princely suitors, and end up married to them and restored to their own high degree. There is material aplenty here to support a diagnosis of Shakespearean drama as essentially conservative in its view of marriage across the tribal boundaries of class. But this is also largely true of his contemporaries, who constructed plots that warn against such risky marriages. In city comedies a poor young gentleman may outmaneuver the greedy citizen and succeed in marrying his daughter, as Touchwood marries Moll in Middleton's *A Chaste Maid*; but the young nobleman who woos a woman who is far beneath him is likely to be reckoned to be moved not by love but by lust.[16]

One Shakespearean instance of this situation that is particularly interesting is Florizels's wooing of Perdita in *The Winter's Tale*. In the pastoral setting of act 4 Florizel, a king's son and heir in disguise, woos and wins a shepherd's daughter, Perdita. Those able to judge her beauty and behavior by courtly standards— Florizel himself, his father, Polixenes, and Camillo—all pay tribute to her elevated qualities, in language that registers her excellence as what is to them, though not to the audience, a social paradox. She herself is the "queen of curds and cream" (4.4.161), and all her "acts are queens" (4.4.146). Camillo praises her:

> *Cam.* There shall not at your father's house these seven years
> Be born another such.
> *Flo.*   My good Camillo.
> She's as forward of her breeding as
> She is i' th' rear our birth.
>
> (4.4.566–69)

Polixenes, however, has no intention of allowing his son and "sceptre's heir" to "affect a sheep hook" (4.4.407–8). Nevertheless, Florizel remains resolute, and his loyalty to the lowly shepherdess reflects well on him. Unlike Dorastus in Greene's *Pandosto*, or Lysimachus in the parallel situation in *Pericles* (21.57–59), Florizel does not wish even for a moment that his humble beloved were of noble birth. He is determined to marry his shepherdess, although even the sympathetic Camillo sees this as a prescription for misery. But as the audience knows, there is in fact to be no princely stooping, since Florizel has found a lost princess to fall in love with. Believing she is the old shepherd's daughter, Perdita defends her own worth, in the aftermath of Polixenes' attack on her, with an eloquent speech on equality:

> I was not much afeard, for once or twice
> I was about to speak, and tell him plainly
> The selfsame sun that shines upon his court
> Hides not his visage from our cottage, but
> Looks on alike.
>
> (4.4.430–34)

Egalitarianism, however, is not to be one of the ideas that structure this play.

Perdita, in particular, cannot ignore rank and its demarcations.
Florizel's disguise as a shepherd makes her anxious. She is troubled by the indecorum of a prince, "The gracious mark o'th'
land," being "obscured" in a "swain's wearing," and also by
being herself "Most goddess-like pranked up" (4.4.8–10) as
queen of the feast. Florizel himself is unconcerned. Like Ferdinand in *The Tempest* who is glad to carry logs to prove his love,
he humbles himself willingly and assures Perdita that the gods
themselves have assumed lowly disguises, a form of conventional
romantic metamorphosis. Rowland Lacy in *The Shoemaker's Holiday* provides a full justification of this practice, which, if conventional in romance, clearly ran against everyday expectations of
rank:

> How many shapes have gods and kings devised.
> Thereby to compass their desired loves?
> It is no shame for Rowland Lacy then,
> To clothe his cunning with the Gentle craft.[17]

Lacy, the nephew of an earl, finally does step down a few degrees
to marry the fair and worthy Rose, the daughter of the recent lord
mayor of London. He does so with the full blessing of the king,
who rebukes the proud earl of Lincoln for opposing the match:

> Lincoln, no more
> Dost thou not know, that love respects no blood
> Cares not for difference of birth or state?
>
> (21.104–6)

But in *The Winter's Tale,* following Greene's *Pandosto,* there is
no mixing of high and low, and the royal blood is not contami-
nated. Greene's story, remarkably realistic in comparison to the
Shakespearean reworking, connects the reader to the real anxieties of lowly fathers whose beautiful daughters are wooed by no-
blemen. Porrus, the old shepherd, fears that his daughter may
find herself pregnant and his whole family feel the king's fury.
Therefore he resolves to inform the king that Fawnia is no daughter of his but a foundling. Fawnia herself, more materialistic than
the high-minded, even philosophical Perdita, rejoices at the prospect of being "advanced from the daughter of a poor farmer to be
the wife of a rich king."[18] Florizel, who more than once avows the
chastity of his love, rules out any danger of the sexual exploita-

tion of Perdita. The old shepherd is driven to reveal all to the king only when Polixenes has proclaimed his opposition to the marriage and threatened the lives of the shepherd and his family.

Throughout Shakespeare's play Florizel remains a thoroughly romantic figure in his devotion to his humble bride. But when Perdita's true parentage is revealed, Florizel's role ceases to be even apparently unusual. It falls in line with a plot formula beloved of the popular Victorian novel and as old as the Greek romances, where the young humble girl is wooed and won by the prince and then discovered to be of high birth herself. Fantasy has turned to reality and is no longer socially disruptive. In a class-conscious world, the equally matched young lovers have a chance of happiness.

All's Well That Ends Well is the true Shakespearean exception. It is the only play concerned with actual discrepancies in rank in a serious affective relationship, and, so Roger Warren suggested, the one occasion outside the sonnets where Shakespeare had allowed himself to treat this painful theme.[19] No Shakespearean comparison for Helena closer than Malvolio, or the Jailer's Daughter, suggests itself. Here is a young woman who loves her social superior, and who is scorned. Critical studies have interpreted the power of the play in terms of a variety of themes, among them forgiveness, education, the nature of honor, erotic energy, and the family romance; but there is no avoiding the notion of rank. It is drummed into the audience's consciousness and simultaneously questioned. As an example of its pervasiveness, it is sufficient to notice the role of the social hanger-on, Paroles, or, on a smaller scale, a moment such as the conversation between Paroles and Lafew in which Paroles takes offence at Lafew's referring to Bertram as his "master." Lafew replies that he himself at least deserves the title of "Man" (2.3.192). Helena's sense of the gulf that, as she feels so intensely, separates her from the man she loves marks one extremity of the play's dramatization of social distinction. In lines that echo the Jailer's Daughter, she complains:

> 'Twere all one
> That I should love a bright particular star
> And think to wed it, he is so above me.
> In his bright radiance and collateral light
> Must I be comforted, not in his sphere.
>
> (1.1.80–84)[20]

At the other extreme of the social scale is the aristocrat's sensitivity to the intrusions of the lowborn. This is a note heard when Hamlet complains of the peasant's toe coming close to the heel of the courtier, or in Richard of Gloucester's sniping at the great promotions of Rivers and Grey,[21] or in *Coriolanus*. But nowhere does the sense of superiority derived from birth have the dramatic impact or prominence of Bertram's. His pride is epitomized in the family ring. In Painter's version of the story the count prizes his ring "for a certain virtue that he knew it had."[22] But in the play its virtue lies in its being the *family* ring: "an honor 'longing to our house," as Bertram explains (4.2.43). Diana underlines the shallowness of his sense of values when, matching word for word, she explains that her "honor" is the "jewel of [her] house" (4.2.46–47). Bertram's snobbishness might seem to be disproved by his affair with this poor gentlewoman, or his alliance with Paroles, but the opposite is the case. In his view, giving up the family ring to Diana presumably simply does not count: he has no intention of marrying her, as is clear to everyone from the start of his liaison. And as for Paroles, Bertram is won by his flattery, just as in Jane Austen's *Persuasion* the snobbish Elliotts are taken in by the ingratiating Mrs. Clay. The king prompts an appropriate view of degree in the audience from the start. He roundly censures pride in rank, one definition of snobbery, in his recollections of the exemplary behavior to inferiors of Bertram's father:

> Who were below him
> He used as creatures of another place,
> And bowed his eminent top to their low ranks,
> Making them proud of his humility,
> In their poor praise he humbled.
>
> (1.2.41–45)

Bertram is of the nobility but, in the eyes of his peers, not noble in his behavior. They all admire the beautiful Helena, the poor physician's daughter. They do so not in any egalitarian spirit but are moved by a high-minded neglect of rank, a romantic denial of difference. They have the capacity to adopt this attitude when it is justified; Bertram, so far, has not. Their feeling is made plausible by the worth of Helena, who proves to be the savior of the king, and whose virtues cannot be ascribed to noble birth. Early in the play, in one of its many passages of moral commentary, the countess introduces a distinction between personal achievements and inherited qualities. She expresses her hopes for her "young gentlewoman," hopes that depend on the influence of Helena's education, her upbringing, and on her "fair gifts," the "dispositions she inherits." Already the countess can praise her, "She derives her honesty and achieves her goodness" (1.1.36–40). Goodness is achieved, not simply inherited. As she takes leave of her higher-born son, the countess's words make the same distinction in the forces that will contribute to his worth: "shape," "blood," and "birthright" as against "manners," "virtue," and "goodness" (1.1.55–57). But in his case the achievement of goodness has not yet begun. So far he has only his "blood" and his youth to give hope to those who look on and wish him well. Helena's worth is able to make rank irrelevant, and this idea is emphasized at several moments in the play. At the beginning of the last scene Lafew, speaking of Bertram, says:

> He lost a wife
> Whose beauty did astonish the survey
> Of richest eyes, whose words all ears took captive,
> Whose dear perfection hearts that scorned to serve
> Humbly called mistress.
>
> (5.3.15–19)

He praises Helena's worth as able to break down notions of rank, to turn masters into servants.

When Bertram first refuses to marry "a poor physician's daughter," he cannot see beyond her low rank, scorning the much-prized physician as well as his daughter. The king indicates Bertram's mistake:

> If she be
> All that is virtuous, save what thou dislik'st—
> "A poor physician's daughter"—thou dislik'st
> Of virtue for the name.
>
> (2.3.117–20)

His point is as clear as can be. Rank is a "tribal difference" that might well have been closer to the lives of Shakespeare's audience than either race or religion, but it is not of prime significance. *All's Well* maintains a lofty romantic view throughout; "radical romanticism" prevails in all, except in Bertram. But though Bertram's prejudiced view of rank seems to be the greatest impediment to the happy marriage, perhaps it is only a convenient excuse.[23] It is only another aspect of his immaturity, like his poor judgment of people and his resentment of authority in any form. Even as the play closes, the problem is that he simply does not love Helena enough to justify a "radically romantic" view of the play. He still does not match her in love; the erotic energy is all Helena's. This, in the end, is the most telling inequality in this unromantic play.

NOTES

1. Michael Pennington, *Hamlet: A User's Guide* (London: Nick Helm, 1996), 41. Pennington then continues: "Marcellus and Barnardo are gentlemen to Hamlet and Horatio, although Barnardo and Francisco are also regular soldiers on guard. Horatio is a loose canon throughout the play moving up and down the hierarchy." For more on Hamlet's snobbishness, see p. 135.

2. *Richard III* 1.3.72–73.

3. On the punishment of the dramatists Chapman, Jonson, and Marston for comment "against the Scots" in their play *Eastward Ho,* including allusion to the selling of knighthoods by James I, see *Eastward Ho,* ed. R. W. Van Fossen (Manchester: Manchester Univ. Press, 1979), 4, 85, and especially the comment made within the play: "I ken the man weel; he's one of my thirty-pound knights" (157).

4. G. K. Hunter, *English Drama, 1585–1642: The Age of Shakespeare* (Oxford: Clarendon, 1997), 474.

5. Marriage within the same social ranks was the norm, as well as the recommended practice; see David Cressy, *Birth, Marriage and Death Ritual, Religion, and the Life-Cycle in Tudor and Stuart England* (Oxford: Oxford Univ. Press, 1997), 255–56; and Ann Jennalie Cook, *Making a Match: Courtship in Shakespeare and His Society* (Princeton: Princeton Univ. Press, 1991), especially chapter 3. Keith Wrightson refers to the research of Vivien Brodsky Elliott, who found a pattern of intermarriage within clusters of status and occupational groups in his essay "The Social Order in Early Modern England: Three Approaches," in *The World We Have Gained,* ed. Lloyd Binfield, Richard M. Smith, and Keith Wrightson (Oxford: Basil Blackwell, 1986), 177–202.

6. "How often have forced contracts beene made to add land to land, not love to love? and to unite houses to houses, not hearts to hearts? which hath beene the occasion that men have turned monsters and women devills. Country and city trials provide some evidence or other on the like tragicall accidents." From Thomas Heywood, "A Curtain Lecture" (1637), quoted by Glenn H. Blayney, "Enforcement of Marriages in English Drama (1600–1650)," *Philological Quarterly* 38 (1959): 459–72.

7. Harriett Hawkins, "Disrupting Tribal Difference: Critical and Artistic Responses to Shakespeare's Radical Romanticism," *Studies in the Literary Imagination* 26, no. 1 (1993): 115–26.

8. Ibid., 124.

9. A. P. Rossiter, *Angel with Horns* (London: Longman, 1961), 92, refers to the uneasiness of the play and of its critics. More recently, Susan Snyder described the ending as an "anticlimax of desire attained" in " 'The King's not

here': Displacement and Deferral in *All's Well That Ends Well*," *Shakespeare Quarterly* 43 (1992): 20–32.

10. *Twelfth Night* 1.3.90–91.

11. *Othello* 3.3.234–36.

12. It is worth insisting on this feeling, given the wide circulation and influence of the passage from G. M. Trevelyan's *History of England*, quoted, for example, by Virginia Woolf in *A Room of One's Own* (London: Hogarth, 1929): "the daughter who refused to marry the gentleman of her parents' choice was liable to be locked up, beaten and flung about the room, without any shock being inflicted on public opinion" (63). In his *English Social History*, 2d ed. (London: Longmans Green, 1946), Trevelyan also observed: "When we reach the age of Shakespeare, literature and drama treat mutual love as the proper, though by no means invariable, basis of marriage" (69).

13. *1Henry VI* 5.5.51–52.

14. Cook, *Making a Match*, 58–60.

15. Some editors assign her scenes to John Fletcher; see, for example, *William Shakespeare: The Complete Works, Compact Edition*, ed. Stanley Wells and Gary Taylor (Oxford: Clarendon, 1988), 1225.

16. This charge is made in, for instance, *The Witch of Edmonton*, by Thomas Dekker, John Ford, and William Rowley, and William Rowley's *All's Lost by Lust*.

17. Thomas Dekker, *The Shoemaker's Holiday*, ed. Anthony Parr (London: A. and C. Black, 1975), 3.1–4.

18. Robert Greene, *Pandosto: The Triumph of Time* (1595), rpt. in *The Winter's Tale*, Arden Shakespeare, ed., J. H. P. Pafford (London: Methuen, 1963), 213.

19. Roger Warren, "Why Does It End Well? Helena, Bertram, and the Sonnets," *Shakespeare Survey* 22 (1969): 79–92, especially 85–86. For another study linking the play to the sonnets, see Richard P. Wheeler, *Shakespeare's Development and the Problem Comedies* (Berkeley and Los Angeles: Univ. of California Press, 1981).

20. Compare the Jailer's Daughter's speech in *The Two Noble Kinsman*, act 2, scene 4.

21. *Richard III* 1.3.54–110.

22. Painter, "The Story of Giletta of Narbona," in *Elizabethan Love Stories*, ed. T. J. B. Spencer (Harmondsworth: Penguin, 1968), 45. Perhaps it is a jewel with healing powers, like that of the Duchess of Malfi.

23. For a psychoanalytically inspired explanation of Bertram's rejection of Helena, as resistance to a love in which he "fears a (forbidden) mother," see Ruth Nevo, "Motive and Meaning in *All's Well That Ends Well*," in *Fanned and Winnowed Opinions: Shakespearean Essays Presented to Harold Jenkins*, ed. John W. Mahon and Thomas A. Pendleton (London and New York: Methuen, 1987), 41–45.

II

Teaching: Technology, Pedagogy, and Ideology

Shakespeare on the Web

Michael Mullin

IMAGINE BEING ABLE TO SUMMON UP SCENES AND ENTIRE PLAYS FROM a worldwide archive of Shakespeare texts, criticism, and performances. Click, and the text appears below the moving image; another click, and the text shifts from English to German or to Chinese. Freeze the frame and go to a video interview with the director and actors. Freeze those frames and shift to other performances of that scene in other cultures. At the same time, users on the other side of the world are also exploring Shakespeare on the World Wide Web. If you wish, you can "chat" with them in real time or leave messages on specialized bulletin boards. Through the Web, scholars, students, and the general public all have access to a vast library of Shakespeare materials, and to each other. Briefly stated, this is a reality toward which "Shakespeare on the Web" is moving swiftly.

As Shakespearean theater historian, as the founder and director of the *Shakespeare Globe USA Website*, and as the developer of *CyberShakespeare* <www.motleyltd.com.au/>, I have been actively involved in this process over a number of years and in different ways. Here I offer first a brief retrospective, then a snapshot of things as they stand and descriptions of the *Shakespeare Globe USA* and the *CyberShakespeare* projects. In conclusion, I speculate on the broader issues involved and the direction of future developments of Shakespeare on the Web.

TEXT AND HYPERTEXT

Overall, the evolution of Shakespeare in electronic form over the past decades retraces the evolution of Shakespeare scholarship over the centuries, beginning with the text, moving outward to commentary on its meaning, and thence to performances of the plays.[1] "Digital Shakespeare"—meaning the text in electronic

119

form—began two decades ago in West Germany, extending a long German tradition of philological analysis of the plays. In the 1960s a team led by Marvin Spevak created a massive concordance to Shakespeare's complete works. At first, the work was slow and arduous. The entire text had to be entered by a double-entry key-punching system, and then the programs had to be run through a punch card system.[2] Although aided by computers, the concordance was essentially a large, printed object, nine volumes overall, not an interactive, digital entity. Today that project has evolved into a sophisticated interrelational database under the direction of H. Joachim Neuhaus at the University of Münster. Going beyond the word-locating functions of a concordance, the *Shakespeare Database*, <ves101.uni-muenster.de/>, links together a vast store of lexical information, permitting users to search the complete works—facsimile quartos, folios, and the Riverside edition—by character, etymology, syntax, variant spellings, inflected forms of words, morphemes, and allomorphs. Like a thesaurus, the corpus may also be searched according to broad areas of meaning, suitably organized and indexed. The result, soon to be available on CD-ROM, will permit sophisticated linguistic analysis of characters and groups of characters. The linguistic traits of the nobility, for example, may be compared to those of the commoners.[3] Already mature and robust, the *Shakespeare Database* makes interrelated linguistic data accessible.

In Great Britain and North America, efforts have ranged across a wide spectrum of scholarly interests. Most Canadian and American Shakespeareans have been trained to think of Shakespeare's plays first as stable texts. Electronic Shakespeare expands the notion of a single text to interlinked texts—hypertexts—that can be searched for every occurrence of a word, these occurrences listed, and any occurrence jumped to by a click of the mouse. Expand from one text to several texts, and one has the ability to compare textual variants and to view footnotes and commentary.[4] Unlike the linear sequence of pages in a book, hypertext allows for instantaneous, nonlinear navigation of the entire textual corpus. Obviously, this saves a lot of page turning, but it does not change the basic conception of Shakespeare as a text with editorial and critical apparatus.

Speaking at the first World Shakespeare Congress in Vancouver in 1971, T. H. Howard-Hill called for a database with old- and new-spelling editions.[5] Only in the past decade has that vision started to be realized. At the Shakespeare Society of America meetings during the mid-1980s, researchers from Brigham Young

University demonstrated a prototype hypertext Shakespeare, which permitted users to bring up commentary on a given line, character, or scene instantly. With some envy at the level of funding and technical support behind the project, many Shakespeareans dismissed it. In part, their reaction came from a technophobia then prevalent, and in larger part, from the perception that the project was limited in use to the authors' Shakespeare classes.

By the early 1990s, Shakespeare in hypertext had become a commercial reality, as *WordCruncher Shakespeare*, based on *The Riverside Shakespeare*,[6] and as *Electronic Shakespeare* from Oxford University Press. *WordCruncher* is easy to use for simple searches, but limited for complex searches. More sophisticated, the Oxford University Press software requires some computer literacy. To date, other digital editions lack the editorial authority and the software of these leaders. Since 1995, the Cambridge University Press's electronic Shakespeare (a cross-platform electronic edition using DynaText) has been another authoritative resource, and with it, illustrations of Renaissance documents, pictures, and production photographs.[7]

In another electronic dimension, the creation of the "Shakespeare Electronic Conference," commonly referred to by its creators and users as "SHAKSPER," is an e-mail listserve. Since the early 1990s SHAKSPER has made possible swifter communications among Shakespeareans with Internet access. From formal announcements of such World Wide Web journals as *Early Modern Literary Studies* <www.shu.ac.uk/em/s/elmshome.html> to informal exchanges—some rather heated—on a variety of subjects, SHAKSPER provides a useful forum. Its moderator, Hardy M. Cook, adopts an egalitarian stance, permitting "postings," or messages, on any subject related to Shakespeare. Primarily a tool for speedy communication, its limitations emerged early. Because it is easy to post a message, SHAKSPER can become so clogged with irrelevant postings that, like a bulletin board with too many messages tacked to it, checking it becomes a chore. One can imagine that in time there will emerge more specialized electronic Shakespearean bulletin boards.[8]

The desire to collect and organize commentary on Shakespeare's plays goes back to the founders of the first Variorum. Judging from his repeated pleas and inducements for assistance in the *Shakespeare Newsletter*, Louis Marder's vision of a Shakespeare database still remains more dream than reality. Questions of practicality have plagued Marder's efforts to digitize roomfuls of published data—everything!—written by or about Shakespeare. A bold vision, first enunciated by Marder in the *Shakespeare Newsletter* in 1984 and echoed playfully in 1989 by Philip Brockbank's ruminations on the possibilities offered by optical disk, the "Shakespeare Database" has yet to take hold outside a small circle of true believers, in part because the project was begun before such an undertaking was technically and practically feasible.[9] The digital *World Shakespeare Bibliography* from Cambridge University Press, *Editions and Adaptations of Shakespeare* from Chadwyck-Healey, *Shakespeare in Context* on CD-ROM from World Microfilms, and other digital library initiatives bring a comprehensive, digital Shakespeare database nearer to reality. These products move beyond digital editions of the plays and so represent the beginnings of a digital Shakespeare library.[10] These and other interactive digital archives will open new opportunities for students and scholars far distant from the great Shakespeare archives, as did the *Variorum* efforts and the waves of facsimile editions earlier in this century.[11]

TEXTS AND IMAGES

From being a peripheral concern of Shakespeare scholarship, during the 1970s and thereafter the performance history of the plays became a central focus of scholarship and teaching. Following this evolution, digital Shakespeare moved beyond texts to include images as well. In the 1990s computer technology has evolved from a technology primarily for text and hypertext into multimedia, a combination of text, hypertext, still images, and moving images. Although it has been awkward to bring clips of Shakespeare performances into the classroom or to assign viewings, Shakespeare on film and video has come to be widely used as an adjunct to reading and discussion of the text. Shakespeare studies and teaching have seized on these developments. For example, impelled by the wish to bring the interactivity of the theater into his Shakespeare classes at Stanford, in the mid 1980s multimedia pioneer Larry Friedlander created a series of interactive programs using the then-new HyperCard application. His "computer tutorials" drew upon an array of unusual resources: performances on videodisk, a library of visual material, an animation program, and a multimedia notebook for student essays that could include "visual quotes."[12] In time, Friedlander's work led to a partnership with Peter Donaldson at the Massachusetts Institute of Technology and an extensive interactive program, still growing, that uses a library of performances on videodisk with software that permits access through text and visual indexing (one may call up all the close-up shots in a given performance, for example). Although the program remains local to MIT, with some clones underway on other campuses, demonstrations at the Shakespeare Society of America meetings and elsewhere have stirred considerable interest both in the Stanford-MIT project and in the wider area of interactive, multimedia Shakespeare.

Because published accounts lag behind work in the field and because information about developments occurs by word of mouth and by e-mail, from here on I draw upon direct personal experience with the caveat that such anecdotal information risks significant omissions. Readers wishing to explore some of the developments herein described may wish to post questions and reactions to SHAKSPER.

My goal in research and teaching has been to join the usually disparate domains of performance and text. In an early attempt to wed the script and its visual realization, in *Macbeth Onstage* I reproduced Glen Byam Shaw's promptbook for the 1955 production starring Laurence Olivier and Vivien Leigh.[13] Angus Macbean's photographs and my written reconstruction of that production helped readers to visualize it moment by moment. In subsequent research and teaching, I came to use commercially available Shakespeare films, later videos, to view and analyze past performances. Just as the rehearsal techniques and acting projects my students undertake are at least one step away from the reality of Shakespeare in performance, films and videos are also at one remove from actual performance. The need for contextual information—the director's and actors' intentions, the reviewers' responses—gave rise to studies of Shakespeare on film and video. In teaching, one can assign viewing and complement it by class notes, or view scenes and discuss them, with the great advantage that, unlike performances in the theater, video performances may be replayed, reexamined, and compared with other videos. Yet the logistics are daunting: wheeling VCRs and monitors into classrooms, or moving classes to a media lab, or hoping that students will schedule and complete out-of-class viewing assignments. As scholars, Shakespeareans have taken the subject seriously, and as teachers, many have made viewing of the plays on film or video an integral part of instruction. Until very recently, however, linking performance with text so that both are easily and simultaneously accessible remained an elusive desideratum.

Only dimly aware of the developments in hypertext Shakespeare, in 1992 I visited the *Perseus* project's computer lab at Harvard University.[14] Published by Yale University Press, *Perseus* is a CD-ROM in which the entire corpus of classical Greek literature has been put into an interactive hypermedia program. The user can move easily from text to glosses on the text to images of objects mentioned. Take as an example a passage from Homer in which a particular kind of sword is named: click on the word and the user finds where this word occurs throughout the corpus of Greek literature and art. One may examine its occurrence in text, in commentary, and in three-dimensional artifacts: vases, statues, mosaics, and the like, which are scattered all over the world and illustrated in hundreds of books. Using *Perseus*, a beginning student can gain access simply and easily to the store of detailed information that once took a classics scholar years to acquire by painstakingly building up expert knowledge of disparate texts and objects. Interpreting what is found, of course, requires expert knowledge. By making access to textual and visual information easy, the emphasis in research and teaching can shift from finding the information to interpreting it.

Videodisks and CD-ROMs

In 1992 at MIT's Media Lab, I viewed an early version of Peter Donaldson's interactive, multimedia, Shakespeare-on-videodisk program. This impressive project had the limitations of high cost, a program that allowed users to view only one play at a time, and reliance on videodisk, a technology that failed to become widely used. Then new, CD-ROM provided an attractive alternative to the MIT videodisk program. CD-ROM offered similar multimedia interactivity, and it was gaining acceptance in the marketplace.[15]

In 1994 two Shakespeare CD-ROMs appeared, *"Macbeth"* by Albert Braunmuller and *Shakespeare's Life and Times* by Michael Best.[16] Braunmuller's *"Macbeth"* includes the text of the play, commentaries, and excerpts from several productions, with a charming "karaoke" feature by which one may suppress the spoken words of one character and speak the lines oneself as the scene plays. The "chunky" moving images reflect the state of the art when the CD-ROM was made, and their poor quality unhappily resulted in the Royal Shakespeare Company withdrawing permission to use the video excerpt from Trevor Nunn's *Macbeth* (somewhat incongruously, the voice track remains). As a teaching resource, however, it is useful for being self-contained and for alerting students to the interplay among text, scholarship, and performance. Its technical limitations may put off students accustomed to the visual sophistication of MYST and other interactive, commercial CD-ROMs.

Michael Best's *Shakespeare's Life and Times*, which first appeared in 1994 and which has subsequently been revised and expanded, is a robust and mature CD-ROM, featuring written materials augmented by sound, still images of Renaissance life and art, and video clips of Renaissance dances. If one imagines the introductory pages of a complete Shakespeare edition coming to life in sound and moving images, one would have a good idea of what Best's work offers. Ironically, Best's simple graphics—mostly text and line drawings—establish their own modest conventions and expectations, delighting when they are exceeded, even as Braunmuller's richer graphics excited higher expectations than the technology could then fulfill.

Besides these two Shakespeare CD-ROMs, there are various Shakespeare CDs that fall under what software developers call "shovelware," meaning that something from another medium is "shoveled" onto a CD-ROM and marketed. The texts of the plays and videos made into CD-ROMs are the low end, whereas interactive multimedia editions are the high end of this undertaking. The Arden and the Cambridge CD-ROMs are perhaps the best of these. The former features not only the Arden text but also facsimile images of earlier texts, especially the folio and the quartos. As with the *Perseus* project, these useful tools enable a beginning student to move easily through the text to trace a word or theme, and to carry the search into the footnotes and related materials.

Instead of full-length performances on videodisk, I chose a different approach: digitized clips of performances, linked to the text being performed and to other materials in an interactive, multimedia CD-ROM environment. During 1993 and 1994 I created a prototype of an interactive multimedia CD-ROM entitled *Our Shakespeares: Shakespeare across Cultures* for a book on the subject. The CD-ROM—or a Web-based equivalent—will provide a selection of the research materials—moving images, stills, and text—upon which my conclusions rest. I think of the CD-ROM as both "digital footnotes" and as a means of providing an independent research resource for scholars who wish to explore the subject.

Taking interactive multimedia even further, the ambitious Open University/BBC Shakespeare Media Research Project is creating a series of instructional CD-ROMs that invite the user not only to view video clips of *King Lear* and *As You Like It*, but also to "edit" the clips so as to create one's own unique video document. Designed for use in an Open University Shakespeare course, these CD-ROMs (or Web versions of them, see below) may also be used as stand-alone instructional resources.

THE SHAKESPEARE WEBSITES

Regardless of how they may expand the possibilities of books and movies for the study of Shakespeare, CD-ROMs have inherent limitations. A CD-ROM is a physical (rather than a virtual) object. It has finite capacity. It must be stored properly so as not to be lost or damaged. Only one person can use it at a time, and one person can use only one CD-ROM at a time, thereby making comparisons among the contents of several CD-ROMs difficult. The World Wide Web promises to overcome these limitations and to offer further possibilities.

The Web is "virtual," that is, its digital information exists on many millions of computers all over the world and not on single CD-ROMs. Instead of loading a CD-ROM into one's computer, one "links" to a Website and its contents, which often contain links to other Websites. Much of this material may be copied (downloaded) to one's own computer, thereby allowing one to create a personal "library" of Web materials. Instead of copying material, most users create a list of "bookmarks" that allow them to return to selected sites without filling up their computer's memory with downloaded information.

Following the growth of the Web, some Shakespeare materials are migrating from CD-ROMs to the Web. Publishers of Shakespeare editions (print and CD-ROM) are putting samples of their electronic texts on their Websites. Further, much Shakespearean print and visual material is appearing directly on the Web without any intermediate CD-ROM version. Copies of the folios, quartos, old-spelling editions, scholarly publications, teaching materials, lectures, illustrations—everything and anything Shakespearean are appearing, with more material being added daily. Even more exciting, new materials are being created specifically for the Web. Eschewing print publication, the *Internet Shakespeare Editions* at <web.uvic.ca/shakespeare/index.html> offer "modern, newly-edited texts of the plays and poems" with source materials, a critical survey, a performance history, and an archive of performance documentation—all "freely available for educational and non-profit use," writes the general editor Michael Best.

However, the rich diversity of Shakespeare resources on the Web presents difficulties for scholars, students, and other Shakespeareans. From the Web's inception, matters Shakespearean have appeared in many forms. Helter-skelter have come individual "home pages" for Shakespeare classes and digital files for the complete works, for scholarly articles, and for illustrations of scenes in the plays. The Web is inherently egalitarian—anyone with Internet access and some simple programming skills can create a rudimentary home page. The Web is easy to explore with "search engines" such as Lycos, Yahoo, and Alta Vista, which search the contents of millions of home pages by keywords. Each time the word occurs, the search engine lists a "hit." In practice, the glut of Shakespeare material, some valuable, some less so, some worthless, is confusing. Using one search engine, for example, one is stunned to find that there are over 100,000 hits listed in response to a search for "Shakespeare" on the Web. The first, "Is Shakespeare Really Dead? Chapter VIII," aptly illustrates the difficulty of separating the wheat from the chaff.

Early in the 1990s, the World Wide Web evolved from the defense-based and scientific Arpanet. Shortly thereafter the National Center for Supercomputing Applications (NCSA) at the University of Illinois developed Mosaic, a "Web browser," which in turn evolved into Netscape, later cloned by Microsoft into Internet Explorer. Responding to these developments by improving access to Shakespeare materials on the Web, in the mid-1990s several Shakespeare Websites sprang up, evolving into useful "bibliographies" of links to Shakespeare resources on the Web. The well-organized *First Folio: Internet and Web Resources* <www.ludweb.com/poetry/sonnets/links.html> and Michael Best's *Internet Shakespeare Editions* represent two continuing individual undertakings.

Inspired by the vision of comprehensive, easy-to-navigate resources for Shakespeare on the Web, in 1996 three Websites were begun, under the joint sponsorship of the International Shakespeare Globe Center's Education Division and the Universities of Illinois, Georgia, and Reading. These "Shakespeare Globe" Websites serve multiple audiences numbering hundreds of thousands—students, teachers, scholars, theater artists, playgoers, and the general public—and multiple uses, from formal instruction in colleges and high schools to research, theater production, and casual interest. Each Website had a somewhat different mission.

The *Shakespeare Globe USA Website* was designed to be a Shakespeare "metasite," a first stop for Shakespeare on the Web. Besides a point-and-click slide tour of the new Globe Theater in London, it contained virtual "rooms"—the Classroom, the Library, the Design Studio, the Players' and Playgoers' Room, the Teachers' Room, and the Viewing Room (real-time excerpts of Shakespeare performances). In turn, this metasite linked to other, freestanding Globe metasites with their own special emphases. *Shakespeare's Globe Research Database*, <www.rdg.ac.uk/globe>, sponsored by Reading University focuses on Shakespeare the Renaissance playwright and the activities of the new London Globe Theater. It also features virtual reality tours of the Globe. At this point, I invite the reader to explore Shakespeare on the Web via *Shakespeare's Globe Research Database*.

MULTIMEDIA ON THE WEB

Because the Web's capacity to transmit information has improved, it can now transmit text, graphics, still images, and also low-resolution moving images. Once a slow and memory-intensive process, transmission of moving images on the Web is now approaching the speed and resolution of broadcast television. Unlike broadcast television, however, moving images stored on a server may be viewed and re-viewed in different sequences. Without going into the complexities of bandwidth and compression, let it be said that present limitations in the size and resolution of moving images on the Web will diminish as the technology evolves. At present RealPlayer is the favored streaming video plug-in for Web browsers. Other streaming video plug-ins such as Vosaic, being developed at the University of Illinois, allow one to view one video clip, freeze-frame it, and then open another, or several others. Further, through "embedded hot links," which appear as one views a video, one may "hopscotch" to other, related videos, images, or text. To these video features is added synchronized text and an index function that allows one to jump from one place in a video to another.[17] Where once "interactive multimedia" meant that the user could choose which path to follow through a library of textual, visual, and video materials, true interactivity means that the user may create a new "Web document" from these materials. Drawing upon videotapes from my research on Shakespeare across cultures and other sources, I am currently experimenting with this application and others like it in the *CyberShakespeare* Project.

For example, various performances of the "kissing scene" in *Romeo and Juliet* may be viewed for comparison. In the Grupo Galpao production from Brazil, we see a street theater company's staging in the mode of the carnival. Drawing upon folk traditions quite remote from Shakespeare's own, they nonetheless make cultural connections much closer to Renaissance England than to modern, first-world conventions. Arranged marriages, concepts of family honor, and a sharp dichotomy between male and female social roles all contribute to a moving evocation of that moment. Following another tradition, the staging of the same scene by students at the University of California, Berkeley, embodies a "classical" Western rendition, in which period costumes and dances, albeit in a contemporary setting, evoke a world far distant from the one their audience lives in. By providing the opportunity to bring such very different interpretations together in sharp contrast, the Web initiates powerful cross-cultural connections for theater, scholarship, and instruction.

WEB-BASED SHAKESPEARE INSTRUCTION: THE *CYBERSHAKESPEARE* PROJECT

Even as these extensive Shakespeare resources on the Web have sprung up, parallel developments in Web-based education have begun to affect Shakespeare teaching, with potential for impact on research. In many Shakespeare courses—Lawrence Danson's at Princeton University, John Gillies's at LaTrobe University, to name only two examples from many—students interact with each other and their instructor through e-mail and electronic bulletin boards. Taking interactivity a step further, in Larry Friedlander's Shakespeare Project at Stanford University and in Michael Best's Shakespeare course at the University of Victoria (British Columbia), students use an interactive CD-ROM to "stage" a scene by placing figures and props on a model of the Globe stage—and to share their results with instructor and classmates over the Web.

In recent years, I have been designing *CyberShakespeare*, an attempt to create yet more interactive Shakespeare teaching on the Web. At <www.motleyltd.com.au>, *CyberShakespeare* is a fresh approach to learning on the Web, inspired by traditional classroom teaching. *CyberShakespeare*'s structured learning modules will explore different areas of Shakespeare study, enabling students and instructors to work together across distance and time. The modules will be designed by scholar-teachers, each a specialist in a different area, each a teacher of proven excellence.

For instructors and students, *CyberShakespeare* will be socially and intellectually interactive, instead of being an impersonal, technology-dominated experience. Instructors will have the opportunity to put their best teaching on the Web—and to share it with other scholars. Students will "meet" other students on the Web, forming pairs or teams who work together. Thus, while working on a *Romeo and Juliet* staging exercise, a young woman in Melbourne might find herself "talking" with a high school teacher in Chicago or even Tokyo. Having worked together on one module, the two could decide to revise their course plans and work together on another module. During a *CyberShakespeare* module, each student will have many opportunities to meet others with different backgrounds.

CyberShakespeare is designed for use both by secondary and tertiary instructors and students as well as by people outside academe. Instead of being the "lonely learners" of online or traditional correspondence courses, *CyberShakespeare* students will interact with each other and with their instructors, helping to improve student retention within courses. Instead of a rigid syllabus, "tailored learning" will allow each student to choose from a range of plays and learning activities. Students will work with several instructors whose comments will be stored so as to be accessible only to the student and the instructors. Instead of time-consuming in-class exercises, *CyberShakespeare* will offer asynchronous instruction. *CyberShakespeare* aims at a full complement of modules, covering the most popular plays and instructional approaches.

It is anticipated that the *CyberShakespeare* learning and instructional environment will lead to applications in other subject areas, setting a pattern for transforming instructors' skills, knowledge, and course materials from the traditional classroom environment to the new interactive environment of Web-based education. Thus *CyberShakespeare* will help others explore the new world of educational opportunities and challenges presented by asynchronous, multimedia instruction on the Web. The reader is now invited to view the earlier and the current states of the project by visiting *CyberShakespeare*.

Shakespeare on the Web: Teaching and Research

Shakespeare on the Web opens many possibilities for collaborative teaching and research. By using a shared interactive database, "authors" (both scholars and instructors) may place "objects" in the database. All authors may have access to all objects in the database. Using selected objects for illustration, the authors may then create documents either as a form of research publication or as instruction—or as a blend of the two. The "users" (students or readers) may then access these interactive documents, usage being recorded by an administrative interface and transmitted, in the case of student users, to universities in which they are enrolled. Where appropriate, users and authors may communicate with each other, and authors may have a record of who their readers or student users are, possibly with royalty payments.

The impact of Web-based instruction engages several concerns of Shakespeare teachers. Viewed positively, Shakespeare on the Web makes new teaching opportunities possible. Besides reaching more students more conveniently through asynchronous instruction, Shakespeare teaching on the Web can reduce the amount of face-to-face time spent by instructors and students. Reduce, but not replace, I should emphasize. Despite the fears of some instructors and the misguided hopes of cost-conscious educational administrators, outright substitution of Web-based instruction for traditional teaching seems out of the question. Printed books helped disseminate knowledge but did not eliminate the desire and need for direct human interaction; so too the Web. However, just as books extend the possibilities of effective instruction beyond those of face-to-face teaching, Web-based Shakespeare offers many other means by which instructors and students can use their time more effectively.

Consider a variation on the traditional Shakespeare course with a single instructor, fixed syllabus, set class meeting times, and a luck-of-the-draw student selection process (often driven by time and place of class meetings). Web-based teaching offers the convenience of a flexible schedule, a varied "tailored learning" approach, and access to more than one instructor. One variation on traditional Shakespeare instruction, for instance, would be to concentrate face-to-face interaction in small groups at the beginning, middle, and end of term, the times in-between being spent on interactive, structured, Web-based exercises. As an alternative to a large lecture series with tutors for marking and group discussions, such an arrangement could give the instructor greater flexibility by taking less time, and give students more interaction with each other and with tutors. Despite the fears, in some cases tinged with Luddite computer phobia, Web-based instruction has already become an important part of many disciplines, and it seems likely to become so for Shakespeare teachers as well.

Web-based research thus far has taken the form of scholarly exchanges through SHAKSPER and other bulletin boards. It is rapidly expanding, however, as a means of publication without paper: electronic journals and, more ambitiously, Michael Best's *Internet Shakespeare Editions*, as mentioned earlier. Drawing upon primary-source materials, the collaborative model sketched above may serve both for the creation of interactive instructional materials and research documents.

BROADER ISSUES: EGALITARIAN ACCESS

Looking beyond the concerns and logistics of the classroom and the study, one can discern yet broader issues. By making access easy, Shakespeare on the Web reduces the exclusive possession of knowledge heretofore maintained by scholars and archives. Whereas access to Shakespeare resources and the scholars-teachers who knew them once depended upon physical proximity in "prestige" departments or at high-profile conferences, the Web makes such access easier and quicker: witness the SHAKSPER exchanges and the many other e-mail messages that take place among individuals. Further, whereas access to texts and performance records once required knowledge of archives and physical access to them, Shakespeare on the Web puts an ever-growing body of rare materials and research publications, easily searched, within the reach of anyone with a computer. How will this affect the shape of Shakespeare teaching and research, and ultimately the profession? It is easy to predict a surge of interest and a leveling of the differences that separate people with different degrees of engagement. Scholars, students, and the general public will all have equal or more nearly equal access to research and educational materials.

Yet with this gain come significant risks. A plethora of knowledge need not lead always to better research and teaching. A classic case in point: American history teachers in a midsize Ohio city created a hypertext corpus of reference readings. Ideally, students could benefit from the combined materials of five different schools. As the experiment proceeded, its initiators found to their dismay that, lacking clear guidance and context, their students' access to diverse information led to errors of fact and interpretation. A search on "Lincoln" could bring up indiscriminately references not only to the president but also to the automobile and to pennies. Multiply this example by thousands, and the need for pathways through the interactive forest of facts and materials becomes apparent. Thoughtful, structured exercises using these newly available materials will challenge Shakespeareans as they introduce their students to the bewildering array of Shakespeareana on the Web.

With ease of access, publication on the Web (as distinct from digitizing print materials) will make possible swifter dissemination of new research. It will also open the door to yet more mushrooming of commentary on Shakespeare's plays. Some scholars might regard this development with distaste, especially if it is seen to dilute the value of their own contributions. Instead, if carefully reviewed, edited, and indexed, such fresh research can escape the limitations imposed by traditional media and rising publishing costs. To name a single example, the changes in editorship at *Shakespeare Quarterly* have been marked by shifts in content. When John Andrews came to the position, he expanded coverage of Shakespearean theater performance around the world; his successor, Barbara Mowat, cut back on the performance component to make room for other areas. Publication of new Shakespeare scholarship has become a zero-sum game, with a sum that grows smaller each year with rising publication costs and shrinking budgets at libraries and university presses. Publication of one article or book precludes publication of others. With inexpensive digital publication, however, Shakespearean scholarship can grow—with the inevitable concern that quantity may overwhelm quality. Digital search engines may ensure easy and accurate access to new scholarship, but that scholarship must itself be evaluated and judged, leading to questions of editorial control in electronic publication. Who will be the gatekeepers?

Despite the concern about quality control, the benefits of Shakespeare on the Web to scholars and students attempting to follow particular lines of inquiry will become more efficient as more and more of past and present scholarship and performance are available in searchable digital form. It will also lessen the often-heard excuse that "so much has been written about Shakespeare that I can't possibly know if my ideas are original." In time, promotion and tenure reviews will take into account the added opportunity offered by digital publication.

CAVEATS AND PARADOXES

Clouding the rosy vision with which I began, however, are several paradoxical issues. What technology makes possible may be impeded by copyright and other commercial considerations. Totally free access to Shakespeare materials with commercial value seems unlikely. More likely, site licenses that could permit open access through local area networks could make it possible for students to view videos over a campus network, rather than having to schedule individual viewings in a media center. It is also conceivable that, as in the case of audiotape and videotape, the ease and frequency with which copyright is ignored will be offset by the decline in quality that occurs with copying. Law-abiding universities that do not tape copyrighted broadcast material without permission will continue to obey the law scrupulously. Individuals may not be so scrupulous, instead making illegal copies and distributing them over the Web, to the consternation of the copyright holders.

One effect will be to filter out of active use some of the benchmark performances—I think here particularly of those at the Globe in London and landmark films—for which no provision has been made for viewing videos offsite. Although the potential for vastly increasing access to Shakespearean materials over the Web exists technologically, unless copyright restrictions can be ameliorated, Shakespeare on the Web will have some inaccessible dark corners. In time actors' contracts and archival policy will recognize the need for Web access, and provisions will be made for it. In the meantime one can foresee teaching and research that is skewed in favor of Web access to materials in the public domain.

Another paradox is that Shakespeare on the Web will enhance teaching and research mightily on the one hand, and on the other, make it possible to do more teaching and research with fewer Shakespeareans. The downsizing of budgets in higher education throughout the world has created a strong incentive for university administrators to increase the efficiency and efficacy of traditional classroom instruction, while at the same time striving to increase the "market" for "educational products" through distance teaching on the Web. These powerful incentives have already begun to have an impact on instructional practice in Australia, North America, and Britain. It has been pointed out to me, for example, that in an Australian university a senior lecturer costs 250 dollars per hour for time spent in the classroom and marking papers, and that a casual instructor on a short-term contract costs about 50 dollars per hour. Recognizing these conditions, large corporations and universities have begun collaborations to offer courses on the Web at lower cost than traditional classroom instruction. If Shakespeare on the Web offers quality instruction at even less cost, will it not mean that Shakespeareans will be replaced by computer-based learning? Put another way, if Shakespeareans retire from a department and are not replaced, would one choose to omit Shakespeare from the curriculum or to use Web-based instruction? Or with fewer Shakespeareans to teach, does one revert to the large lecture format with classes of 250 students or to a blend of face-to-face teaching extended through Web-based instruction?

To these questions there are no simple answers. In some cases, Shakespeare instruction will be entirely Web-based. Shakespeare on the Web certainly is better than none at all, especially for students without any other access to instruction—those in remote areas, in prison, or disabled. In other cases, Web-based Shakespeare will enhance traditional distance and classroom instruction, making more effective use of instructors' time. Will most Shakespeareans be replaced by a few who create classes on the Web? Most certainly not, but Shakespeare on the Web will certainly change the way in which we teach and research. Just as the demographics of the student population is changing to include off-campus students and adult learners, so too the learning environment is expanding from the polarity of on-campus or off-campus instruction. Even as the absolute number of Shakespeareans may decline, a grim demographic fact in view of decreases in funding for higher education, the resources on which Shakespeareans may draw will increase. One can imagine Shakespeare instruction and research tied to the productions of a Shakespeare festival, for example, through Web-based materials that are geared to a particular season and then archived for continued use after the lights in the theater have gone out.

CHALLENGES AND OPPORTUNITIES

While important, these challenges and opportunities ought not to obscure the main story. Shakespeare on the Web is creating an extensive, ever-growing, virtual library of important Shakespeare materials. Shakespeare on the Web offers a vast array of resources to which everyone—playgoers, theater artists, students, teachers, and scholars—can have access. The library never closes—an important consideration for students and for users in different time zones. People in the new Shakespeare library can leave notes for each other and collaborate over distances in time, space, and status. It is impressive that students and scholars communicate directly and publicly through SHAKSPER. Any great library creates new opportunities for informal and scholarly exchanges, and, as have such outstanding Renaissance libraries as the Folger, the Huntington, and the Newberry, this new Shakespeare library on the Web may even alter both the contents and the underlying assumptions of scholarly publication.[18] With other Shakespeareans I look forward to the rapid growth and continuing evolution of Shakespeare on the Web.

Notes

1. A shorter, earlier version of this essay, entitled "Digital Shakespeare," appears as a chapter in *Teaching Shakespeare through Performance*, ed. Milla Riggio (New York: MLA, 1998). For research assistance I gratefully acknowledge the aid of my honors Shakespeare students Brian Choi, Jill Mulligan, Hiten Patel, Kim Whittaker, and Sofia Zats.

2. Double-entry means that all the data are entered twice, then the two large files are compared and inconsistencies corrected. It was a time-wasteful but necessary and standard procedure in those days.

3. For further information, see H. Joachim Neuhaus, "Integrating Database, Expert System, and Hypermedia: The Shakespeare CD-ROM Project," *Literary and Linguistic Computing* 6 (1991): 187–91; or write to H. Joachim Neuhaus, Director, Centre for Applied Computer Science, Westfälische Wilhelms-Universität, Münster, Germany. For publication information write to Olms Neue Median, Georg Olms Verlag, Hagentorwall 7, D-31134 Hildeheim, Germany <olms@oln.comlink.apc.org>. The author thanks Dr. Marga Munkelt for her assistance in visiting the Centre in June 1995.

4. For information on HyperCard, DynaText, and other hypertext engines, one should seek technical expertise; the programs evolve too swiftly to make a description here accurate by the time this book is printed.

5. See Anita Lowry, "Electronic Texts in English and American Literature," *Library Trends* 40 (1992): 704–23, where Howard-Hill's remarks are cited.

6. Electronic Text Corporation, Johnson and Company, American Fork, Utah; *The Riverside Shakespeare*, ed. G. Blakemore Evans (Boston: Houghton Mifflin, 1974).

7. For information about this edition, I am grateful to Michael Hattaway, University of Sheffield, the director of the project, with whom I spoke in the

summer of 1995. For current information, contact Hattaway or Sarah Stanton at Cambridge University Press. Since this book has gone to press, various other CD-ROM editions have of course begun to emerge.

8. In no way am I faulting the valiant efforts of Hardy M. Cook, whose tolerant diligence suffers both fools and novices without a murmur. To subscribe, e-mail him: HMCook@boe00.minc.umd.edu (the 00 are zeros).

9. "Optical Discs: A Shakespearean Proposal," *International Journal of Micrographics and Optical Technology* 7 (1989): 115–19. Ironically, as general editor for the New Cambridge Shakespeare, Brockbank's half-serious proposal for an interactive variorum using optical disks is now being implemented, on a smaller scale than he may have foreseen, through CD-ROM technology.

10. Adding to this body of digital material comes the recent collaboration among the Folger Shakespeare Library, the Shakespeare Centre Library (Stratford-upon-Avon), and the Massachusetts Institute of Technology presently underway. How this digital material will be made available has not yet been announced. For further information, contact Peter Donaldson, Department of Literature, MIT, or the Shakespeare Centre Library in Stratford.

11. *Shakespeare Newsletter* (1995): 21, 37.

12. For a full account, see Larry Friedlander, "The Shakespeare Project: Experiments in Multimedia Education," *Academic Computing* 2, no. 7 (1988): 26–29, 66–68.

13. Columbia and London: Univ. of Missouri Press, 1976.

14. My involvement with computer-assisted research dates back to the late 1970s, when I used computers at the University of Illinois at Urbana-Champaign to create *Theater at Stratford-upon-Avon: A Catalogue-Index to Productions at the Shakespeare Memorial / Royal Shakespeare Theater, 1879–1978* (Westport and London: Greenwood, 1976). Subsequently, I collaborated with Alan Somerset (University of Western Ontario) and Marian Pringle (Shakespeare Centre Library) to create an interactive database at the Stratford library and to produce a 1979–93 supplement to the earlier two-volume catalog-index.

15. "Computer Disk Read-Only Memory" or CD-ROM may be conceived as locked floppy disks with the capacity to store large files required by moving images. Depending on the quality of the images, a CD-ROM can hold two or three hours of digital video; rapid improvements in image quality and capacity are expected as the technology evolves.

16. Albert Braunmuller, *"Macbeth"* (New York: Voyager, 1994); and Michael Best, *Shakespeare's Life and Times* (Santa Barbara, LA: Intellimation, 1994).

17. For current information, please see www.vosaic.com.

18. See Peter Holland, "Authorship and Collaboration: The Problem of Editing Shakespeare," in *The Politics of the Electronic Text*, ed. Warren Chernaik, Caroline Davis, and Marilyn Deegan (Oxford: University of London, 1993), 17–23, where Holland argues that digital Shakespeare editions will modify editors' silent control of the text.

Cultural Appropriations of Shakespeare in the Classroom

Susan Gushee O'Malley

> the worst thing we can do is to foster in them [students] an
> attitude of reverence before texts.
> —Robert Scholes, *Textual Power:*
> *Literary Theory and the Teaching of English*

> The force of hegemony . . . is in the use of the plays as a whole,
> in how they have been "naturalised" into the dominant ideol-
> ogy. That is, the ruling-class views seem to arise from the
> plays themselves rather than to be imposed on them.
> —David Margolies, "Teaching the Handsaw to the Fly:
> Shakespeare as a Hegemonic Instrument,"
> in *The Shakespeare Myth*

> [Shakespeare] does not have to be a crucial stage in the justi-
> fication of elitism in education and culture. He has been ap-
> propriated for certain practices and attitudes, and can be
> reappropriated for others.
> —Alan Sinfield, "Give an Account of Shakespeare
> in Education . . ." in *Political Shakespeare*

MY STUDENTS AT THE CENTER FOR WORKER EDUCATION, A BRANCH
campus of The City College of The City University of New York
(CUNY), too often believe that studying Shakespeare is a marker
of ascendance into elite culture. Their Shakespeare is not the
popular Shakespeare of New York City's Central Park but the hegemonic Shakespeare of "universal truths" and "timelessness"
that they have been led to believe all educated and cultured people should know. Because of their hostility toward or false reverence for Shakespeare, they approach the plays with trepidation
and have great difficulty engaging with the texts. They want me
to tell them what a play means so they may write their papers
and exams with certainty. This situation is complicated by the
fact that all of the students are working-class adults and the ma-

jority are women of color, many of whom have immigrated from countries that were colonized by England.

For these students to read Shakespeare as the repository of universal truths of the dominant culture is a schizophrenic act. This is true for working-class students, both African-American and white, as well as students who grew up reading Shakespeare in schools of former British colonies still dominated by the British educational system. Student comments such as "In comparison to Prospero, whose learned sorcery is 'Art,' is the 'natural' Caliban, with his lust and his beastlike resistance to education" or "Kate in her submission to Petruchio has finally learned to love and be loved," while they may or may not be true in the world of the play, are destructive when they are elevated to "universal truths." When an African-American student whose ancestors are also Native-American makes statements about the base nature of Caliban, or a woman who is struggling in an abusive marriage praises Kate's submission to Petruchio and then generalizes these statements as universal truths, what does this say about the student's consciousness?[1]

In an attempt to challenge what I consider to be the false consciousness with which my students too often approach Shakespeare, I designed a course, entitled Cultural Appropriations of Shakespeare, that focused on three Shakespearean plays, *The Tempest*, *Othello*, and *King Lear*, and appropriations of them. I use the word "appropriation" in the sense of "to take to or for oneself" or "to take possession of." In *Talking Back to Shakespeare* Martha Tuck Rozett uses "transformations," instead of "appropriations," to mean "stretch[ing] the texts in new directions,"[2] but I thought that using the term "appropriation" would lead more easily to my desire to speculate on the cultural, political, and ideological work of each of the texts. Here I was influenced by Althusser's essay "Ideology and Ideological State Apparatuses"; I wanted the students to begin to understand how Shakespeare has been used ideologically in our culture. Clifford Geertz's definition of culture as "the framework of beliefs, expressive symbols, and values in terms of which individuals define their world, express their feelings, and make their judgments" informed our discussion of culture.[3]

It was difficult to decide which plays and appropriations to include in the syllabus. I decided on *The Tempest*, *Othello*, and *King Lear* for the following reasons. First, many of the students at the Center for Worker Education are from the Caribbean, so it seemed appropriate to begin the course with *The Tempest*. I wanted them to be free to do "positioned" readings of the play. Also, my friend Barbara Bowen had just taught a course at the CUNY Graduate School entitled Postcolonial Shakespeare, which focused on *The Tempest*, and I was eager to read her syllabus. Second, I chose *Othello* because of Leslie Dunn's fascinating paper on her teaching both *Othello* and Tayeb Salih's *Season of Migration to the North* to first-year students at Vassar College, a paper that she presented at the Sixth World Shakespeare Congress in Los Angeles in April 1996. Third, I chose *King Lear* because I was intrigued by Jane Smiley's rewriting of the play in *A Thousand Acres,* although I was aware that New York City students might be bewildered by the extensive amount of farming information in the novel.

Growing out of an extension program for public employees, the Center for Worker Education of City College was established in 1981 to educate adults who work in New York City. Today the center offers two degrees, a bachelor of arts degree in interdisciplinary liberal arts and a bachelor of science in early childhood education. Of the nearly one thousand students at the center in 1998, more than half are public employees and most are union members. The average age of the students at the center is forty, and about 75 percent of the students are women. Although the majority of the students are people of color from the United States, the Caribbean, and Africa, students come from many different countries. Each year the center graduates about one hundred students, some of whom win prestigious graduate fellowships to continue their studies. What has impressed me as an instructor at the center is its engaged intellectual atmosphere and the working-class identity of many of the students.

Classes at the center are held once a week for three-and-one-half hours, a challenge in itself. I structured the syllabus so that we would spend two classes on each of the Shakespearean plays, six classes in total, and eight classes on the appropriations. For each class, the students had to write a one-to-two page reaction paper on the assigned text. Once during the term a student had to pair up with another student to begin the class discussion with a series of questions to engage the class with the text. I find that this often causes the discussion to go in directions I would never have imagined. After about twenty or thirty minutes I would begin to shape the discussion to ensure that points I thought were crucial to an understanding of the text were covered. I also required a final paper and an exam that asked the students to choose four of the appropriations that they had read and, using

Althusser if they wished, to write an essay on the cultural, political, and ideological work of each of the appropriations. To my surprise, many of the students asked me if they could write their own appropriations instead of a final paper. This worried me, but I agreed, thinking that the final would force the students to draw some conclusions about what they had read during the term.

To my amazement, the appropriations were marvelous. In reading the uses to which others had put the Shakespearean plays, the students had found their own voices. Prospero became a drug lord in a Queens housing project in one student's paper and the head of the National Academy of Television Arts and Sciences (where the student worked) in another; Iago was transformed into a black woman in love with Maurice, a black journalist from the United States engaged with the Sandinistas in Nicaragua. He, of course, was in love with the light-skinned daughter of the commandant; Lear, now an older woman forced to live in a nursing home in Staten Island, bewailed how her daughters were treating her in an appropriation entitled "O'Leary's Trash and Treasures." One student appropriated Tayeb Sahib's *Season of Migration to the North*, a novel influenced by *Othello*, transforming it into a neocolonial story of two girls in Guyana, one of whom left to study in England, married an Englishman, and returned with her husband to Guyana to experience racism and eventual suicide. The appropriations used elements of the plot, images, and verbal echoes of the Shakespearean plays imaginatively and effectively. Many were concerned with race, colonialism, and explorations of power. What I had conceived as a vehicle to get students to engage more fully and more honestly with Shakespearean plays had worked beyond my wildest imaginings. Gone was Robert Scholes's fear of undue "reverence before texts," as quoted in the first epigraph to this essay. Instead, in Alan Sinfield's words, the plays were being "reappropriated" for other "practices and attitudes," or as Margaret W. Ferguson suggests in her afterword to *Shakespeare Reproduced*, perhaps the effect of the juxtaposition of the Shakespearean text with the appropriation was "disrupt[ing] the processes of ideological reproduction."[4] Because the students had written their own appropriations, they had a much better sense of Shakespeare's rewriting his sources and were able, as a consequence, to read the plays with a much more courageous and developed critical perspective.

But to return to the course. After having a discussion on what might be meant by the terms "appropriation" and "culture," I began the course by showing segments of *Kiss Me Kate*, produced in 1953, and *West Side Story*, released in 1961, with relevant passages from act 2, scene 2, of *The Taming of the Shrew* and act 2, scenes 1 and 2, of *Romeo and Juliet*. I wanted to show the students two popular reworkings of the plays and how they were situated in the time in which they were written.

The following two weeks we read *The Tempest* and began to work with the appropriations. For *The Tempest* the appropriations I chose were Aime Cesaire's *A Tempest*, Michelle Cliff's *No Telephone to Heaven*, and George Lamming's *The Pleasures of Exile*. In addition, we read Robert Browning's "Caliban upon Setebos," a number of poems from Edward Brathwaite's *Islands*, and Lemuel Johnson's *Highlife for Caliban*. Film appropriations included segments of Paul Mazursky's 1982 *Tempest*, with John Cassavetes, Susan Sarandon, and Raul Julia; Peter Greenaway's *Prospero's Books*, with John Gielgud, produced in 1991; and the 1956 science fiction version, *Forbidden Planet*, with Walter Pidgeon and Anne Francis.[5]

After reading and discussing *The Tempest*, we began our analysis of appropriations with a consideration of George Lamming's *The Pleasures of Exile*, published in 1959, the year of the Cuban Revolution but before the liberation of other African and West Indian colonies.[6] Students read several chapters, including "A Monster, a Child, a Slave" and "Caliban Orders History." Although several writers before Lamming, such as Rubén Darío, Ernest Renan, and Octave Mannoni, used *The Tempest* to analyze colonization or to indict imperialism, Lamming was the first, according to Barbara Bowen, "explicitly to recuperate Caliban for a politics of resistance to colonialism."[7] Lamming, who left Barbados to live in England, says his subject is "the migration of the West Indian writer, as colonial and exile, from his native kingdom, once inhabited by Caliban, to the tempestuous island of Prospero's and his language" (13). Caliban, according to Lamming, is Prospero's "convert, colonized by language, and excluded by language" (15). Because of Prospero's gift of language, Caliban is "exiled from his gods, exiled from his nature, exiled from his own name!" (15). In Lamming's reading, Caliban "has no self which is not a reaction to circumstances imposed upon his life" (107) because he does not have the power to see. Caliban is "a state of existence which can be appropriated and exploited for the purposes of another's development" (107). Lamming sees Prospero as an imperialist and a sadist who needs Caliban "in order to escape the purgatory which has been crystallised by their encounter" (15).

Students much preferred Cesaire's *A Tempest*, published in 1969, to Lamming's *Pleasures* because Caliban, in addition to speaking the colonizer's language, had retained his own language, Swahili, and his own god, Shango.[8] To Prospero, Caliban says "Uhuru," the Swahili word for freedom that was used as the watchword of Mau Mau rebellions in Kenya as early as the 1940s. Prospero objects to Caliban's use of his "native language" (11), which Prospero himself has not bothered to learn. When Caliban marches off with Trinculo and Stephano to attack Prospero, he calls upon his god, Shango, the Yoruba god of thunder, who causes "lies" to "expire" (52) when he strikes with his big stick. Students were also fascinated with the juxtaposition of Caliban with Ariel, who tries to convince Caliban to work nonviolently to help Prospero "acquire a conscience" (22), a kind of Malcolm X versus Martin Luther King or, in another reading, the slave who worked in the field versus the slave who worked in the master's house. At the conclusion of *A Tempest*, however, Prospero does not leave the island, but stays to "protect civilization" (68) and to answer Caliban's violence with his own. Caliban charges him with being "an old [colonial] addict" (65). The final words of the play are Caliban's: "FREEDOM HI-DAY, FREEDOM HI-DAY!" which suggest the possibility that Prospero's kingdom might soon collapse. Although students felt that there was more possibility for Caliban in *A Tempest* than in Lamming's *Pleasures*, they also felt that the colonizer was "caught," in one student's words, "in a codependent power struggle, dancing a sadistic tango with the colonized,"[9] and that the colonized suffered from false consciousness in attempting to organize Trinculo and Stephano to defeat Prospero. In other words, the struggle is ongoing.

Michelle Cliff's *No Telephone to Heaven*, the third appropriation we read, is written from the point of view of Clare Savage, a "new world" Miranda.[10] Although Shakespeare's *The Tempest* is only a "residual presence" in the novel,[11] I wanted to include a woman's writing on anticolonialism. Barbara Bowen's contention that both Lamming and Cesaire are "complicit with Shakespeare's play in suppressing the agency of women within and against colonialism,"[12] also reinforced my decision to include a woman's perspective.

No Telephone to Heaven takes place in an extended flashback in the mind of Clare Savage while she is riding in a truck with a group of revolutionaries to blow up a British and American movie set for a film that belittles Jamaican history. Clare is a light-skinned Jamaican from a wealthy family who has immigrated to the United States where her Prospero-like father, Boy Savage, has insisted that the family pass for white. Clare or Miranda has broken away from her father and returned to Jamaica to do something for her people. There she meets Harry/Harriet, a man who has become a woman and who works as a healer. Harriet is the child of a black maid and her master who fired his maid when he discovered that she was pregnant and raised their child himself. Harriet educates Clare on how the Jamaican people have internalized the values of their masters (127), speaks Jamaican with her, and initiates her into a group of revolutionaries.

I first taught this novel in a course on gender without reading it as an appropriation of *The Tempest*, but I think Thomas Cartelli's essay, "After *The Tempest*," makes a good case for reading *No Telephone* as an appropriation of *The Tempest* and perhaps Cesaire's *A Tempest*. Cliff prefaces several chapters with quotes from Cesaire and includes Caliban in her lists of associations with Bertha from *Jane Eyre*, a woman Clare realizes she is closer to than the Jane her father wanted her to be.

For the students *No Telephone* was about the harsh realities of colonialism. Some students read Clare as Cesaire's mulatto Ariel. Because she can pass but chooses to be black, she will never really be accepted.[13] Another older student vividly described the lowering of the Union Jack and the raising of the Jamaican flag in 1962, and explained to the class that the people's hopes when Norman Manley came to power were dispelled with the rule of Seaga and Manley's second term. She saw *No Telephone* as "the tempest . . . representative of the experiences of a people in transition from colony to independent nation discarded by England, the motherland, without a legacy to fend for itself. . . . *No Telephone to Heaven* suggests hopelessness for its Calibans." She did, however, point to Cliff's belief that "when you come from a culture that is not mainstream . . . you really can use that in a way to admit that you don't have much loyalty to [the tradition] and that you can play with the forms more," a liberating possibility for a writer.

The appropriations for *Othello* and *King Lear* were less extensive as the term was already in its seventh week. For *Othello* we read the Sudanese novel, *Season of Migration to the North* (1969) by Tayib Salih, and viewed excerpts from Janet Suzman's 1987 South African production of *Othello* with John Kani as Othello, Orson Welles's 1952 *Othello* with Welles as Othello and Michael Maclaimmoir as Iago, and Oliver Parker's 1995 *Othello* with Laurence Fishburne as Othello and Kenneth Branagh as Iago.

In *Season of Migration to the North* Mustapha Sa'eed has just returned to the Sudan from England where he had been imprisoned for seven years for killing his English wife.[14] A brilliant student, Mustapha Sa'eed was sent by the colonial power to England where he studied economics and deliberately seduces as many women as he can by appealing to their orientalist and racist fantasies of black men. Unlike Othello whose identity disintegrates by the end of the play, Muatapha Sa'eed is aware of his position as a colonial other and exploits it. He refers to Othello three times in the text, once to say he is no Othello because he [Mustapha] is a lie (33), then to claim he is like Othello because he is Arab-African (38), and then to assert he is "no Othello. Othello was a lie" (95). Both Mustapha Sa'eed and Othello create lies about themselves: Othello to arouse Desdemona's "pity," and Mustapha Sa'eed to feed the fantasies of the five women with whom he lives. In contrast to Shakespeare, Salih's sexual relationships between the colonial subject and western women do not produce idealized Desdemonas. The western women and Mustapha Sa'eed are all implicated in the destructiveness of their relationships, distorted in the political and racial power struggles of colonialism.[15]

Season of Migration to the North participates in the Arabic literary classification called "mu arandeh," which means "opposition" or "contradiction," a formula in which a writer responds to another writer but reverses the meaning. Salih contradicts Shakespeare's *Othello* by deconstructing the orientalist creation of the colonized African and the innocent Desdemona.

The students were pained by *Season of Migration to the North*. They saw Mustapha Sa'eed as a symbol of the colonized, one forced into becoming a neocolonist by the British and intent at colonizing the colonized, or "polluting" the women of the "polluters." Othello is a lie, said one student, because he is a sentimentalized fiction of a white man. The novel "demonstrates what can happen when whites objectify blacks. They might get more than they bargained for when they get their fantasy, one based on a racist ideological apparatus about the sexual nature of black men." In an appropriation of both *Othello* and *Season*, Bhomatie Leopold, a student from Guyana, wrote a moving story of what happened to Sadia, who was sent to university in England to study, while the narrator of the story, whose ancestors came from India as indentured servants, worked at the sugar estates in Guyana owned by the English. The story addresses the stripping of cultural identity in the British educational system in Guyana, the racism of the society, and the impossibility for Sadia to exist in either England or Guyana after she returns.

The last play we read together was *King Lear*. Film versions included excerpts from Michael Elliott's 1983 *Lear* starring Laurence Olivier, Akira Kurosawa's 1985 version entitled *Ran*, and the 1954 appropriation, *Broken Lance*, with Spencer Tracy. Jane Smiley's *A Thousand Acres* (1991), the one appropriation we read besides a quick read of David Denby's "Queen Lear," an account of his mother published in the *New Yorker*, is a feminist reworking of *Lear* from the point of view of Ginny or Goneril.[16] Nowhere in the novel is the play mentioned, but it is obviously a reworking of *King Lear*: Larry Cook, an older man, decides to form a corporation to avoid estate taxes and to give his one thousand acres of land to his three daughters and their husbands, the youngest of whom questions her father's wisdom and is disinherited. Patriarchal Larry moves from one of his daughter's houses to the other until, enraged at his daughters, he spends the night in a violent storm. This Lear, however, has physically and sexually abused his two older daughters, although this is a family secret. The farm that Larry and his two sons-in-law farm together is an environmental disaster. Ginny has repeated miscarriages and her sister Rose (Regan) contracts fatal breast cancer, probably caused by the DDT used as a pesticide in her father's farm. This is revealed by Jess Clark, the Edmund character, a Vietnam veteran who sleeps with both sisters.

Initially angry at Ginny's inability to be decisive, students read *A Thousand Acres* as a story of sexual abuse that cripples the independence of the two older daughters. Caroline, the youngest, has escaped the farm and her father's sexual exploits because she was protected by her sisters, but she is not a sympathetic character. Neither is Larry, who has tried to control his daughters' lives. "O'Leary's Trash and Treasures," the one student appropriation I received based on *Lear*, deals with the relationship of narrator, Grace, and her elderly mother, who resides in a nursing home in Staten Island. Matriarch O'Leary ran an antique shop that she decided in her old age to split among her three daughters. The youngest, who has managed to escape Staten Island for Manhattan, refuses. The story is the juxtaposition of the stream of consciousness in matriarch O'Leary's head during her Sunday afternoon outings away from the nursing home with Grace, her daughter, who is trying to understand how her mother has controlled her entire life.

So what was accomplished by English 317.34, Cultural Appropriations of Shakespeare? I like to think that the students left the course with an increased ability to read Shakespearean plays more critically and honestly and also to explore issues that are important to them by reading the appropriations. Too often in my experience we want the Shakespearean text to be more politically correct than it is, to say more about sexism or anti-colonialism than it does. Juxtaposing the Shakespearean text with appropriations in some ways levels Shakespeare, but makes for more honest readings of the plays.[17] Instead of either genuflecting before the Shakespearean text or dismissing Shakespeare as irrelevant—which they had expected to do before they took the class— these working-class adults ended the course with an increased ability to read the plays critically and more courageously because of having read the appropriations of the plays and then having written their own appropriations. Working through the three levels of play, appropriation, and their own appropriations gave the students a greater understanding of the original play and made Shakespeare and his language more accessible to them. It allowed them both to understand how many writers have, in Rozett's phrase, "talked back" to Shakespeare by rewriting his plays to express current concerns and to find their own voices by talking back to Shakespeare in their own appropriations.

If I teach the course again, I might try first to work with Shakespeare's source material, the play, and then the appropriation, in other words, adding an extra level of appropriation, and ask the same questions: what cultural, political, and ideological work does each text do? I would also insist on a prerequisite that all of the students had read several Shakespeare plays. The students who had never studied Shakespeare had a very difficult time in the course.

ADDENDUM

In spring 2001 I again taught Cultural Appropriations at the Center for Worker Education. I changed the syllabus somewhat: I omitted George Lamming's *The Pleasures of Exile* and Michelle Cliff's *No Telephone to Heaven* and added Gloria Naylor's *Mama Day* and Paula Vogel's *Desdemona: A Story about a Handkerchief*. The students liked these readings better than the readings they replaced from my previous class. Gloria Naylor's *Mama Day* is a loose reworking of *The Tempest*; it changes Prospero to Mama Day, a matriarchal African-American woman who resides in a mythical island off the coast of the Carolinas and plies her healing magic to save Cocoa, her grandniece, who has moved to New York City.[18] It is an African-American woman's vision that takes *The Tempest* and creates a story of the importance of faith and the healing possibilities of Southern herbal folklore as opposed to the limits of rationality in urban New York City.

Vogel's *Desdemona: A Story about a Handkerchief* tells the Othello story from Desdemona's point of view, but this Desdemona is spending time with Bianca and working as a prostitute one night a week.[19] Cassio is the one man that she has not slept with, but Othello suspects her of infidelity with him. Students raved about *Mama Day*, but many were upset at Vogel's making Desdemona a part-time prostitute. Jane Smiley's *A Thousand Acres* taught even more successfully than before because of the excellent articles in Marianne Novy's edited volume, *Transforming Shakespeare*,[20] one of which is by Jane Smiley, who explains why she could not write *A Thousand Acres* today as her reading of *King Lear* has changed. I also showed the recent movie of *A Thousand Acres*.

Students wrote appropriations of the plays we read—one wrote a prequel to *King Lear* that explained how the Lear family became so dysfunctional—but the appropriations lacked the political bite of the previous appropriations. That may have been because of the substitution of the Naylor for more markedly political appropriations of *The Tempest* or because I assigned appropriation writing rather than the students' demanding to write them or because this group was younger and less political than my earlier class. These appropriations were more concerned with sexual politics, in particular homosexuality and incest. An appropriation entitled "Queer Lear" attests to this. They also criticized Smiley for making Larry, her Lear figure, commit incest with his two older daughters. They astutely felt that this was reductive and did not give Larry a chance in the reader's estimation.

I am still convinced that reading Shakespeare's plays and the appropriations of them and then encouraging students to write their own appropriations is productive in enabling students to become mature critical readers of Shakespeare. When I teach only the plays of Shakespeare, there is less engagement with the texts and an unhealthy reverence for and distance from the plays. In the words of Agustin Rodriguez, a Puerto Rican student who took the course this spring, "The Shakespeare plays we read became my own because of the appropriations we read and wrote."

NOTES

1. My thinking about the uses to which Shakespeare has been put in the service of elite culture is influenced by Ania Loomba's discussion of curricula in India in "Imperialism, Patriarchy and Post-colonial English Studies," in *Gender, Race, Renaissance Drama* (Manchester: Manchester Univ. Press, 1989), 10–37. My experience teaching O and A levels to Jamaican, Pakistani, Nigerian, and Ghananian students at Vauxhall College of Further Education in South London from 1982 to 1983 has also influenced my thinking. When I asked why there were no texts from the Caribbean included on the set syllabus, I was told that they had no culture and no literature. Later I was told that there was a Caribbean and African syllabus, but it was considered inferior as it included no Shakespeare.

2. Martha Tuck Rozett, *Talking Back to Shakespeare* (Newark, Del.: Univ. of Delaware Press, 1994), 7.

3. Louis Althusser, "Ideology and Ideological State Apparatuses," in *Lenin and Philosophy and Other Essays*, trans. Ben Brewster (New York: Monthly Review Press, 1973); Clifford Geertz, *The Interpretation of Cultures: Selected Essays* (New York: Basic Books, 1973), 144–45.

4. Margaret W. Ferguson, afterword to *Shakespeare Reproduced: The Text in Ideology and History*, ed. Jean E. Howard and Marion F. O'Connor (New York: Methuen, 1987), 281.

5. Students were amazed that *Forbidden Planet* reduced the story to psychological terms: Caliban becomes the id of Morbius, the Prospero figure.

6. George Lamming, *The Pleasures of Exile* (1959; reprint, Ann Arbor, Mich.: Univ. of Michigan Press, 1992).

7. Barbara Bowen, "Writing Caliban: Anticolonial Appropriations of *The Tempest*," *Current Writing* 5, no. 2 (1993): 87.

8. Aime Cesaire, *A Tempest*, trans. Richard Miller (New York: Ubu Repertory Theater Publications, 1969).

9. These are the words of Jacqueline E. Sutton in her final exam.

10. Michele Cliff, *No Telephone to Heaven* (New York: Random House, 1987).

11. Thomas Cartelli uses this phrase in "After *The Tempest*: Shakespeare, Postcoloniality, and Michelle Cliff's New, New World Miranda," *Contemporary Literature* 36, no. 1 (1995): 82–102.

12. Bowen, "Writing Caliban," 90.

13. Michelle Cliff discusses this in an interview by Judith Raiskin, "The Art of History: An Interview with Michelle Cliff," *The Kenyon Review* 15, no. 1 (1993): 57–71.

14. Tayeb Salih, *Season of Migration to the North*, trans. Denys Johnson-Davies (1978; reprint, Portsmouth, NH: Heinemann, 1995).

15. I am indebted to Jyotsna Singh's "Othello's Identity, Postcolonial Theory, and Contemporary African Rewritings of *Othello*," in *Women, "Race," and Writing in the Early Modern Period*, ed. Margo Hendricks and Patricia Parker (London: Routledge, 1994), 287–99.

16. Jane Smiley, *A Thousand Acres* (New York: Fawcett Columbine, 1991); David Denby, "Queen Lear," *New Yorker*, October 3, 1994, 88–96.

17. Here I am thinking of my teaching Shakespearean acting with my brother in his New York studio and of the ways we made the texts appear relevant. Often I felt uncomfortable in our attempts to make the text do more than it possibly could.

18. Gloria Naylor, *Mama Day* (1988; reprint, New York: Vintage, 1993).

19. Paula Vogel, *Desdemona: A Play about a Handkerchief*, in *The Baltimore Waltz and Other Plays* (New York: Theatre Communications Group, 1996).

20. Marianne Novy, ed., *Transforming Shakespeare: Contemporary Women's Re-visions in Literature and Performance* (New York: Palgrave, 1999).

The Uses of Shakespeare in Criminal Rehabilitation: Testing the Limits of "Universality"

Laura Raidonis Bates

"THE USES OF SHAKESPEARE" IS A POPULAR CATEGORY OF SCHOLARLY inquiry. I have participated in seminars under that title at recent conferences of both the Shakespeare Association of America and the International Shakespeare Association. At each conference, the range of "uses" explored was as wide as the range of participants involved. But while conference seminars and scholarly papers have tended to analyze this topic on a more theoretical level, the idea that the plays would have some *practical* application is an appealing one. (Indeed, my own doctoral dissertation dealt with the contest for appropriation of Shakespeare's works during the nationalist movement in nineteenth-century Eastern Europe). In this essay, therefore, I will explore the practical application of Shakespeare's work in a tangible, literally concrete setting: prison. Working with Shakespeare in particular in this context can provide a range of positive personal, educational, and social outcomes for criminal offenders.

Studies on recidivism rates, conducted by those involved in correctional education, unanimously claim a significant correlation between higher education and the avoidance of a return to criminal activity—or, at least, a return to prison. Both inmates and society seem to benefit from programs that develop the basic skills that are essential in making a successful transition following incarceration. To scholars and educators, the necessity of literacy and the humanizing effects of literature are self-evident. But they are also evident to criminal offenders. As one of my students said, "Illiteracy will only kill us; education will only heal us."

I embarked upon this project a few years ago, while still a doctoral student at the University of Chicago, specializing in Shake-

151

speare studies and completing a dissertation under the direction of David Bevington. At the time, I saw it as a way of testing the limits of Shakespeare's alleged "universality." Although critics have for centuries agreed with Ben Jonson's assertion that Shakespeare's plays are "not of an age, but for all time," it seemed to me that it did not necessarily follow that they were for all places and all people. What would happen if I took Shakespeare into prison (even if it were necessary—and it was in some cases—to literally smuggle in the texts as contraband)? Could his works reach even *this* audience?

Some fifteen years earlier, I had conducted a drama workshop in a prison setting, inspired by the work of the Geese Theater Company of London, which under the direction of John Bergman performed its play scripts to audiences of inmates. In my workshop, however, I took Bergman's approach one step further: under my guidance, the inmates themselves wrote and performed their own original script—a prison comedy with a moral. When I conducted my first Shakespeare workshop in a prison setting, my work was further inspired by that of the Kentucky Shakespeare Company, which under the direction of Curt Tofteland performs "the Bard behind bars." But once again, my work attempted to go one step further: rather than attempting to turn inexperienced and often semiliterate inmates into Shakespearean actors, I encouraged my students to rewrite Shakespeare's text into their own words, to engage in both linguistic and cultural translation.

The work began with an informal introduction to Shakespeare, through readily accessible video excerpts, followed by the painstakingly slow and careful reading aloud of the same text— ensuring that *every student* fully understood the meaning of *every word*. The final step was adapting Shakespeare's text (including adding original material), through group discussion and improvisation aimed at identifying the relevance of the text to the students' own experiences. The goal was to bring Shakespeare— allegedly the most "universal" playwright of all time—into the inmates' environment through this process of "cultural translation." For the inmate-students, other benefits included improved communications skills and literacy, the ability to work as part of a team within a casual but structured setting, and an enhanced self-confidence that comes of having "worked with" Shakespeare (perhaps for the first time). One student summed it up this way: "I have heard people discuss Shakespeare like he was a genius. I look forward to reading his work for two reasons. One, to see what all the hype is about. Two, because I feel that it would be a good learning experience for myself."

Since that initial Shakespeare workshop, I have taught and studied Shakespeare's plays with male and female inmates in the complete range of correctional facilities: from minimum to maximum to supermaximum security (solitary confinement). The essay that follows draws on three of these experiences: *Romeo and Juliet* in minimum security; *Macbeth* in maximum security; and *The Taming of the Shrew* in a women's prison.

ROMEO AND JULIET IN A MINIMUM-SECURITY FACILITY: "CIVIL BLOOD MAKES CIVIL HANDS UNCLEAN"

On the first day of the workshop, I asked the volunteers who had assembled in my makeshift classroom what they wanted to get out of their study of Shakespeare. "I want to get out of cleaning toilets!" Antwon replied.* The "classroom" in which I conducted my first workshop, in Chicago's Cook County Jail (under the auspices of the PACE Institute), was an empty auditorium, located just down the hall from the retired electric chair. Although it was located on a floor separate from the regular classrooms, I had requested it as a space in which the students could move around, improvise their responses to scenes, and feel free to express themselves physically.

While some had no doubt come merely to get out of cleaning the toilets, and others (I would later learn) were hoping that the visiting instructor would be less aware of gang interaction in the classroom and saw this as an opportunity for meetings, still others were sincerely eager to become acquainted with Shakespeare. Some had a faint recollection of a high school reading assignment they never completed; others had no Shakespearean experience whatsoever. "Did he write all that?" someone else asked, picking up the *Collected Works* I had smuggled in (hardbound books—especially of the size of Shakespeare's *Collected Works*—are considered potential weapons). "Two thousand pages! And I thought he'd only written a couple novels!"

Romeo and Juliet may seem, at first, an odd choice to study with an all-male group of students. "Are you going to be our Juliet?" one student called out when I introduced the text. Joseph, at fifty-six years of age, was my oldest student and had already

---

*All names have been fictionalized.

spent most of his life behind bars. I thanked him for the invitation but explained that instead we would focus on the scenes of male-male relationships, which are numerous in this play, and crucial. Addressing the issue of gang violence head-on, we viewed Baz Luhrmann's version of the initial encounter between the houses of Capulet and Montague in act 1, scene 1. These inmate-students had an intimate knowledge of gang violence, both as perpetrators and as victims. But they rejected *Romeo + Juliet*'s outrageous rendition, watching attentively but silently as the gas station in "Verona Beach," California, exploded amid the gunfire. Not one of them laughed at the ridiculously exaggerated depiction of street violence, as have many cinema audiences (myself included). Instead, they asked, "So, what was *that* supposed to be?"

Undaunted by their rejection of the 1996 film version, I circulated copies of Shakespeare's original text to be shared among the fifteen students (I had asked for a maximum of eight). Together we read line-by-line, until every student understood every word. They quickly mastered "thee" and "thou" and such antiquated curses as "marry" and "zounds"; they had no trouble translating guns for swords. After they had achieved a thorough understanding of the original text, we began the process of improvising each scene verbally and physically, shouting out lines and moving around the room. Throughout the summer, we progressed at the rate of one scene (at times, no more than one speech) per day.

"For now, these hot days, is the mad blood stirring" (3.1.4): the gang encounter that ends in the murder of Mercutio was on the agenda on an unbearably hot day in Chicago, when the temperature inside Cook County jail was enough to stir mad blood indeed. Inner city inmates know exactly why Shakespeare emphasizes heat: "On a hot summer day, the dudes are out and the streets are full of tension. There's the feeling that anything could pop." In a potentially risky exercise in improvisation, real-life gang members were called upon to portray rivals and encouraged to improvise their responses to a tense situation. Dozens and dozens of gangs roam Chicago's streets; most of them are represented—and active—in jail. With no way of knowing my students' individual gang affiliations, I also had no way of knowing whether my volunteers in this scene were real-life rivals, who might choose to act out. There was no guard in attendance.

Instead of a prison riot, the result of this session was a meaningful foray into Shakespearean textual analysis, focused on the question of why the combatants in this scene are reluctant to move into a private realm. The inmates explained that Tybalt, in coming to Mercutio and Benvolio, has entered Montague turf, and therefore he wants a *public* show of triumph. At first, he's "viewing the consequences," aiming for psychological effect. He's looking to gain power, not necessarily respect. But once the fight escalates, Tybalt has little choice: he needs to kill Mercutio—and he needs to do it in public.

Following this discussion, we began to explore the question of whether Romeo did the right thing in trying to stop the fight between Mercutio and Tybalt. "No!" was the unanimous response—the code of the streets requires that you let your partner fight his own fight—"But you have to stop it before it ends in murder," someone added. Just then a guard leaned into the room and called out, "PACE is walking!" meaning the end of the school day. But no one made a move to go. Instead, the spirited discussion continued, until the call came again, this time more insistently: "PACE is *walking!*" It was the inmates' dinner hour, but Joseph insisted, "We would rather eat the bread of this knowledge than the chicken in the cafeteria!" I couldn't argue with that but the guard could. "Let's go!" he shouted. Then he came over and whispered to me, "I've never seen them refuse to leave class before."

MACBETH IN A MAXIMUM-SECURITY FACILITY: "I AM AFRAID TO THINK WHAT I HAVE DONE / LOOK ON'T AGAIN I DARE NOT"

When, the following year, the opportunity arose to teach college writing and literature courses at several correctional facilities in the Indiana Department of Corrections through Indiana State University's prison program, I pursued the possibility of expanding my "Shakespeare experiment." If inner-city gang members could relate to the elements of violence in *Romeo and Juliet*, I reasoned, then convicted murderers would surely have unique insights into *Macbeth*. I requested a position in a notorious maximum-security facility downstate. ("It's been good knowing you!" said one of my on-campus students—a corrections officer—when I announced my new teaching appointment.)

To teach Shakespeare to these inmates, I passed through a series of checkpoints, several rows of razor wire, x-ray detectors, and a pat-down search. Held in a small, locked, unguarded concrete-block room, my first class in the level-four division at the Wabash Valley Correctional Facility consisted of male offenders whose sentences ranged from twenty years to life. Although it was neither my business nor my inclination to seek to know any of my students' particular records, I eventually learned that two (and, I assumed, many more) had been convicted of murder: "Macbeth and I have both caused problems in our time," wrote one student in response to the work we were studying.

Although these students posed special challenges, I quickly learned that the increased severity of the prison terms (and crimes) by no means indicated a less-intelligent student population; quite possibly, the reverse. The length of sentence already served, however, resulted in a less-responsive group, one that had learned to survive through passivity and resignation. The intellectual aggressiveness and high energy that I had come to relish as a challenge in the minimum-security setting were now replaced by an even greater challenge: awakening a student population that—although it had been awarded a "life" sentence—was, in some ways, already dead. Bob had spent most of his forty-eight years behind bars, starting with juvenile detention centers. Juan was from Puerto Rico and severely limited by the fact that English was his second language. Joe had been "down" for eleven years—and had an attitude. Having spent years, even decades, behind bars, they had put up equally impenetrable barriers around themselves. Some, like Joe, seemed virtually unreachable, as he was a quiet student, exhibiting less overt opposition than minimal participation, or even attention. (He would end up in solitary confinement, after trying to kill a fellow inmate.) Very few of these students had had any previous encounter with Shakespeare. None had had a pleasant one.

In a start-of-semester survey, I found it more perplexing than disturbing that the most popular leisure reading material among inmates in a maximum-security prison was, overwhelmingly, "true crime" stories. Perhaps in the same way that gruesome war narratives appeal especially to those who have suffered the same in real life, this population reveled in the literature that reflected their lives. And what was *Macbeth* if not a "true crime" narrative?

My approach to *Macbeth* was the same that I had taken toward *Romeo and Juliet* the previous year. We began by reading aloud act 1, scene 3: Macbeth's first encounter with the witches. Student volunteers read the roles of Macbeth and Banquo; I asked Joe to read the witches' lines. We paused during the reading often enough to ensure comprehension of this challenging text and unfamiliar vocabulary. Immediately, they understood why Macbeth seemed to fear the witches' "fair-sounding" tidings: "He's gonna

ice the old man!" In the subsequent soliloquy, they could relate
to the agony of the decision: to kill or not to kill. Perhaps surprisingly, they supported Macbeth's initial decision to let chance
crown him—without his stir. And the following week, they condemned Lady Macbeth's manipulative maneuverings, and especially her attack on Macbeth's manhood.

The "true crime" approach to the play was emphasized by our
plot-driven analysis. At the end of each day's scene, I asked the
group to summarize the events of the scene at hand and to speculate what would happen next. Early on, some believed that Macbeth would, in fact, stay true to his own convictions and *not* kill
Duncan. But once the murder had been committed, they immediately realized the need to cover up. Without stopping to consider
the possibility of regret or remorse, they addressed the question
of whether Macbeth was "smart" to kill the king's drunken
grooms: "He covered his tracks good, so it must be good"; "Always get rid of all evidence of a murder, including any witnesses";
"I think it was a smart move for Macbeth to kill the guards because he got rid of the only witnesses there were—or did he?"
They were perceptive in their reading of the events to come, perhaps inspired by their own circumstances in their interpretation
that "crime doesn't pay": "Something is going to go wrong, and
Macbeth and his wife are going to get caught." Clearly, they understood the difference between anonymous wartime killing and
premeditated murder: "Although he is a great war hero and can
get into a certain *zone* in wartime and kill, for Macbeth to kill
someone he knows is going to get the best of him."

They recognized the pattern, that "Blood will have blood"
(3.4.121): "I think what is coming next is more killing, because
he has done it before and now that he knows what it's like, he
has no fear of it." But they were completely surprised by—and
offended by—Macbeth's murder of Banquo, whom they had seen
as a loyal partner. The day we studied the banquet scene (3.4), I
distributed a handout that had conveniently eliminated the "Our
fears in Banquo / Stick deep" (3.1.50–51) passage in the preceding material. As they read the scene aloud and the events un-
folded, including the arrival of the ghost of Banquo, shaking his
gory locks at Macbeth, the awful truth slowly dawned on the students. In disbelief, one of them cried out: "He done killed his
roadie!"

Once again, the most significant insight into the play came not
from me but from my students. Though they may never have
studied *The Poetics*, they taught me that Macbeth's tragic

flaw—in a truly Aristotelian sense—is not his ambition or his ability to kill, but his inability to remain detached after the killing. It was, after all, an art that the murderers among us—to the extent that they could be said to be survivors—had had to master themselves. And they, especially, knew that Macbeth's inability would lead to his ruin: "Wake Duncan with thy knocking. I would thou couldst" (2.2.72).

Each of the daily *Macbeth* readings was followed—as had been the *Romeo and Juliet* readings—by exercises in improvisation, in which students were invited to create their own collaborative version of this scene, following the Shakespearean model. Rewriting Shakespeare certainly did not fit the "norm" in these students' experience, and their imaginations were indeed engaged. At the end of the first session, the students registered a sense of satisfaction. Joe lingered behind after the others had left, but he seemed unsure how to express what was on his mind. Finally, he flashed a shy, toothless smile and said, "I dig this Shakespeare stuff."

THE TAMING OF THE SHREW IN A WOMEN'S FACILITY: "THESE KITES THAT BATE AND BITE AND WILL NOT BE OBEDIENT"

It is, perhaps, impossible to study *The Taming of the Shrew* without resorting to sexist observations—and this paper is no exception. This experiment served to highlight some instances of gender inequity while challenging others. In terms of "crime and time," there was little inequity between the male and female inmates. The women I worked with at the medium-maximum security Rockville Correctional Facility were serving from ten- to thirty-year sentences for crimes that could range from drugs to murder. These women were not afraid of anything, not even *The Taming of the Shrew*. Where politically correct angels fear to tread, these "foolhardy" ladies were delighted to rush in.

Early writing samples, however, had indicated a distinct inequity in terms of education and skill. I have to admit that the men's work—in general—was superior (more thoughtful, analytical, creative) to that of the women. And, as with most of the men, my first-day questionnaires had indicated that these students had had very limited previous Shakespeare experience; some had had none. Most had not heard of this play; none had ever seen or read it. (One woman had boasted to an officer that she was going to be reading *The Taming of the Shrew* in class; he told her that she would find it "interesting.")

Once again, the work began with a slow reading aloud of the text, pausing at the end of every speech to ensure that each student understood each word. The scene I chose as perhaps the most accessible was the initial encounter of Katherine and Petruchio. (They giggled at the idea that a man had read the part of Juliet when I had taught *Romeo and Juliet* in a men's facility, but they had no hesitation in volunteering to read the part of Petruchio.)

In each of my experiences teaching Shakespeare in a correctional facility, I have been impressed with the inmates' ability to quickly pick up on details that are lost on traditional students. In this respect, the women were equal to the men, as was indicated by their reading of Petruchio's opening lines to Katherine:

> You lie, in faith, for you are called plain Kate,
> And bonny Kate, and sometime Kate the curst . . .
> Hearing thy mildness prais'd in every town,
> Thy virtues spoken of, and thy beauty sounded—
> Yet not so deeply as to thee belongs—
> Myself am moved to woo thee for my wife.
>
> (2.1.183–92)

Although it is buried, in mid-speech, among the numerous witty plays on the offensive nickname "Kate" and the sarcastic references to Katherine's "mildness" and "virtues," the women immediately recognized the unintended slip that reveals Petruchio's sincere attraction (and, as they saw it, a hint of true love) in the words, "Hearing . . . thy beauty sounded—yet not so deeply as to thee belongs."

They laughed immediately at Katherine's retort, despite the fact that the humor is entirely dependent on the multiple, and at times obscure, meanings of the word "move":

> Moved? In good time. Let him that moved you hither
> Remove you hence. I knew you at the first
> You were a movable.
>
> (2.1.193–94)

Though Petruchio has to ask, "Why, what's a movable?" (2.1.195), the women did not. When I asked them to explain all of the levels of this Shakespearean wordplay, they could. Indeed, I gradually came to realize that the women needed *less* explication and glossing of terms than any of the "academically superior" male groups with whom I had worked.

The most surprising discovery, however, has to be the women's response to Petruchio's aggressive treatment of Katherine in this initial encounter. I admit that I prefaced the introduction of this work with the caveat that some women find this text offensive. One woman defended the work in terms of context: "You have to look at it as a product of its own time period." Another defended it in terms of an attack on censorship, adding that whenever someone suggests censoring a work "it says more about the person than the work." And what did it say about these women, then, that they unanimously saw Petruchio's behavior as acceptable and understandable, and as "Pete's" way of indicating his love for "Kate"? As one student put it, "Kate is fierce by nature and Pete did her good by taunting her. To the world she felt that she had to be professional at all times, but Pete knew that she had a side of her that was wanting to get out." Another remarked, "Pete loves a challenge. He sets his sights upon this beautiful nightingale to cage her, if you will. Scars he will have. Nurse maid she will be."

After the reading and discussion of this key scene, we viewed the entire Stratford, Ontario, production on videotape. At the risk of making another sexist observation, I would have to observe that the women were significantly more vocal and demonstrative in their reactions. As they huddled around the tiny Department of Corrections television set, they literally cheered Petruchio on with each witty retort. Even the highly manipulative strategy to claim that it was bargained betwixt them in private that Kate "shall still be curst in company" (2.1.297) was not condemned but applauded.

These women (ranging in age from twenty-something to fifty-something) are vastly experienced in painful relationships. They know all-too-well the warning signs of a seriously abusive dominant man, and they did *not* see that in this scene: "It was a happy scene to me. They enjoyed talking to each other a lot. Pete was telling her all the things he thought would make her get upset, but she came back strong and he likes the challenge of her conversation." Furthermore, it was precisely in the superficially "offensive" dialogue that these women saw evidence of Petruchio's sincere affection: "I believe Pete has an honest care and concern for Kate, even though he tries to cover it up with his jokes. They seem to be very drawn to each other. They taunt and tease each other, get each other's interest to peak and then back off. I like this playful stage of a relationship. I'd like to see Kate marry Pete: all's well that ends well." These women knew, from their own experiences, that affections of such a personal nature are often expressed in a roundabout manner. It is, after all, a fact of prison life that feelings and emotions must find an indirect means of expression.

The only aspect of the play that these female criminal offenders were truly offended by was the treatment of Sly in the prologue. Seeing the harmless drunkard as a humorous and sympathetic character, they were again unanimous in their responses—this time, of condemnation. In her end-of-day comments, one student wrote, "I am upset about how Christopher is being tricked by everyone. I feel it is immoral to do so. They may laugh now, but I wonder if they will laugh at the end: 'I shall have the last laugh upon where it is due. Thou has been made a fool by a drunken man.'"

CONCLUSION

"Shakespeare is garbage!" were the words that greeted me when I began my very first prison session, as Antwon strolled in and slumped defiantly into one of the chairs outside of my friendly semicircle. I quote him now as representative of the resistance with which many students—in prison, just as in the traditional classroom—approach Shakespeare. "You can lead a student to Shakespeare, but you cannot make him quote," wrote one of my students in response to a survey question that asked him to describe his earlier experiences with these works.

In general, these are not the kinds of students that stand to gain much Shakespearean insight by being handed an assignment—"Read *Hamlet* by next week"—and being left alone to deal with the fardels and bodkins. And yet that is exactly what the public school system offered them in high school. It is little wonder, then, that these students walked away not just from Shakespeare but from education in general. On the other hand, what did the students get from working with Shakespeare now, in prison? Certainly, working with Shakespeare's texts offers inmates a vehicle by which to improve their basic reading skills. A high school dropout or an adult who reads at a child's level feels a special sense of accomplishment that comes from having mastered the "undisputed master" of the English language. Additionally, workshopping the scenes as a group provides inmates desperately needed training in collaborative skills. And, perhaps most significantly, Shakespeare's unbiased treatment of issues such as violence and social accountability allows the inmate to view his own situation from another's perspective.

As I was walking out of one of my prison-classrooms late one evening, a guard called out after me: "Did they learn anything?" I called back: "I hope so. I know I did!" In each of my experiences, my students have taught me as much (if not more) than I have taught them. From them, I have learned to appreciate the theme of violence in *Romeo and Juliet* that underlies and undermines the relationships not only of Romeo and Juliet, but also of Mercutio and Tybalt and the rest. From them, I have gained a unique insight into the terror and complexity of Macbeth's conscience. From them, I have come to see that strong women can laugh at Shakespeare's comic portrayal of "male dominance" in *Taming of the Shrew*.

Finally, my students have also provided an answer to my original question: is there a limit to Shakespeare's universality? Can his works reach this audience? I confess that I began this project somewhat skeptically. And, no doubt, some of my students have left the classroom as indifferent as they had arrived. But gradually, I had discovered that at least some of the plays are even *more* relevant to this group than to other, more traditional student populations. In the final words of Antwon, "Maybe Shakespeare ain't garbage—maybe he ain't no different from what is going on in my own life!" Awaiting sentencing in Cook County Jail, Deon agreed. He had been involved with a girl from a rival gang and was now facing attempted murder charges. "If only I'd a read this before," he said, "I'd a looked at what happened to Romeo and I'd a left the girl alone—and I wouldn't a ended up in here!"

As perhaps an ultimate challenge to Shakespeare's "universality," I smuggled his texts into a segregated housing unit (solitary confinement), to present to inmates serving *years* in isolated concrete-and-steel boxes. With each range remote controlled from a central terminal, these inmates receive little or no human contact. (And who but a Shakespeare scholar would volunteer to spend a summer in such a Dantean inferno, where those who enter must surely abandon all hope?) In this stiflingly hot environment, amid the din of fans and the shouts of caged creatures, communicating through a metal grill that permitted only a partial and distorted view, I read Shakespeare—one-on-one—with more than thirty inmates, sharing my photocopied text on the small surface of the metal cuff-ports (the slots through which food trays are provided, and through which inmates place their hands to be handcuffed prior to any forced "extraction" from their cells).

I recall one particular conversation with Don, a long-term resident who, in response to my question about the opportunity for "peer work" in solitary confinement—that is, the possibility of inmates shouting out study questions instead of obscenities to one another—insisted that education was the one topic that *never* gets discussed here. That day, I had distributed to those who were interested (and that was nearly everyone) Richard II's soliloquy on solitary confinement: "I have been studying how I may compare / This prison where I live unto the world" (5.5.1–2). The next day, Don reported that a heated debate had taken place that evening among several inmates regarding the interpretation of the text. When I reminded him of his insistence that literary topics would never be discussed here, his smile indicated a recognition that the impossible had occurred. In the unlikeliest of settings, the question of Shakespeare's "universality" had been, in my mind, answered.

Whose Will, or Who's Will? Teaching Shakespeare Him-Self

Sara Jayne Steen

ONE OF THE FEW DIFFICULTIES OF TEACHING SHAKESPEARE AT THE undergraduate level is that students often have little cultural context for the works. To relocate Shakespeare within his cultural context, and at the same time lead students to ask of themselves the kinds of useful questions that current scholars are asking, I sometimes juxtapose Shakespeare's works with thematically related texts by other early modern male and female writers, most recently in a topics course entitled In Search of the Self. In this upper-division undergraduate course, which includes Shakespeare's sonnets and *Twelfth Night*, clusters of related works allow students to make multiple connections. (I should add that thematic pairings work less well in my experience than clusters of works; students see the pairings as contained units for comparison and are reluctant to extend ideas beyond that pairing.) For this course, the primary texts in addition to Shakespeare's were Anne Askew's *Examinations*, Edmund Spenser's *Faerie Queene*, Lady Arbella Stuart's *Letters*, John Webster's *Duchess of Malfi*, and Margaret Cavendish's "Assaulted and Pursued Chastity."[1]

The topic, In Search of the Self, is one of a number of topics I have investigated over the years, and I chose it for a variety of reasons.[2] As Frank Whigham recently has noted, "the struggle to gain or constitute or achieve personal identity was a central concern of early modern England."[3] Since the Victorian era, in fact, when Jacob Burckhardt claimed the Italian Renaissance was the point where mankind—and he did mean upper-class males—moved forward into the light of individuality and self-fulfillment, scholars have discussed the Renaissance as the era propelling a renewed respect for and joy in the self. Religious scholars have emphasized the role of the Reformation in the new individuality, as worshippers developed a personal relationship with God. Philosophers have seen the seventeenth century as the "great divide" in our understanding of human consciousness.[4] More recently, and perhaps extending from Stephen Greenblatt's *Renaissance Self-Fashioning*,[5] our own field has seen a wealth of books and articles exploring the topic, some arguing for the self as a critical element of modernity and as a significant issue for postmodernists. As a result, I knew students would have a strong pool of secondary resources on which to draw.[6] And since the majority of my students would be in their early twenties and searching for their own identities, I hoped the topic would provide a happy confluence of personal and scholarly interests.

I had other theoretical goals for the course as well, as anyone who has read the text list probably has deduced. Many older accounts of the emergence of identity in the early modern era focused on male identities, as though only men had subjectivities.[7] Recent editions of works by women allow us to place women beside men and examine both within a larger context. Most of my students find it exciting to be part of what is a wholesale reexamination of the early modern literary and cultural landscape. The topic also lends itself to varied forms of self-presentation such as the spiritual autobiography and the letter, genres in which early modern men and women both wrote, but with which my undergraduates have little familiarity. I hoped we could learn together how to read more broadly, as Margaret Ezell advocated in *Writing Women's Literary History*.[8] Finally, I wanted to insure that the course's focus on cultural studies and broad contextualization would be accompanied by thoughtful textual analysis and enriched, not obscured, by the emphasis on social and cultural interrelationships.[9]

Rather than begin the course with a lengthy work, I adapted Josephine Roberts's method for teaching Shakespeare's sonnets and opened the course with brief pieces by Queen Elizabeth.[10] "On Monsieur's Departure" and the "Tilbury Speech" and "Golden Speech" allow for a concise, concrete introduction to issues related to the self and literary production. Let me quote one stanza from Elizabeth's lyric poem:

> I grieve and dare not show my discontent,
> I love and yet am forced to seem to hate,
> I do, yet dare not say I ever meant,
> I seem stark mute, but inwardly do prate.
> I am and not, I freeze and yet am burn'd,
> Since from myself, my other self I turn'd.[11]

Students recognize the questions to consider. Who is the "I" of the poem, and who is the "other self" from whom the speaker has turned? How do we explore a divided self? Should the poem be read autobiographically as representative of deep emotion? If so, which of the proposed "Monsieurs" might it have been written about? Or should it be read as political self-presentation? Can we distinguish between a "self" engaging with us and a constructed persona? Does the poem reflect social and political tensions between private life and public responsibilities, suggesting the queen's two bodies? The speeches suggest additional questions. For example, when the queen says in the "Golden Speech," "Shall I ascribe anything to myself and my sexly weakness? I were not worthy to live then,"[12] in what gendered social context shall we interpret the words? How do we "read" a speech? Is it literature? These introductory discussions set the stage for more in-depth work to follow, which for ease of presentation I will explore under three categories: subjectivity, narrativity, and gender.

SUBJECTIVITY

Anne Askew's account of her examinations, presented with commentary by John Bale, raises many questions about early modern concepts of the soul and martyrdom. Askew's text is powerful: the words of a woman who defied the social code, joined the Protestant reformers, was charged with heresy, tortured, and burned at the stake in 1546. She was dead at about age twenty-five. Students are intrigued by the idea of spiritual autobiography as testimony to a life and mind and are surprised to discover that autobiographies, journals, diaries, and memoirs were rare before 1500.[13] They find the contrast between Bale's voice and Askew's startling, and Askew clearly is the subject "I" with whom they identify. They cheer as Askew by her account repeatedly and humorously bests her interrogators: "And then doctor Standish desyered my lorde, to byd me saye my mynde, concernynge that same text of S. Paule. I answered, that it was agaynst saynt Paules lernynge, that I beynge a woman, shuld interprete the scriptures, specyallye where so manye wyse lerned men were" (54).

Following our exploration of Queen Elizabeth's texts, however, students are ready to question the autobiographical method, complicating their own first readings. They are suspicious of Askew's consistent wit and irony, though not because they doubt female psychological endurance. They wonder whether anyone in such a situation could avoid shading the truth, recasting the conversations to create the strongest self-presentation in prose. They consider the lure for the writer to assume a cloak of stoic martyrdom that, like Renaissance family portraits that included dead or absent members, was more ideal than actual. They examine carefully Askew's rhetorical and fictional techniques, such as her dramatic dialogue and narrative structure.

At this point, students are in a good position to discuss subjectivity in Shakespeare's sonnets without becoming lost in the myriad questions the sonnets provoke. Few works have been interpreted autobiographically more often. To Wordsworth, writing in 1827, in them "Shakespeare unlocked his heart."[14] W. H. Auden in 1964 was similarly astonished at "the impression they make of naked autobiographical confession," and concluded that although "Shakespeare may have shown the sonnets to one or two intimate literary friends—it would appear that he must have—he wrote them, I am quite certain, as one writes a diary, for himself alone, with no thought of a public."[15] Much effort has been spent on useful and less-than-useful inquiries about the identification of everyone from "the only begetter" to the Dark Lady.

To interpretations of the sonnets as private, personal expressions, students who have read Queen Elizabeth and Anne Askew and explored persona and audience quickly raise objections;[16] for example, they point out the persona's repeated awareness of an audience well beyond the individual seemingly addressed: "So long as men can breathe or eyes can see, / So long lives this, and this gives life to thee" (Sonnet 18). Introducing the idea of a manuscript culture at this point allows students to evaluate with some historical perspective critical arguments concerning the sonnets' manuscript circulation. Students make other connections as well. They compare the persona's confusion and conflicting desires to Queen Elizabeth's similar sense of a divided self. They place Askew's dramatic dialogue beside the sonnets and discuss the degree to which each sonnet is a speech to someone else, a dramatic dialogue in which we as readers create the absent Young Man and Dark Lady. They look to rhetoric and ask how imagery and shifts in time shape the reader's sense of "I," as well as the degree to which our response is colored because the voice we hear in our heads is our own.[17]

In a course on selfhood, *Twelfth Night* also has a different cul-

tural context than it usually might. The foundation of comedies
of mistaken identity is identity, a true self that can be mistaken
and then revealed at the conclusion of the play. The way in which
early modern comedies differ from their classical predecessors is
in the key role of the soliloquy, a technique that assumes the inte-
riority of a thinking individual.[18] Since by convention no character can lie in a soliloquy, the soliloquy purports to offer the
audience access to the true self, to the character's mind. The
aside serves much the same purpose. Understanding this, my students argue, for example, that we must accept the longing in
Viola's "myself would be his wife" (1.4.41), no matter how unrea-
sonable such longing may seem to them, and that Malvolio is fundamentally a narcissist. Disguise also fits this paradigm. As Lloyd
Davis has pointed out, disguise becomes "a process of personal
palimpsest," establishing the difference between the essential
and the nonessential. Within the disguise, a character can try on
other roles, as Viola does, while the audience reads the true
through the assumed; this concept offers students another point
of entry into the play. Moreover, to take on a disguise and speak
as another is to create a persona, a connection that allows students to cross genres and compare the "I" of the autobiography
and the sonnets with characterization in the play.[19]

NARRATIVITY

By the time my students reach the upper-division level, they
usually are comfortable reading an individual sonnet, but decid-
edly uncomfortable about making sense of the ongoing narrative
in a sonnet sequence and thus of evaluating the subject "I" on
the broader scale. As one student said after he realized that Sonnet 18 ("Shall I compare thee to a summer's day?") probably was
addressed to the Young Man, "Professor Johnson didn't tell me
that in my survey course!" Students find it useful to think about
what a given sonnet means as a separate poem, in another context such as a friend's wedding, and within the larger narrative
of the sequence. Initially, students—like most of us when we
confront the unfamiliar—want the narrative to be readily com-
prehensible and straightforward, with each sonnet adding a chronological "and then" to the storyline. It is not easy for students
to relax and accept a more amorphous structure in which sonnets
are clustered, where pivotal sonnets provide unexpected shifts of
ground, and movement of the narrative is not always linear.[20]

Ironically, one way to put students more at ease is to introduce them to textual issues that have complicated other readers' interpretations of the sonnets and thus to let students know that they are not alone in finding the sequence difficult. I supply a photocopy of the 1609 version of "Sonnet 20" ("A woman's face, with nature's own hand painted") and the modernized version from Stephen Booth's *Shakespeare's Sonnets* and ask students to note differences in spelling, capitalization, and punctuation.[21] They consider how editorial practice might affect their interpretation of this key sonnet and thus of the relationship between the Poet and the Young Man throughout the sequence. The implications of the absence of manuscript evidence are great: the sequence as printed in 1609 might reflect more the printing house's style than the author's. Students also are intrigued to learn that scholars do not know exactly how the 1609 order for the sonnets was determined, or by whom. At this point, students visit the Rare Books Room of the campus library to examine early modern books and learn about their material production, from watermarks to compositors' sticks. Consistently such visits evoke enormous enthusiasm, and the processes of production and interpretation are foregrounded.

Another method is to extend similar questions to other genres. With *Twelfth Night*, for example, I circulate a facsimile of the first folio, which we use as a resource for thorny textual issues.[22] More important in terms of narrativity, however, is that students see that the play, too, is not straightforward and chronological, but constructed in ways that parallel the sonnet sequence: interwoven plot elements; clusters of scenes, which Jean E. Howard in her work on Shakespeare's orchestration calls theatrical "movements";[23] shifts in place, time, and tone; thematic contrast and recurrence. All lead in *Twelfth Night* to a conclusion in which identity is revealed. Although undergraduate English majors are confident that they can read a play well, and for most purposes they are correct, few have examined dramatic technique in this way or made structural connections across genres.

The letters of Lady Arbella Stuart add additional twists to this discussion. A letter, although a highly personal document, was an art form in the Renaissance, and for a woman as politically prominent as Stuart, a potential heir to Queen Elizabeth's throne, appropriate self-presentation was critical.[24] Students quickly engage with Stuart's compelling drama of confrontation, clandestine marriage, imprisonment, cross-dressed escape, and eventual death in the Tower of London. With the exception of Frank

Whigham and Lynne Magnusson, however, few scholars and fewer students have developed reading strategies for a social and interactive genre such as the letter.[25] One advantage of using Stuart in a course on selfhood is that some drafts of her letters are extant; through examining the revisions in these drafts, students can consider her reasoning as they watch a rhetorically talented woman craft a "self" in prose. They ask what it means in terms of our larger construct of "self" that she once in a marginal note to a draft explicitly denies the version of herself that circumstances forced her to present: "I bely my selfe extreemely in this" (Letter 101).

When students look beyond individual letters to the sequence, they see that the letters can be clustered, sometimes by audience, sometimes by goal, and that the letters, like the sonnets, can be read according to placement in the sequence, from which readers evaluate the juxtaposition of ideas and shifts in persona. Since letters obviously were composed in chronological order, the order of the sequence here would seem fixed. However, because many of Stuart's letters are undated, the "correct" order is impossible to determine, except insofar as the manuscript evidence extends. Undated letters will have been ordered by the editor, whose choices can suggest quite different subjectivities and storylines.[26] Students find the idea of narrativity and the associated issues of material production intriguing, a reminder that good reading demands active participation, even to the point of seeing and challenging the editorial decisions that underlie authors' texts.

GENDER

Issues of gender are woven throughout these texts, beginning with the introductory pieces by Queen Elizabeth in which she calls attention to her "sexly weakness" and masculine heart. That the Virgin Queen repeatedly refers to herself as "prince" or "king" in an era when women were believed unfit to rule seems significant to students in terms of identity and immediately establishes the problem. Students question John Bale's sometimes-odd commentary on Anne Askew's words and ponder Askew's need to assert her right as a woman to read and interpret Scripture.[27] Spenser's handling of gender and selfhood in *The Faerie Queene* is controversial, especially with the cross-dressed Britomart in book 3. By the point in the course at which students begin Shakespeare's sonnets, they already see gender as a cultural issue associated with individual and collective identity and understand that gender roles appear to have been in flux in early modern England, with an accompanying confusion about masculine women and feminine men. It is also valuable for students to think about literary production and reception in gendered terms. Both early modern women writers and Shakespeare had to develop ways to work within a tradition that was heavily gender-marked.[28] The phrase "woman of letters" would have been viewed as a contradiction in terms, and the Petrarchan sonnet tradition was a heterosexual one. According to Bruce R. Smith, women's writings and the sonnets have been culturally contained in similar ways: until the eighteenth century, when editor Edmund Malone convinced readers that Shakespeare's addresses to another man were acceptable after all, "Shakespeare's sonnets were 'marginal' texts like those that feminist critics of the past twenty years have been . . . rehabilitating."[29] As a result of these discussions, students are more prepared than they otherwise might be to deal seriously with the issues of gendered address, same-sex desire, and female sexuality in the sonnets.

The gender of the addressees is the first consideration. Do we know which sonnets are addressed to a man and which to a woman? How do we know? Some sonnets clearly indicate the addressee, but others are less obvious; and a number are not clear at all, especially if taken out of sequence. As we begin to examine the relationship between the Poet and the Young Man, students may read sections of Bruce R. Smith's *Homosexual Desire in Shakespeare's England* for early modern attitudes toward same-sex desire or Peter Stallybrass's "Editing as Cultural Formation: The Sexing of Shakespeare's Sonnets" for the cultural development of the "sexual identity" of the poet.[30] I provide some background, including the attack of George Steevens, who registered his "disgust and indignation" about the relationship; Edmond Malone's 1780 response that "such addresses to men . . . were customary in our author's time, and neither imported criminality, nor were esteemed indecorous"; and Coleridge's comment that "the sonnets could only have come from a man deeply in love, and in love with a woman; and there is one sonnet which from its incongruity, I take to be a purposed blind."[31] That sonnet, of course, is Sonnet 20, "A woman's face, with nature's own hand painted," which Coleridge imagined as a deliberate deception intended to deflect attention from Shakespeare's heterosexual passion. We discuss Sonnet 20 in detail, examining possible readings and then considering how each might affect our understanding of the relationship over time and of the Poet's affair with the Dark Lady. Students are fascinated by the Dark Lady, whose darkness is contrasted with the Young Man's fairness and whose appeal is unambiguously sexual. Although she in many ways fulfills early modern stereotypes of the unchaste woman, students always comment on the sheer fun of that relationship, as shown in pun-filled sonnets such as Sonnet 135 ("Whoever hath her wish, thou hast thy *Will*"). Nothing in the sonnets is uncomplicated.

Both gender stereotypes and homoeroticism emerge in different forms in *Twelfth Night*, a comedy that focuses on confusions of sexual identity. Viola's cross-dressing as Cesario allows her to achieve insight into and intellectual intimacy with a member of the opposite sex: Orsino talks honestly with another male but poses in the presence of a woman. The comedy contains varied forms of seeming same-sex desire, Viola and Olivia, Cesario and Orsino, only to reveal Viola's "true" identity and reestablish heterosexuality as the norm, although the character of Antonio, alone at the end of the play, continues for students the questions of homoeroticism raised in the sonnets.[32] The play raises useful questions about gender. Is sexual identity fixed and stable, part of the essential "true" self revealed at the end of the play? Or is sexuality unstable? Are gender roles little more than clothing? If gender roles are fluid, what defines us? Is there something essentially human that transcends gender? Boy actors and moral debates over theatricality lead students to a consideration of drama's effect on society.

The discussions of succeeding works double back and incorporate the sonnets and *Twelfth Night* into considerations of Lady Arbella Stuart, who fled cross-dressed to France, of Webster's Duchess of Malfi, who flouts her brothers' authority to marry as she chooses, and of Margaret Cavendish's cross-dressed Travellia in "Assaulted and Pursued Chastity," who flees rape and eventually wins battles and governs the land of Amity. Taken together, the works form for students a reasonably broad cultural context in which to consider Shakespeare and gender.

By including works in nontraditional genres, a course such as this one invites students into discussions of the canon. My choices of Anne Askew and Lady Arbella Stuart provoked thoughtful discussions of what literature is. Such a course will not please all students—one said he was going to "hold me accountable" for having included Anne Askew and not John Milton—but almost all gave it high marks, and one student has received permission from Oxford University Press to produce a studio recording of Askew's *Examinations* in order to make the work more widely available.[33] What the course did do was lead students to sophisticated questions about identity, literature and history, and literary production and reception.

There are a number of benefits to teaching Shakespeare in relation to other writers of his era, male and female. Students can compare and contrast female and male subjectivities. They can compare styles, goals, audiences, and genres. And a topics-based course such as this one accommodates an abundance of writers, allowing students to make connections between Shakespeare and, for example, John Donne or Ephelia. Not all students found the Shakespeare they expected, or perhaps desired, but they did find a complex Shakespeare who was part of his culture, and saw that Shakespeare is not diminished by being of his era as well as for all time. What are the answers to the questions posed in my title "Whose Will, or Who's Will?" Not being as clever as Shakespeare, I may have trapped myself in playing with Shakespearean puns. By way of response, however, I ask you to consider the concluding couplet of Sonnet 136 and what you might make of it in the context of a course on selfhood: "Make but my name thy love, and love that still, / And then thou lovest me for my name is *Will*."

NOTES

1. Anne Askew, *The Examinations of Anne Askew*, ed. Elaine V. Beilin, Women Writers in English, 1350–1850 (New York and Oxford: Oxford Univ. Press, 1996); Hugh Maclean and Anne Lake Prescott, eds., *Edmund Spenser's Poetry*, 3d ed. (New York and London: Norton, 1993); William Shakespeare, *The Sonnets, Narrative Poems: The Complete Non-dramatic Poetry*, ed. Sylvan Barnet (New York: Signet, 1989); William Shakespeare, *Twelfth Night, or What You Will*, ed. David Bevington (Toronto and New York: Bantam, 1988); Arbella Stuart, *The Letters of Lady Arbella Stuart*, ed. Sara Jayne Steen, Women Writers in English, 1350–1850 (New York and Oxford: Oxford Univ. Press, 1994); John Webster, *The Duchess of Malfi*, ed. Elizabeth M. Brennan (London: A and C Black, 1993); Margaret Cavendish, *The Blazing World and Other Writings*, ed. Kate Lilley (London: Penguin, 1994). Subsequent quotations from these works will reflect these editions and be cited in the text.

2. The idea was sparked by the honors course Self and Society in English Renaissance Literature, developed by Elaine Beilin and shared with members of the Shakespeare Association of America seminar on "Teaching Judith Shakespeare: Early Modern Women Writers and the Bard" in the spring of 1997.

3. Frank Whigham, *Seizures of the Will in Early Modern English Drama* (Cambridge: Cambridge Univ. Press, 1996), 3.

4. Roy Porter, introduction, to *Rewriting the Self: Histories from the Renaissance to the Present*, ed. Roy Porter (London and New York: Routledge, 1997), 3–4.

5. Stephen Greenblatt, *Renaissance Self-Fashioning: From More to Shakespeare* (Chicago and London: Univ. of Chicago Press, 1980).

6. In addition to Porter and Greenblatt (cited above), students and scholars might look to Charles Taylor, *Sources of the Self: The Making of the Modern Identity* (Cambridge: Harvard Univ. Press, 1989); Marshall Grossman, *The Story of All Things: Writing the Self in English Renaissance Narrative Poetry* (Durham, N.C., and London: Duke Univ. Press, 1998); Camille Wells Slights, "Notaries, Sponges, and Looking-Glasses: Conscience in Early Modern England," *English Literary Renaissance* 28 (1998): 231–46; Julia M. Walker, *Medusa's Mirrors: Spenser, Shakespeare, Milton, and the Metamorphosis of the Female Self* (Newark, Del.: Univ. of Delaware Press, 1998); and works by and about Michel Foucault. The subject has been treated in relation to Shakespeare in a number of recent articles, such as Donald L. Guss, "The Power of Selfhood: Shakespeare's Hamlet, Milton's Samson," *Modern Language Quarterly* 54 (March 1993): 483–511; Burton Hatlen, "The 'Noble Thing' and the 'Boy of Tears': *Coriolanus* and the Embarrassments of Identity," *English Literary Renaissance* 27 (1997): 393–420; and Camille Wells Slights, "Slaves and Subjects in *Othello*," *Shakespeare Quarterly* 48 (1997): 377–90.

7. On this point, see Porter, *Rewriting the Self*, 12; Catherine Belsey, preface to *The Subject of Tragedy: Identity and Difference in Renaissance Drama* (London and New York: Methuen, 1985); and Mark Breitenberg, *Anxious Masculinity in Early Modern England* (Cambridge: Cambridge Univ. Press, 1996), 7–8.

8. Margaret Ezell, *Writing Women's Literary History* (Baltimore and London: Johns Hopkins Univ. Press, 1993).

9. Russ McDonald describes his *Shakespeare Reread: The Texts in New Contexts* (Ithaca, N.Y., and London: Cornell Univ. Press, 1994) as a similar attempt to merge the cultural and textual (introduction).

10. Josephine Roberts, " 'Thou maist have thy *Will*': The Sonnets of Shakespeare and His Stepsisters," *Shakespeare Quarterly* 47 (1996): 408–9. (This essay appears in a special issue, "Teaching Judith Shakespeare," that I coedited with Elizabeth H. Hageman; the issue includes ten essays on teaching Shakespeare in relation to women writers.)

11. Elizabeth I, "On Monsieur's Departure," in *Women Writers of the Renaissance and Reformation*, ed. Katharina M. Wilson (Athens, Ga., and London: Univ. of Georgia Press, 1987), 536.

12. Elizabeth I, "Golden Speech," in *Women Writers*, 545.

13. Peter Burke, "Representations of the Self from Petrarch to Descartes," in *Rewriting the Self*, 21.

14. William Wordsworth, "Scorn Not the Sonnet," in *Wordsworth: Poetical Works*, ed. Thomas Hutchinson (London: Oxford Univ. Press, 1969), 206.

15. W. H. Auden, introduction, reprinted in Shakespeare, *The Sonnets, Narrative Poems*, xxxiv–xxxv.

16. At this point students also would have read books 1 and 3 of Spenser's *Faerie Queene*. After having compared Spenser's fictional spiritual biography with Askew's text and Spenser's shadowings of Queen Elizabeth with the

queen's self-presentation, students read Virginia Woolf's essay "The Faery Queen" (from *The Moment and Other Essays*, reprinted in *Edmund Spenser's Poetry*, 672–75) and debated her idea that in Spenser's work "we are confined in one continuous consciousness, which is Spenser's."

17. Although I did not ask my students to read *Shakespeare's Perjured Eye* and respond (as Josephine Roberts did) to Joel Fineman's thesis that in the sonnets Shakespeare developed "a subjectivity altogether novel in the history of lyric," a subjectivity emerging from the poetry of praise, these undergraduates did discuss his theory and were capable of approaching so complex an idea with some sophistication; see Joel Fineman, *Shakespeare's Perjured Eye: The Invention of Poetic Subjectivity in the Sonnets* (Berkeley and Los Angeles: Univ. of California Press, 1986), 48.

18. Porter, *Rewriting the Self*, 3, 10; Belsey, *Subject of Tragedy*, 42–43.

19. Lloyd Davis, *Guise and Disguise: Rhetoric and Characterization in the English Renaissance* (Toronto and Buffalo: Univ. of Toronto Press, 1993), 10–11.

20. Roberts, "Sonnets of Shakespeare," 411–12; Roberts suggests that students read Mary Wroth's sonnets in order to examine the design of sonnet collections.

21. Stephen Booth, *Shakespeare's Sonnets* (New Haven and London: Yale Univ. Press, 1977), 22.

22. *The First Folio of Shakespeare*, prepared and introduced by Doug Moston (New York and London: Applause, 1995).

23. Jean E. Howard, "The Orchestration of *Twelfth Night*: The Rhythm of Restraint and Release," in *Shakespeare's Art of Orchestration: Stage Technique and Audience Response* (Urbana, Ill., and Chicago: Univ. of Illinois Press, 1984), 172–206.

24. Sara Jayne Steen, "Fashioning an Acceptable Self: Arbella Stuart," *English Literary Renaissance* 18 (1988): 78–95; reprinted in *Women in the Renaissance: Selections from "English Literary Renaissance,"* ed. Kirby Farrell, Elizabeth H. Hageman, and Arthur F. Kinney (Amherst, Mass.: Univ. of Massachusetts Press, 1990), 136–53.

25. See Lynne Magnusson, *Shakespeare and Social Dialogue: Dramatic Language and Elizabethan Letters* (Cambridge: Cambridge Univ. Press, 1999); and Frank Whigham, "The Rhetoric of Elizabethan Suitors' Letters," *PMLA* 96 (1981): 864–82; and his *Ambition and Privilege: The Social Tropes of Elizabethan Courtesy Theory* (Berkeley and Los Angeles: Univ. of California Press, 1984).

26. Sara Jayne Steen, "Manuscript Matters: Reading the Letters of Lady Arbella Stuart," *South Central Review* 11 (1994): 24–38.

27. See Megan Matchinske's analysis of Anne Askew in *Writing, Gender and State in Early Modern England: Identity Formation and the Female Subject* (Cambridge: Cambridge Univ. Press, 1998), 24–52.

28. Here and in what follows on the sonnets, I draw again on Roberts, "Sonnets of Shakespeare," 412–13.

29. Bruce R. Smith, *Homosexual Desire in Shakespeare's England: A Cultural Poetics* (Chicago and London: Univ. of Chicago Press, 1991), 269.

30. Peter Stallybrass, "Editing as Cultural Formation: The Sexing of Shakespeare's Sonnets," *Modern Language Quarterly* 54 (1993): 91–103.

31. Cited in ibid., 94–95, 99.

32. Laurie E. Osborne explores the homoerotic dimensions of the play and

delineates how nineteenth-century productions altered scenes with Antonio and Sebastian, indicating an anxiety about that pairing, in *The Trick of Singularity: Twelfth Night and the Performance Editions* (Iowa City, Iowa: Univ. of Iowa Press, 1996).

33. The studio compact disk, featuring Michele Sanborn as Anne Askew and Justin Kitto as John Bale, recorded by Tony Sacco, is nearly complete at this writing; for materials on availability, contact me at Montana State University.

Teaching the Environment of
The Winter's Tale: Ecocritical Theory
and Pedagogy for Shakespeare

Simon C. Estok

Recent accounts of Shakespeare have done a lot of useful work in exploring discursive intersections between gender and categories such as class, race, and sexual orientation,[1] but there has been almost no work done that looks seriously at how representations of the early modern natural environment fit into such equations.[2] While it is true enough that until recently fairly "little attention has been paid, in cultural analysis, to material means employed in cultural production,"[3] it is perhaps less obvious to question how material resources (outside of the processes of the physical production of texts and their distribution) are figured in, called up, called into being, recalled, produced, and so on in processes of cultural work (such as plays by Shakespeare, for instance). Can we make "a case for an environmental basis of history?"[4] How can a materialist criticism investigate the ways that the environment is worked in discourse? What are the ideological purposes and conditions for which the natural environment is produced in literature?

Critical tradition has read *The Winter's Tale* as political, religious, and autobiographical allegory; as fantasy; as geographically improbable; as the work of someone other than Shakespeare; as realism par excellence; as the literature of escape; as a sophisticated vegetation myth; as boring; as a falling off; as a structural, thematic, or philosophical experiment; as a general failure; as a perfect example of symbolic technique; and so on. There have been reams written on that nasty bear who runs off with Antigonus; discussions about the tension between art and nature in the play are everywhere; and there have certainly been enough analyses of the role and function of natural imagery in the play. Sustained ecocritical readings of *The Winter's Tale*, however, are not

177

part of the play's critical history. Part of the reason is simply that the necessary critical and pedagogical terms for meaningful discussion are only now becoming available.

It is possible for at least two reasons to debate such well-established issues as misogyny, racism, homophobia, and anti-Semitism in Shakespeare: first, in each case the estranged and disaffected subjects are material things that walk among (often as a threat to) fully enfranchised subjects; and second, it is possible to debate the issues because there is a whole litany of terms with which to describe and then examine the concepts. If, for example, "misogyny" is a hatred of women; "racism," of racial difference; "homophobia," of same-sex issues; and "anti-Semitism," of Jewishness and Jews—then what should we call a fear and contempt for the environment? Perhaps we might use a term such as "ecophobia," but whatever the terminology, the ways in which the environment is perceived and represented—for better and for worse—are concerns of ecocriticism.[5]

There are, of course, several important questions here: what on earth is ecocriticism, how does one do it, what does it do, and, most important, why bother? Are there revealing links between environmentally and socially oppressive systems, overlapping and interlocking structures that need to be examined? Keith Thomas maintains that "it is impossible to disentangle what the people of the past thought about plants and animals from what they thought about themselves";[6] but *is* it possible to proceed on (or avoid) such an assumption without reproducing the anthropocentrism that undergirds our current environmental crises?

For a play that foregrounds the pastoral tradition so heavily, that stresses so insistently a relationship between nature and art, that is so deeply rooted at many levels in conceptual dividedness, an ecocritical approach can help to give the student an understanding of the literary traditions at work in the text. It can also give insights about "interconnectedness" (a keyword of ecocriticism); of ways in which nonliterary texts and assumptions about nature come to bear on the play; of ways that the division between men and women in the play might be viewed as part of a larger dynamic (larger than simple anthropocentric models) through which difference is designated; and of ways that the play might be seen to participate in our own relationship with the natural world. If our critical work is really directed toward helping people change the way they think and behave, then there has certainly never been a better time to look at these kinds of issues.

Yet as Jean E. Howard and Marion F. O'Connor point out, "it is only too easy to read and/or write as a born-again postructuralist/ Marxist and still teach like an unregenerate New Critic."[7] It is a position that Richard Paul Knowles develops in his brief but evocative article, which seeks, as its subtitle suggests, a way "Towards a Materialist Pedagogy." The problem, Knowles understands, is that the shift in theoretical analysis "has not yet made much impact on classrooms and curricula."[8] Consequently, when we start talking about the environment in *The Winter's Tale* in ways that are clearly not directed toward thematic or imagistic readings, it is not only strong curiosity but often a sense of bewilderment that students express in response. Students want to know what ecocriticism is and how it can be applied to a text such as *The Winter's Tale*.

ECOCRITICAL THEORY

The Association for the Study of Literature and the Environment (ASLE) recently posted a number of position papers on the Internet that attempt to define ecocriticism. Some are proudly antitheoretical. Some are dogmatic and prescriptive in their listing of ecocritical principles. Some claim that no such lists have yet been given and hunger for ecocritical theory. Some think they offer answers. Some only raise questions. All of them struggle with the hard reality that ecocriticism is a thing that was named before it was properly born.[9]

The 1999 PMLA Forum on Literatures of the Environment, also posted on the ASLE Website, registers a continuing dissatisfaction with the status of ecocriticism, with many of the contributions (my own included) griping about ecocriticism's shortcomings. One of the recurring complaints (one that this current essay addresses) is that the boundaries of ecocriticism have been far too constricted.[10] A primary question, inextricably linked to these discussions must be, what is ecocriticism, if it is anything at all? What counts as ecocriticism, and what doesn't?[11]

Cheryll Glotfelty's 1996 *Ecocriticism Reader* did a tremendous amount in helping to formalize the critical status of ecocriticism. It was the first of its kind—an anthology of essays devoted to organizing an area of study whose efforts had, until then, not been "recognized as belonging to a distinct critical school or movement."[12] In it, Glotfelty defines ecocriticism as "the study of the relationship between literature and the physical environment."[13] She argues that it is difficult to defend the traditional failure of the literary profession to address "green" issues. Glen Love, paraphrasing Glotfelty's point, puts it best: "race, class, and gender are words which we see and hear everywhere at our professional meetings and in our current publications . . . [but] the English profession has failed to respond in any significant way to the issue of the environment."[14] That was then, and, as Love knows, things are changing: the English profession is responding, but the direction of the response may not be very revolutionary. Love has recently noted that "the study of literature and the environment and the practice of ecocriticism has begun to assume an active place in the profession"; however, he also seems to feel some unease about "what that place is to be, particularly in its theoretical and methodological base."[15]

In the same year that Glotfelty's collection came out, Lawrence Buell published *The Environmental Imagination,* where he defines " 'ecocriticism' . . . as [a] study of the relationship between literature and the environment conducted in a spirit of commitment to environmentalist praxis."[16] Buell acknowledges that there is some uncertainty about what the term exactly covers but argues, "if one thinks of it . . . as a multiform inquiry extending to a variety of environmentally focused perspectives more expressive of concern to explore environmental issues searchingly than of fixed dogmas about political solutions, then the neologism becomes a useful omnibus term for subsuming a large and growing scholarly field."[17]

Buell's definition is valid, as far as it goes. Like Glotfelty—indeed, like many people who are calling themselves ecocritics these days—Buell uses ecocriticism as if it were designed only for nature writing.

Examining nature writing is, of course, one of the things ecocriticism does, and does well; but when nature writing constitutes the sole purview of ecocriticism, the lack of theoretical diversity, conceptual in-breeding, and a weakening of contacts with the wider literary world will spell disaster for the approach. Focusing exclusively on nature writing wrongly suggests an essential link between ecocriticism as a methodology and nature writing as the natural object of its inquiry. As Ursula K. Heise poignantly asserts, "ecocriticism has nothing specifically to do with *nature* writing."[18] Environmental issues are written into many nooks and crannies of canonical literature, in much the same way that issues of concern to other kinds of theorists are embedded in "the canon." As Glotfelty herself acknowledges, feminist theorists do not confine themselves to works about feminism any more than

Marxist theorists confine themselves to works about Marxism or commodity fetishism. The next logical question, then, is simple: why should ecocriticism restrict itself to the genre of nature writing?

Assuming that ecocriticism need not (and, in fact, should not) restrict itself to texts *about* nature, the ecocritic is immediately faced with another obstacle: namely, that the polyphony of critical voices articulate at times seemingly opposed purposes—and, indeed, definitions—resulting in a hydra-headed monster that often seems to be speaking in tongues or at cross-purposes.

Stephanie Sarver goes as far as to say that ecocriticism has remained less a theory than a focus: " 'Ecocriticism' is . . . an unfortunate term because it suggests a new kind of critical theory. The emerging body of work that might be labeled ecocritical is united not by a theory, but by a focus: the environment. This ecocritical work draws on a variety of theories, such as feminist, Marxist, post-structuralist, psychoanalytic and historicist."[19] In a sense, Sarver has a point, but it is a point that may be applied to any kind of theory, indeed the very theories she mentions as being theories in themselves: feminist, Marxist, poststructuralist, psychoanalytic, and historicist theories. All of these draw heavily on other theories that preceded them. Such borrowing, however, is exactly what goes on in the articulation of a new critical practice. All theories are a synthesis, and Sarver's apparent failure is in not recognizing this fact. Nevertheless, the argument Sarver is making is valid insofar as it calls ecocriticism to task for not being theorized enough.

Patrick D. Murphy offers the most promising synthesis of material that works toward articulating a methodology for ecocriticism. For him, the problem with ecocriticism is that too much of it "remains theoretically unsophisticated. Too often, there remains an anti-theoretical, naive, realist attitude expressed in" the work of ecocritics.[20] In place of these theoretically unsophisticated stances, Murphy offers a Bakhtinian "dialogical orientation," which, he maintains, "reinforces the ecofeminist recognition of interdependence and the natural need for diversity."[21] Sarver would argue that this is simply not good enough. In her own words, "Literary scholars who are environmentalists seem not to be creating a new critical theory; rather, they are drawing on existing theories to illuminate our understanding of how human interactions with nature are reflected in literature."[22] The dialogic answer would be that such borrowing is exactly what goes on in the articulation of a new critical practice. If nothing else, Murphy succeeds in taking ecocriticism out of the hands of the theoretically unsophisticated. If Murphy is to be critiqued, it is for the theory that he chooses rather than for the choosing of theory. We might debate the usefulness of Bakhtinian dialogics, for instance, but that is not part of my project here.

While ecocritical debates are developing, one thing is agreed on: ecocriticism must create change. In a sense, though perhaps few practitioners would agree, ecocriticism is an approach with heavy leanings toward various materialist critiques. We can answer the question about why bother with ecocriticism in the same way that we answer detractors who ask why, for example, bother with materialist-feminist approaches. We bother with ecocriticism because there are problems in these times; because understanding the relationship of humanity with the natural environment, both in contemporary times and in earlier periods, can help us to understand how we got to where we are; because it is time to start looking at the ways that we conceptualize the natural world, and how these conceptualizations affect our behaviors toward the natural environment; in short, because it is important.

ECOCRITICAL THEORY AND PEDAGOGY FOR SHAKESPEARE:
A BRIEF STUDY OF *THE WINTER'S TALE*

What *does* ecocriticism have to do with *The Winter's Tale*, a text written hundreds of years before we noticed the hole in our sky?[23] Students and teachers alike have wildly mixed responses to *The Winter's Tale*, and teaching the play (not to mention environmental issues within it) is no easy task. Part of the difficulty for students is that the play seems disjointed—the pastoral scene of act 4 radically counterposed to the court scenes, in terms both of physical and temporal scene, is one of the most immediate problems. Acknowledging the perceived disjunctions *and* continuities of the play is a useful pedagogical maneuver that helps students begin informed discussions.

One of the more fruitful lines of comparison for students looks, for example, at the dynamic similarities between representations of the natural environment and of women in the play. This approach is easily accessible because it resembles (and can too easily swing into) a formalist thematic groove (which students tend to prefer because it is easier to do than materialist criticism). The representations of women and the environment clearly articulate values about patriarchal power that the text carries. Both the environment and women are characterized in ideologically highly charged terms. The environment and women are often *either* good *or* bad in Shakespeare: in *The Winter's Tale*, the environment is a vicious space of bears and wolves, or else a beautiful place of fertility and abundance; women are liars, shrews, and lechers all, or else they are chaste, guiltless, or otherwise guileless. There is no ambiguity in this play. Paulina is a good woman, as is Hermione,[24] but the spectator (constructed with all of the insecurities of a man like Leontes) is dragged along and made complicit in the testing of these women. Justifiably or not, the audience may wonder about Hermione and about whether Leontes has just cause in his worries. This possibility raises several questions that are difficult to answer but useful for students to consider. Do men and women in the class have the same thoughts about Hermione? Where do these responses come from? What ideological positions do these responses to Hermione support?

Of course, students soon see that there really are no evil women in the play, that Hermione is evil only in the mind of Leontes, and that Paulina's open revolt against constituted authority is for a higher moral good than that which the Crown pretends to represent. It is then worth pointing out to students that phobic reactions toward Hermione cannot be rationalized,[25] and that misogynistic fear is the only foundation for Leontes' rage and jealousy.

We cannot, however, say the same of the fear and loathing that the play generates for the natural environment. If the play challenges gynophobia (no matter how weakly, ineffectively, or inadvertently), it fails to challenge ecophobia. After all, the hapless Antigonus *does* have an unfortunate and fatal encounter with a bear, which "tore out his shoulder bone" (3.3.89) and ate him. And moments before this, "the sea mock'd" (3.3.92) and "swallowed with yeast and froth" (3.3.87) the equally unfortunate mariners who accompanied Antigonus. The anthropocentric image is of the environment as some kind of disaffected subject (in competition with the men), whose raison d'être is to cause chaos, pain, suffering, or loss. It is ruthless, both in the anthropocentric language that the characters in the play use to describe it, and in the audience's understanding of it as a hostile threat to order and goodness.[26]

David Laird argues that the main problem for Leontes is in keeping a sense of order and goodness, and that it is a linguistic problem: "To control language, to exercise the power to name, categorize, and classify is an essential weapon in the arsenal" of things Leontes uses to control his world;[27] so, when Leontes thinks that Hermione uses "a discourse where meanings are multiple, ambiguous,"[28] we may want to encourage students to talk about the various ways that the play talks about disruptions of order, transgressions, and, in particular, pollution.[29] There may be times when we really do not like the environment that this play describes, and the two-dozen references, oblique and direct, to pollution in *The Winter's Tale* contribute to this ecophobic reaction.

Often metaphorical, pollution in the play covers a broad field: epistemological pollution (rotten opinions [2.3.90] and infected knowledge [2.1.43–44]), gender pollution (the blurred gender boundaries of the "mankind witch" [2.3.68]), sanguinary pollution (Polixenes' infected blood [2.1.58–59], "an infected jelly" [1.2.417–18]), and air pollution (the infected air of Sicilia [5.1.167–69], an instance of environmental pollution working allegorically as a metaphor for the pollution of the body politic). But by far the most important kind of pollution in *The Winter's Tale* is perhaps best described as "genetic." It is on this string that most of the plays thematic issues hang, and its acme is reached in the play's pastoral interlude. It is a formal debate between Polixenes and Perdita on the division between art and nature, resting on anxieties first about crossbreeding, and second about definitions, classifications, and naming.

The question of crossbreeding has numerous implications, both in the play and in early modern culture in general. It is an important question in regard to the protagonist couple, Perdita and Florizel, who, to all appearances, are mismatched: Perdita, ostensibly a country lass; Florizel, a prince. The whole section on what Perdita calls "Nature's bastards" (4.4.83) smacks heavily of allegory: if there is any doubt about whom the gentler scion or the wildest stock might refer to, it is dispelled a moment later by Perdita when she talks about Florizel breeding or reproducing by her (4.4.103). In an instant, she has colocated women with breeding animals and fertile flora. Yet this is the same woman who sees crossbreeding as a diluting of nature, a hybridization and infection of natural processes: "I care not to get slips from them [crossbred things]" (4.4.83–84), she insists, because she thinks that selective breeding "shares / With great creating Nature" (4.4.87–8). The argument that Polixenes makes is that Perdita (of ostensibly wild stock) and Florizel (a gentler scion) can crossbreed profitably and without fear of the kind of pollution Perdita seems to imagine. Polixenes has argued that in a material sense crossbreeding, rather than polluting nature is, in fact, natural: it uses natural materials.

Crossbreeding, nevertheless, a form of pollution in the text as in the larger culture of which the text is a part, disrupts classification systems, blurs "natural" with "unnatural," culturally acceptable with unacceptable, fair issues with monstrous ones.[30] While we are, for the most part, spared real disaster in the play (perhaps because the play is generically confused, beginning in high tragic style and switching abruptly to comic mode with the sudden appearance of the bear in act 3, scene 3), what we do get is a jiggling of classificatory schemata, and people suffer when there is this kind of jiggling.[31] With all the images of monstrosity, disease, infection, and pollution that run through this play, and with all of the implied and explicit questions about what is what, people (children and women in particular) suffer. Mamillius dies; Hermione has half her life taken away and for sixteen years has no daughter. And why? We might ask our students if they think that Leontes is terribly strange in his feelings about women. We might also point out that there is a long history in Western culture of perceiving and constructing women as sources of pollution, and that we see this history in much early modern drama.[32] We will ask our students to think things through, to try to understand how materials are manipulated in this and other plays. Camillo argues that "'tis safer to / Avoid what's grown than question how 'tis born" (1.2.432–33), but doing this doesn't get us anywhere.[33]

The methodological ground of ecocriticism is interdisciplinary, regardless of Stephanie Sarver's views, and there are numerous routes we could take to continue an ecocritical reading of *The Winter's Tale*. We could use theories from social and feminist geography to help us think about space, place, and the widely disjunctive geographies in *The Winter's Tale*. We might argue that because the pastoral scenes represent not only a different geographical space but a different political economy, it is a mistake to think that we can talk meaningfully about social relations in the play without talking about how the production of space bears on these relations. Another issue that we could look at is the spatial dimensions of the play's patriarchy: the patriarchal assumptions of Sicilia remain essentially unchallenged, and the space of Bohemia remains an unrealistic ideal (with a few fatal exceptions),[34] insofar as it represents the "flower power" dream of the play, the never-never land where all is happy and peaceful but which cannot actually be located on a map. Certainly space and its conceptualization in this play are very significant, not only for the choppy plot but, more important, because they determine the structure of the lived experiences of the people in those spaces. Discussing such things is the heart and soul of literary criticism, and there are many more discussions to be had: ecocriticism is in its infancy.

Thematic and symbolic readings of green issues have had, as I noted earlier, a substantial history in Shakespearean criticism, but ecocritical readings, which position themselves on par with feminist, Marxist, and materialist readings have, for the most part, been ridiculed. I have tried to suggest what shape an ecocritical reading of *The Winter's Tale* might take, and though I suspect that I have not provided much more than a truncated, fragmentary study, I hope I have also provided at least the beginnings of a convincing argument for ecocritical Shakespeares and for confronting the "inevitable difficulties" that attend such an approach.[35]

NOTES

1. My wording here is only slightly different from that used by Newton and Rosenfelt in their remarkable book that brilliantly sketches possible parameters for a materialist-feminist criticism (xi). See Judith Newton and Deborah Rosenfelt, preface and "Introduction: Toward a Materialist-Feminist Criticism," in *Feminist Criticism and Social Change: Sex, Class and Race in Literature and Culture*, ed. Judith Newton and Deborah Rosenfelt (New York and London: Methuen, 1985), xi–xiv, xv–xxxix.

2. The most promising recent gesture vowing to link ecocritical approaches and Shakespeare texts came in March 2001 in Toledo, Ohio, at the Ohio Shakespeare Conference. This conference, entitled The Nature of Shakespeare, took as its focus the relationships between nature and Shakespeare and showed a remarkable openness to discussions that ranged far outside the thematicism that has so long beleaguered other similar discussions.

3. H. Gustav Klaus, "Cultural Materialism: A Summary of Principles," in *Raymond Williams: Politics, Education, Letters*, ed. W. John Morgan (London: St. Martin's, 1993), 91.

4. Clarence J. Glacken, "Environmental Theories of Early Modern Times," in *Traces on the Rhodian Shore: Nature and Culture in Western Thought from Ancient Times to the End of the Eighteenth Century* (Berkeley and Los Angeles: Univ. of California Press, 1967), 445.

5. I use the term "ecophobia" to denote fear and loathing of the environment in much the same way that the term "homophobia" denotes fear and loathing of gays, lesbians, and bisexuals; see my "Conceptualizing the Other in Hostile Early Modern Geographies: Situating Ecocriticism and Difference in Shakespeare," *Journal of English Language and Literature* 45, no. 4 (December 1999): 877–98.

6. Keith Thomas, *Man and the Natural World: Changing Attitudes in England, 1500–1800* (London: Allen Lane, 1983), 16.

7. Jean E. Howard and Marion F. O'Connor, introduction to *Reproducing Shakespeare: The Text in History and Ideology*, ed. Jean E. Howard and Marion F. O'Connor (London: Methuen, 1987), 5.

8. Richard Paul Knowles, "Otherwise Engaged: Towards a Materialist Pedagogy," *Theatre History in Canada* 12, no. 2 (fall 1991): 193.

9. William Rueckert coined the term in his 1978 article entitled "Literature and Ecology: An Experiment in Ecocriticism," which is reprinted in *The Ecocriticism Reader: Landmarks in Literary Ecology*, ed. Cheryll Glotfelty and Harold Fromm (Athens, Ga., and London: Univ. of Georgia Press, 1996), 105–23. It is only since the mid-1990s, however, that the term has gained relatively popular currency.

10. The boundaries and methodologies of ecocriticism are the central concern of the recently published Karla Armbruster and Kathleen R. Wallace, eds., *Beyond Nature Writing: Expanding the Boundaries of Ecocriticism* (Charlottesville, Va., and London: Univ. Press of Virginia, 2001).

11. Much progress has been made connecting environmentally oppressive structures with social ones. Discussions looking at dynamic similarities between the representation of women and animals are extensive; see particularly Carol J. Adams, *The Sexual Politics of Meat: A Feminist-Vegetarian Critical Theory* (New York: Continuum, 1991); Carol J. Adams and Josephine Donovan, eds., *Animals and Women: Theoretical Explorations* (Durham, N.C., and London: Duke Univ. Press, 1995); Carol J. Adams, ed., *Ecofeminism and the Sacred* (New York: Continuum, 1993); Carol J. Adams, *Neither Man nor Beast: Feminism and the Defense of Animals* (New York: Continuum, 1995); and Donna Haraway, *Simians, Cyborgs, and Women: The Reinvention of Nature* (New York: Routledge, 1991). There is also a growing body of work that looks at women and geography; see Gillian Rose, *Feminism and Geography: The Limits of Geographical Knowledge* (Minneapolis: Univ. of Minnesota Press, 1993); Doreen Massey, *Space, Place, and Gender* (Minneapolis: Univ. of Minnesota Press, 1994); and Annette Kolodny, *The Lay of the Land: Metaphor as Experience and History in American Life and Letters* (Chapel Hill, N.C.: Univ. of North Carolina Press, 1975). A flurry of greatly diversified discussion has recently appeared linking racism and fear and contempt for the natural enviroment; see Lawrence Buell, *The Environmental Imagination: Thoreau, Nature Writing, and the Formation of American Culture* (Cambridge and London: Harvard Univ. Press, 1995), 53–82; Gretchen Legler, "Body Politics in American Nature Writing: 'Who may contest for what the body of nature will be?'" in *Writing the Environment: Ecocriticism and Literature*, ed. Richard Kerridge and Neil Sammells (London and New York: Zed Books, 1998), 71–87; Anna Bramwell, *Ecology in the Twentieth Century: A History* (New Haven: Yale Univ. Press, 1989); Janet Biehl and Peter Staudenmaier, *Ecofascism: Lessons from the German Experience* (Edinburgh: AK Press, 1995); and Richard H. Grove, *Green Imperialism* (Cambridge: Cambridge Univ. Press, 1995). Discussions that draw links between ecophobia and homophobia, on the other hand, are more difficult to locate; see Barbara White, "Acts of God: Providence, the Jeremiad and Environmental Crisis," in *Writing the Environment*, 91–109. Links between geographies of exclusion and dissident sexualities are raised by many of the essays in *Mapping Desire: Geographies of Sexualities*, ed. David Bell and Gill Valentine (London and New York: Routledge, 1995), and by Gill Valentine, "'(Hetero)Sex-

ing Space: Lesbian Perceptions and Experiences of Everyday Spaces," *Environment and Planning D: Society and Space* 11 (1993): 395–413. Despite all of this, mountains of work remain. As Jonathan Levin succinctly observes, "nature and culture are mutually entangled in complex and inherently elusive ways": "Contribution to the *PMLA* Forum on Literatures of the Environment," *PMLA* 114 (1999): 1098. If ecocriticism is to stand on its own, clearly distinguishable from "nature studies," then how it relates with social matters *matters*.

12. Cheryll Glotfelty, "Introduction: Literary Studies in an Age of Environmental Crisis," in *The Ecocriticism Reader*, ed. Glotfelty, xvi–xvii.

13. Ibid., xviii.

14. Glen A. Love, "Revaluing Nature: Toward an Ecological Criticism," in ibid., 226.

15. Glen A. Love, "Science, Anti-science, and Ecocriticism," *ISLE: Interdisciplinary Studies in Literature and Environment* 6, no. 1 (winter 1999): 65.

16. Buell, *Environmental Imagination*, 430 n. 20.

17. Ibid.

18. Ursula K. Heise, "Contribution to the *PMLA* Forum on Literatures of the Environment," *PMLA* 114 (1999): 1097.

19. Stephanie Sarver, "What Is Ecocriticism?" January 2, 1998, <http://www.people.virginia.edu/~djp2n/conf/WLA/sarver.html>.

20. Patrick D. Murphy, *Literature, Nature, and Other: Ecofeminist Critiques* (Albany, N.Y.: State Univ. of New York Press, 1995), 165.

21. Ibid., 22. See also Murphy's "Anotherness and Inhabitation in Recent Multicultural American Literature," in *Writing the Environment*, 42.

22. Sarver, "What Is Ecocriticism?"

23. There is no shortage of books and articles that look at the representations of natural environments in Shakespeare. In general, these books and articles fall under two general catergories: the formalist camp and what I would call the proto-ecocritical group. The formalists have looked at birds, plants (especially flowers), gardens, the relationship between nature (as a general theme) and genre, the way the natural environment could be seen to fit into cosmic patterns, and so on. The difference between the group I am calling proto-ecocritical and the earlier group is in the *kind* of analysis that is being undertaken. While the former is structuralist (concerned primarily with enumerating instances of thematic clusters, with comparing such clusters, with trying to get idealist pictures of the English Renaissance, and so on), the latter is poststructuralist in its various movements toward theoretical analyses of the ways that thinking and talking about the natural world interrelate with other early modern discourses. In *The Shakespearean Wild: Geography, Genus, and Gender* (Lincoln, Neb., and London: Univ. of Nebraska Press, 1991), Jeanne Addison Roberts "marks the stages in the evolution of Shakespeare's ideas" about the wild (84) in a largely formalist attempt to analyze discursive relationships, "how the construction of Culture and Wild [in Shakespearean literature] shapes our perceptions of females" (12). In *Shakespeare and the Geography of Difference* (New York and Cambridge: Cambridge Univ. Press, 1994), John Gillies relies heavily on detailed discussions about the influence of classical texts on Shakespeare and elegantly maps the coordinates linking geographical difference with social exclusion and otherness. Richard Marienstras, a proto–new historicist, tries, among other things, to unearth early modern environmental laws, the background against which Shakespeare wrote; see his *New Perspectives on the Shakespearean World*, trans. Janet Lloyd (Cambridge: Cambridge Univ. Press;

Paris: Editions de la Maison des Sciences de l'Homme, 1985). Linda Woodbridge looks at interconnected representations of land and body, penetration and pollution, at how sexualized landscapes form part of semiotic systems that she calls "the discourse of fertility" (159), and at ways that this discourse overlaps and interacts with discourses of magic; in particular, see "Protection and Pollution: Palisading the Elizabethan Body Politic" and "Green Shakespeare," in *The Scythe of Saturn: Shakespeare and Magical Thinking* (Urbana, Ill., and Chicago: Univ. of Illinois Press, 1994), 45–85, 152–205. There is a lot that has been written about the environment in Shakespeare, but *none* of it is properly ecocritical. None of it is, at core, ecologically revolutionary, and the goals are not explicitly to effect change in the way we think about and produce the environment. Nevertheless, much of the work, both from the proto-ecocritics and by the formalists and structuralists, is very useful.

24. Howard Felperin seems inclined to argue that Hermione is "tongue-tied" and that her contorted and tortuous syntax perhaps partly justifies the wild imaginings of Leontes; see "'Tongue-tied our queen?' The Deconstruction of Presence in *The Winter's Tale*," in *Shakespeare and the Question of Theory*, ed. Patricia Parker and Geoffrey Hartman (New York: Methuen, 1985), 10–12. It is more productive for my purposes to look not at how her words might damn her, but at the ideological effects of her silence, at the workings of the words that are inscribed in the space left empty by her silence. What we are presented with is not merely a silencing, though, nor even an erasure, but an ossification, a pause held for Leontes to work out his matters. Hermione, a very real material presence, must, in this play, be denied her material realities for the man whose matters weigh more heavily in the sexist scales that the play presents. Hermione's presence can be turned on or off, depending on what the matters demand in the male arena that views and controls her. Such is her dramatic function, and it is one that is startlingly similar to the dramatic function of the bear. When it is needed, it is called in, and it is abandoned just as easily.

25. Dorothea Kehler argues this position in "Teaching the Slandered Women of *Cymbeline* and *The Winter's Tale*," in *Approaches to Teaching Shakespeare's* The Tempest *and Other Late Romances*, ed. Maurice Hunt (New York: MLA, 1992), 80–86. Drawing heavily on the work of Jean Baudrillard, she argues that depictions of women in *The Winter's Tale* follow Baudrillard's concept of simulacra, models "without origin or reality" (80).

26. This is perhaps not so surprising, since Judeo-Christian society has a long history of allegorizing the environment; one has only to think of the tree that bears the fruit that yields knowledge of good and evil.

27. David Laird, "Competing Discourses in *The Winter's Tale*," *Connotations* 4, nos. 1–2 (1994–95): 27.

28. Ibid.

29. Laird goes on to say that "Hermione speaks a discursive skepticism that measures the distance between words and things" (27); unfortunately, he doesn't explore how this relationship between words and things functions in the objectification of Hermione, how words "thingify" her. She is a palpable material presence in the text, yet the text vigorously excludes her from much of the material action of the drama, the male action that determines her material fate. Made passive, excluded, and ossified, Hermione may be, as Laird implies, "singularly daring" (30), but she suffers singularly in a way that singularly daring men in Shakespeare don't.

30. Witness the anxieties about crossbreeding in the many early treatises about monstrosities, deformities, and so on.

31. We don't see disaster of the kind that we see, for instance, in other plays of Shakespeare where there is similar substantial boundary transgression. *Othello*, *Titus Andronicus*, and even *Romeo and Juliet* come to mind (the latter because the warring families could be argued to constitute a version of class conflict and can unquestionably be said to profile a forbidden inter-breeding).

32. Linda Woodbridge explains that if pollution is primarily the transgression of culturally significant boundaries, bodily orifices being one such set of boundaries, then it is easy to see why men constitute women as a site of pollution: "women have more orifices than men to start with, which may be why the female body offers the more frequent image of society endangered" ("Protection," 52). Leonard Tennenhouse urges much the same position, claiming that early modern tragedy "defines the female body as a source of pollution . . . any sign of permeability automatically endangers the community": *Power on Display: The Politics of Shakespeare's Genres* (New York and London: Methuen, 1986), 117–18. The female rape victim becomes a site of pollution (as her tousled hair perhaps signifies), and the woman with her own sexuality is also a site of pollution (and a threat to the patriarchal hegemony). But the tradition that seeks to identify women as a source of pollution is not merely concerned with what goes in but with what comes out of the body as well. Thus, women who speak out of order become sites of pollution as do menstruating women.

33. Much of what I have been talking about in this essay centers on birthing—perhaps an unfortunate metaphor, since it genders my topic in ways that indict me for my own sexism. Nevertheless, I began by saying that ecocriticism is a thing that has been named but not properly born, and the question of *how* something is born—the methodologies of its birth—strikes me as vitally important.

34. The fantasy of an idyllic paradise, in part, is what fueled the imperial drive to the New World at precisely the time the play was written, as many people have noted over the last couple of decades.

35. Raymond Williams, "Problems of Materialism," *New Left Review* 109 (May–June 1978): 3.

Wrangling Pedantry: Education in *The Taming of the Shrew*

Kim Walker

In an essay on *THE TAMING OF THE SHREW* AND EDUCATION PUB-
lished in 1994, Dennis S. Brooks argues that Shakespeare proposes a kind of education in the play in which the theater operates as a model classroom, an alternative to rote learning and to
the private tutorials advocated by humanist pedagogues.[1] In both
the induction and the play proper, Brooks suggests, Shakespeare
explores the use of the arts, particularly the theater, to "tame humanity's asocial passions in the interests of civility."[2] He argues
that "on- and off-stage audiences would have seen Kate's tan-
trums as a mirror of their own lack of self-control, her transformation into a submissive wife as a reflection of their potential for
Renaissance versions of educated civility, and Petruchio's approach to courtship and marriage as exemplary of a pedagogy
that might move them from incorrigibility to civility."[3] On the
other hand, the courtship of Bianca illustrates for Brooks a "mis-
education that fails to socialise and results in misfits like Sly who
press what knowledge they possess into the service of their asocial appetites."[4] By reading Katherine's shrewishness as a "caricature of Sly's lack of self-control," Brooks generalizes the
function of the taming stories to all "humanity."[5] Likewise, he
generalizes early modern educational attitudes, largely ignoring
the gender and class specificity of pedagogical theory and practice, and seems to assume a homogeneous, male, middle-class audience: "English grammar schools constituted, of course, the
educational experience of most of Shakespeare's audience (Sly,
too, one could assume)."[6] Effectively, then, Brooks writes women
and the lower classes out of his discussion.

   In this essay I wish to argue that, on the contrary, the play is
very much concerned with gender- and class-specific education,
and that there is a crucial doublethink at work in the play in relation to the education of women. On the one hand, Latin and

mathematics as well as music and needlework are seen as appropriate acquisitions for a gentlewoman, making her a fit wife for a gentleman. Bianca is praised for her love of learning, and Katherine demonstrates her shrewishness partly in her opposition to learning, when she beats her music teacher around the head with her lute. On the other hand, Bianca's education becomes the means for her to make her own romantic choice of a husband and so deceive her father. Given the way in which Bianca is positioned as incipient shrew at the end of the play, while Katherine is positioned as the model wife by means of a very different kind of schooling, the humanist classroom, as related to women, might well be understood as a "shrew-making" school.

It is now commonplace to read back from Bianca's refusal of the summons of her husband, in the final scene of *The Taming of the Shrew*, to argue that "her earlier docility may have been a calculated pose."[7] Correspondingly, act 3, scene 1, in which Bianca is courted by her two false tutors, has often been interpreted as the space in which Bianca's "whiteness" is tainted by means of the witty and flirtatious behavior she engages in with her supposed Latin master, Cambio/Lucentio. Her modesty can thus be considered "conventional posturing."[8] Such notions of Bianca's duplicity read her character in dichotomous terms, much as Hortensio does when the woman he first describes as "my treasure . . . the jewel of my life" (1.2.112–13) later becomes whorelike for him, a woman who casts her "wandering eyes on every stale" (3.1.88). The scenes can be interpreted in quite different terms: in my reading, the play reproduces the anxieties attendant on the education of women that are visible in humanist pedagogical treatises and conduct books of the sixteenth century.

Shakespeare's *Shrew*, unlike *The Taming of a Shrew*, whose relationship with Shakespeare's play is still in debate,[9] puts education—a humanist education in the liberal arts—into the foreground immediately. In *A Shrew*, the taming play opens with the gentleman-scholar Polidor welcoming his friend, the nobleman Aurelius, to Athens, which is located educationally by means of Polidor's reference to "Platoes schooles and Aristotles walkes."[10] Yet this stranger comes to Athens solely to find Polidor, whose "faithfull love" has made him "second selfe" Aurelius (3.8–9). Scholarship, at least in relation to the plot, is quickly left behind, and the disguise of merchant's son that Aurelius takes on to court the second of three sisters is purely an evasion of his superior class origins. As his father, the duke of Cestus, later says to the father of Aurelius's beloved Philena, the Bianca figure, "Alfonso

I did not thinke you would presume, / To mach your daughter with my princely house" (16.64–65). The only schooling Aurelius makes available involves ordering his servant to teach music to the shrewish sister, Kate, in order to keep her occupied: "by this devise," we are told, "Shall we have leisure for to courte our loves, / For whilst that she is learning on the lute, / Hir sisters may take time to steele abrode" (5.149–52). Likewise, in Gascoigne's play *Supposes*, commonly accepted as a source for the Bianca-Lucentio plot,[11] there is no equivalent for the humanist classroom. The Lucentio figure, Erostrato, leaves his studies in law to his servant Dulippo and becomes a mere servant in the house of his beloved for two years in order to sleep with her. Schooling in this play is not associated with the education of women and can therefore remain uncomplicatedly privileged. Indeed, it acquires for the servant Dulippo both a good reputation and a rise in social status, although his social mobility is authorized by the "discovery" at the end of the play that he is the lost son of the wealthy Cleander.

The Taming of the Shrew, on the other hand, is built around a contrast of two kinds of schooling, each bound up with the education of a woman. The play proper opens with Lucentio arriving in the Italian university town of Padua, which he calls a "nursery of arts," to "institute / A course of learning and ingenious studies" (1.1.2, 8–9). His aim, in good humanist fashion, is to "deck his fortune with his virtuous deeds" (1.1.16). Tranio's advice, that Lucentio should follow his desires, simultaneously suggests the comic direction that the play will take and repeats the humanistic argument that "no profit grows where is no pleasure ta'en" (1.1.39). As Rebecca Bushnell points out in *A Culture of Teaching*, humanist writers like Erasmus, Vives, Ascham, and Elyot "idealized the schoolroom . . . as the 'house of play and pleasure, and not of fear and bondage,' " despite the anxiety they also displayed about the need for control, and despite the powerful influence of the biblical proverb, "spare the rod and spoil the child."[12] Tranio insists that music, poetry, and rhetoric should supplement philosophy, logic, mathematics, and metaphysics; Ovid should supplement Aristotle (1.1.25–37). Tranio bespeaks the breadth of subjects associated with the humanist education of a gentleman, while at the same time, he echoes pedagogues such as Erasmus in their concern that each student should be steered in the right direction by paying close attention to their "natural" talents or proclivities.[13] In effect, Tranio's voice here seems less the voice of the witty servant of classical comedy and more the voice of a humanist tutor, both master and servant to his gentlemanly student at once. This ambiguous position is literalized when Tranio is transformed into Lucentio for the duration of his master's courtship of Bianca.

Tranio barely mentions Ovid, of course, before Lucentio falls in love with Bianca, in a street scene that Tranio announces as a "show" to welcome them to Padua (1.1.47). This "show" most obviously contrasts Katherine's shrewish tongue with Bianca's silence, in a scene that seems to corroborate the warnings of many early modern conduct books and treatises about the horrors of women's speech.[14] Less explicitly, it also corroborates warnings about the dangers for women of going outside the house, their proper sphere. Joel Fineman, in his essay on the "turn of the shrew," points to the way that Bianca's silence is inscribed in a scopic economy, as something that is seen rather than heard. Bianca, he says, "does in fact speak quite often in the play—she is not literally mute—but the play describes this speech, as it does Bianca, with a set of images and motifs, figures of speech, that give both to Bianca and to her speaking a specific phenomenality which is understood to be equivalent to silence . . . that is to say, Bianca and her language both are silent because the two of them are something to be seen."[15] Given the arguments often made in contemporary pedagogical tracts and other treatises about the home as the proper sphere for women (and particularly unmarried women), I would argue that Bianca's very visibility puts her modesty and chastity at risk here, even as she is claimed as the model woman by each of the men around her. Vives, for example, becomes particularly expansive on this topic in his popular humanist treatise on female education, *The Instruction of a Christen Woman* (1529): "A woman shulde be kepte close, nor be knowen of many, for hit is a token of no great chastite or good name, to be knowen of many, or be songen about in the cite in songes, or *to be markedde or named by any notable marke*, as whyte, lame, gogle eied, lyttell, great, fat, maymed, or stuttynge, these ought nat to be knowen abrode in a good woman."[16] As I have argued elsewhere, inscribed in this statement is an elision of physical marking ("notable markes" on the woman's body) and verbal or visual marking (by men who visually mark or verbally name these "markes"). By means of this elision, bodily defect slides into defect in virtue, outer mark into inner taint, "a token of no great chastite."[17] Because Bianca can be and is seen by men, in public, she can be read both as the perfect silent woman and as the immodest visible woman, putting her body on "show," regardless of anything she is or is not, regardless of anything she does or does not do. As a woman, in other words, she cannot escape the (varying) judgments of men, any more than her more voluble sister can, and this has nothing to do with her behavior. Within such a framework of ideas about women, Bianca is always available for construction as a duplicitous potential shrew, a construction taken up at the end of the play and repeated by so many critics. As Lorna Hutson has argued, in the context of a much broader project, such a critical response "accurately conveys how the play works to create uncertainty around Bianca's speech and action, so that readers, actors and audience are obliged to interpret her in retrospect, revising an initial 'mistaken' impression of her modesty in the conviction that the error in judgement that produced it must mean that she is to be read as deceitful." Shakespeare, Hutson says, "relocates the sense of anxiety once associated with [clandestine courtship] in the duplicity of 'Bianca's love.' "[18]

At this early point in the play, Baptista orders Bianca back into the house, and her submissive response tells us what she will do to amuse herself:

> Sir, to your pleasure humbly I subscribe.
> My books and instruments shall be my company,
> On them to look and practise by myself.
>
> (1.1.81–83)

Here, then, her humility and acquiescence are linked to her learning. When she has left the stage, Baptista goes on to organize a humanistic education, to satisfy her "delight / In music, instruments, and poetry" (1.1.92–93). He decides to patronize "cunning men," to keep schoolmasters in his house, as a way of being "liberal / To mine own children in good bringing-up" (1.1.98–99). Baptista is represented here as the good father and a good patron of the (liberal) arts at the same time, even as he lays down the law in relation to the marriage of his two daughters and insists on Bianca's retirement.

But it is in act 3, scene 1, that early modern anxieties specifically about women's education become the clear focus of attention. In this scene, which has no equivalent in either *Supposes* or *A Shrew*, we see Bianca with her two young male tutors. The scene centers on two metamorphoses (the disguising of Bianca's two suitors, signalled by Lucentio's adopted name Cambio, "I change") and an Ovidian text. That text is not taken from Ovid's

Metamorphoses or his *Art of Love*, but is rather an apparently harmless citation from Penelope's complaint in the *Heroides*.[19] Ovid was expressly forbidden to women readers by humanist pedagogues and reformist writers of the sixteenth century because of the perception that his works had the capacity to incite amorous desires in a sex prone to licentiousness. Even in the relatively liberal program of reading for women that he outlined, Vives excluded Ovid, calling him a "schole maister of baudry" (sig. B2v).[20] Moreover, the youth of Bianca's tutors also works against the strictures of the humanist pedagogues who argued, with a similar anxiety in mind, that daughters should be educated either by women or by grave old men. Shifting his ground to the dangers of male desire, Vives suggests that if no "holy and well lerned woman" was available, then "let us chuse some man either well aged, or els very good and vertuous, which hath a wyfe, and that ryghte fayre ynough, whom he loveth well, and so shall he nat desyre other" (sig. E2).

The play's third act opens with a struggle over priority between Lucentio, disguised as Latin tutor Cambio, and Hortensio, disguised as music tutor Licio. Cambio calls Licio "too forward" and reminds him of the rough treatment he received from Katherine in his role as music teacher (3.1.1–3). The tutors' rivalry puts in question the nature of an appropriate female response to education. Licio tells Bianca that he is going to teach her the "gamut," or scale, as the "rudiments of art" before he lets her "touch the instrument / To learn the order of my fingering" (3.1.62–65). Such fingering of instruments comes up elsewhere in Shakespeare, with bawdy double entendres. In *Cymbeline*, for example, Cloten's courtship of Imogen includes asking his musicians to "penetrate her with [their] fingering" (2.3.12), and in *Pericles*, Antiochus's daughter is compared to a viol "Who, fingered to make man his lawful music, / Would draw heav'n down . . . / But, being played upon" by her own father in an incestuous relationship, makes that music hellish (1.2.122–24).[21] Licio's phrasing here recalls his earlier complaint about Katherine's shrewish abuse:

> I did but tell her she mistook her frets,
> And bowed her hand to teach her fingering,
> When, with a most impatient devilish spirit,
> "Frets, call you these?" quoth she, "I'll fume with them,"
> And with that word she struck me on the head . . .
> While she did call me rascal, fiddler,

And twangling jack, with twenty such vile terms,
As she had *studied* to misuse me so.

(2.1.147–57; emphasis added)

On the one hand, this is one of the many instances in the play
where language itself becomes a source of confusion or a site of
struggle, as the frets of the instrument are reinterpreted as the
frets of a moody woman. But Katherine's abuse is placed in the
context of teaching her fingering, and in that context it is significant that Lucentio refers back to this rough response when he
accuses Licio of being "too forward" with Bianca. Katherine's
"studies" in verbal abuse put her tongue, that "glibbery member" associated with the penis, to the defense of her chastity.[22] It
is as though that very response is not only to be interpreted as
unwomanly shrewish behavior, but also to be read as a response
that prevents inappropriate sexual forwardness on the part of the
male tutor. Her antagonism to her music lesson may also be read
with reformist writers such as Thomas Salter in mind, whose
translation of a treatise by Giovanni Bruto forbade music to
women: "For as Musicke if it be used to a laudable and good intention, hath no evill in it, but deserveth a place among the other
Artes, the whiche appertainyng properly to menne, be called Lib-
erall: Yet, it beareth a swete baite, to a sowre and sharpe evill.
Therefore I wishe our Maiden, wholie to refrain from the use of
Musicke, seeyng that under the coverture of Vertue, it openeth
the dore to many vices."[23] Bianca, of course, rejects Licio's advances in a more restrained mode than Katherine: "I am not so
nice," she says, "To change true rules for odd inventions"
(3.1.78–79). But she does allow Lucentio's odd inventions to
change the rules in his Latin lesson.[24]

Bianca intervenes to stop the two tutors quarreling:

Why, gentlemen, you do me double wrong
To strive for that which resteth in my choice.
I am no breeching scholar in the schools.
I'll not be tied to hours nor 'pointed times.
But learn my lessons as I please myself.

(3.1.16–20)

Her words here echo Katherine's rebellious response to her
father's direction in the opening scene where, in a disruptive shift
away from verse to prose, she says: "Why, and I trust I may go
too, may I not? What, shall I be appointed hours, as though, be-
like, I knew not what to take and what to leave?" (1.1.102–4).

Critics have accordingly read back from the final scene of the play to find the incipient shrew here, in Bianca's voiced desire to please herself and in the "preposterous" reversals of the student's and teacher's roles that follow, such as her demand that her Latin tutor "construe" the Latin text for her (3.1.30).[25]

Yet it is above all the contradictory position of the schoolmaster/tutor in relation to his students in humanist pedagogical practice that allows for a way of reading Bianca as potential shrew, at the same time as she stops the quarrel and "chastely" defends herself from what turns out to be the amorous advances of her "wrangling pedants." As Bushnell has argued, the schoolmaster occupied an ambiguous position as both master and servant at once, particularly in relation to a student of gentle or noble birth.[26] Because Bianca is not a "breeching scholar of the schools," but a well-off student receiving tuition at home, she takes up an equally ambiguous position in relation to her two tutors. Similarly, because she is a woman, she is in an ambiguous position in relation to the hierarchy of master and servant. As a result, her intervention into the quarrel of the two tutors may be read either as the appropriate voice of the good housewife in the home who keeps her servants in order, or as the incipiently shrewish voice of a woman resisting male authority.

Here, I want to take up that reference to the "breeching scholar in the schools." Karen Newman has argued that, in both Sly's desire in the induction for the page-boy "wife" and Petruchio's desire at the end of the play for his "wife," played by a boy actor, "woman" is exposed as a cultural construct by "the very indeterminateness of the actors' sexuality, of the woman/man's body, the supplementarity of its titillating deconstruction."[27] That argument is aimed at deconstructing the image of the model wife that appears in Katherine's final speech, partly at least to enable the play's acceptance in an age of feminism. A similar reading might be made here in act 3, scene 1. When Bianca, speaking as a gentlewoman, distances herself from the "breeching scholar in the schools," she distances "herself" also from the boy actor who plays her role, a boy actor who presumably was or had been just such a breeching scholar. Who is speaking here? Bianca's voice may be read as a voice that exposes the shrewish woman as a cultural construct through this moment of overt artifice. But it may also be read as a voice that reaffirms the incipient shrew by doubling it with the boy actor's resistance to "proper" adult male authority.

The interrelation of class- and gender-specific expectations reappears in Hortensio's rejection of Bianca at the end of the scene. His anxiety about Cambio's looks of love is quickly displaced onto anxiety about Bianca's behavior. As has often been noted, she is imaged as a hawk—in the same way that Petruchio figures Katherine in his taming speech in act 4, scene 1,—a hawk that here has "wand'ring eyes" that are cast toward "every stale" or decoy (3.1.88). Class values are involved as well as gender values. Bianca, he assumes, is looking "humbly" at a mere schoolmaster—a master who is also a servant—and that implies the possibility of lustful behavior with regard to "every stale," any man who comes along. One slip for a woman, in those terms, is a complete fall from virtue: "If *once* I find thee ranging, / Hortensio will be quit with thee by changing" (3.1.89–90; emphasis added). Hortensio's class consciousness may be mocked when he brings the fake master Tranio, as Lucentio, to observe Bianca's behavior, but Bianca herself can still be read as "tainted" by the association with her Latin tutor Cambio and, once again, by her very visibility. Her Latin lesson becomes a sight/site of female duplicity. As Hutson argues, this "extraordinary scene of voyeurism . . . makes us rather aware of a disturbing gap in our knowledge about Bianca herself, as she appears to respond with ambiguous facility to the instructions of her private tutor." Our sense of Bianca's "character," she continues, "thereby partakes . . . of Hortensio's own error in supposing this to be proof of her promiscuity, entertaining honest suitors while she flirts with a household servant."[28] The sight/site bespeaks not only the warnings of writers such as Thomas Salter, who saw women's education in anything other than piety and housewifery as a corrupting influence,[29] but also the ambivalence present in humanist pedagogical treatises toward the education of women.[30]

The anxiety that humanist education is itself a source of potential disorder in the hierarchy of gender is apparent here, even at the same time as the play values a humanist education in philosophy, languages, poetry and the arts—for men. It is in this context that the introduction of the pedant is best seen in act 4, scene 2 (replacing both the merchant of *A Shrew* and the Sienese gentleman of *Supposes*).[31] Again we are presented with a man who is positioned as master and servant, a substitute father and at the same time a rather foolish nonentity. For Lucentio, this pedant, like his own pedagogy, helps him to the well-born wife of his choice. Education provides him with both profit and pleasure, as it does Bianca. But in Bianca's case, her appearance as incipient shrew at the end of the play encourages us to read back onto act

3, scene 1, the dangers of humanist education for women, just as it has encouraged so many critics to read her behavior in these early scenes as duplicitous posturing. The popular perception, which Margaret King and Lisa Jardine have discussed, of a link between learning in women and their aggression or sexual deviancy seems to be reinforced here, undercutting the early humanist idea that learning for gentlewomen provided a training for superior wifehood.

Neither *Supposes*, the source play for the Lucentio-Bianca plot written about thirty years earlier, nor *The Taming of a Shrew*, for all its likenesses to *The Shrew*, appear remotely interested in the education of women. Nor does Fletcher's "sequel," *The Woman's Prize, or The Tamer Tamed* (first acted c. 1611), in which Petruchio is tamed by his second wife, Maria, after Katherine's death, with the assistance of her (apparently husbandless) cousin, Byancha.[32] By the time the first adaptation of the play was written in the Restoration, the scene of wrangling pedants has been shorn of its anxiety. *Sauny the Scott*, a revision of *The Shrew* by the comic actor John Lacy in the early 1660s, was probably written to precede Fletcher's *Woman's Prize*, which along with other Fletcherian drama would prove popular on the Restoration stage.[33] Lacy's prose version turns Padua into London (as does *The Woman's Prize*) and Lucentio into Winlove, an English gentleman newly come up to the city to educate himself in all that London has to offer. His father, Sir Lyonell, has an estate in the Vale of Evesham (an agriculturally rich area southwest of Stratford-upon-Avon). Appropriately for this revised city context, the substitute father who takes Sir Lionel's place at the end of the play is no longer a pedant but Snatchpenny, a petty criminal, "a rare old Sinner [found] in the Temple Cloysters" (3.21).

When Winlove falls in love with the Biancha of *Sauny the Scott*, he disguises himself as an "ordinary French master" (1.3), aligning himself with the Restoration court newly returned from exile in France. The books he offers Bianca's father for her education are French romances rather than *The Shrew*'s Greek and Latin texts; as Woodall (the Gremio figure) explains, "your French books treat most of love" (2.7). The "lesson" scene has Winlove telling Bianca (now of course played by a woman, not a boy) he is to read her the story of Apollo and Daphne, "der ver fine Story in de Varle of Mounsieur Appollo, And Madomoselle Daphne" (3.14); this suggests a domesticated French translation of Ovid's *Metamorphoses*, with "Mr." Apollo replacing the classical god. But Winlove does not attempt to interweave any French text into his lesson. Like the lute master of the play, he merely hands over a paper telling Biancha who he is, with no "show" of teaching anything. The education of Biancha has become attenuated here, and there is none of the anxiety of Shakespeare's play bound up with it. This is also evident in the Hortensio figure Geraldo's rejection of Biancha. Instead of a class-bound concern that Biancha is humbling herself to a mere schoolmaster, he betrays an anxiety about the French infiltration of the city: "These damn'd French men, have got all the trade in Town[;] if they get up all the handsome Women, the English must e'en march into Wales for Mistersses [sic]" (3.15) Given a Francophile court, this comment helps mark the comic inadequacy of Geraldo rather than the waywardness of Biancha.

Biancha's incipient shrewishness is also downplayed at the end of *Sauny the Scott*, since Katherine is given a more extended taming when she proves still rebellious after she arrives home in London. The taming is extended into a tooth-pulling exercise and into Petruchio's pretense that she is dead. Biancha, meanwhile, shows herself concerned at such rough treatment of her sister, exiting on the line, "I'll be gone, I can't endure to see her put to so much Pain" (5.43). Katherine is "won over" only when Petruchio publicly attempts to bury her alive; but even here, her own "taming" speech is only two lines long, looking "forward" to the assumption in Fletcher's play that Katherine was never tamed, and perhaps also revising the marriage in line with the new "gay couple" of Restoration comedy, for whom marriage meant a loss of freedom, and satisfaction of desire meant, in Hobbesian terms, a loss of desire. Petruchio's epilogue points beyond the boundaries of the play to his return in Fletcher's play: "I've Tam'd the Shrew, but will not be asham'd / If next you see the very Tamer Tam'd." The "ideal wife" of *The Shrew* no longer dominates the end of the play, and as a result her opposite, Bianca as incipient shrew, fades away too.[34] The Restoration theater, with its more courtly audiences, its necessarily literate female actors, and its increasingly suspicious attitude to marriage, makes more of Katherine's rebellion and less of Bianca's education and "change."[35]

CODA

In this coda, I address two twentieth-century adaptations of *The Taming of the Shrew*—a play by Charles Marowitz and the popular film version of the musical *Kiss Me Kate*—to glance at two rather different contemporary "revisions" of the lesson scene. Marowitz's *Shrew* was first written in 1974, then revised and published in 1978.[36] Characteristically, Marowitz reorders and revises the taming plot to emphasize its violence. By dropping the farce and focusing on Petruchio as a "scheming adventurer as cruel as he is avaricious,"[37] his play disallows a reading of shrew taming as bourgeois romance. Kate is beaten down through brainwashing and public rape until she becomes an automaton in institutional dress, who mechanically mouths her final speech at the prompting of both husband and father. The Bianca plot is transformed into contemporary scenes between an unnamed Girl and Boy. Education, here, is something associated simply with class. The Girl is upper-middle class while the Boy is working class, and the Girl's education is part of her attraction, at least initially, for the Boy. It is not the Girl's education per se that is problematic here; it is education as a mark of class difference, of the gap between the two. Interestingly, the Boy is doubled in the taming plot not by a Lucentio figure, who never appears, but by Hortensio, whose contempt of Bianca's flirting with a schoolmaster in *The Shrew* is inverted as the Boy's anger and jealousy at the Girl's conversations with other more educated men:

> *He.* You were cooped up with that guy for almost three hours. I might just as well have been the hatstand. . . .
> *She.* Look. The boy had read a book I'd just finished. He had opinions about it. They were interesting, different from mine, and we just discussed it. . . .
> *He.* I heard little flashes of all that hyper-intellectual stuff all night, and I suppose I just got angry because I was, well, barred.[38]

Her education, as a marker of social standing, becomes something that the Boy resents and perceives as the source of "infidelity" on her part, set against his own more flagrantly physical infidelities.

In Marowitz's introduction to the play, however, it is neither class nor gender that he blames for the degeneration of the couple's relationship. He pinpoints the problem of the first version of his play (subsequently revised for the published edition) as its suggestion that nothing very much has changed since the seventeenth century. Yet he goes on to lay the blame on a generalized human nature, arguing that the "tragedy" of the Boy and Girl "is built into their human metabolism":[39] "What I wanted to say was, in fact, that no human relationship has the stamina to withstand long periods of intimate exposure . . . that there was something at the core of human nature which was irrevocably abusing and self-consuming."[40] Nevertheless, I would argue that what the contemporary scenes actually show is precisely that such corrosive relations are a product of a class-based society, a society marked and marred by differences in education. Interestingly, passages from the induction of Shakespeare's play, which deals with class in a way that *The Shrew* proper does not do, are attached to Kate's taming in the main scenes of Marowitz's play.

Class is again at issue in the popular 1953 film version (directed by George Sidney) of *Kiss Me Kate*, though the 1950s United States clearly provides a very different context from the 1970s Britain of Marowitz's play. The musical has been associated with postwar attempts to re-domesticate women in the home and, as Barbara Hodgdon has written, is "less interested in shrewing around than in placating, through song and dance, the cultural tensions of screwing around."[41] In the early scenes, for example, Lois (the Bianca figure) is contrasted with Lilli (the Katherine figure) in ways that spell out their distinct class origins. Lois-Bianca appears initially in a brief scarlet chorus girl's outfit, with her long legs on full display, looking for ginger ale and tap-dancing her way across Fred-Petruchio's living room. Lilli-Kate watches with refined distaste, elegant in calf-length black dress, tapered to fit, fur stole, long black leather gloves, and neat fitted cap. As Fred-Petruchio is later told, "she's got breeding, and culture. . . . She's a real classy broad." The terms of the contrast between Katherine and Bianca in Shakespeare's play have obviously changed. Lois-Bianca's outgoing energy and loud mouth (features that one might associate with Katherine in *The Shrew*) make her less of an incipient shrew in this context than an incipient cheerleader. Lilli-Kate's mocking silence and sartorial self-containment, on the other hand, bespeak the independence of the divorced woman. It is a self-containment that the film will have to explode before the romantic ending can be imposed.

Education plays no role in the Bianca scenes of the musical within the film. *The Shrew*'s lesson scene is replaced by a scene between Bianca and her three suitors, who operate more like the three suitors of *The Merchant of Venice*—patrician, rich man, and poor-but-loving lover. Bianca sings, "I'm a maid who would marry," and her suitors join her in an almost explicitly sexual chorus that announces that any Harry, Tom, or Dick will do. The "duplicitous posturing" of Bianca is here taken as a given, made visible through such moments as Lois's "bad" acting of Bianca's tears, which is immediately transformed into a sidelong smirk as she launches into her exuberant song and dance routine. For Lois herself, "playing the field" is a means of acquiring material possessions—diamond clips, sable coats, and Paris hats—possessions that are also, of course, markers of status in a consumer society. Nevertheless, Lois, like a twentieth-century bourgeois Bianca, finally longs for the domestic idyll of a "farm near her old home town" with a "white picket fence," where she and her indigent gambler boyfriend Bill can "settle down."

Education in this musical is displaced completely from the scene of the courtship of Bianca via Latin and lute music onto the two lower-class hoodlums who sing "Brush up your Shakespeare" to Fred-Petruchio. By means of the titles of his plays, in this song "Shakespeare" becomes the way to ensure female submission to every sexual advance, from initial encounter to rape:

> Brush up your Shakespeare, start quoting him now;
> Brush up your Shakespeare, and the women you will wow.
> Just declaim a few lines from Othella,
> And they'll think you're a heck of a fella. . . .
> If she fights when her clothes you are mussing
> Well, clothes is Much Ado About Nothing.
> If she says your behaviour is heinous,
> Kick her right in the Coriolanus.
> Brush up your Shakespeare, and they'll all kow-tow.[42]

The two gangsters recommend a use of Shakespeare that harks back less to the wrangling pedantry of *The Shrew*'s lesson scene than to Petruchio's violence in his taming of Kate, a violence now to be directly applied to the women. An education in Shakespeare becomes a new way to tame women in the gangsters' more contemporary but equally violent heterosexual courtship practices.

The gangsters are used to provide a farcical contrast to the more "cultured" world of the theater and the wooing of Fred and Lilli. But this appropriation of Shakespeare points out the way that *Kiss Me Kate* as a whole recommends an education in Shakespeare to men and women as a way of reconstituting women in their proper domestic roles as wives, mothers, and sexual objects. "Brush up your Shakespeare" may also provide us with a rueful reminder that Shakespeare as cultural capital may be put to many uses, some of them not at all what we—wrangling pedants?—might wish.

NOTES

1. Dennis S. Brooks, " 'To show scorn her own image': The Varieties of Education in *The Taming of the Shrew*," *Rocky Mountain Review of Language and Literature* 48 (1994): 7–32.

2. Ibid., 8.

3. Ibid., 7.

4. Ibid., 8.

5. Ibid., 11.

6. Ibid., 12.

7. Jean E. Howard, introduction to *The Taming of the Shrew*, in *The Norton Shakespeare*, 135.

8. Andrew Gurr, *Playgoing in Shakespeare's London* (Cambridge: Cambridge Univ. Press, 1987), 149.

9. See Leah Marcus's materialist analysis of the history of this debate, in "The Shakespearean Editor as Shrew-Tamer," *English Literary Renaissance* 22 (1992): 201–22. Marcus comments that Katherine, "by learning to speak the pedagogue's language of social and familial order . . . shows herself to be a better student of standard humanist doctrine than her sister" (204).

10. *The Taming of a Shrew*, in *Narrative and Dramatic Sources of Shakespeare*, ed. Geoffrey Bullough (London: Routledge, 1957), 1:73 (3.1–2).

11. See, for example, Richard Hosley, "Sources and Analogues of *The Taming of the Shrew*," *Huntington Library Quarterly* 27 (1964): 303–6. Gascoigne's play (1566) is a prose version of Ariosto's *I Suppositi* (1509), itself related to the classical comedy of Plautus and Terence.

12. Rebecca Bushnell, *A Culture of Teaching: Early Modern Humanism in Theory and Practice* (Ithaca, N.Y.: Cornell Univ. Press, 1996), 30. Ascham, for example, cites the instance of Lady Jane Grey, whom he comes upon "in her Chamber, readinge Phaedon Platonis in Greeke, and that with as moch delite, as som gentleman wold read a merie tale in Bocase [Boccaccio]." Her eagerness to learn, she tells him, derives from her tutor, who, unlike her parents, "teacheth me so gentlie, so pleasantlie, with soch faire allurementes to learning, that I thinke all the tyme nothing,whiles I am with him. . . . And thus my booke, hath bene so moch my pleasure, and bringeth dayly to me more pleasure and more, that in respect of it, all other pleasures, in very deede, are but trifles and troubles unto me" (*The Scholemaster* [London, 1570], 1.11–12). Like Prospero in *The Tempest*, such writers urged differential treatment on the basis of the student's nature, a nature that often merged implicitly with class. Bushnell comments that writers such as Henry Peacham "believed that flogging was an inappropriate way to train one inherently 'gentle' " (31). Peacham argued in his *Compleat Gentleman* (London, 1622), that "one and the selfe-same Method agreeth not with all [students] alike," and that "The Noble, generous, and best Natures, are won by commendation, enkindled by Glory . . . to whom conquest and shame are a thousand tortures. Of which disposition for the most part, are most of our young Nobilitie and Gentlemen, well borne" (22–23).

13. Bushnell argues that humanist pedagogical writings are contradictory in regard to the force of the child's nature. It is both something that can never be fully expelled or altered, and something that can be shaped like a growing plant (*Culture of Teaching*, 100–108).

14. See my *Women Writers of the English Renaissance* (New York: Twayne, 1996), 8–11.

15. Joel Fineman, "The Turn of the Shrew," in *Shakespeare and the Question of Theory*, ed. Patricia Parker and Geoffrey Hartman (New York: Methuen, 1985), 147.

16. Juan Luis Vives, *A very frutefull and pleasant boke called the Instruction of a Christen Woman*, trans. Richard Hyrde (London, 1529), sig. N3; emphasis added.

17. Walker, *Women Writers*, 11.

18. Lorna Hutson, *The Usurer's Daughter: Male Friendship and Fictions of Women in Sixteenth Century England* (London: Routledge, 1994), 214–18. Hutson's book "interprets sixteenth century fictions of women in relation to what men understood was happening, under the combined impact of print and humanism, to the meanings of 'friendship' and 'service' in this period" (2).

19. Thomas Moisan argues, however, that on the one hand Lucentio's selection of the description of Troy from Penelope's complaint has the effect of "silencing and suppressing a radically different and far unhappier perspective on the domestic arrangements Katherina's exposition dutifully idealizes" in her final speech, while on the other hand, in Ovid's translation of Homer, and in Turbervile's translation of Ovid, Penelope's complaint makes her kin to the Elizabethan "querulous wife"; see his "Interlinear Trysting and 'Household stuff': The Latin Lesson and the Domestication of Learning in *The Taming of the Shrew*," *Shakespeare Studies* 23 (1995): 112–13. Moisan adds that Penelope's complaint "hovers conspicuously about the translation scene of the Shrew as its unvoiced lesson, as one more intrusive, albeit invisible, tutor," a lesson in which "women's behavior and potential as domestic partners become the stuff of male speculation . . . and public examination" (114–16).

20. As Patricia B. Phillippy points out in, " 'Loytering in Love': Ovid's *Heroides*, Hospitality, and Humanist Education in *The Taming of the Shrew*," *Criticism* 40 (1998): "annotated Latin texts reflect the revamping of Ovid as a teacher of virtue rather than praeceptor amoris within the rhetorical education of boys, [but] annotated vernacular editions indicate a similar effort directed toward a female readership. When educating women, however, the commentators stressed not rhetorical mastery but moral behavior" (32).

21. See also John Webster's *Duchess of Malfi*, where the Cardinal addresses his mistress, Julia, comparing his own (sexual) prowess with that of her husband, the old Castruchio: "Thou hadst onely kisses from him, and high feeding, / But what delight was that? 'twas just like one / That hath a little fingring on the Lute, / Yet cannot tune it: (still you are to thanke me)" (2.4.44–47), in *The Complete Works of John Webster*, vol. 2, ed. F. L. Lucas (New York: Gordian Press, 1966).

22. Cf. Richard Brathwait, *The English Gentlewoman* (London, 1631): "[women's] tongues are held their defensive armour; but in no particular detract they more from their honour, than by giving too free scope to that glibbery member" (88). For the link between the tongue and the penis, see Lisa Jardine, *Still Harping on Daughters* (New York: Harvester, 1983), 121–33.

23. *The Mirrhor of Modestie* (London, 1579), sig. C6–C6v.

24. Here I am in agreement with Patricia Phillippy's argument that the play casts "humanist education itself—or more specifically, its all-too-easy manipulation—as a dangerous and seductive interloper in the household" (42).

25. Patricia Parker has commented on Lucentio/Cambio's use of the rhetorical term "preposterous" (3.1.9) in relation to Hortensio/Licio's attempt to reverse the proper order of philosophy (in the Latin lesson) and music. She argues

that "the fact that Lucentio's intended mastery of Bianca in Act III summons the notion of the preposterous, in lines that recall the prescribed and 'natural' ordering of the genders from the Ceremony of Matrimony, gives . . . support to readings of the play that see its apparent affirmation of patriarchy as the self-conscious following of yet another script": *Shakespeare from the Margins: Language, Culture, Context* (Chicago: Univ. of Chicago Press, 1996), 34.

26. See in particular the chapter in Bushnell's *Culture of Teaching* entitled "The Sovereign Master and the Scholar Prince" (23–72).

27. Karen Newman, "Renaissance Family Politics and Shakespeare's *The Taming of the Shrew*," *English Literary Renaissance* 16 (1986): 100.

28. Hutson, *Usurer's Daughter*, 216.

29. Salter's translation of Bruto argues that "it is not mete nor convenient for a Maiden to be taught or trayned up in learnyng of humaine artes, in whome a vertuous demeanouor and honest behaviour, would be a more sightlier ornament, then the light or vaine glorie of learnyng, for . . . every woman ought wholelie to be active and diligent about the governmente of her housholde and familie . . . and seing also that in suche studies, as yeldeth recreation and pleasure, there is no lesse daunger, that they will as well learne to be subtile and shamelesse Lovers, as connyng and skilfull writers, of Ditties, Sonnetes, Epigrames, and Ballades" (sig. C1–C1v).

30. This ambivalence is clearly charted in Anthony Grafton and Lisa Jardine's *From Humanism to the Humanities* (Cambridge: Harvard Univ. Press, 1986), 29–57; see also Jardine's *Still Harping on Daughters*, 37–67, and my *Women Writers*, 4–23.

31. Clearly, I disagree with Richard Hosley and those editors of the play who replace the pedant with a merchant on the grounds that a merchant was more likely to be carrying "bills for money by exchange" (4.2.90): see Hosley, "Sources and Analogues," 305. This argument seems unsound, given the folio text's consistent use of "Pedant" in speech prefixes, and the need for the equivalent of today's travelers' checks at a time when highway theft was common.

32. See vol. 4 of *The Dramatic Works of the Beaumont and Fletcher Canon*, ed. Fredson Bowers (Cambridge: Cambridge Univ. Press, 1979); all references are to this edition. Fletcher's Byancha, derisively called "Colonell Byancha," the "Engineir [who] commands the workes" of Maria's barricade against her husband, by Petruchio's servant (1.3.63–65), has been read as "an extension of Shakespeare's manipulative Bianca" by Molly Smith in her essay, "John Fletcher's Response to the Gender Debate: *The Woman's Prize* and *The Taming of the Shrew*," *Papers on Language and Literature* 31 (1995): 48. Certainly, Fletcher's choice of name for his female "engineir" suggests that the reading of Bianca as incipient shrew at the end of Shakespeare's play was available to early modern audiences, just as Katherine's tamed/taming speech was able to be put in question: in *The Woman's Prize* we are told that Petruchio's first wife was never tamed: "What though his other wife, / Out of her most abundant stubbornesse, / Out of her daily huy and cries upon him, / (For sure she was a Rebell) turn'd his temper, / And forc'd him blow as high as she?" (1.1.16–20).

33. Fletcher's play was produced on the Restoration stage as early as June 1660, while Lacy's revision may have been written in 1663; see Michael Dobson, *The Making of the National Poet: Shakespeare, Adaptation and Authorship, 1660–1769* (Oxford: Clarendon, 1992), 22–23. Sauny the Scot is the Grumio figure of *The Shrew*, whose comic part is much expanded. The name recalls the parallel figure in *A Shrew*, Saunders/Saunder/Sander. All further references to

Lacy's play are taken from *Sauny the Scott, or The Taming of the Shrew* (London, 1698).

34. In *Players' Scepters: Fictions of Authority in the Restoration* (Lincoln, Nebr.: Univ. of Nebraska Press, 1979), Susan Staves argues that Lacy's play seems to reflect "some loss of belief in the traditional ideological underpinnings of a husband's claim to authority" (134).

35. It is interesting to note an advertisement published in 1673 for Bathsua Makin's London boarding school for gentlewomen. Makin's school distinguishes itself by its claim that it will spend only half the time "in all things ordinarily taught in other schools" for women—dancing, music, singing, writing, keeping accounts and needlework—while the other half will be employed "in gaining the Latin and French tongues; and those that please, may learn Greek and Hebrew, the Italian and Spanish [and] some general Knowledge in Astronomy, Geography, Arithmetick and History": *An Essay to Revive the Antient Education of Gentlewomen* (London, 1673), 42–43. Despite (or because of) the breadth of the humanist curriculum offered by Makin, the advertisement is appended to an anonymous pamphlet defending the education of women. The defense makes clear that the popular link between learning in women and their deviancy has not vanished: "A learned Woman is thought to be a Comet; that bodes Mischief, when ever it appears. To offer to the World the liberal Education of Women is to deface the Image of God in Man, it will make Women so high, and men so low, like Fire in the House-top, it will set the whole world in a Flame. These things and worse then these, are commonly talked of, and verily believed by many, who think themselves wise Men: to contradict these is a bold attempt" (sig. A2). Nevertheless, that "bold attempt" is made, and presumably by Makin herself; Makin's defense and her school argue for a somewhat less-constrained position for women in the Restoration.

36. Charles Marowitz, *The Marowitz Shakespeare* (1978; reprint New York: Marion Boyars, 1990).

37. Charles Marowitz, "Shakespeare Recycled," *Shakespeare Quarterly* 38 (1987): 471.

38. Marowitz, *Marowitz Shakespeare*, 156, 158–59.

39. Marowitz, introduction to ibid., 19.

40. Ibid., 17.

41. Barbara Hogdon, "Katherina Bound, or Play(K)ating the Strictures of Everyday Life," *PMLA* 107 (1992): 547.

42. *Kiss Me Kate*. Directed by George Sidney. 116 min. Warner, 1953.

Beyond Shakespearean Exceptionalism

Barbara Bowen

IF SHAKESPEARE STUDIES, LIKE MUCH LITERARY AND CULTURAL CRIT-icism, stands at a critical crossroads, our collective task, at least as readers and teachers of Shakespeare, is to think our way through this crossroads and figure out how to go forward from here. How do we make use of the astonishing discoveries of the last twenty years, particularly the rich knowledge from the textual and material archive of early modern Europe, without sinking into repetition and historicist parody? And a related issue: how do we build on the advances of feminist theory, queer theory, and postcolonial theory that have made crucial interventions in the field, while not setting up a competition among them or retreating into an aestheticized Shakespeare? In Shakespeare studies, responses to these kinds of questions often confront a paradoxical obstacle in seeking to remake our critical practice: the surprisingly resilient paradigm of Shakespearean exceptionalism.

Despite the massive amount of information scholars have unearthed about the early modern world and the vastly enriched sense of history in which we can now read Shakespeare, there is something in the formation of Shakespeare criticism that is still resistant to seeing him as one writer among others. The Romantic veneration of Shakespeare as a solitary genius has cast a long shadow. Despite the new understanding, for instance, of women's lives, of early imperialism, of other theatrical writers, or of the links between slavery, women's consumption of commodities, and the writing of colonialism, it remains permissible to treat Shakespeare as a field of knowledge, indeed an industry, in himself. Obviously Marxist and other forms of historicist criticism have always been a challenge to this extreme version of author-centric criticism, and part of what I am describing may simply be lingering resistance to the historicist approach. But despite the efforts of a whole generation of critics to ask questions about race, sexuality, and gender in Shakespeare's works, and of these and other critics to insist that Shakespeare be read alongside his (male) contemporaries, Shakespeare studies remains reluctant to let go of the most-favored-author status it has enjoyed for so long.

I borrow the term exceptionalism from the Left analysis of American capitalism as sui generis, an expression of capitalism so different from any other that it forms a world unto itself, exempt from the usual protocols of analysis. But the application to Shakespeare studies is clear. As Shakespeareans, our training was in some way deformed by the notion that Shakespeare was so great in himself that his works could be studied in isolation, first from social and political history, and still, perhaps, from other writers. Eve Kosofsky Sedgwick has explained that the danger of the literary canon is not so much that it does not represent certain writers, certain knowledges, but that it insulates texts from each other and thus occludes potential political connections between them.[1] She breaks through what has been called "the denial of coevalness,"[2] and develops a queer epistemology by reading Oscar Wilde against Herman Melville. I want to attempt a related move by reading Shakespeare with and against and in the shadow of Aemilia Lanyer, a contemporary English writer whose isolation from Shakespeare in literary analysis is the result of gender, not nationalist, apartheid. My project is to discover whether we can escape what I see as a roadblock in Shakespeare studies, the persistence of exceptionalism, by looking hard and long at literate women—not just as writers, but as readers. What difference does it make, both to our sense of Shakespeare and to our epistemological commitments as critics, that Shakespeare was read by women?

Early in his book *Archive Fever*, Derrida poses the puzzle of a "retrospective science fiction" that he claims he does not have time to explore. Of course he does explore it, but even in outline the puzzle raises important questions for materialist critics, and for all of us in a field that has been transformed primarily by the plunge into the archive. What if Freud and his contemporaries, Derrida asks, instead of writing thousands of letters by hand, had had access to faxes, computers, cell phones and especially e-mail? Would the archive of psychoanalysis be unrecognizable to the past century? He answers: "This archival earthquake would not have limited its effects to the . . . printing and to the conservation of the history of psychoanalysis. It would have transformed this history from top to bottom and in the most initial inside of its production, in its very *events*." "No," he goes on, "The technical structure of the *archiving* archive also determines the structure of the *archivable* content even in its very coming into existence and its relation to the future."[3]

The early modern period, as a liminal point in the history of another revolution in communication technology, suggests similar questions. How does the introduction of printing determine not simply the form but also the content of the archive in which we work; how does it structure the relation of the archive to the future? Printing has already been the focus of much important work in our period, especially as a gendered and gendering technology—an area totally unexplored in Derrida's book—and there is still much to be learned and asked. But my interest here is in the possibility of a different kind of archival earthquake: would the archive be transformed retrospectively in the way Derrida imagines—"from top to bottom and in the most initial inside of its production"—by an epistemological revolution as much as by a technological one? What if Shakespeare and his contemporaries had had access not to e-mail but to feminism? Or what if we knew that Shakespeare had been read by women? Would that make "Shakespeare" different, not just in the future but in the past?

Of course we know that Shakespeare was read and his plays seen by women. The presence of women in the playhouse has been one of the important discoveries of historicist analysis. We also know, thanks to feminist investigations of the archive, that women in significant numbers in early modern England were writing and publishing their works. But I am interested in the idea of retrospective transformation because I do not think we have yet allowed our Shakespeare to be remade by the presence of women writers, and certainly not by women readers. The Shakespeare presented in the groundbreaking critical work of new historicists and, sometimes, even of feminists is a Shakespeare largely unchanged by the presence of literate women.

The above claims about the resistance of Shakespeare studies to deep transformation through the scholarship on race, sexuality, even other male playwrights may well be correct and are no doubt contentious, but for now I want to focus on how Shakespeare studies resists knowing that women in the period wrote and read. Both sides of the critical enterprise are culpable here; it would be too easy just to target the major male Shakespeare critics and show how rarely their work takes women seriously as producers of knowledge. Criticism of early women writers is itself in something of a political time warp. The field has been characterized by beautiful archival work but remains caught in what

Gayatri Spivak long ago diagnosed as the pattern of "isolationist admiration" that distorts Anglo-American feminists' approach to white women writers.[4] Even the most powerful writers on early modern women, such as Margaret Ferguson, have too often had recourse to biography as a touchstone for criticism in a way they seldom allow themselves when writing about men. Shakespeare criticism, on the other hand, while it has arguably been reshaped by other new questions arising from and brought to the archive, has yet to allow its deep landscape to be altered by the presence of women.

Think about how rarely the major works of Shakespeare criticism entertain the possibility that Shakespeare is something different because he was read by women, or how rarely Shakespearean criticism acts as if women writers mattered. A pertinent example might be Steven Mullaney's history of new historicism in *Alternative Shakespeares Two*, which polices the norms of acceptable feminism and fails even to consider the recovery of women writers.[5] To call for such a change is in one sense to call for what has often been the usual progression of feminist literary projects: first, the recovery of women's works; then, the revision of the field with these works in view. What I am suggesting here is that Shakespeare—because of his history in criticism and on the stage—has remained amazingly resistant to revision, despite the revisionary scholarship going on all around us. On an optimistic day we might argue that the study of American literature has been transformed by the knowledge that African Americans were literate. *Moby Dick* is not the same text, in the past or in its future, as Derrida would put it, because Frederick Douglass and Harriet Jacobs and Harriet Wilson were writing and reading at the same time as Melville. But I do not think we can yet say that *Hamlet* is not the same *Hamlet* because of *The Tragedy of Mariam*; or that the sonnets have now become different poems because we know they would have been read by Mary Sidney.

I focus on reading as much as writing because I think it is as readers that literate women of this period have been most dramatically misrepresented. Despite the indispensable work on women writers by such scholars as Barbara Lewalski, Elaine Beilin, Susanne Woods, Mary Beth Rose, Josephine Roberts, Margaret Ferguson, and others, I feel that women writers have been consistently underread, and underread particularly as readers. The failure of Shakespeare criticism to take women writers seriously originates in the failure of feminist criticism to do the same thing. That few of the fine essays on Aemilia Lanyer, an English writer who lived from 1569 to 1645, discuss her reading of other writers is a sign of an inhibition that hangs over feminist critics.[6] We have been on the one hand chastened by a Shakespeare establishment that consistently refuses to acknowledge feminism in its account, say, of the corporeal turn in Shakespeare studies,[7] and on the other hand mesmerized by the possibility of contact with writing women and yet unwilling to claim too much for them, perhaps because there is a special kind of derision reserved for excessiveness in women. But imagine what kind of reader a seventeenth-century woman would have to be to produce a volume of verse or drama. Imagine how that woman must have devoured the male writing she got her hands on, how men's writing must have been meat and drink but also poison to her; think of the complexity of her readings of other women writers. The specter of "vulgar feminism," I fear, has kept many of us from imagining the psychological and epistemological drama of women's reading that lies behind every piece of women's writing. Feminist critics of early modern women, still haunted as we are by the spectacle of Virginia Woolf's desire both to find and not to find Shakespeare's sister, recoil from a similar desire in our own scholarly work, with the result that it remains dangerously undertheorized.

Aemilia Lanyer's raw and deeply citational writing gives us permission—compels us, I would say—to adopt a different critical practice, and much of the rest of this essay aims to sketch out the beginning of an analysis of her reading of Shakespeare's narrative poem on rape. My argument is not just that such a reading deepens our understanding of Lanyer, but that it fundamentally changes Shakespeare, revises him retrospectively, as Derrida would have it. *Salve Deus Rex Judaeorum*, Lanyer's 1611 poem on Christ, makes a different Shakespeare available to Lanyer's readers. In thinking these differences through, a more congenial model of archival revision than Derrida's ungendered and rather depoliticized one in *Archive Fever* is offered in Walter Mignolo's 1995 book, *The Darker Side of the Renaissance*. Mignolo's study of the Amerindian writing systems that were invisible to and displaced by the alphabetic writing of the Spanish colonists is also an investigation of how to "decolonize scholarship and decenter epistemological loci of enunciation."[8] Mignolo wrestles with the significant problem of simultaneity. How do you think two cultures at once? How do you think both feminism and Marxism, both gender and sexuality? His focus is on the coevalness of cultures and the specific problem of reading the European Renaissance from the Amerindian margin, but I think it suggests a way out of exceptionalism as a practice of reading. "I insist," he writes, "first on the coexistence of languages, literacies, memories, and spaces; second, on the dominance that makes it possible for one of the coexisting elements to occupy a position of power over the others as if it were the only truth; third, on the need of the politicization of hermeneutics to deal with these questions."[9] Trying to "understand the past by speaking the present," Mignolo reminds us that the "drive toward understanding arises not only from disciplinary and rational, but also from social and emotional, imperatives." The past, he writes, cannot be rendered "in a neutral discourse."[10] His model of a politicized hermeneutics is one in which a coexistence of literacies and a competition to be the only truth are always made present. Thus even without the counternarrative to Shakespeare provided by a writer such as Lanyer, Shakespeare's works, according to Mignolo's model, need to be read as the result of a competition against other ways of knowing, other memories and literacies.

Aemilia Lanyer's poem on Christ's Passion and Crucifixion is an explicit expression of the knowledges crowded out by the discourse of Shakespeare's 1594 *Lucrece*. There is not the scope in this paper for a full reading of the relation between these two poems, but I hope to suggest by reading Lanyer what we would gain if Shakespeare's exceptionalism were unsettled. In 1611 Aemilia Lanyer published a poem entitled *Salve Deus Rex Judaeorum*, or *Hail God King of the Jews*. Lanyer's volume has received attention because it begins with a unique series of dedications exclusively to women, it includes an all-female pastoral that may be the first English country-house poem, and it rewrites Matthew's Gospel account of the Crucifixion to emphasize the role of gender, rather than religious or political difference, in the death of Christ. Its signal intervention comes in the expanded narrative Lanyer allows to Pilate's wife, which is included in the section titled "Eves Apologie." After claiming that Eve's sin in the Garden of Eden was only desire for knowledge, nothing compared to the sin *men* committed at the Crucifixion, she cries:

> Then let us have our Libertie againe,
> And challendge to yourselves no Sover'aingtie;
> You came not into the world without out paine,
> Make that a barre against your crueltie;
> Your fault being greater, why should you disdaine
> Our being your equals, free from tyranny?

> If one weak woman simply did offend,
> This sinne of yours, hath no excuse, nor end.[11]

The phrase Pilate's wife uses to define the crucifixion as a male crime is a direct quotation from Shakespeare's *Rape of Lucrece*—"no excuse, nor end." It occurs in Shakespeare as Tarquin argues with himself about whether to go through with the rape of Lucrece, the wife of his fellow soldier and friend, Collatinus:

> Had Collatinus kill'd my son or sire,
> Or lain in ambush to betray my life;
> Or were he not my dear friend, this desire
> Might have excuse to work upon his wife
> As in revenge or quittal of such strife.
> But as he is my kinsman, my dear friend,
> The shame and fault finds no excuse nor end.
>
> (ll.232–38)

"No excuse nor end": it sounds as if it might be proverbial, but I have not been able to trace the phrase as a proverb, nor is it glossed in the Variorum *Lucrece*. Even if the expression is proverbial, however, Lanyer's positioning of the words makes it clear that she is thinking of Shakespeare's poem. She places the phrase in exactly the same position Shakespeare does—at the end of a couplet that concludes a stanza—but uses it to signal that her poem reads his at the same time as it enlarges her own through reference to the Roman story. I have argued elsewhere for the intellectual ambitiousness of Lanyer's work and specifically for her critique of the association of whiteness with womanhood.[12] I want to suggest here that her reading both of the Crucifixion and of Shakespeare is at least as oppositional as her reading of whiteness. (It might be useful to know that Lanyer's poem meditates repeatedly on her own "darkness" in comparison to her patrons' supposed "whiteness," and that she was herself the daughter of an Italian Jewish father and an English Protestant mother.)

Calling attention to the moment in Shakespeare when the male perpetrator of rape hesitates because of his relationship to another *man*, Lanyer both complicates Tarquin's crime by aligning it with the Crucifixion and sexualizes Christ's death by aligning it with the rape of Lucrece. *Salve Deus* hints at the idea that the violation of Lucrece is of the same magnitude as the Crucifixion of Christ; one story the foundational narrative of republican government, the other the foundational narrative of Christianity. The Crucifixion of Christ, like the rape of Lucrece, is revealed as a *male* crime—a point Lanyer makes in the narrative itself as she stresses episodes in which men betrayed Christ and women comforted or understood him. Daringly, *Salve Deus* uses the scene of rape to uncover an eroticism at the heart of the passion narrative: the poem allows the suggesting that Christ's death, like Lucrece's, is somehow *caused* by the beauty of his body, though in his case the beauty is visible only after the Crucifixion. In one of several moments in *Salve Deus* where the masculinist rhetoric of praise, with its fetishized colors red and white, is employed to describe the crucified Christ, this blazon offers his body to both male and female gaze:

> His joynts dis-joynted, and legges hang downe,
> His alabaster breast, his bloody side . . .
> His count'nance pale, yet still continues sweet,
> His blessed blood watring his pierced feet.
>
> (ll.1161–76)[13]

Perhaps most tellingly, though, is that the line Lanyer quotes from *Lucrece*—with Tarquin hesitating because of his ties to Lucrece's husband—insists that the Crucifixion, again like the rape of Lucrece, is essentially a negotiation *between men*; as Nancy Vickers has argued about the Shakespeare poem, rape is the punishment for being praised by men, and women's silence is the inevitable result.[14] Lanyer in a sense speaks Lucrece's part, drowned out in Shakespeare by Lucrece's obsession with the pollution of her *husband* through the rape—"I will not poison thee with my attaint" (l.1072)—and then displaced by her mediation on Hecuba. Like Hamlet, Lucrece is drawn to the Trojan queen as the image of articulate female suffering; like him too she becomes a writer in the presence of the story of Troy. For the silent Hecuba painted on her wall, Lucrece ventriloquizes a lament, concentrating on the link between Paris's "heat of lust" (l.1473) and the destruction of a city:

> Why should the private pleasure of some one
> Become the public plague of many moe?
> Let sin alone committed light alone
> Upon his head that hath transgressèd so;
> Let guiltless souls be freed from guilty woe.
>   For one's offence why should so many fall,
>   To plague a private sin in general?
>
> (ll.1478–84)

The poem ends with another homosocial rhetorical contest: when Lucrece kills herself in the poem's final section, the response of her father and husband is to struggle over ownership of her body, and her story:

> Then one doth call her his, the other his,
> Yet neither may possess the claim they lay.
> The father says, "She's mine"; "O mine she is,"
> Replies her husband, "do not take away
> My sorrow's interest; let no mourner say
>   He weeps for her, for she was only mine,
>   And only must be wail'd by Collatine."
>
> (ll.1793–99)

My argument, still at a preliminary stage here, is that Lanyer was enabled by her critical reading of *Lucrece* to develop an analysis of the Crucifixion as a gendered and eroticized transaction between men. Thus while her poem answers Shakespeare's by offering a critique of its silencing of Lucrece's position, it also uses the earlier poem to formulate its own argument about the Crucifixion. Lanyer's poem, which offers women readers the tricky position of identifying with the crucified Christ, is in a sense her response to Lucrece's act of locutionary surrender. At risk of becoming a byword for infidelity, Lucrece realizes that her body will become her voice. She is persuaded not to kill herself during the rape because Tarquin fiendishly swears that if she does, he will kill a servant and arrange his body beside hers, allowing Tarquin to claim afterward that he surprised her in an act of adultery:

> Yea, the illiterate that know not how
> To cipher what is writ in learnèd books
> Will quote my loathsome trespass in my looks.
>
> (ll.810–12)

In a gesture that bears resemblance to the subaltern "speech" identified by Gayatri Spivak, Lucrece decides to kill herself after publicly identifying her rapist in order to prevent the misreading of her body after death. Spivak famously gives the story of Bhuvaneswari Bhaduri, who was unable to go through with the task of political assassination and then committed suicide only *after* her menstrual period had begun, providing a sign that she had not killed herself out of sexual shame. My point is not that Lucrece is Spivak's subaltern—the crucial difference is that as a

Roman aristocrat she *can* speak publicly and be believed—but that a seventeenth-century woman reader could find in Shakespeare's poem an invitation to replace the silence of the woman's body with her own voice.

Yet Lanyer is also an anti-Lucrece, as a second quotation of *Lucrece* in *Salve Deus* makes clear. Shakespeare's poem, is set in motion by "a descriptive occasion, by a competition between husbands each blazoning his wife,"[15] which leaves Tarquin inflamed with lust for "Lucrece the chaste" (1.7). In the next stanza we learn why: Lucrece's husband has made the mistake of boasting that his wife possesses the impossible combination of beauty and virtue:

> Haply that name of chaste unhapply set
> This bateless edge on his keen appetite,
> When Collatine unwisely did not let
> To praise the clear unmatchèd red and white
> Which triumphed in that sky of his delight.
>
> (ll.8–12)

Lanyer directly answers this opening passage at the moment her passion narrative begins. She withholds the narrative of Christ's death one final time in order to highlight the virtue of her patron with "An Invective against outward beuty unaccompanied with virtue," as the passage is titled in the margin:

> That outward Beautie which the world commends,
> Is not the subject I will write upon,
> Whose date expir'd, that tyrant Time soon ends;
> Those gawdie Colours soone are spent and gone:
> But those fair Virtues which on thee [the Countess of
> Cumberland] attends
> Are alwaies fresh, they never are but one:
>   They make thy Beautie fairer to behold,
>   Than was that Queenes for whom prowd *Troy* was sold.
> As for those matchlesse colors Red and White,
> Or perfit features in a fading face,
> Or due proportion pleasing to the sight,
> All these doe draw but dangers and disgrace.
>
> (ll.185–96)

Given her poem's interest in *Lucrece*, I am convinced that Lanyer's pointed phrase, "As for those matchlesse colors Red and White"—a rare foray into irony for her—is an answer to Shakespeare's "unmatched red and white" (1.11), the phrase that announces one of the organizing tropes of his poem. Red and white are woven in and out of the fabric of *Lucrece*, personified as beauty and virtue in the "heraldry" of Lucrece's blushing face (1.64), invoked in the metaphor of the "white fleece" (1.678) that stands in for the action of the rape itself, repeated at the moment of Lucrece's death, when "two slow rivers" of "crimson blood" flow from her breast (1.1738). By quoting—and contesting—the first appearance of the colors in *Lucrece*, Lanyer signals her oppositional reading of Shakespeare's poem and its project of displaying the woman's raped body. For the body of Lucrece, Lanyer substitutes the body of Christ, drawing both on the Christ-like image of Lucrece's death in Shakespeare and perhaps the visual tradition that linked the two.

I do not want to write out the genuine religious impulse that produces Lanyer's poem, but it might not be too much to say that she finds in the Crucifixion the only image capable of displacing the silenced, raped woman at the center of patriarchal rhetoric. Although I would insist that *Salve Deus* is a religious poem, I would suggest that it is simultaneously and just as deeply a counternarrative to *Lucrece* and to the rhetorical tradition in which it participates. Lorna Hutson has argued beautifully that Lanyer's poem is a contestation of the masculinist rhetoric of praise. I am proposing that the contest is waged directly with a contemporary male-authored poem. Shakespeare is not the only male author Lanyer quotes—the invective on beauty also contains a citation of Lyly—and my point is not that she was singling out Shakespeare for an epistemological contest. More likely, his poem was one of many—some not yet discovered in her work—that she read viscerally, brilliantly, as she made the leap from reader to writer.

Walter Mignolo writes that his hope in studying Amerindian systems of writing is to identify the spaces in between produced by colonization as a location and energy of new modes of thinking.[16] My intention, with this reading of Shakespeare, is something similar. I hope to suggest that new sources of energy arise in the interaction between men and women writers, and that this interaction creates a space for new thought, perhaps even a new epistemology. But in doing so I would insist that we remain alert to this moment not only as one of crisis for materialist criticism of Shakespeare, but also as affecting how all of our scholarship is being used in the current academy. Again, there is not scope here to do a thorough analysis of the neoliberal paradigm for the academy, but its symptoms are widely, internationally familiar: withdrawal of funds from education, increasing privatization, assessment of scholarly and pedagogical work according to marketplace values; the instrumentalization of knowledge; and most acutely, the collapse of the job market and replacement of full-time faculty lines with part-time and temporary positions. I want to suggest that the only way forward for us as Shakespeareans, and particularly as historicist critics, is to turn our powerful materialist gaze on the academy itself, and to do scholarship in light of what we discover there. The way forward in Shakespeare studies is not to blame radical criticism for the shortage of academic jobs. If anything, the opposite is true: one of the subtler motives behind the current assault on the academy is the attempt to wipe out our new knowledges. Nor is the way forward, I would argue, to call for a return to an aestheticized, timeless Shakespeare.

My sense of the direction we might take from this crossroads is to embrace the new knowledge, insisting on detailed, radical critique, and standing up for the complexity of thought available in Amerindian literacy systems and Aemilia Lanyer's vigorous readings. But we need to pursue the new spaces for thought with an understanding of the role we want cultural critique to play in the current crisis. I cannot offer an answer to how our critical practice might progress. I would, however, suggest that progress would have to include a politicized hermeneutic, as Mignolo asserts, and that it would have to see what we do in the academy as in a complicated relation to the drive to marketplace hegemony. The way forward for us as Shakespeareans, then, has to include a contestatory model of knowledges, a sense of new formations for the academy, including a conscious relation as academic laborers to other sectors of labor. This is one way of saying that if we want to resist the instrumentalization of what we do in the academy, we could begin by resisting and changing what we do with Shakespeare.

NOTES

1. Eve Kosofsky Sedgwick, *Epistemology of the Closet* (Berkeley and Los Angeles: Univ. of California Press, 1990), 48.

2. Johannes Fabian, *Time and the Other: How Anthropology Makes Its Object* (New York: Columbia Univ. Press, 1983).

3. Jacques Derrida, *Archive Fever: A Freudian Impression*, trans. Eric Prenowitz (Chicago: Univ. of Chicago Press, 1996), 16–17; original emphasis.

4. Gayatri Spivak, "Three Women's Texts and a Critique of Imperialism,"

in *"Race," Writing and Difference*, ed. Henry Louis Gates Jr. (Chicago: Univ. of Chicago Press, 1986), 262.

5. Steven Mullaney, "After the New Historicism," in *Alternative Shakespeares Two*, ed. Terence Hawkes (London: Routledge, 1996), 17–37.

6. For a notable exception, see Lorna Hutson's discussion of Lanyer in *The Usurer's Daughter: Male Friendship and Fictions of Women in Sixteenth-Century England* (London: Routledge, 1994).

7. For an example of this kind of omission, see Keir Elam, " 'In What Chapter of His Bosom?': Reading Shakespeare's Bodies," in *Alternative Shakespeares 2*, 140–63.

8. Walter Mignolo, *The Darker Side of the Renaissance: Literacy, Territoriality and Colonization* (Ann Arbor, Mich.: Univ. of Michigan Press, 1995), ix.

9. Ibid., 4.

10. Ibid., 5.

11. Aemilia Lanyer, *The Poems of Aemilia Lanyer: Salve Deus Rex Judaeorum*, ed. Susanne Woods (New York: Oxford Univ. Press, 1993), ll.825–32.

12. See my "Aemilia Lanyer and the Invention of White Womanhood," in *Maids and Mistresses, Cousins and Queens: Women's Alliances in Early Modern England*, ed. Susan Frye and Karen Robertson (Oxford: Oxford Univ. Press, 1998), 274–303.

13. The visual tradition of Lucrece representations, as Linda C. Hults has shown, had already established a connection between Lucrece and the crucified Christ: Hans Baldung made the connection in parallel woodcuts of Lucrece and Christ in 1511, and Dürer appears to have amplified the analogy in his influential 1513 oil painting, *The Suicide of Lucretia*: see Hults's essay, "Dürer's *Lucretia*: Speaking the Silence of Women," *Signs* 16, no. 2 (1991): 205–37.

14. Nancy Vickers, " 'The blazon of sweet beauty's best': Shakespeare's *Lucrece*," in *Shakespeare and the Question of Theory*, ed. Patricia Parker and Geoffrey Hartman (New York: Methuen, 1985), 95–115.

15. Ibid., 96.

16. Mignolo, *Darker Side*, xv.

III

Performance:
Texts and Productions

Material Boys: Apprenticeship and the Boy Actors' Shakespearean Roles

Richard Madelaine

THE PREDOMINANT DISCOURSES IN RECENT CRITICISM OF ENGLISH Renaissance drama—new historicism, cultural materialism, and feminism—have at least one thing in common: a tendency to underestimate the *theatrical* context of the plays in question, for all their emphasis on social context, or occasionally on performance in a more general sense. This is never so apparent as in discussions of the boy actors' presentation of female roles. New historicism teaches the salutary lesson that we can only construct the past in terms of present consciousness, but there are different ways of carrying one's cultural baggage.

Many of the recent accounts of the way in which boys appropriated gender, Renaissance audiences viewed the boys as sex objects, or patriarchy was anxious about gender roles seem to commodify the boys rather than focusing on their "laboring bodies as means of production."[1] That is not surprising, given the paucity of information about the boys' training and about the careers of individuals (especially boy actors' baptismal dates and the first performance dates of plays).[2] But we have many of the scripts the boys used (the play-texts), and it is time to approach Shakespearean boy actors in a way that recognizes the implications of their apprenticeship and its influence on the attitudes of the dramatists and adult actors to the boys and their roles. It is, after all, fairly clear that the boy actors were apprentices in terms of circumstances and training, even if, for conventional or legal reasons, they were not always called "apprentices."[3]

Michael Shapiro's book *Gender in Play* is a stride in the right direction, making good use of evidence in the play-texts, but Shapiro often accepts old assumptions under the guise of fact. Stage historians distinguish boy actors in adult companies from those in all-boy companies by asserting that the former only played women's parts, though of course they know that many of those female roles involved male disguise. Shapiro, working on the disguises and their literary sources, and deciding that the boys play their roles successively, in layers,[4] sees that as a way for them to cope, rather than envisaging the boys as tackling the disguises as male roles that will develop their versatility as actors. Despite Dympna Callaghan's claim that theatrical "economic and sexual practices molded the boys, aesthetically, if not surgically, into the shape of eunuchs,"[5] there is no evidence that master-apprentice relationships in the public theatre were *entirely* exploitative of the boys.[6] It therefore seems logical to assume that dramatists and sharers saw disguise-roles, for example, as acting opportunities for boys who wanted to become adult actors and who no longer wanted to play women's parts. In other words, though the concept of the disguised heroine may derive from literary convention, and its theatrical use may be the exploitation of the audience's anxieties about gender, the theatrical choice of story or source was probably partly made in the light of the availability of boy actors and their particular talents. If the Henslowe model was followed by the Lord Chamberlain's/King's Men,[7] then presumably the question of which boys were available was considered by the sharers at the plotting stage of a new play, before the roles were developed by the dramatist.

T. W. Baldwin, though holding a number of false assumptions, may have been right in a more general sense about Shakespeare writing parts for particular actors, and clearly the actors included the boys.[8] Experienced dramatists and actors in a star-oriented system must have recognized the likelihood of sparkle when there was a high degree of compatibility between actor and part, not to mention between actors. It is tempting to think of Shakespeare as writing, say, Cleopatra's part with a specific boy in mind,[9] just as he presumably had Burbage's style and capabilities in mind when he wrote Antony's part. Such a large and daring role as Cleopatra, with its three supporting female roles, certainly suggests that Shakespeare was confident that a virtuoso boy and three other highly competent ones would be available.[10] And, to go a step further, presumably Shakespeare thought it worthwhile to give some instruction to the unknown boy who first played the part of Cleopatra. We know nothing for certain about the Jacobean equivalent of directorial intervention, though many modern scholars think that dramatists at least attended rehearsals of their own plays in Shakespeare's time.[11] Whether boy actors in major female roles were more carefully instructed than the adult actors is another issue; it may be that their apprentice status

meant their instruction was left to their master in the public theatres; in the private ones, where they were nominally apprenticed
to the manager of the company, the dramatist may well have been
expected to take responsibility.[12] If Stephen Orgel is right in insisting that only guild members were able to take on apprentices
in the public theaters,[13] then presumably a master might encourage his apprentice to seek guidance from other sources where appropriate. In the case of a groundbreaking new role, such as
Cleopatra, what seems to be needed is a combination of the dramatist's advice on the conceptualization of the role and the master's practical help with the pyrotechnics. Perhaps, in any case, if
a boy was near "graduation," he might be treated more like an
adult actor and expect to receive instruction from the dramatist.

Another assumption that can be challenged is the supposed
need for an unbroken voice in a boy playing women's parts. Some
historians point to evidence for delayed puberty in the period.[14]
Bruce R. Smith, who seems to favor fourteen as the usual age for
boys' puberty in the period, writes of the interchangeability of
boys' and women's voices in terms of smallness and shrillness.[15]
We do know, however, that some "boy" actors went on playing
female roles until seventeen, eighteen, or even twenty-one years
of age.[16] The sticking point is probably the famous passage in
Hamlet, where Hamlet jocularly hopes the boy player's "voice,
like a piece of uncurrent gold, be not cracked within the ring"
(2.2.410–11). Callaghan reads this as meaning that a broken
voice was "the end of effective female impersonation,"[17] but of
course the boy in question is still in employment, and Hamlet is
alluding to a temporary disablement in which the breaking voice
is neither reliable nor resonant. Boys in that condition were probably given small parts, perhaps (if naturalistic considerations and
theatrical opportunity converged) old women's parts, such as
that of Queen Margaret in *Richard III*.[18]

Perhaps the challenge to the notion of unbroken voices can best
be made in the light of the limited experience we have (necessarily from outside the convention of boy actors) of modern youths
playing female parts. That experience suggests that the combination of youth and fine features allows a willing suspension of disbelief. This was true of Toby Cockerell's Princess Katherine in
the Red Company's *Henry V* in the opening season of the Third
Globe; conversely, the large-featured Christian Camargo made an
unlikely Queen Isabel, despite his good acting. The combination
(probably causally connected) of age, coarser features, and inability to identify with the role was a real problem for the men who

played the daughters in the Parsons/Harrison *King Lear* of 1991 for the Sydney Theatre Company: they looked and acted like pantomime dames, or like slimline versions of Falstaff in drag (whose gross features and facial hair are remarked on in the text).[19] On the other hand, the fine-featured Lorne Gerlach, who originally played Lady Macbeth in the Frank Productions' *Macbeth*, performed at the 1996 ANZSA conference in Sydney, was entirely convincing. This may tell us something about the selection of boy actors in Shakespeare's day; at any rate, it suggests that the successful playing of female roles by young men has less to do with unbroken voices than some have claimed. On the contrary, it is highly likely that more mature boy actors were trained to speak major female roles in a voice "ever soft, / Gentle, and low, an excellent thing in woman" (*King Lear* [Conflated Text] 5.3.271–72), for the same cultural reasons as modern actresses of major female roles such as Cleopatra ideally have a good contralto voice. Such training may well have preceded the breaking of their voices: Bartholomew the page is expected to perform his imitation of a gentlewoman in a "soft low tongue" (*Taming of the Shrew* induction.1.110).[20] The maturity of the first Cleopatra's voice is attested to by the demands of the part and by his being asked to speak the lines "I shall see / Some squeaking Cleopatra boy my greatness" (5.2.215–16), which depends entirely upon his *not* coming across as a boy squeaking them; the character is voicing her anxiety about being played as a minor role by an inexperienced boy, in a way that would reflect the Romans' belittling view of her greatness.[21] Boy actors with unbroken voices were presumably given unimportant roles: pages, precocious boys (such as Arthur in *King John*), singers,[22] and women with few lines or none. But such uses may have been incidental in the public theaters; the main reason why boys started their apprenticeship with unbroken voices was probably the perceived training period required and a sense that the optimum time for an experienced boy to play a major female role was his late teens.[23] It is likely that the extant three-year theatrical contracts were given to boys with previous acting experience, possibly in the private theatre.[24]

Obviously we have to be careful in making assumptions about "naturalistic" illusion on a nonlocalized stage, where actors and audience colluded in the use of numerous conventions. From this point of view it is worth reconsidering the roles of Princess Katherine and Lady Macbeth, since both examples raise another issue that may need to be taken into account—the relationship between self-consciousness and stylization. Katherine's part incorporates adolescent female self-consciousness about the gestures and moods of enticing womanliness. It was thus ideal for a young modern actor from outside a convention in which it is "natural" for men to play female parts. It may well have been a part Shakespeare wrote with a comparatively inexperienced boy actor in mind. Certainly at the other end of the spectrum is Cleopatra's part, which requires a middle-aged female self-consciousness and an experienced and especially talented actor. Lady Macbeth is a "masculine" female role, which would suit a boy of some experience, capable of subtlety in highlighting the "masculine" elements in a female character. Andrew Gurr may be right in thinking that, because of their rhetorical training, the actors in the Elizabethan all-boy companies used more stylized gesture than the boys in the adult companies;[25] but Shapiro surely seems wrong in suggesting that on the public stage the boy actors played in a more stylized fashion than the men did, as a result of their self-consciousness.[26] The convention made their playing women's roles seem "natural"; their audiences, and presumably the adult actors, valued "natural" impersonation, and the boys were supposedly being trained to take on male roles. But apprentices in their early years might have been given roles that allowed or encouraged self-conscious imitation of theatrical female gait and gesture. Many scholars have noted the preponderance of self-conscious roles, male and female, in plays written for the all-boy companies, many of whose actors did have the unbroken voices needed for the kind of singing that was a hallmark of the private theatres.

Boy actors did not have much status, inside the theater or outside it (where the adult players had little more).[27] Theatrical and trade apprentices were bought, sold, and rented out by men, as some women might be,[28] and similarities between the social positions of youths and women were widely recognized.[29] In the public theater, the boy actors seem to have been noticed more as their master's boys than as people, in their own right, if we are to trust surviving plots and some stage directions.[30] We have a text, unfortunately from neither Shakespeare nor the public theater,[31] which dramatizes some of the burning social issues for apprentices, both to trade and to theater.[32] In Rafe's exit from *The Knight of the Burning Pestle*, where the boy actor draws double attention to himself as an apprentice, in trade by role and in acting by profession, the earthly pleasures he regrets are those of Shrove Tuesday, when apprentices compensated for their social (and sexual) repression by subversive and violent interventions.[33]

They were not only given to attacking brothels, as in Rafe's fond reminiscence, but also taverns and, on at least one occasion, a private theater. The price of admission was probably the cause of resentment in each case.[34] Violent annual eruptions are, it seems, the means by which Rafe has managed to remain a model apprentice. Jasper, whom citizen values construct as a bad apprentice turned prodigal, is dismissed by his master and also freed from the care and control of his parents. He is thus given the opportunity to come of age by fending for himself and his beloved, showing his ripeness for marriage. His apprenticeship status had marginalized him in love (indeed, one of the reasons for the city fathers' extension of the age for terminating apprenticeships to twenty-four was the prevention of youthful marriages),[35] and it is not surprising that so many of the boy actors' roles are concerned with such issues. Ironically, Jasper's position as discharged apprentice becomes an apprentice's dream come true: self-motivation and initiative of the Shrove Tuesday sort, together with marriage to the master's daughter. Theater apprentices were not likely to do so well: Richard Robinson, who had probably been an apprentice of Richard Burbage's, married Burbage's widow in 1619, by which time he was a sharer in the theatrical company; this kind of marriage is usually regarded as a "decent" and loyal way of providing for the master's widow, but it may well have elements of apprentice dreaming in it too. Beaumont's two apprentices represent contrasting views of apprenticeship in the larger theatrical context: Jasper enacts a parodic role typical of the private theater, whilst Rafe's "huffing" part is a role from the downmarket public theaters, the Red Bull and the Fortune, which were favorite haunts of trade apprentices.[36] *The Knight of the Burning Pestle* incidentally supports the view that theatrical apprentices were potential sex objects for female, as much as for male, audience members: the master's wife Nell's mainly motherly interest in the pretty boys is complicated by her unintentional bawdry and her vivid recollection of the freak show "little child that was so fair grown about the members" (3.278–79).

Developed male parts were what older boys in the private theater could expect but public theater boys had mainly to aspire to, along with adult status.[37] Meanwhile, their apprenticeship status must have given them some fellow feeling for the female characters they were usually required to play and who, like them, were marginalized by patriarchal values, power, and sense of ownership. As far as the boys' presentation of female parts is concerned, there is some textual basis for thinking they tried to create the illusion that they had them. If costume was a sign of gender in the period, it was also a means of enhancing the illusion of a transformed body.[38] We know the boy who played Cleopatra wore a bodice and farthingale from the words "Cut my lace, Charmian" (1.3.71), but he probably also wore his bodice low-cut, and the lacing of his bodice might have helped produce the theatrical illusion of a bosom. The most dramatic part of the stage picture of Cleopatra's death, her putting an asp to her breast, is a detail Shakespeare did not find in Plutarch,[39] and, for all the emblematic implications of the "suckling," Shakespeare's initial interest in Cleopatra's breast may well have been fired by the fashion for décolletage.[40] It may be that Cordelia's references to her false sisters' "professèd bosoms" (1.1.269) and Lear's to his expectation of Cordelia's "kind nursery" (1.1.122) glance at similar dresses in the opening scene of *King Lear*.

In a culture accustomed to reading both costume and gesture emblematically, it would be surprising if boy actors were not trained, in the public theater as much as in the private theater, to make the most of nonverbal language; and of course we have eyewitness evidence for it in Henry Jackson's well-known description of the boy who played Desdemona in 1610.[41] Before playing a deeply affecting corpse, the boy actor presumably made Desdemona's body attractive in a different sense, but by equally nonverbal means, to both Othello and the audience. The Puritan I. H. may have been specifically thinking of boy actors when he denounced players "who by their wantonizing stage-gestures can ingle and seduce men to heave up their hearts and affections . . . by how much more exact these are in their venerean action, by so much more highly are they seated in the monster-headed multitude's estimation."[42] The verb "ingle" means "coax," but the noun means "catamite," an interesting and possibly cross-dressed connection. Stubbes had already suggested that cross-dressing can actually transform gender,[43] but I. H. seems conscious of the nature of theatrical illusion, even if he sees it as the devil's work. It is more helpful to emphasize the connection between illusion, eroticism, and subversion than to try to specify the kind of eroticism it is, for two reasons. First, the erotic trigger depends on individual eye and brain,[44] and second, in performance an actor's status is always, in a sense, suspended, and for the boys this meant partial liberation from being both gender-specific adolescents and lowly apprentices. But the suspension, for actors and audience, occurs only in one sense, and the relationship between the boys and their roles is obviously a complex one. The role of a sexually, socially, and culturally subversive woman is the kind that must have most appealed to and most challenged an experienced boy actor, familiar, as an apprentice and as a young man, with the tension between established codes of behavior and an impetus in the marginalized to subvert. It might have provided the kind of psychological safety valve that Rafe could only use once a year.

Boy actors seem to have done a little doubling, usually minor female parts with minor male parts such as pages, and these doubled parts were almost certainly given to the less-experienced boys.[45] A probable exception is the part of the Doctor in *The Duchess of Malfi*, doubled with Cariola by Robert Pallant,[46] though we do not know at what age. It is, of course, possible that he played the Doctor as a younger boy: the Doctor's main speech may have been cut in performance, the role has burlesque elements, and Ferdinand draws attention to the boy actor's long beard and eyebrows.[47] The more challenging parts were doubtless taken by boys of experience, which might have been quite considerable. Theatrical apprenticeships seem to have varied in length from three to twelve years,[48] and the actors of major boys' roles were certainly youths rather than boys in the modern sense, who may well have had some ten years' acting experience.[49]

In the earlier part of Shakespeare's career, the major parts for boys, such as Rosalind in *As You Like It*, are long and depend on male disguise for subversive freedom, variety, and pathos (of course, issues of genre are involved here too). Shakespeare is interested in contrasting pairs of female roles, and in *Much Ado* he exchanges disguise for mistaken identity and uses theatrical dynamics to compensate for the risks posed by the likely casting: the good girl is nominal and can be played by any inexperienced boy who can do feminine silence and a swoon, and the experienced boy rises to the challenge of Beatrice's "masculine" wit, which engages the audience. This is not entirely satisfactory, and the major boys' role, Cleopatra, is given franker dominance over the role of the good girl, Octavia. Cleopatra's essence is the playing of female "variety," but it is also partly a "masculine" role on the princely model provided by Elizabeth I, who had the "heart and stomach of a king," and the violent temper too. Webster provided comparable models in Vittoria and the Duchess of Malfi, and this complex kind of female role is doubtless the product of many factors: cultural change, genre, writing skills, but also faith in the ability of experienced boys. These roles are more openly transgressive, but also more clearly transitional in terms of the boys' ripeness for "graduation."[50] For Shakespeare, though, the disguised heroine remains a possibility. Imogen is an interesting example, with a feminized male disguise that Shapiro has remarked on.[51] The roles for experienced boys remain marked by length, though length is not necessarily a function of the number of lines spoken. It may involve an intensity derived from the silence and other sore trials that patriarchy imposes on women, and that the dramatists impose on boy actors, challenging their nonverbal skills.

Shakespeare also seems to capitalize on the competitiveness between apprentice roles and adult roles. An early play such as *The Taming of the Shrew* seems to provide a model in Katherine for the eventual subjugation of the subversive female/apprentice, but this process is ironized by the (admittedly less dynamic) countermovement in which Bianca "develops" in the opposite direction. It is tempting to think that each pair was played by the master and his apprentice.[52] Again, the late play *Antony and Cleopatra* provides a more emphatic model: Juliet Dusinberre, writing about the competitiveness built into the protagonists' roles, sees the boy actor as "playing the part of an Empress, possibly to his own master, Burbage himself, whom he is allowed, in theatrical terms, to supersede."[53] It is a pleasurable speculation, but Richard Robinson, at any rate, does not seem to have been a member of the company at that stage.[54] Of course the necessary kind of chemistry, which has been elusive in the entire stage history of the play, may have been more likely with someone else's apprentice.

Some major roles for boys may have served as, even been conceived of as, "apprentice-pieces" for boys at the end of their apprenticeship and about to "graduate."[55] The marks of such a test piece would have been virtuosity and an emphasis on boundary crossing: at the end of *The Knight of the Burning Pestle* both apprentices are freed from their masters, one by death and the other by marriage. There are potential test pieces in Shakespeare, though none is as directly about the transformation of apprentices as Beaumont's roles. An obvious example involving male disguise is the role of Portia, who makes such a success of doing what a man has to do as Balthazar, the young doctor of laws who preserves Antonio's flesh, and also delivers one of Shakespeare's most famous set speeches. At the end of the play, the boy actor has to revert to a female role, but, as recent commentators on the giving and returning of the rings have pointed out, the post-Balthazar Portia challenges the subjugation of women in the world of the play.[56] The best all-female example of the potential Shakespearean test piece is the role of Cleopatra, unequalled in the repertory of the day: at the end of the play, she has a whole act to herself, to test Caesar's intentions, to become "marble-constant" (5.2.236), and to look for another life in Elysium.

How, then, might an awareness of the boy actors' apprenticeship affect an approach to the issues of gender and self-consciousness? It further complicates the relationship between actor, role, and audience, since Shakespeare's audiences must have shared, to some degree, the actors' awareness of the boys' apprenticeship in role playing. Such an awareness might encourage readers to speak less readily about gender blurring than about consciousness of role playing, and to perceive different dynamics between player, persona, and the male disguise adopted by female characters. A boy actor playing a female character in male disguise has a different motivation for disguising than the character, even if both wish to play, temporarily, a more privileged role in a patriarchal world.

NOTES

1. An allusion to Jean E. Howard's keynote address, "Material Culture and Historical Materialism" delivered at *Material Shakespeare*, conference of the Australian and New Zealand Shakespeare Association, Brisbane, July 11–15, 1998.

2. Cf. T. J. King, *Casting Shakespeare's Plays: London Actors and Their Roles, 1590–1642* (Cambridge: Cambridge Univ. Press, 1992), 19: John Honyman (baptized 1613) played an adult role possibly at seventeen and definitely at eighteen.

3. Cf. Stephen Orgel, *Impersonations: The Performance of Gender in Shakespeare's England* (Cambridge: Cambridge Univ. Press, 1996), 65–67. In *The Shakespearian Playing Companies* (Oxford: Clarendon, 1996), Andrew Gurr writes that a boy actor's bond was "not the kind of regulated seven-year contract that the guild companies operated, though it did have a rough parallel in that a successful boy player, like an apprentice turning journeyman, might expect eventually to graduate into the profession as an adult player" (100). It is worth noting that Augustine Phillips, who was apparently not a guild member, refers to Samuel Gilbourne and James Sands as his "Late Aprentice" and "aprentice" respectively in his will of 1605 and that William Hovell also uses the term in his will of 1615: see *Playhouse Wills, 1558–1642*, ed. E. A. J. Honigmann and Susan Brock, Revels Plays Companion Library (Manchester: Manchester Univ. Press, 1993), 3, 73, 100.

4. Michael Shapiro, *Gender in Play on the Shakespearean Stage: Boy Heroines and Female Pages* (Ann Arbor, Mich.: Univ. of Michigan Press, 1994), 51.

5. Dympna Callaghan, *Shakespeare without Women: Representing Gender and Race on the Renaissance Stage* (London and New York: Routledge, 2000),

67; Callaghan's claim that theatrical apprentices were more visibly susceptible to exploitation than boys in other trades is based on the malpractice of press-ganging boys for one of the all-boy companies, and the well-known Puritan intimations of sexual impropriety.

6. In *The Profession of Player in Shakespeare's Time, 1590–1642* (Princeton: Princeton Univ. Press, 1984), G. E. Bentley emphasizes the familial side of such relationships (129, 133).

7. Cf. King, *Casting Shakespeare's Plays*, 6.

8. In T. W. Baldwin, *The Organization and Personnel of the Shakespearean Company* (Princeton: Princeton Univ. Press, 1927): cf. Bentley, *Profession of Player*, 113–46.

9. It has been suggested that major female roles such as Cleopatra were played by adult rather than apprentice actors. Carol C. Rutter extrapolates this from one costume payment of doubtful significance: see *Documents of the Rose Playhouse*, ed. Carol C. Rutter, Revels Plays Companion Library (Manchester: Manchester Univ. Press, 1984), 124–25. In *Renaissance Drama in Action: An Introduction to Aspects of Theatre Practice and Performance* (London and New York: Routledge, 1998), Martin White invokes the precedent of the Tudor interludes and considers it "unclear" whether "mature males" played leading female roles on Shakespeare's stage (83). Bruce R. Smith, in *The Acoustic World of Early Modern England: Attending to the O-Factor* (Chicago and London: Univ. of Chicago Press, 1999), believing that Robert Pallant doubled the Duchess of Malfi and Cariola as an adult actor, goes on to imagine a vocal contrast between the female parts in which the servant has the bass line and suggests that an adult actor played Maria in *Twelfth Night* (232). The problem with this speculation is that, even when the play was revived, Pallant was still in his teens.

10. King calculates an average of four boys per play in principal female roles, but he defines such roles as consisting of ten or more lines (*Casting Shakespeare's Plays*, 1). On boy actors' roles in *Antony and Cleopatra*, see my "Cleopatra and the Apprentice Hierarchy," *QWERTY* 10 (2000): 33–38.

11. Some Restoration actors liked to trace the provenance of their interpretation back to Shakespeare; see John Downes on Betterton in *Roscius Anglicanus*, ed. Montague Summers (London: Fortune Press, 1928), 24. In 1613 Johannes Rhenanus wrote that English actors "are daily instructed, as it were in a school, so that even the most eminent actors have to allow themselves to be taught their places by the dramatists": cited by David Klein, "Did Shakespeare Produce His Own Plays?" *Modern Language Review* 57 (1962): 556; cf. Meredith Anne Skura, *Shakespeare the Actor and the Purposes of Playing* (Chicago and London: Univ. of Chicago Press, 1993), 48. However, Peter Thomson, in *Shakespeare's Theatre* (London: Routledge and Kegan Paul, 1983), notes that, in trying to sidestep the trouble over *Byron*, Chapman claimed, "I see not mine own plays" (81). In *Rehearsal from Shakespeare to Sheridan* (Oxford: Oxford Univ. Press, 2000), Tiffany Stern suspects that Rhenanus is writing about academic productions and is cautious about dramatists' involvement in rehearsals in the public theatre (40).

12. This point is made by Alexander Leggatt in his essay "The Companies and Actors," in J. Leeds Barroll et al., *The Revels History of Drama in English* (London: Methuen, 1975), 3:113; cf. Gurr, *Shakespearian Playing Companies*, 349.

13. Orgel, *Impersonations*, 65. The theaters were, however, outside normal

city jurisdiction, and the boys may have been called "servants" simply to avoid demarcation problems; Gurr suggests that Augustine Phillips was an exception to the guild rule (100).

14. Shapiro also seems to accept this notion (*Gender in Play,* 34). But the early age (nine or ten) at which many boys were castrated for continental church choirs throws doubt on the supposition of delayed puberty: A. Heriot's assumption that "the later a child was castrated, the lower its voice would be" rests on the anticipated onset of puberty; see *The Castrati in Opera* (London: Secker and Warburg, 1956), 44.

15. Smith, *Acoustic World,* 226. As Smith also notes, fourteen is the age nominated by the English translator of *The Problemes of Aristotle* (227). He continues that the pitch of boys of fourteen is similar to that of women, but that the sound is "purer," more carrying and penetrating, and that it would have made a striking aural contrast with the men's voices in both pitch and timbre, the "female" sounds being more isolated in the theater (pp. 228–29).

16. Cf. Andrew Gurr, *The Shakespearean Stage, 1574–1642,* 2d ed. (Cambridge: Cambridge Univ. Press, 1980), 93.

17. Callaghan, *Shakespeare without Women,* 71. She envisages an actor in "late adolescence or early manhood" in a "taxing role" such as Desdemona's and curiously imagines a vocal crisis over the singing of the willow song, either in falsetto or in unbroken voice. I suspect that the cracked voice to which Hamlet alludes is the nearest thing to a vocal crisis on Shakespeare's stage, and that the actors of major female roles had left such anxieties behind them.

18. On the casting of boys in this play, see my " 'Who intercepts me in my expedition?': The Structural Function of the Boy Actors' Roles in *Richard III,*" *QWERTY* 9 (1999): 25–31. I would argue that the confrontational power of the female characters in the play outweighs their vocal strength and that in *The Acoustic World of Early Modern England,* Smith undervalues the other theatrical elements in asserting that "the king takes firm command of the aural field" (23).

19. Cf. *The Merry Wives of Windsor,* where Evans's spying "a great peard" (4.2.168) under the muffler of the "fat woman of Brentford" (4.2.61) convinces him that she is a witch, as Ford claims.

20. Octavia (probably an intermediate part) is described as "low-voiced," as opposed to "shrill-tongued," in *Antony and Cleopatra* (3.3.12–13).

21. I argue this position at length in "Cleopatra and the Apprentice Hierarchy." The passage tests critical positions nicely: Callaghan regards it as marking "a crisis in the enactment of masculinity itself" (*Shakespeare without Women,* 53), whilst Smith, assuming that Cleopatra is a treble part, regards the play as an exception to the rule about the predominance of the bass line in adult plays (*Acoustic World,* 236). Martin White says of the passage, "If Cleopatra was played by a teenager this was a daring moment of theatrical self-reflexivity, whereas if the lines were spoken by an older actor it would have sustained the appropriateness of the *character's* image" (*Renaissance Drama in Action,* 83).

22. Whilst he does not in fact sing, the eunuch Mardian was possibly such a part, though documentary evidence indicates that at least one eunuch was played by an adult player (King, *Casting Shakespeare's Plays,* 65,); the Mardian role does have affinities, in its self-conscious badinage about sexual desire and performance, with the satirical roles apparently given to younger boys in the satirical plays written at the turn of the century for all-boy companies by dramatists such as John Marston.

23. The trade apprentice model seems not to have been appropriate to theatrical circumstances; it was a seven-year period originally terminating at twenty-one, but changed to twenty-four in London by the late 1550s; see Margaret Gay Davies, *The Enforcement of English Apprenticeship: A Study in Applied Mercantilism, 1563–1642* (Cambridge: Harvard Univ. Press, 1956), 2.

24. Former private theater boys may have been regarded as having gained specific technical advantages, as well as acting experience, from their earlier training as choir boys, in terms of vocal agility; as ex-singing students, they may have been more likely to possess a natural vibrato, which could be put to "expressive" use in speech; see John Potter, *Vocal Authority: Singing Style and Ideology* (Cambridge: Cambridge Univ. Press, 1998), 49, 58.

25. Gurr, *Shakespearean Stage*, 94–96.

26. Shapiro, *Gender in Play*, 37.

27. See Skura, *Shakespeare the Actor*, 37, 46.

28. Cf. Herbert Berry, "The Player's Apprentice," *Essays in Theatre* 1 (1983): 73–80 and Skura, *Shakespeare the Actor*, 43.

29. See Sue-Ellen Case, *Feminism and Theatre* (London: Methuen, 1988), 22; cf. Shapiro, *Gender in Play*, 41 and Orgel, *Impersonations*, 60–61, 70.

30. Cf. Bentley, *Profession of Player*, 124. On the other hand, in *An Apology for Actors* (London, 1612), Thomas Heywood asks of the audience, "who cannot distinguish them by their names, assuredly?" (sig. C3v).

31. It looks fairly certain that *The Knight of the Burning Pestle* was conceived for performance at the private theater, and first performed at the Blackfriars in 1607 by the Children of the Queen's Revels.

32. For a discussion of this issue, see my "Apprentice Interventions: Boy Actors, the Burning Pestle and the Privy Mark of Irony," *QWERTY* 5 (1995): 73–77.

33. Francis Beaumont, *The Knight of the Burning Pestle*, ed. Sheldon P. Zitner, Revels Plays (Manchester: Manchester Univ. Press, 1984), 5. 333–41.

34. See Ann Jennalie Cook, *The Privileged Playgoers of Shakespeare's London, 1576–1642* (Princeton: Princeton Univ. Press, 1981), 253.

35. Cf. Davies, *Enforcement of English Apprenticeship*, 2–3.

36. In *Shakespearian Playing Companies*, Gurr notes a history of clashes between trade apprentices and the Inns of Court students who frequented the private playhouses (325).

37. Sebastian in *Twelfth Night* may have been an intermediate role for a "boy," if, as Smith suggests, Sebastian is also Viola's aural twin (232). The age of both actors remains open to question, however, since Viola/Cesario is described as neither boy nor man, and any equation of this state with an unbroken voice may be dubious.

38. Cf. Laura Levine, *Men in Women's Clothing: Anti-theatricality and Effeminization, 1579–1642* (Cambridge: Cambridge Univ. Press, 1994), 4; also Orgel, *Impersonations*, 104.

39. He probably got it from Thomas Nashe or from contemporary paintings of Cleopatra: see G. Watson, "The Death of Cleopatra," *Notes and Queries*, n.s., 25 (1978): 409–14.

40. See C. W. and P. Cunnington, *Handbook of English Costume in the Seventeenth Century* (London: Faber, 1972), 82.

41. Writing about the King's Men's performance of *Othello* in Oxford, he singles out for praise the boy actor playing Desdemona, who "pleaded her case very effectively throughout, yet moved (us) more after she was dead, when, lying on

her bed, she entreated the pity of the spectators by her very countenance";
many commentators have noted the feminine forms in Jackson's original Latin.
The excerpts are in the Fulman Papers, in the Library of Corpus Christi College
(10.83v–84r), and are translated in *The Riverside Shakespeare*, ed. G. Blakemore Evans (Boston: Houghton Mifflin, 1974), 1852.

42. I. H., *This World's Folly* (London, 1615); quoted in David Wiles, *Shakespeare's Clown* (Cambridge: Cambridge Univ. Press, 1987), 50.

43. Philip Stubbes, *The Anatomie of Abuses* (London, 1583), sig. F5v; cf. Levine, *Men in Women's Clothing*, 3–4.

44. White suggests a more socially conscious context for the response of audience members to the boy actors: "different groupings in an audience would have
focused on different readings of single actions or recognised the particular significance of those actions for sections of the audience other than themselves"
(*Renaissance Drama in Action*, 86).

45. See King, *Casting Shakespeare's Plays*, 15.

46. This is according to the cast list of the 1623 quarto; John Russell Brown
thinks it unlikely that Pallant played the Doctor in the first performance of the
play, when he would only have been nine. In his introduction to *The Duchess of
Malfi*, ed. John Russell Brown, Revels Plays (London: Methuen, 1964), Brown
suggests that Pallant first doubled the roles in a revival, when he was sixteen or
seventeen (xxi).

47. "Let me have his beard sawed off, and his eyebrows filed more civil"
(*Duchess of Malfi*, 5.2.59–60).

48. See Bentley, *Profession of Player*, 120.

49. They are called "youths" by Thomas Heywood in *An Apology for Actors*,
sig. C3v; in *Twelfth Night*, Malvolio calls Viola, in disguise as Cesario, "not yet
old enough for a man, nor young enough for a boy" (1.5.139–40).

50. The all-boy plays have corresponding virtuoso, if rather less complex,
roles for experienced boys too, such as Franceschina in John Marston's *The
Dutch Courtesan*.

51. See Shapiro, *Gender in Play*, 173.

52. Such a pairing would both capitalize on and complicate the usual stage
contrast between adult and apprentice roles; White comments, "The 'difference' of the boys and youths who played female roles in the adult companies
could be accentuated not only by costume but by juxtaposing them with the
physical and vocal presence of adult male actors" (*Renaissance Drama in Action*, 80).

53. In Juliet Dusinberre, "Squeaking Cleopatras: Gender and Performance
in *Antony and Cleopatra*," in *Shakespeare, Theory, and Performance*, ed. James
C. Bulman (London and New York: Routledge, 1996), 55.

54. See Roslyn L. Knutson, *The Repertory of Shakespeare's Company, 1594–
1613* (Fayetteville, Ark.: Univ. of Arkansas Press, 1991), 180.

55. "Apprentice-piece" is a term from craft apprenticeships and refers to an
article made to demonstrate mastery of the trade skills; perhaps it has metaphorical application to theatrical practice.

56. See, for example, Orgel, *Impersonations*, 76.

"Betwixt" and "between": Variant Readings in the Folio and First Quarto Versions of *Richard III* and W. W. Greg's Concept of Memorial Reconstruction

Adrian Kiernander

In THE NINETEENTH AND THE EARLY TWENTIETH CENTURIES, SCHOL-arly opinion was divided over the relative merits of the folio and first quarto texts of *Richard III*, and the consensus swung in both directions.[1] But the publication in 1936 of David Lyall Patrick's *The Textual History of Richard III* moved the scholarly pendulum in the direction of the folio as the better text, indeed the only authoritative one.[2] The result was a consensus, which prevailed until recently,[3] that the first quarto text is inferior and indeed defective, specifically that it is an unreliable memorial reconstruction of a missing "prompt book" by the actors of the Chamberlain's Men. Antony Hammond's influential Arden edition perpetuates the theory of the memorial reconstruction of the first quarto, though with some hesitations,[4] and it has been enshrined in Stanley Wells and Gary Taylor's *Textual Companion*: "At present, Patrick's hypothesis holds the field, and has held it, virtually uncontested, for half a century."[5] There is a considerable irony here because the most memorable twist in the narrative attributed to Patrick—the detective-fiction "case of the missing prompt book"—is one which Patrick himself explicitly rejected:

> It is unnecessary to assume that the original copy was lost, stolen, missing, or left behind in order to believe that the company caused a new copy to be made, and set down in this new copy the lines and words that they were speaking upon the stage when they presented the play. Where the play had divergence in many respects from the original text there would be a definite advantage in having an accurate, up-to-date prompt copy. This copy may have been made in longhand during rehearsals, possibly, as we have said, at the time when

the company was preparing to take the play on tour with a reduced cast. It would be simple enough to have a scrivener on hand to take down the changes as they were being worked out and so produce a new prompt copy. Or the printed quarto might become the new prompt copy. There are other possibilities, of course. Players' parts modified by the actors may have been used to some extent. The prompter unquestionably had a good deal to do with the making of the quarto text.[6]

The idea of the missing prompt book was attached to Patrick's research in what looks like a brazen attempt at claim-staking by W. W. Greg in his 1938 review of Patrick's book.[7] Here Greg typically reacted against the threat of a junior academic from overseas encroaching too far into his own territory.[8] Greg's review begins, "Dr. Patrick, who is assistant professor of English in the University of Arizona," and then continues, "No doubt I am prejudiced in Dr. Patrick's favour, since his conclusions are very much what I had arrived at myself." In the course of the review, Greg sides with Patrick on the question of the inferior status of the first quarto, making assertions with a vehemence in inverse proportion to the substance of his evidence: "To suppose that Shakespeare, or for that matter any competent writer, could have written the quarto text as it stands, seems to me out of the question; given the quarto text, to suppose that the folio was produced by a process of revision, mere fatuity." But Greg demolishes those conclusions of Patrick's book that diverge from his own views, labeling his major suggestion as "fantastic," and he proceeds to build on the rubble his own edifice, the idea of memorial reconstruction of the lost book. Greg went on to expand on this theory in his subsequent *The Editorial Problem in Shakespeare*:

the company [that is, the Chamberlain's Men] in general could perfectly well have produced from memory the quarto text of *Richard III*; and like Patrick I am driven to conclude that this is actually what happened. An occasion is provided by the restraint of London acting in the summer of 1597, which sent the Chamberlain's men, with others, into the country. They were in Kent in August, at Bristol in September. Their numbers were presumably reduced and their repertory limited. We may suppose that when they wished to act *Richard III* they found that the prompt book had remained in London. It would have been some trouble to fetch it, and it would anyhow have needed altering to fit their smaller cast; so instead they reconstructed it by a feat of communal memory, adapting it at the same time to altered circumstances. The absence of some of the minor actors who had taken part in the performance in London was made up for by the

presence of the book-keeper, who had a general knowledge of the dialogue and could regulate the succession of the scenes. He would be
more likely than the actors themselves to conflate their parts. On
their return to London some time in the autumn they would have no
further use for the improvised prompt-book: it may have gone astray,
or it may have been deliberately sold for publication, perhaps with
the idea of forestalling piracy, a fate that overtook *Romeo and Juliet*
the same year. In any case the play was duly entered in the Stationers' Register on 20 October.[9]

Despite its complexity, this surmise has a seductive attraction, offering a tantalizingly detailed (though I will argue fanciful)
glimpse into the working world of the Chamberlain's Men. Yet it
depends on several dubious premises, including a low opinion of
the abilities of the actors. Patrick and Greg in fact share this part
of the argument; Patrick dismisses the first quarto as an "actors'
version" and talks at one point about "the changes which an
actor invariably makes in uttering his lines on the stage."[10]
Greg's theory also ignores the possibility that Shakespeare, as a
member of the Chamberlain's Men, was on the tour and would
therefore have been one of the actors who was responsible for the
reconstruction, undermining the idea that the first quarto is an
unreliable text.[11]

Furthermore Greg does not make it clear what would be the
use of such a text to the actors on their tour. It would not be the
legally required "allowed book," not having been submitted for
censorship. A full reconstruction of the entire play, including all
of Richard's long speeches for example, would be unnecessary if
they merely wanted to give a few performances of the play on
tour, especially if, as Andrew Gurr has suggested, there was no
prompting in the Elizabethan theater and that what have become
known as "prompt books" were really designed for backstage
management of the entrances of the actors.[12] Indeed, because of
the misleading and anachronistic assumptions associated with
the idea of the prompt book, many scholars have recently re-
verted to the term "play book."

Throughout both Patrick and Greg there is repeated acknowledgment that their conclusions are tenuous, and they constantly
reiterate that the argument depends entirely on there being no
counterevidence and no more plausible explanation for the facts.
However, in the subsequent sixty years there have been some
considerable assaults on aspects of their evidence, notably from
Kristian Smidt, E. A. J. Honigmann, and more lately Gary Tay-

lor, Laurie E. Maguire, and John Jowett.[13] Even Hammond, who supports the theory, provides evidence (drawn from MacD. P. Jackson's research) that some of the clearest memorial features of the first quarto could be attributable to Simmes's Compositor A, who probably set sheets A-G, rather than the actors;[14] and Steven Urkowitz has demonstrated serious flaws in Patrick's evidence and argument in a witty, sophisticated essay.[15]

After the arguments of Honigmann and Urkowitz, the Patrick-Greg explanation stands on shaky ground, to say the very least. There have been compelling counterarguments and more plausible explanations of most of the facts that supported the idea of memorial reconstruction.[16] More recently, Laurie E. Maguire has elegantly pointed out the flaws in much of the argument on which the general theory of memorial reconstruction was originally based, and her conclusion with regard to *Richard III* is that it is not a memorial reconstruction.

With so much of the argument for memorial reconstruction demolished, the main feature of the text of the first quarto that remains to be explained, if the theory is to be laid to rest, is the presence of many strangely pointless or indifferent variations between the two versions, variations between words such as, for example, "slew" and "kill'd," "King" and "Sovereign," "betwixt" and "between." These variations have been consistently attributed by Patrick, Greg, and Davison to the supposedly faulty memories of actors who, according to this argument, changed the words written by Shakespeare, as recorded in the folio, to the apparently inferior words found in the first quarto, and they have thus been used as evidence for memorial reconstruction. There is the real danger of a circular argument here: the first quarto must be a memorial script because its variant readings are inferior, and its variant readings must be inferior because it is a memorial script. Nevertheless, the variants are an unusual feature of this play, and they need to be accounted for if explanation of memorial reconstruction of the text is discarded. What I plan to do here is to outline three pieces of evidence that might contribute to alternative explanations. This is not an attempt to prove what happened but to respond to Patrick's assertion that "the case for the memorial transmission of the quarto text is offered as proved by reason of the quantity and completeness of the evidence and the exclusion of other hypotheses."[17]

I would like to begin by drawing attention to a feature of printing that was made explicit by Fredson Bowers: "The printing of a quarto may be taken as implying the destruction of its manuscript." Honigmann comments: "The owner of a private transcript—or for that matter, of foul papers or of an authorial fair copy—would be unwilling to lend it to a printer because the printer would mark it, smudge it, and return it (if at all) very much the worse for wear."[18] Peter W. M. Blayney concurs:

> After the first edition was printed, the publisher would usually keep that part of the manuscript on which the authority to publish and the license to print were recorded. What happened to the rest of it might depend on how extensively the printer's workmen had marked or mishandled it—but the person from whom it had been bought would not usually have expected it back. . . . So if a play still in repertory was offered to a publisher by the players, or by the playwright himself with their consent, the manuscript supplied would not usually have been "the allowed book" then being used for performance.[19]

If the suggestion is taken seriously that any manuscript that was used to set a printed edition was destroyed, then we have to suppose that a special copy of the play, not previously used for any other purpose, was prepared for the printer. This would be in addition and subsequent to any working copies for the bookkeeper and the actors, and any other kind of script or cue sheet for the musicians and other playhouse uses. Traditional narratives about the printing of these plays seem to assume that the compositors worked directly from manuscripts that had previously been used for other theatrical purposes, with little or no alteration specifically for the printing process. This seems to be the assumption underlying Janis Lull's recent suggestion that "the missing manuscript from which F was set may have been a 'fair copy' or cleaned up draft of Shakespeare's original, *perhaps made for theatrical use.*"[20] The use of such a manuscript by the compositors implies that the theater company would have no further need for it. In the case of a popular play still in the repertoire, this seems unlikely, and it is more probable that a special one-off transcript was made expressly for the purposes of publication. Such a specially prepared version might easily have included some changes initiated by the actors in performance, even if it were being transcribed by the author.

In any case, we now have to posit a more casual, rather scruffier system of script management than Greg's neat, linear, and binary formulation of authorial foul papers and theatrical prompt copy, which has been called seriously into question by Paul Werstine.[21] Barbara A. Mowat has pointed out "the possibility that there may have been a large flow of manuscript copies of Shakespeare's plays, copies marked by the idiosyncrasies of manuscript transmission, idiosyncrasies that would inevitably have made their way into the printed copies."[22] As Jowett makes clear, the situation is "at a far remove from the New Bibliographical definition of ideal copy as '*a fair copy, made by the author himself*,' apprehended at the moment before it passes into the hands of the theatre personnel."[23]

This view provides a rather different understanding of early modern play scripts, as having their existence in various, perhaps ad hoc, versions simultaneously, in both written form and in the memories of actors, the variants arising partly from the need to cope with external contingencies such as, in the case of *Richard III*, a transfer from the Theatre to the Globe, and the changing availability of actors. It also facilitates the idea of texts as commodities to be transformed for trading in differing markets and the possibility that the text deemed suitable for acting and hearing might have been rather different from that suitable for printing and reading. These conditions might well result in variants between the published versions that owe nothing to memorial reconstruction and could account for many if not all the differences between the first quarto and the folio.

Let me now consider more closely the question of synonymous variants themselves. Many of them are almost completely indifferent, although reasonably convincing attempts have been made to justify them as the kind of minute editorial revision typically taken by an author in reworking old material.[24] If Shakespeare were preparing a special draft of the play specifically for the publisher Andrew Wise in about October 1597, it is possible that the alterations are his deliberate revisions of one of the available manuscript versions, together with those blemishes, irregularities, and infelicities that have come through as the result of normal printers' errors, haste, and the compositors' difficulties with Shakespeare's handwriting, which Honigmann has claimed was less than easily legible.[25]

But there is another possible explanation involving the use of Elizabethan shorthand.[26] This possibility was advanced by Alexander Schmidt in 1879 in relation to the text of *King Lear*, and Adele Davidson has recently revived the theory that the text of *King Lear* shows traces of stenography.[27] There was one form of Elizabethan shorthand in use at the time that *Richard III* was published that was based not upon sounds but on meanings. Dr. Timothy Bright's 1588 Characterie was a shorthand system that consisted of a master list of over five hundred key words represented by symbols.[28] Where a word not included in Bright's master list was required, the symbol for a synonym from the list would be used, with a superscript mark representing the initial letter of the actual word placed to the left. For example, there is a symbol for the word "forsake" but not for "abandon." The word "abandon" has to be represented by the symbol for "forsake," but with a small (and easily overlooked) diacritical stroke indicating an initial "a" to its left. In transcribing the shorthand text to longhand, transcribers confronted by this symbol would have to find a synonym for "forsake" beginning with the letter "a." This clearly results in certain ambiguities in the system and the possibility of a different synonym, or the keyword itself, being chosen.[29]

A detailed study of Characterie by Otto Pape, published in 1906, demonstrated that a significant number of variant readings in *Richard III* coincide with the inherent weaknesses in Bright's system.[30] But Pape, fixated on the idea of textual piracy, proposed that, given the clumsy nature of the shorthand, six surreptitious stenographers would be needed to record the play in performance. Patrick, Greg, and Duthie all dismissed the idea that the system could have been used in this way, Greg claiming characteristically that "[t]he suggestion seems to me utterly fantastic."[31]

However the problem with their rejection of Pape is that they all (including Pape) assumed that the only use for shorthand in this process would be the illicit transcription of a pirate text by audience members during performance. None considered the possibility that such a form of shorthand was used simply for the sake of speed or convenience during the legitimate composition and copying of the texts of *Richard III*. If a version of *Richard III*, fully or partly in Characterie, had been made and then transcribed in longhand at any stage in the preparation of the texts that were to become either the first quarto or folio (or both), it could account for many of the pointless synonymous variants in the texts. And the transcriber preparing a text specifically for the printer might conceivably have been the author, especially as he was a member of the company.[32] If this were the case it would raise the status of the first quarto and explain some of its apparent strengths relative to the folio text. The use of shorthand is not direct evidence that the hypothesis of memorial reconstruction is wrong, but it renders it unnecessary as an explanation for these features of the text.

A further suggestion has to do with the question of oral influence on the texts. This is something that Patrick refers to, but he habitually conflates the words "oral" and "memorial" as if they were the same thing. Until very recently, nobody has seriously explored the possibilities of a nonmemorial oral component in the copying of the texts of *Richard III*.[33] Now, we know that the Elizabethan actors' companies worked fast in the preparation of performances. One necessary and potentially time-consuming stage in the process was the copying of the actors' parts. This process would have to be extremely accurate in particular ways, especially in terms of the correct sequence of speeches within each part and the brief cues that preceded each speech, because any errors would be complicated to correct and could result in considerable waste of precious rehearsal time as confusions were sorted out. Errors would also lead to the mislearning of a role by an actor and, in extreme cases, the possible breakdown of an under-rehearsed play in performance as the result of a defective cue or a misplaced speech in one written-out part.

The standard consensus is that the preparation of the parts was the work of a single scribe. In *Shakespeare's Theatre*, Peter Thomson creates a vivid though suspiciously neat picture of this process: "The playhouse scribe would write out the play from the author's copy. . . . The scribe's copy was chopped into 'parts,' and the parts pasted together in sequence [into long rolls]."[34] This seems to mean that each separate speech would be cut out of the whole text and incorporated into the appropriate part, where it would be glued to the preceding speech for that character. Thomson repeats this understanding of the process in *A New History of Early English Drama*.[35] However, I am aware of no evidence that would support this version of the process. On the contrary, the single professional actor's part that we still have, Alleyn's script for the title role in *Orlando Furioso*, does not consist of single speeches glued together to form a scroll. Instead the speeches have been written out continuously on narrow sheets of paper that have then been glued together to form the roll, with as many speeches copied onto each sheet of paper as will fit.

This means that if we hold to the single-scribe view, we have to imagine a rather less simple process, a scrivener surrounded by his master copy and up to forty or fifty piles of papers, one for each separate speaking role, copying each separate speech from the exemplar onto the correct piece of paper from the correct pile. The task becomes more and more complex wherever the number of characters onstage increases and the length of speeches dimin-

ishes, with added difficulties in the case of lines spoken simultaneously by more than one character. Potential for serious error is
great, the possibilities for checking and correction very slight,
and there would be a considerable waste of precious time as the
scribe juggled and shuffled multiple piles of papers. It is not a
very sensible way of proceeding, and there is no evidence that it
actually happened.

An alternative explanation is that the parts might have been
copied out by a number of scribes taking dictation, with a much
smaller number of parts each, perhaps one major or a few minor
roles per scribe. If this dictation took place, it would also be possible for a complete play book to be written out at the same time,
along with any other copies and versions that might be needed
for musicians and so on. All of these texts could have been produced in the time it took to produce a single copy. The scribes
might have been, or might at least have included, some of the
more literate actors in the company who could have used this
transcription process as the start of their memorization of the
lines, though my argument does not depend on this.[36] Furthermore, it is not impossible that the person dictating to the scribes
was, on some occasions at least, the author (or authors), giving a
first reading of the new play to the cast and working from a text
that could have been complete but might equally have been a
good rough copy, or even notes if the play had been prepared in a
rush to meet a deadline. An author giving dictation in this way
might have taken the opportunity to do some on-the-spot revision
as he spoke the lines aloud, perhaps for the first time ever, with
possibly some input and advice from his fellow actors, who might
already have contributed substantially to the drafting of the
script.[37] It would also have provided a chance to check that the
intricate details of doubling were workable, and perhaps to make
decisions about some stage management issues such as unusual
entrances and exits. This process would produce a version, or
more probably versions, that might have many indifferent variations as well as some significant differences from and improvements over the original. The extent of variation might be
unevenly distributed throughout the texts and between characters. It would also almost inevitably result in minor errors such
as omissions, mislineations, and confusions.

I cannot prove that this happened, but I know of no evidence
against such an apparently sensible process, and there is some
evidence to support it. David Carnegie has described parts, from
four different amateur plays performed at Christ Church, Oxford,

surviving in a manuscript held at Harvard.[38] In this case, the parts have been written into a book that was already bound at the time. Writing parts onto separate sheets of paper is one thing, but working with a stack of separate books, one for each character, all of which need to be opened at the right page for every new speech, adds a further level of difficulty and delay.

In the case of the *Orlando Furioso* part there is a further strange feature: every now and again the scribe has left out words, many of which are unusual proper nouns,[39] some of which have been filled in later in a different hand. Greg attributes this to the scribe encountering illegible passages in the text he was copying from, but the spaces are in many cases too small for the word to be written in neatly. If the scribe had been copying from a manuscript, he would have had a reasonably accurate idea of the length of the illegible words and could have left adequate space. This feature of the text could at least as well be explained by the scribe taking dictation at speed and leaving gaps for unfamiliar-sounding words, with consequently less idea of the length of these words on the page. One telling gap is followed by the words "& mirh"; a scribe who was working at his own speed from written copy might be expected to have supplied the correct reading "frankincense," as Greg did,[40] but this kind of scribal backtracking is considerably more difficult in the case of rapid dictation.

In short, then, I am proposing a process for the copying of the texts of *Richard III*, and their later preparation for publication, which may have included at some points, as perfectly standard playhouse practice, either or both the use of a shorthand system and oral dictation,[41] and that the texts that have been printed may have been dictated to, rather than by, the actors. This suggestion may seem cumbersome, but the orthodox theory, though more familiar, is even more labored and has no more evidence to support it. Such an alternative explanation accounts for some of the strange features of the text of *Richard III*, especially the indifferent variants, while avoiding the need to blame actors and theater practice for faulty memorial reconstruction, as Patrick does in the final words of his book. "With the exceptions named," he wrote with a positivist confidence and a scholarly aloofness from theater practice that now look rather dated, "the Folio text best represents *Richard III* as Shakespeare wrote it. The quarto is peculiarly a practical stage version of the play."[42]

More recent scholarship has rejected the antitheatrical prejudice betrayed by such statements and has begun to embrace the mutably theatrical qualities of these plays, which seem to have been readily adapted by their first performers, "at short notice to take account of new developments, topical, circumstantial, or aesthetic."[43] The original players perhaps did not regard a play script as high art or as immutable holy writ, but rather as the raw materials from which ad hoc performances could be created. Many theater practitioners still regularly do this with Shakespeare and other "classic" plays, cutting sections that seem too long or that are irrelevant to a director's or actor's particular approach, selecting readings from whichever available text is preferred at a particular point, modernizing vocabulary or grammar, including allusions to contemporary events, and introducing passages of dialogue from outside the text. Even the titles of classic plays are subject to modification. All of these are standard in much current theater practice.

One consequence of this proposal might be a quite new paradigm for modern editions of the plays. Rather than attempting to provide a coherent and seamless text based on a single published version or a conflation of several versions, with every crux neatly solved and alternative readings, spellings, and punctuation relegated to the notes or silently "corrected," the editor could decide to produce a working document whose text highlights the reading and performance options available from all major sources, including the play's subsequent production history, and to flag the significance and historical provenance of the alternatives. They might thus encourage their readers—scholars, students, theater practitioners, and others—to make their own informed choices about which features of the text they want to use for whatever are their immediate needs, as it seems the plays' first users might have done.

NOTES

1. In the introduction to his 1981 Arden edition of *Richard* III, Antony Hammond quotes Clark and Wright, the editors of the 1864 Cambridge Shakespeare: "The respective origin and authority of the first Quarto and first Folio texts of *Richard III* is perhaps the most difficult question which presents itself to an editor of Shakespeare," and then adds that "a definitive solution is still to seek": see introduction to William Shakespeare, *King Richard III*, ed. Antony Hammond, Arden Shakespeare (London: Methuen, 1981), 1–2.

2. See David Lyall Patrick, *The Textual History of Richard III* (Stanford, Calif.: Stanford Univ. Press, 1936): "If the quarto text in its passage through the memories of the men who acted it has acquired certain errors recognizable as the variations incidental to oral repetition, then no line and no single word

of the quarto, much less any of the spelling or punctuation, can be taken, with the least assurance, to be the original text. . . . If this theory be accepted . . . then the received text of the play should be purged of all readings drawn from the quarto at the expense of a satisfactory reading [in the folio]" (148). Note that variations in the first quarto automatically become errors according to Patrick. It is because of this conclusion that I wish to argue against aspects of Patrick's book.

3. John Jowett's recent edition, published after this paper was first written, argues strongly against the superiority of the folio and uses the first quarto as the basis for the text; see *The Tragedy of King Richard III*, ed. John Jowett (Oxford: Oxford Univ. Press, 2000).

4. Hammond's doubts about the matter are reflected in contradictions in his argument: "It is a meagre harvest of evidence to support the theory of memorial reconstruction occasioned by the loss of the promptbook during a tour . . . the evidence concerning the nature of the manuscript underlying Q is inconclusive. There are strong reasons for believing it to have been produced by an act of collective memorial reconstruction involving virtually the entire company. . . . The evidence supporting the memorial theory of Q is too strong to be rejected. The various unusual features of Q may be largely accounted for by supposing that the reconstruction was made by the co-operative efforts of most of the company in the absence of the official prompt book, perhaps during a provincial tour (that of 1597 is a possible candidate). The company involved was almost certainly the Chamberlain's Men" (introduction to *Richard III*, 19–20).

5. Stanley Wells and Gary Taylor, with John Jowett and William Montgomery, *William Shakespeare: A Textual Companion* (Oxford: Clarendon, 1987), 228.

6. Patrick, *Textual History*, 147–48.

7. W. W. Greg, review of Patrick's *The Textual History of Richard III*, *The Library* 4, no. 19 (1938): 118–20.

8. See Laurie E. Maguire, *Shakespearean Suspect Texts: The "Bad" Quartos and Their Contexts* (Cambridge: Cambridge Univ. Press, 1996), 61.

9. W. W. Greg, *The Editorial Problem in Shakespeare*, 2d ed. (Oxford: Oxford Univ. Press, 1951), 85–86. Greg's hypothesis, for all its detail, leaves us unclear about what actually happened. If the Chamberlain's Men had planned in advance to perform a reduced-cast version of *Richard III* on the tour, they would presumably have prepared an appropriate script before leaving, which they then must very carelessly have left behind; this implies the possible existence of two reduced-cast versions of the script. If, on the other hand, the decision to stage the play was a spur-of-the-moment one while on tour with a reduced cast (as Greg seems to imply), they would presumably have to go back to London anyway to get the costumes and props.

10. Patrick, *Textual History*, 18.

11. In the introduction to his edition of the play, Peter Davison attempts to counter this flaw in the argument: "We cannot be sure that [the sharers] would all tour and Professor Park Honan (who is working on a biography of Shakespeare) believes that Shakespeare would take this opportunity to visit 'his native Countrey,' as John Aubrey put it in his 'Brief Life' "; see *The First Quarto of King Richard III*, ed. Peter Davison, New Cambridge Shakespeare (Cambridge: Cambridge Univ. Press, 1996), 15. Hammond also mentions the possibility of Shakespeare's involvement in the supposed reconstruction (introduction to *Richard III*, 20).

12. Andrew Gurr, "Maximal Editions and Minimum Performances" (paper delivered at *Material Shakespeare,* conference of the Australian and New Zealand Shakespeare Association, Brisbane, July 11–15, 1998).

13. See Kristian Smidt, *Injurious Impostors and "Richard III"* (Oslo: Norwegian Univ. Press, 1964) and *Memorial Transmission and Quarto Copy in "Richard III": A Reassessment* (Oslo: Norwegian Univ. Press, 1970); see also *William Shakespeare, The Tragedy of King Richard the Third: Parallel Texts of the First Quarto and the First Folio with Variants of the Early Quartos,* ed. Kristian Smidt (New York: Humanities Press, 1969); E. A. J. Honigmann, "The Text of *Richard III,"* *Theatre Research* 7, nos. 1–2 (1965): 48–55, "On the Indifferent and One-Way Variants in Shakespeare," *The Library* 5, no. 22 (1967): 189–204, and *The Texts of "Othello" and Shakespearean Revision* (London: Routledge, 1996); John Jowett, *"Richard III* and the Perplexities of Editing," *Text: An Interdisciplinary Annual of Textual Studies* 11 (1998): 224–45; Maguire, *Shakespearean Suspect Texts*; and Gary Taylor, "Copy-Text and Collation (with special reference to *Richard III*)," *The Library* 6, no. 3 (1981): 33–42.

14. Hammond, introduction to *Richard III,* 26; see also MacD. P. Jackson, "Two Shakespeare Quartos: *Richard III* (1597) and *1Henry IV* (1598)," *Studies in Bibliography* 35 (1982): 173–91.

15. Steven Urkowitz, "Reconsidering the Relationship of Quarto and Folio Texts of *Richard III,"* *English Literary Renaissance* 16 (1986): 442–66.

16. However, Peter Davison's recent edition of the first quarto text reinstates in full the idea of memorial reconstruction by actors. Davison refers to the article by Urkowitz, but it makes no apparent impression on his line of reasoning; many of Davison's arguments seem to ignore the counterevidence outlined by Urkowitz and others.

17. Patrick, *Textual History,* 18.

18. Fredson Bowers, "Authority, Copy, and Transmission in Shakespeare's Texts," in *Shakespeare Study Today,* ed. Georgiana Ziegler (New York: AMS Studies in the Renaissance, 1986), 15, quoted by Honigmann, *Texts of "Othello,"* 80.

19. Peter W. M. Blayney, "The Publication of Playbooks," in *A New History of Early English Drama,* ed. John D. Cox and David Scott Kastan (New York: Columbia Univ. Press, 1997), 392.

20. Shakespeare, *King Richard III,* ed. Janis Lull (Cambridge: Cambridge Univ. Press, 1999), 217; emphasis added.

21. Paul Werstine, "Hypertext and Editorial Myth," *Early Modern Literary Studies* 3, no. 3, special issue 2 (1998): 1–19, <www.shu.ac.uk/emls/03-3/wersshak .html>, December 12, 2001, and "Plays in Manuscript," in *New History,* 481–97.

22. Barbara A. Mowat, "The Problem of Shakespeare's Text(s)," in *Textual Formations and Reformations,* ed. Laurie E. Maguire and Thomas L. Berger (Newark, Del.: Univ. of Delaware Press, 1998), 136.

23. Jowett, "Perplexities," 240.

24. For example, Urkowitz, "Reconsidering."

25. See Honigmann, *Texts.*

26. Hammond claims that Patrick suggested that the actors dictated their reconstruction to a scribe who transcribed it in shorthand (introduction to *Richard III,* 9). On the contrary, Patrick specifically argues that the transcript was taken down in longhand.

27. George Ian Duthie, *Elizabethan Shorthand and the First Quarto of King*

Lear (Oxford: Blackwell, 1949), 1; Adele Davidson, " 'Some by stenography'? Stationers, Shorthand, and the Early Shakespearean Quartos," *Papers of the Bibliographical Society of America* 90, no. 4 (1996): 417–49, and *"King Lear* in an Age of Stenographical Reproduction, or 'On Sitting Down to Copy *King Lear* Again,' " *Papers of the Bibliographical Society of America* 92, no. 3 (1998): 297–324.

28. Duthie, *Elizabethan Shorthand,* 2–12.

29. There are other inherent weaknesses in the system that might have contributed to features of the first quarto. See E. K. Chambers, *William Shakespeare: A Study of Facts and Problems* (Oxford: Clarendon, 1930), 1:159–62.

30. Otto Pape, *Über die Entstehung der ersten Quarto von Shakespeares "Richard III"* (Berlin: G. Reiner, 1906).

31. Greg, *Problems,* 85.

32. The idea of shorthand was not unknown in the playhouse, as evidenced by Heywood's (much later) claim that the 1605 edition of his play *If You Know Not Me, You Know Nobody* was based on copying of the "plot" by stenography; the piracy theory was partly based on this statement, though it could equally be a complaint about incompetent in-house copyists. Andrew Gurr has pointed out to me that "plot" here may mean not the script but rather the summaries of the action that were hung up backstage during performance, in which case Heywood's complaint has no bearing on this issue other than to reinforce the connection between shorthand and the theaters.

33. Since this paper was initially written, Scott McMillin and Sally-Beth MacLean have published a detailed study of the Queen's Men. They propose that in-house dictation may have been used in the preparation of the play books, especially when they were being revised, and this might have involved the actors dictating from their parts. It is an attractive and convincing proposal; my slightly different but not incompatible suggestion is that dictation might have been used at an earlier stage of the process, and that the dictating may have been made to, rather than by, the actors. See Scott McMillin and Sally-Beth MacLean, *The Queen's Men and Their Plays* (Cambridge: Cambridge Univ. Press, 1998).

34. Peter Thomson, *Shakespeare's Theatre,* 2d ed. (London: Routledge, 1983), 122.

35. Thomson, "Rogues and Rhetoricians: Acting Styles in Early English Drama," in *New History,* 322.

36. Interestingly, Greg notes that the hand of the scribe who wrote the *Orlando Furioso* part was "unusual"; he goes on to say that "from its calligraphic qualities [it] would seem to be that of a professional scribe who was familiar with this class of work"; see *Two Elizabethan Stage Abridgements: "The Battle of Alcazar and Orlando Furioso,"* Malone Society Extra Volume (Oxford: Oxford Univ. Press, 1922), 137. The unusual qualities of the hand seem to contradict the idea that it was a professional scribe, and Greg's sense that the scribe was familiar with this class of work might support the view that it was one of the actors. In any case it seems clear that the scribe was not Alleyn, the actor who played the role. His handwriting is apparently different and is visible in corrections and annotations to the text as the result of his study of the part.

37. See Werstine, "Plays," 489.

38. David Carnegie, "Actors' Parts and the 'Play of Poore,' " *Harvard Library Bulletin* 30, no. 1 (January 1982): 5–24.

39. Words omitted and supplied later include "Clora," "Ate," "Galaxsia," "Nymosene," and "Tyms."

40. Greg, *Abridgements*, 198.

41. Patrick, following Malone and Dover Wilson, suggested that the actors' parts might have been used in the preparation of the printed texts, but this too was rejected by Greg, though his argument only applied to plays characterized by few stage directions and initial massed entries; see W. W. Greg, *The Shakespeare First Folio* (Oxford: Clarendon, 1955), 156–58, and also Chambers, *William Shakespeare*, 1:153–54. The rejection of the use of actors' parts seems nevertheless to have been more widely applied.

42. Patrick, *Textual History*, 150.

43. Maguire, *Suspect Texts*, 335.

The Case of the Rouged Corpse: Shakespeare, Malone, and the Modern Subject

Ron Bedford

THIS REPORT, OR MEDITATION, REFLECTS ON SOME HIGHLY SELEC-tive features of the ongoing debate about the materiality of Shakespeare's texts (and by extension of any text), and the new challenges thrown down, often in a spirit of revolutionary fervor, to contest what had been thought of as received notions of schol-arship, editorial practice, and even the pursuit of literary study itself. Over the last few years a series of articles (many of them in the journal *Textual Practice*) have debated the protocols, value, and implications of idealistic versus materialistic approaches to the play texts (and indeed the sonnets) that stemmed from Mar-greta de Grazia's *Shakespeare Verbatim: The Reproduction of Au-thenticity and the 1790 Apparatus* (1991) and from de Grazia and Peter Stallybrass's later article "The Materiality of the Shake-spearean Text," which appeared in *Shakespeare Quarterly* in 1993.

The whole question of editorial practice has become a topic of intense theoretical discussion—not only regarding editorial prac-tice in relation to the texts of Shakespeare but also regarding early modern literature at large and, by a logical extension, edito-rial intervention in all texts. Something of what is at issue here may be gauged from recent textual products themselves: for ex-ample, by comparing the *Oxford Shakespeare* (1986) or the more recent *Norton Shakespeare* (1997), at nearly three and a half thousand pages, with one of the slim texts in the Early Quarto Series of *The New Cambridge Shakespeare*—for example, Jay L. Halio's *The First Quarto of King Lear* (1994), or Peter Davison's *The First Quarto of King Richard III* (1996), or some of the early "bad quartos" (for instance of *Hamlet*) promoted by Graham Holderness and Harvester Press. In the first we have the "traditional" products of centuries of editorial labor: textual comparisons and reconstructions, act and scene divisions, stage directions, emendations, glossings, annotations—though they contest and revise some of the more speculative and supposedly "improved" practices of the older tradition. In the second we have the earliest, barest, unmediated, and (supposedly) most "authentic" printed texts. It is the ambition of Margreta de Grazia's project to shake us all free of the editorial, scholarly, and ideological practices bequeathed to us by previous generations, as it is too of Leah S. Marcus in her *Unediting the Renaissance: Shakespeare, Marlowe, Milton* (1996), in which she proposes the "temporary abandonment of modern editions in favor of Renaissance editions that have not gathered centuries of editorial accretion round them."[1]

Such proposals are not new; even Dr. Johnson made a similar point. In a sense, they are at bottom philological and antiquarian and are no doubt part of the program implicit in the larger interpretative shifts of new historicism and cultural materialism. Marcus, for instance, is preoccupied with recovering specific verbal meanings available to contemporary readers of these early published works that have been obliterated or emended into something else by modern editors. She gives as an opening example the description of Sycorax in *The Tempest* as a "blew-ey'd hag," variously emended to "blear-ey'd" or "blery-ey'd"; or, in a larger frame, she examines and prefers the 1602 quarto of *The Merry Wives of Windsor* over the "gentrified" 1623 folio text, arguing that it is not a "corrupt version" of a definitive text but rather the textual record of an actual topical performance that names the local targets of its satire.

Some general points might be made even at this stage. The first point is that, since all of us probably rely on modern editions of Shakespeare for both our scholarly work and our teaching (trusting that we are better off in the hands of experts than in venturing inexpertly into the confusing world of early unedited printed texts), a proposal such as Marcus's seems unlikely to succeed. Relatively few of us have access to extensive rare book collections, and even if we did we would soon discover that sixteenth- and seventeenth-century books can vary alarmingly from one copy to another. A second point could be that we might want to resist, or at least question, the fundamental assumption that the most important item of knowledge about, say, a Shakespeare play is its historical origin. As Michael D. Bristol asks as an aside, while reviewing recent studies in Tudor and Stuart drama: "And why is

history the discipline to enforce on students of literature anyway?
Why not geography, or psychology, or even moral philosophy, as
the basis for the interpretation of texts?" Bristol presses his
point: "To say that these orientations would be unhistorical obviously won't do; this response is exactly what is meant by the expression 'begging the question.' One is obliged to give reasons for
the claim that a historical approach is definitely better than an
unhistorical one."[2]

Another point to note, no doubt, is the way in which issues of
authorship and the nature of human agency in the creation of literary artifacts are also bound up in these debates. I am not about
to rehearse the theoretical problems involved in trying to answer
the question What is an author? though Tom Stoppard, author of
the screenplay for the 1999 film *Shakespeare in Love*, has a characteristically sharp comment on the issue when a theatrical
backer points to the young Shakespeare, asks the theater owner
Philip Henslowe, "Who's that?" and receives the reply, "Nobody,
sir. He's the author."[3] Cultural materialist opponents of traditional editorial practices and assumptions often raise an objection
to the high cultural or "romantic" elitism and, in their view, the
anachronism of the notion of an actual literate and literary author bearing some proprietorial and originating relationship
to the textual artifact (an argument de Grazia pursues in the introduction to *Shakespeare Verbatim*). It remains noteworthy,
nonetheless, that the writers themselves, whether stridently re-
formatory or ludically attenuated in manner, appear to have a robust sense of their own authorship.

A further readily recognizable dimension of the debates is their
political and ideological orientation. There are frequent aggressive rhetorics condemning and exposing the villainy of editors
and the interpretive practices they foster, from the eighteenth
century to the present, and the accompanying scandals of ideological distortion or appropriation—particularly sensitive issues in
the case of a national and international monument such as
Shakespeare. The emphasis instead is upon an apparently undis-
torted, unappropriated textual product, unauthored, demotic,
and democratic, preferably thoroughly fingered by an acting
troupe, perhaps badly printed by an illiterate apprentice and still
smelling of printer's ink. Such Marxist-materialist emphases co-
exist with a radical "Protestant" kind of discourse that upholds
the authority of Scripture (the marks on the page) over the authority of tradition and its "priestly interpolations." In this view,
the object of higher scholarship (that is, of academic institutions

and, in particular, departments of English studies) is not to maintain and enhance a vitally evolved and evolving textual resource but, in Marcus's phrase, to *unedit* it, and to preserve and disseminate in its place a random gathering of historical artifacts.

What follows is not a direct contribution to these debates but is rather a contemplation, or triangulation, of three material items that may occur within it. The first is a pile of uniformly produced books, paper, card, calfskin and buckram artifacts, inked, paginated, stitched, bound in eighteen volumes with three additional volumes, or 1800 pages, plus prolegomena, and weighing in at many kilograms; the second is a single, slim paper artifact or book in duodecimo to be weighed in grams; and the third is a lump of stone. And lurking behind (if that is indeed the right preposition) is a ghost—not this time the ghost of Hamlet's father, but, as if in some quite other spatial and temporal dimension, what is often called in these debates "the ghost of Shakespeare."

First the lump of stone. Edmond Malone is accused of many corrupting and misleading practices by recent critics, but in his own day he was seen as guilty of one in particular, the notorious case of his editorial work on Shakespeare's Stratford monument. Despite the fact that Malone had virtually purloined boxes of paper and manuscripts from the Stratford Corporation and either returned them only after years of reminders or never returned them at all,[4] the authorities seemed grateful for Malone's offer in 1793 (three years after the publication of his great editorial project on Shakespeare's works) to render the famous monument "authentic," which he did by returning it, with a suitable pot of paint, to what he believed to be its original stone color.[5] Curiously, Malone insisted that the colored, make-uplike paint on the monument was unbearably inauthentic. He was in fact mistaken: the statue had never been monochrome, and the original colours were eventually restored in 1861. Malone thought of himself of having performed, as he said, "a public service," but others thought differently. Some years later an epigram appeared in a Stratford *Visitors' Book:*

> Stranger, to whom this monument *is* shewn,
> Invoke the Poet's curse upon Malone;
> Whose meddling zeal his barbarous taste betrays,
> And daubs his tombstone, as he mars his plays![6]

Samuel Schoenbaum observes: "No other act of Malone's did such lasting damage to his reputation as his tampering with the Shakespeare bust."[7]

There are some strange paradoxes about this episode. The first lies in the paradox of Malone's fit of neoclassicism in the restoration of the bust; for it was the very neoclassicizing or adaptation of the "original" Shakespeare that he most deplored and from which, in his editorial practice, felt impelled to rescue or recover Shakespeare. (Or perhaps he was responding to the rediscovered 1609 *Sonnets*: "I never saw that you did painting need, / And therefore to your fair no painting set" [Sonnet 83, ll.1–2].) Paradoxical too is his belief that the colored paint on the bust was not original but the irresponsible work, he claimed, of "some strolling players" about forty years earlier,[8] players who, one could think, might have been closer inheritors of that Shakespeare of the theater and the people in whom Malone professed to be most interested.

The episode—like the other episodes I want to highlight, and like the current materialist debate—is of course highly charged politically. The neo-Augustan restoration of a demotic desecration is exercised upon vagrant, itinerant theatrical players by a member of, if not the actual aristocracy (though close to it in Malone's privileged and extensively propertied Irish background in County Westmeath),[9] certainly of the cultural and intellectual aristocracy or elite of eighteenth-century London. Malone was the friend of, among others, Samuel Johnson, James Boswell, Sir Joshua Reynolds, James Caulfield (first Earl of Charlemont), and Edmund Burke. His action thus lays itself open to charges of elitist appropriation, a further paradox that will be returned to.

It is perhaps a tribute to Malone's enormous and continuing prestige that the original colored paint was not restored until 1861. For nearly seventy years Malone's version of Shakespeare's bust presided at Stratford. Victor Hugo, in exile on Guernsey, recalled Malone's obliteration. In his *William Shakespeare* he wrote, "An imbecile, Malone made commentaries on his plays, and, as a logical sequence, whitewashed his tomb."[10] In this comment, one can perhaps recognize the germens of, for example, Margreta de Grazia's opening to *Shakespeare Verbatim* where, on the first page, she explains her conviction that "authentic" texts and the accompanying historical and biographical baggage "are not necessary in any absolute sense" and asks "why should [this construct] still prevail?" Contemporaries of Malone had made similar points. One reviewer of Malone's Shakespeare enterprise took up the editorial claim that "if even every line of his plays were accompanied with a comment, every intelligent reader would be indebted to the industry of him who produced it," replying that every reader "of common sense" could understand nearly all of Shakespeare that is "worth understanding" without assistance from an editor with the annotating sickness.[11] Malone suspected his great antagonist George Steevens was behind this stinging riposte, even if Steevens had not written the review himself. An anonymous letter, signed *Philalethes*, appeared in the *Gentleman's Magazine*, indignantly defending Malone, reminding the reader of the great harvest of new material in the edition, and defending Shakespeare's commentators over the past thirty years and with them, implicitly, the scholarship that produced Malone's huge prolegomena and extensive editorial apparatus. The letter has been thought the work of Boswell, but Malone's recent biographer, Peter Martin, is convinced Malone wrote it himself.[12] Malone, perhaps hoping to emulate Swift—whose correspondence he also edited—had several times tried his hand at irony in satirical pieces on Irish politics. A notably flat piece was his lamentation on the Irish consumption of millions of eggs a year when a little self-discipline could yield more substantial food in the form of chickens.[13] Here in the letter he tries a rhetorical flourish that may serve as a warning of the dangers of ironical writing, for it oddly prefigures responses to Malone by some present-day critics. Malone claims that if Shakespeare is teeming with "absurdities" and "vapid nonsense," then Dr. Johnson, Mr. Steevens, and Mr. Malone have all most "egregiously mis-spent their time these thirty years past; and it is highly incumbent on the relations of the two latter gentlemen to put them in some place of confinement, appropriate[d] to those unfortunate persons whose minds are deranged."[14]

Michael Dobson, in his *The Making of the National Poet* (1992), alerts us to another paradoxical dimension of Malone's repainting exercise. Dobson comments on the outrage, both historical and modern, that habitually repudiates vulgarizing "adaptations" of Shakespeare (whether Dryden's or Baz Luhrmann's) and its customary vocabulary of "mutilation," "desecration," or "perversion." He quotes George C. D. Odell's *Shakespeare from Betterton to Irving*, published in the early 1920s, as an example of such outrage: "Literally, Shakespeare is 'smeared over' by the inferior stuff so proudly vaunted by the perpetrators. It is almost a rouged corpse—a thing too ghastly to conceive of."[15] Odell, contemplating the alterations of Tate or Cibber, finds himself staring in horror at a "rouged corpse," and Dobson points out that what is at stake here is the preservation not only of the *Complete Works* from adaptation but also "the integrity and indeed masculinity of

Shakespeare himself." In a footnote he suggests that "[t]his image inevitably calls to mind" Malone's renovation of the Stratford monument. Indeed it does, but not in a way that is without complication. Dobson suggests that for Odell "adaptation likewise turns a dignified, classical image of the dead Shakespeare into some thing tackily pretending to be alive."[16] But, as noted earlier and paradoxically, the historicizing thrust of Malone's enterprise was to *retrieve* the once living and historical Shakespeare and his texts, to re-cover them with an "authentic" and "original" paint to a depth, as it were, of eleven volumes in the 1790 edition and twenty-one volumes in the Malone and James Boswell 1821 Variorum Edition, including three on Shakespeare's biography, learning, language, theater, versification, chronology, and text. But to represent Shakespeare in the present (the present of 1790) is to cut off access to the actual plays with a vast barricade of apparatuses, or, to change back the metaphor, to "smear over" Shakespeare's textual effigy with such layers of historicizing makeup (making him over in his origins of place and time so as to view him as though he were still alive) that the corpse is again thoroughly rouged, if in a quite different way. Perhaps there was something after all understandable in Malone's otherwise quite inconsistent desire to whitewash the monument, a desire, no doubt quite unconscious, to mitigate the effects of all the makeup, to reach for something simple, severe, and clean.

Malone is indeed, as Howard Felperin points out, the first new historicist.[17] At the very moment that Malone was laboring away, identifying the Bermuda pamphlets as an "historical" source for *The Tempest*, Coleridge was idealizing, universalizing, and dehistoricizing the plays in his public lectures. The complex currents in the period generated by the impulse, on the one hand, to editorial and archival recovery and, on the other, the impulse to transcendentalize, to deliver Shakespeare from both Elizabethan historicity and the textual baggage of his commentators, might lead us to wonder whether it was not in fact Coleridge rather than Malone who effectively recast the bust of Shakespeare into an unpainted effigy presiding timelessly over centuries, past and future, of seamless and universal human experience.

So far, monument and corpse. In his recent literary biography of Malone, Peter Martin targets especially Gary Taylor's *Reinventing Shakespeare* (1989) and Margreta de Grazia's *Shakespeare Verbatim* and flatly denies de Grazia's contention that Malone was freezing Shakespeare with his rigidly documentary and factual criteria, making him what de Grazia calls a "relativized enclave," or that Malone prescribed and dictated the terms according to which Shakespeare is accepted and read.[18] Certainly, in contemplating the considerable pile of volumes that constitute Malone's Shakespeare, de Grazia accuses him (and it is rhetorically in the nature of an accusation) of having set editorial practice on the wrong path for two hundred years, supported by collaborators (with many of whom Malone disagreed, and sometimes vehemently, but no matter): the long line of eighteenth-century editors—Rowe, Pope, Theobald, Warburton, Johnson, Capell, Steevens—who are all in fact very different from each other but are brought together in conspiracy because each was commissioned by the powerful Tonson publishing house. The compilation of the 1790 edition is (inevitably) a *political* act, and de Grazia's own prolegomena discourses on the nature of individualism and subjectivity and the emergence of the bourgeois subject, and defines Malone's edition of Shakespeare as an ideologically driven apparatus designed to protect, in late-eighteenth-century Europe, the unique character of the metonymic Shakespeare-England-Englishness. While the ideological nature and origins of the edition may hardly be called reprehensible (just as there is no such thing as an unedited Shakespeare text, so there is no such thing as an un- or apolitical discourse), it is certainly seen as unfortunate, antiquated, and anachronistic. In its place is an inevitably ideologically constructed materialism whose political agenda is equally accessible to scrutiny. As Jerome McGann puts it (and his "texts" here would naturally include academic books and articles): "Texts are produced and reproduced under specific social and institutional conditions, and hence . . . every text, including those that appear to be purely private, is a social text. The view entails a corollary understanding, that 'text' is not a 'material thing' but a material event or set of events, a point in time or a moment in space where certain communication interchanges are being practiced."[19]

Indeed, the conflicts between social and political positions in the recent debates have given rise to some curious interchanges and assertions: for example, Edward Pechter's claim that for the materialists (de Grazia and Stallybrass), "authors do not write books" (misunderstanding, quite deliberately, the materialists' point that authors write only manuscripts or typescripts, not actual physical objects called books), and his mockery of the "radical change indeed" of the proposed materialist disciplinary shift "whereby we renounce the study of literature and move into the study of the history of printing," "the *paper*, the *ink*."[20] Here, as in the renovation of the Stratford bust, the conflict between the elite and the demotic reappears. Pechter claims that it is traditional literary study—and by implication the program outlined by Malone and the resources he brought to it—that is an "inherently democratic discipline," while it is materialist historians who "serve the interests of the elite." He continues: "Although they identify themselves as inclusive and egalitarian, conferring value upon the honest labor of printshop workers, the consequence of pursuing their project is to restrict Shakespeare to a privileged group, exclusively academic and exclusionary even within the precincts of the academy."[21]

Laying aside the archly rebarbative point-scoring here, the arguments do describe some elegantly paradoxical circles. The effort of the universalizing and idealizing Coleridge to deliver Shakespeare to the people and release him from the fetters of the historicist Malone is matched by the effort of the materially historicizing revisionist equally designed to deliver Shakespeare from the toils of Malone. And yet most theoretically oriented cultural materialists would be appalled to think they had not Marx, or even God, on their side but *Coleridge*. Pechter suggests that what may be going on here is a tendency of materialist historians simply to "collapse Coleridge into Malone" and a failure properly to notice the Coleridgean ambition, similar in so many respects to their own, to liberate Shakespeare from the proprietorship of an aristocratic and literary elite, a push that Howard Felperin diagnosed as "the first realization of the democratic potential of his work."[22] According to Pechter, in returning to the historicism of Malone, the quasi-democratic materialist historians now serve the interests not of a democratic Shakespeare but of an academically elitist Shakespeare.

To reply, as Peter Stallybrass does, that Malone and Coleridge are not just different ways of interpreting Shakespeare (historicizing or universalizing), but that "Malone has constructed the text that Coleridge reads: Coleridge's responses are responses to *Malone's* Shakespeare," hardly seems to meet the case.[23] Whatever text of Shakespeare Coleridge reads, *someone* has constructed it. To argue, by way of an example, that Coleridge read Malone's recovered 1609 text of the *Sonnets* and became very confused by its homoerotics (it is, after all, very different from the 1640 text "constructed" by John Benson that everyone had been reading up till then) is, I would suggest, to make a point very clearly in Malone's favor. But perhaps the real issue of contention about Malone resides in the fact that (to recall McGann's words) a text "is not a 'material thing' but a material event or set of events, a point in time . . . where certain communication interchanges are being practiced." What material event or set of events accompanies Malone's 1790 apparatus? At what point in time does it enter its multivolume material space? And what communication interchanges may be taking place?

The slim volume, the third material object here, is of course Edmund Burke's *Reflections on the Revolution in France,* also published in 1790, a copy of which Burke sent to his friend Malone in return for Malone's gift to him of the 1790 edition of Shakespeare. The two clearly shared common intellectual and political ground: both were men antirevolutionary in sentiment, and both their texts were dedicated in their different ways to a reassertion of the sanctity and inviolability of the past. De Grazia, pouncing upon the word, invites us to consider that the Malone "apparatus" functions ideologically like an Althusserian state apparatus that shapes and positions its subjects—a claim propped up by citations from Marxist critics. Burke certainly saw Malone's Shakespeare as a bulwark against anarchy. This is not the context here to critique de Grazia's reading of the Burke-Malone relationship, except to say that there are many unresolved paradoxes in her interpretation, not the least of them the way in which she appears to argue two contradictory positions: first, that Burke (and implicitly Malone) sought to resist what Foucault calls "the invention of man" in the late eighteenth century,[24] the emergence of the individual sovereign subject or consciousness (for Burke this bourgeois subject, without a community to support and succor it, was only "the dust and powder of individuality");[25] second, that Malone's "apparatus" created the individual authorial consciousness of "Shakespeare himself" as "an exemplary instance of the autonomous self, the self whose autonomy entitled him to his works."[26] Instead, I would conclude with a quotation from Burke's *Reflections* which, if we substitute (in a not entirely arbitrary way) the word "Shakespeare" for Burke's "the state," may provide an at least interesting gloss on both Malone's project and the polarities of the current debate:

> To avoid therefore the evils of inconstancy and versatility, ten thousand times worse than those of obstinacy and the blindest prejudice, we have consecrated [Shakespeare], that no man should approach to look into its defects or corruptions but with due caution; that he should never dream of beginning its reformation by its subversion; that he should approach to the faults of . . . [Shakespeare] as to the

wounds of a father, with pious awe and trembling solicitude. By this wise prejudice we are taught to look with horror on those children of their country who are prompt rashly to hack that aged parent in pieces, and put him into the kettle of magicians, in hopes that by their poisonous weeds, and wild incantations, they may regenerate the paternal constitution, and renovate their father's life.[27]

NOTES

1. Margreta de Grazia, *Shakespeare Verbatim: The Reproduction of Authenticity and the 1790 Apparatus* (Oxford: Clarendon Press, 1991); Leah S. Marcus, *Unediting the Renaissance: Shakespeare, Marlowe, Milton* (London and New York: Routledge, 1996), 5.

2. Michael D. Bristol, "Recent Studies in Tudor and Stuart Drama," *Studies in English Literature* 38, no. 2 (1998): 374.

3. *Shakespeare in Love.* Directed by John Madden. 123 min. Miramax, 1998.

4. Peter Martin, *Edmond Malone, Shakespearean Scholar: A Literary Biography* (Cambridge: Cambridge Univ. Press, 1995), 179–82.

5. Samuel Schoenbaum, *Shakespeare's Lives* (Oxford: Clarendon, 1991), 130.

6. As quoted in E. K. Chambers, *William Shakespeare: A Study of Facts and Problems* (Oxford: Clarendon, 1930), 2:184. The epigram also appears in *Gentlemen's Magazine* 75 (1815): 390.

7. Schoenbaum, *Shakespeare's Lives*, 130; this judgment is repeated in Martin, *Edmond Malone*, 181.

8. See Malone to Boswell and Charlemont, 1 September, *B-M Corrrespondence*, 472, and 15 November 1793, *Reports of Historical Manuscripts Commission*, 13:8.221; cited in Martin, *Edmond Malone*, 181.

9. Martin, *Edmond Malone*, 1–2.

10. Victor Hugo, *William Shakespeare*, trans. Melville B. Anderson (1887); cited in Schoenbaum, *Shakespeare's Lives*, 130.

11. *Critical Review*, December 1791, 369; cited in Martin, *Edmond Malone*, 140.

12. Martin, *Edmond Malone*, 141.

13. Ibid., 14.

14. *Gentlemen's Magazine* 62 (1792): 41–42.

15. George C. D. Odell, *Shakespeare from Betterton to Irving* (1920–21), cited in Michael Dobson, *The Making of the National Poet: Shakespeare, Adaptation and Authorship, 1660–1796* (Oxford: Clarendon, 1992), 9.

16. Dobson, *Making of a Poet*, 10, n. 22.

17. Howard Felperin, "Historicizing Bardolatry, or Where Could Coleridge Have Been Coming From?" in *The Uses of the Canon: Elizabethan Literature and Contemporary Theory* (Oxford: Clarendon, 1990), 7–12.

18. Martin, *Edmond Malone*, 25, 134.

19. Jerome McGann, *The Textual Condition* (Princeton: Princeton Univ. Press, 1991), 21.

20. Edward Pechter, "Making Love to Our Employment, or The Immateriality of Arguments about the Materiality of the Shakespeare Text," *Textual Practice* 11, no. 1 (1997): 51–67.

21. Ibid., 62.

22. Felperin, "Bardolatry Then and Now," in *The Appropriation of Shakespeare: Post-Renaissance Reconstructions of the Work and the Myth*, ed. Jean I. Marsden (Hemel Hempstead: Harvester, 1991), 129–44.

23. Peter Stallybrass, "Response to Pechter," *Textual Practice* 11, no. 1 (1997): 69–79.

24. Michel Foucault, *The Archaeology of Knowledge and the Discourse of Language*, trans. A. M. Sheridan Smith (New York: Pantheon, 1972), 387.

25. Edmund Burke, *Reflections on the Revolution in France*, ed. Conor Cruise O'Brien (London: Penguin, 1968), 194.

26. De Grazia, *Shakespeare Verbatim*, 10.

27. Burke, *Reflections on the Revolution in France*, 194.

Determination and Proof: Colley Cibber and the Materialization of Shakespeare's *Richard III* in the Twentieth Century

Gillian M. Day

HOWEVER DEFORMED AND PREMATURE HE MAY ACTUALLY HAVE BEEN, Richard III came fully fledged and monstrously humped into the universe of legend. At first he was cursed simply for his name, chroniclers having already found reason to condemn the fated foreign name of "Richard" for the early deaths of Richards I and II.[1] Later histories read evil in his shape. By 1548, this was a shape embodied in his life—the rise and fall of evil—as the record patterned Richard's history to a teleological account of England's decline during the Wars of the Roses and its renaissance under the Tudors—a renaissance determined, providentially, by Richard III's death.[2]

Shakespeare's play *Richard III* follows this dynamic but differs from the chronicle by failing to fit Richard's form neatly to history's frame. The playwright destabilizes the monological structure of his source texts by combining the roles of historical narrator and dramatic protagonist in the potentially unreliable Richard. He even presents himself as a player-fiction who is enacting a determination, "I am determined to prove a villain" (1.1.30), a term for a rhetorically constructed demonstration of a truth. The unfolding drama continues this complex interplay of form and content by counterpointing the immediate intimacy of Richard's performance of events with historiography's prescribed account. Shakespeare reinforces his ironic structure by invoking audience preconceptions of the Richard story as one thread in a tapestry of official record, oral report, verbal reiteration, popular myth, and narrative convention, which challenges the fixity of chronicle truth. *Richard III* sets up a dialogue, therefore, between Richard and the pattern of his history. Defining villainy in terms of intellectual virtuosity and not monstrous deformity, Shakespeare pits

266

Richard's wit against his official allegory. Since Richard's shape (both in his proportion of the play-text and his embodiment on stage) and the play's structure are so finely balanced, to alter one is to re-form the other, as this essay seeks to show.

Shakespeare's play represents the most lasting and perhaps the most consistent public imaging of Richard. Rarely offstage since the late 1590s, the popularity of *Richard III* in Shakespeare's lifetime required five reprintings of the quarto text, and records of performances throughout the eighteenth and nineteenth centuries confirm one of the longest uninterrupted stage histories in the Shakespeare canon. Indeed, the play's central figure has become so much part of popular perception that the image of the historical Richard III in people's minds is almost always Shakespeare's. It remains, however, a record and a public image sustained by constant adaptation of the play.

Perhaps its most famous adapter is Colley Cibber, who restructured the text in 1700 to fit the demands of his time, his theater, and, primarily, his career.[3] Seeking to elevate his position on the London stage but finding a dearth of material to suit his unheroic appearance, Cibber discovered in Shakespeare's Richard an ideal combination of heroism and evil, a figure whose witty villainy would showcase the actor's comic skills. Cibber the theatrical practitioner also kept an eye on audience taste. In line with the Restoration preference for clarity of exposition, he streamlined the play's historical background, removed "unnecessary" scenes and characters that competed for attention, and not unflatteringly focused his text on Richard.

Cibber's changes aimed to set Richard center stage, but that is not quite what he achieved. By placing seven new soliloquies *after* the relevant action, where they became more introspective than informative, and by introducing spectators to comment on events, he confined Richard increasingly within the play. This psychologically realistic treatment denied Richard the artistic flexibility and dramatic ambiguity of Shakespeare's villain. Moreover, his metadramatic intimacy with the audience was weakened by the structure of the Restoration stage. The abstract Elizabethan playing space, which is localized in *Richard III* almost at Richard's behest, is lost in a Restoration theater where scenes are "revealed" not by characters but by sliding screens. There Richard does not so much present the play but is presented by it, placed at the mercy of a performance that, in part at least, he should control. The liminal space that Shakespeare designates as

Richard's is prevented, therefore, by both the staging and the dramatic construction of Cibber's piece.

In diminishing Richard's metadramatic role, Cibber also divested him of symbolic status within the play. This is a diminution reinforced by motivation clearly founded in Richard's sense of deprivation and jealousy; such human vulnerability is less evident in Shakespeare's text. The result focuses on an inner conflict between Richard's self-advancement and his virtue and marginalizes his role in the broader history. Villainous deception turns into psychological displacement as each of Richard's performances shows him "acting out" the monster, and not his skilful playing of the man, as in Shakespeare. Thus Richard's self-fashioning as the tyrant-villain becomes an insecure attempt to recreate the legendary villain figure missing from Cibber's play. Hence, though he is in many ways the antithesis of the chronicles' evil king, Cibber's human Richard, framed within the rational uniformity of his text, neatly restores both narrative and structure to the monological pattern of the chronicle accounts.

Cibber's adaptation dominated the stage for almost two centuries. What sustained its performability? No doubt the removal of obscure and often awkwardly delivered historical detail eased some of the play's problems for later audiences. After the Interregnum, diminishing awareness of those nonrealistic narrative and theatrical conventions to which Shakespeare's *Richard III* alludes must have weakened its dialogic dimension to a point that advantaged adaptation. And, perhaps inevitably, such historically contingent impediments to understanding the original text's complexity increased with time. Fortunately, Cibber's adaptation proved adaptable. It fed interest in "Richard the man," giving the melancholic villain motivation bound up with personality rather than role, and rooted in this world not beyond, to create a character who was essentially the same as those who watched him. So human was he that the eighteenth century could consider him heroic, his struggling conscience exemplifying the conflict of mind and soul by which that century defined its heroism. And actors such as Garrick played the part as if it were Hamlet or Macbeth.

The increasing humanity of Richard reflected changes in critical emphasis that Cibber's adaptation happily accommodated and may even have inspired. So it is ironic that the theater's return to Shakespeare's text in the late-nineteenth century was prompted by belief in its superiority in realizing the complexity of characterization that critics then desired and defined—the admired cad of audacious intellect whom Henry Irving portrayed in his acclaimed restoration of Shakespeare's *Richard III* at London's Lyceum Theatre in 1877. This was less of a revelation than it might have seemed, however, since Irving achieved his combination of the intellectual and the noble hero by adaptation. He simply fitted Shakespeare into Cibber's frame.

Cibber's influence survived in the structure of Irving's text. He too diminished all characters but Richard, muting his victims and enemies and reducing his deeds to punishable crimes or, as F. A. Marshall put it, to the "audacious criminality . . . [of] a splendid ruler of men."[4] The production's second half utilized this admiration to suggest a developing moral sensitivity and a vulnerability even more characteristic of Cibber's Richard than of Shakespeare's. On awaking from the ghost-filled dream, he held up a crucifix and declared, "no creature loves me" (5.5.154), neatly ending the scene there, before Richard's self-recrimination. The image was repeated at the final curtain, when the dying Richard held high the cross-shaped hilt of his sword; and on this occasion nothing of Richmond's epilogue was allowed to spoil the pathos.

Irving claimed to be the first to restore Shakespeare's *Richard III* to the stage in 1877. In fact he was preempted by Samuel Phelps's brief return to Shakespeare in 1845, and more significantly by Charles Calvert's production at the Palace Theatre, Manchester, in 1870. Calvert also adapted Shakespeare's text, but with an emphasis quite different from Irving's. For here the chronicle elements, which Irving and Cibber so disliked in the original, were celebrated in a pageant—or grand historical revival—of Plantagenet history, "perfect in correctness of detail and accuracy of mis-en-scene."[5] But then it was a historicizing of Richard that played to current events: the anticipated invasion of Britain by Napoleon III in the autumn of 1870. Calvert even announced his forthcoming production on Bastille Day.

Calvert staged Shakespeare's play as history. Irving played it as pathetic tragedy. Each made Richard a figure of the time: the political enemy without or the psychological threat within. And this is the divide, with its human denominator, which characterized most major twentieth-century stagings of the play, at least in Britain. Cibber's focus on Richard was subsumed into Shakespeare's play, assisted by adaptation that either echoed Cibber's structure or reflected his rationalizing, humanizing intent. And the reasons for this seem remarkably similar to those that prevailed in 1700. The twentieth century focused on man's role in a world increasingly of his own making. Post-Enlightenment scepticism of providential patterning, alongside trust in a self-determined psychosocial state, fostered interest in the complex mentality of a realistic Richard within a material world.

Written at an equivalent turning point in history, with action bridging the medieval and modern worlds, the play provided a particular focus for interwar disillusion. Directors such as Henry Cass and Tyrone Guthrie, at the Old Vic in 1936 and 1937, offered a psychological interpretation of Richard but also looked beyond him to illustrate their theme. His tyranny became the manifestation of a mind warped by internecine strife and a tragedy caused by society's dysfunction. Guthrie signalled this transition by developing the action from morality to psychological drama. His Richard (Emlyn Williams) was seen to evolve from a devil-figure, acting divine, to a creature of society's corruption, or from monster to mankind.

The stagings of *Richard III* that have since amplified this relativist-materialist perspective can be divided into two main groups. Some Richards have worn the mantle of mankind as Christ-like victims of a self-destructive society. Evil deriving not from a realm beyond man's understanding, but specifically within the social or political structures by which Richard controls his world, became a disability that was socially or psychologically created. This line of interest in Richard has found its most sustained representation in the four productions of *Richard III* directed by Terry Hands, at the Liverpool Everyman Theatre in 1965, with the Comédie Française in Paris in 1973, and for the Royal Shakespeare Company (RSC) in 1970 and 1980.

Both of Hands's RSC productions presented a world filled with religious symbols, Christian and pagan, but one in which moral and spiritual disillusionment meant that such traditional structures offered little more than superstitious scaffolding for instinctual fears. As a result the female figures, presented in the 1970 and 1980 productions as simultaneously objects of patriarchal adoration and as the sole means by which that society could renew itself, seemed to bear some almost witchlike responsibility for its deformed offspring and, by implication, for Richard's later deeds. His demise seemed less the result of conscious villainy than of his calculated victimization by those from whom Richard had originally acquired his perverse view of life. This ambiguous apportioning of responsibility hung a question mark over the play's final justice. It was a doubt endorsed in the 1980 version by the ghosts' assistance in Richard's death, divesting him of those items of clothing—the jacket, the right shoe, and the left glove—that had defined his disability. Nonetheless, the conclusion drawn by each production was positive. If it is material, human deprivation that deforms such men as Richard, then society at least has access to its cure.

Other directors cast more active Richards but offered less hope. For them he was the tragic challenge to a political order that, shorn of beneficent divinity and social responsibility, became the determinism of a nihilistic world. His acts represented the cumulative result of internecine conflict and power struggles that predated his appearance on the scene. This view has been characterized in particular by the popular trilogy conflations of Shakespeare's *Henry VI* plays with *Richard III* devised over the past half-century—*The Wars of the Roses* (RSC adaptation, 1963), *The Plantagenets* (RSC adaptation, 1988), and *The Wars of the Roses* (English Shakespeare Company adaptation, 1988). Framing Richard within a recognizably materialist world, all three cycle-sequences have illuminated the darker ages of English history by the light of twentieth-century power politics and viewed past conflicts as popular chronicles of our time.

A key feature of an adapted trilogy cycle is its structure, into which the separate plays must coalesce. In over nine hours of performance, the interests of clarity require continuity and coherence, which adapters impose through textual and visual patterning. By its very nature, the exercise rejects difference and favors analogue. Events develop logically, characters psychologically, and homogeneity requires the rationalization of historical detail. In fact, by interlinking and reorganizing scenes into a logical sequence of causation and effect, adapters enact the process of narrative construction that they claim to identify in the texts themselves.

Both the Hall-Barton and English Shakespeare Company (ESC) adaptations underscored the plays' contemporary relevance. The ESC staged the plays in different periods, from Regency to the present day. Hall and Barton alluded to modern democracy by replacing spiritual references with political terms and substituting for the throne a council table, a democratic symbol eventually demolished by Gloucester's storm troopers. The reduction of spiritual references in all three cycles placed an additional emphasis on individual motivation. The reassignment of Richard's rhetoric to his brothers in the Hall-Barton text, for example, delineated a quietly calculating, secretive nature not unlike that of the kingmaker, Warwick. Such an emphasis facilitated closer comparison between the rise of Richard and the political careers charted in the earlier plays.[6]

However, these dramatic devices, intended to draw the three or four parts into a coherent whole, frequently conflicted with the self-conscious artifice of the final play. The added symbols and recurrent images, by which adapters signposted the unfolding rationale of events in the *Henry VI* plays, carry a quite different weight in *Richard III*, where Shakespeare's dramatic and linguistic devices already signal a self-consciously and ironically unrealistic interplay of forms. Each cycle attempts a uniformity of voice and structure that *Richard III*'s dialogic inconsistencies, whether in solo performance or in sequence, seem to qualify. And the cyclical patterning that results, albeit underpinning a secular rationale, is strikingly like that endorsed by the source chronicles.

A complicating consequence of the popularity of this Shakespeare-Cibber interpretation has been the play's own incorporation into the myth-history that it ironizes. And it was Laurence Olivier's 1955 film of *Richard III*, both famed and blamed for its Cibberean echoes, which was quick to acknowledge the paradox. Olivier's performances as Richard spanned a decade, from John Burrell's 1945 stage production (at the New Theatre) to the 1955 film, directed by Olivier himself, and the interval inspired key differences between the stage and celluloid accounts. Like the stage performance, the film drew openly on the realist line of inheritance, but it looked away from that tradition in acknowledging the play's ambiguity and artifice through subtle shifts in reading Richard and in the settings and framework of events.

Initially the film's structure follows Cibber. Minor details, however, edge it away from the narrow focus on Richard's personal concerns that this structure invites. Where Irving replaced Richard's conscience soliloquy (5.5.131–60) with his silent prayer, Olivier's camera moves from Richard's tent onto Bosworth Field. There Richard's offscreen waking cry, "Have mercy, Jesu" (5.5.132), hangs in the air as the ghost lights fade. An eleven-second silence, punctuated by two cock crows, conveys deaf heaven's response. The sound, instead, rouses Richard's enemies. The seemingly minor differences between Irving's and Olivier's versions of this moment marks an important shift in our view of Richard, and of Providence, and introduces a significant element of equivocation into the film's final movement. A similar shift takes place at its close. Olivier follows Irving in cutting Richmond's final speech, but his editing accentuates the victor's silence. Framed in long-shot against the close-focused empty crown, Richmond's mute, bareheaded figure denies the film an unambiguously heroic end.

The settings and framework of the film endorse this ambivalence. The action moves from patent artifice in the pseudo-medieval interiors of the court scenes (act 1–act 4, scene 3) to the locational reality of Bosworth Field. It marks a switch from artifice to realism that reinforces a duality in the film's reading of Richard, from witty villain to sympathetic victim, and in the play's narrative focus, from protagonist to chronicle account. And as the film's internal form indicates the play's structural ambiguity, so an added framework signals its historical instability. An opening crawler title details the legendary aspects of Richard's tale, while, at the close, a close-up of Richard's leg-armor and garter motto—"Honi soit qui mal y pense" (evil be to him who evil thinks)—quietly reasserts the distance between historical fact and myth. By implying the artifice of dramatizing history in the film's framework and structure, therefore, Olivier reestablished something of a dialogue between the play and the shape of Richard's history.

In the last twenty years, stagings of *Richard III* have begun to explore this ironical dimension, thus focusing fresh attention on those ambiguities in the play's form suppressed by socially and politically orientated accounts. Fissures have become important, not because they negate the logic of the text but because they complicate it. The developments were advanced in various innovative stagings of radically adapted versions of *Richard III* undertaken by small-scale theater companies during the 1970s and early 1980s, by Jane Howell for BBC television in 1983, and by Bill Alexander for the RSC in 1985. Frequently the necessary limitations of small, usually touring companies were turned to advantage by doubling or even trebling roles, reducing staging requirements to a minimum and exposing the structure and techniques of performance. In the process, it was noted how appropriately this staging endorsed aspects of the play's inherently self-conscious form.

Elements of these experimental productions, particularly of Barry Kyle's 1975 *Richard III* at Stratford's Other Place theater, appeared in Sam Mendes's 1991 RSC production, where Margaret and Richard broke the stage frame by entering from different points in the auditorium, where doubling modified realistic characterization (particularly when those playing Anne and Elizabeth became the young princes), and where ritualizing executions and the final confrontation required the audience to read the play as a performance, and the performance itself as play. Drawing on a repertoire of known theatrical genres, including music hall,

stand-up comedy, surrealist theater, and melodrama, the production asked its audience both to recognize and to switch between
different performance conventions. It thereby replicated that dimension of theatrical self-reference evident in Shakespeare's allusions to contemporary dramatic and literary forms.

Steven Pimlott's main stage production at Stratford in 1995 literally foregrounded this dimension of the play's metatheatrical-
ity. His color-coded subdivision of the proscenium-arch stage into
performance areas defined the text's collage of dramatic styles in
spatial terms. A black half-frame linking the overhead walkway,
on which the grief-stricken Elizabeth emerged, to the prosce-
nium-front pit where the ghosts gathered, outlined the text's de-
livery of chronicle narrative as classical tragedy. Within this, the
front stage separation into rock-edged wasteland and mobile platform stage distinguished ritualistic procession from interior court
argument, highlighting Richard's transgressive control of both in
a visual correlative of his verbal dexterity. In a spatial symbolism
that matched the significance of Richard's platea / locus flexibility
on the Elizabethan stage, Margaret and Richard moved freely between all but the overhead arena, a transition that signalled their
figurative status in the play. Pimlott thereby invited his audience
to read on a range of nonrealistic levels, revisiting convention by
translating narrative structures into staging terms.

At the close, Richard was not killed by Richmond. Instead he
returned himself to physical wholeness, standing upright, relax-
ing his arm, and moving with ease to the ghosts' side-stage space
from where he slowly applauded Richmond's closing speech, delivered from "above." On each occasion that I saw the production, the audience was uncertain whether to join in this applause.
Breaking the play's conventional closure disturbed their place in
the performance. The presence either of a Richard liberated from
myth-history or of the actor freed now from the villain role invited alternative readings of the formal end. Audience applause
here might signify collusion in historiography or endorse the
player-Richard's seeming scepticism at that determining narrative. Thus the dramatic artifice of the play's own multilayered
framework was itself exposed, disclosing the possibility of other,
untold versions of the tale.

The opening of the production was similarly ambiguous. Richard was limping painfully downstage as if about to address the
auditorium audience, when he was prevented from speaking by
Edward IV's highly stylized coronation procession, which
emerged unexpectedly onto the rear-stage balcony. Richard im-

mediately scurried back through doors in the rear wall and appeared again, dressed this time as a court jester, to the delighted applause of the audience above. Now in spotlight, he performed his opening speech—the first thirteen lines of the play—to that audience. In the light of Richard's closing action, this initial sequence could have been offering the tantalizing possibility of an alternative opening speech, perhaps another version of history, had Richard been allowed to deliver it in private. Thus both the opening and closing moments of this interpretation confronted the audience with its need to distinguish between reality and fiction and invited it to recognize the difficulty of doing so, in spite of, or perhaps because of, the polyphony of fictional forms made manifest in Pimlott's account.

Supplementing these narrative frames of reference within the text is a range of external dramatic and historical references accrued through the play's influential interpretative history. This was a dimension examined in Richard Eyre's 1991 production for the National Theatre, where allusions to stage and celluloid versions of Shakespeare's Richard, as well as to this century's artistic imaging of other villain figures, set the play's role in history alongside history's role in the play. The result was an intertextual reinforcement of the play's intrinsic challenge to notions of fixed truth, which also established uncomfortable parallels between modern media mythopoesis and the dramatic representation of history.

The production drew attention to image making, from its filmic opening title, *Edward IV,* projected onto the rear-stage curtain, to similar titles—*Richard III* and *Henry VII*—that concluded each half of the play. Staging Baynard's Castle (3.7) as a propaganda rally was not new, but here the performance was defined in cinematic terms, the auditorium audience becoming not a citizen crowd but a cinema audience. Neither was Ian McKellen simply identifiable as Hitler-Richard. The Hitler he imitated was drawn from newsreel and propaganda footage, a figure who played not to the theater audience but to cameras and television monitors set on the circle front. It was a transformation that reworked images familiar from newsreel, propaganda, and television film to underscore the interpretation's two-dimensional artifice more than its historical realism.[7] The audience's awareness of this double frame illustrated how the modern parallels themselves relied on historical image making, with images whose instant recognition derives from their repeated transmission through the lens of recorded account.

The allusion in McKellen's performance to Edward VIII's alliance to Hitler-Richard was an added irony (an irony omitted from the 1995 film). Playing on newly publicized doubts about the duke of Windsor's wartime loyalty, it constructed a fascist king of England from archive footage to flesh out what has become, in retrospect, another monstrous fear. Parallels with the Richard legend were evident here and in the complication of realist comparisons between Richard III and Hitler. By inviting the audience to recognize an archetypal pattern in the performance of its villain-hero's tale onstage and on screen, this interpretation alerted its audience to that pattern and identified the play's place in the myth-making process. As a reenactment of our recent past, reenacting an earlier past, Eyre's production directed attention to our own century's media-focalized potential for representing modern history as myth, and myth as material history. It was, I suggest, a dialogic ambiguity not incompatible with that of the play.[8]

NOTES

1. In *The Croyland Chronicle*, Richard is styled as the last of three kings "who after the Conquest of England were called Richard," a possible allusion to the foreign origin of the name, which is in fact German not Norman. See *The Crowland Chronicle Continuations, 1459–1486*, ed. Nicholas Pronay and John Cox (London: Sutton, 1986).

2. Edward Hall, *Hall's Chronicle*, ed. Sir Henry Ellis (London: J. Johnson, 1809).

3. Colley Cibber, *The Tragicall History of King Richard III*, in *Five Restoration Adaptations of Shakespeare*, ed. Christopher Spencer (Urbana, Ill.: Univ. of Illinois Press, 1965), 274–344.

4. F. A. Marshall, Introduction to *The Henry Irving Shakespeare*, ed. Henry Irving and F. A. Marshall (London: Blackie and Son, 1870), 13–14.

5. Charles Calvert, introduction to *The Life and Death of Richard III* (Manchester: A. Ireland, 1890).

6. With Richard and Buckingham taking "the greatest care . . . to act constitutionally," the Hall-Barton adaptation muted the final play's emphasis on the illegitimacy of almost every move that Richard makes: Peter Hall, Program for *Richard III* (Stratford: RSC, 1963).

7. Richard Loncraine and Ian McKellen's 1995 film adaptation of *Richard III*, which was based on this National Theatre production, did something of the same, although it underpinned the Richard-Hitler story with allusions to the cinematic conventions of fictional gangster movies rather than newsreel and newspaper report.

8. Parts of this essay have been included in my introduction to *Richard III at Stratford* (London: Arden, 2001) in the Arden Shakespeare at Stratford series.

New Faces for Shakespeare in Contemporary Australia

Philippa Kelly

> The Sydney Corps Drama attempted to perform *King Lear* on Monday evening last. Let them not be offended at the word *attempted*—for who can perform the play of *Lear*? . . . Still there was no necessity that they should transform the play of *Lear* into a jumble of nonsense. . . . One of the audience in the dress circle was heard to enquire, "What was it all about?" Knowles *could* play the part of Lear in a manner above mediocrity; but really he ought not to come upon the stage so utterly imperfect as he sometimes does. It is not only an affront to the audience, but it is also a very serious injury to his own reputation as an actor. We could adduce instances of the almost total ignorance of their parts in all the performers from the first scene to the last. . . . In the last scene—which was the author's, not Tate's alteration—[when] Mr. Knowles came on bearing the *dead* body of Cordelia (Mrs. Cameron), an awkward circumstance occurred . . . Mr. Knowles could get no further than the words, "Howl, howl!" when *dead* Cordelia, "perforce," laughed in his face!
>
> —unsigned review, *Sydney Morning Herald* (January 26, 1837)

THE LAUGHING CORDELIA

AN INDIGNANT REVIEWER'S RESPONSE TO AUSTRALIA'S VERY FIRST performance of *King Lear,* held in 1837 at the Theatre Royal in Sydney, might serve to highlight some unanticipated relationships between Shakespeare and the contexts in which his plays are performed and read. By laughing in Lear's face the actor breaks with convention in two ways. In refusing to "stay dead," she takes Cordelia's disobedience of her father's wishes in act 1, scene 1 to new levels of metadramatic self-parody: not only does Cordelia defy the prone and passive expectations of her postmortem comportment in act 5, scene 3, but she "laughs in the face" of them. And the actress also adds her own idiosyncratic repudiation of Australian nineteenth-century interpretive approaches to the play, which generally tamed its excesses into visions of moral redemption.[1] Far from the prone martyr, the memory of whose voice is "ever soft, / Gentle, and low" (5.3.246–47), we can imagine Cordelia's laughter ringing out into a hushed and embarrassed auditorium.

The laughing Cordelia has further implications for a contemporary point of view. Though the nineteenth-century reviewer receives the unfortunate actor's lapse as the last gasp in an appalling production, in terms of more recent reestimations of Shakespeare's value the scene can be interpreted very differently. Not exactly the best moral medicine, Cordelia's laughter might be seen instead to mock the very idea that the brutalized and chaotic world of *King Lear* can be healed. Perhaps it irreverently reinforces Edmund's vision of an unyielding nature, oblivious to the forces of human love and longing. For this vision is what the play leaves us with if we do not apply the salve of redemptive moralizing. It seems, then, that if the laughing Cordelia offended sturdy nineteenth-century conventions that advocated tragic propriety, this judgment might be dismantled by a contemporary theorist who turns her laughter from embarrassing to productive transgression. The performance event challenges patterns of interpretation that have historically contained this huge, relentlessly cruel play. Such a perspective, moreover, would celebrate the potential of "Shakespeare's book" not only to resist received ways of reading, but also to be variously embodied in the actions and speeches of actors, night after night. *King Lear* is a performance text, open to all the vagaries of directorial and performative whim. After all, if Cordelia gets the giggles, no one can stop her.

The relatively trivial incident of the laughing Cordelia gives rise to a number of complex questions. First, is there anything uniquely "Australian" about the disruption of canonical tragic drama by inopportune laughter? Second, are we to see this scene as one of the bad moments of Australian culture—a moment hardly worth hauling into the spotlight of critical analysis—or is it rather a moment of glorious insurrection? Third, does the incident unsettle notions of emotional extravagance that have so often been associated with *King Lear* as a journey of self-discovery and with Shakespeare as the embodiment of our most lofty emotions? Does Cordelia's laughter offer (albeit unintended) a challenge to the celebration of Shakespeare's "universal" voice and to the cultural predominance that his plays have enjoyed since the moment of colonization?[2]

While the first question is certainly worth thinking about, an attempt to generalize the incident of Cordelia's laughter in terms of a uniquely "Australian" moment would go beyond the scope of the present discussion; it would need to be addressed though a comprehensive, ongoing study of Australian cultural representations. The second question—how are we to read the scene—highlights the perspectival shifts through which Shakespeare's plays are endlessly reevaluated and reinterpreted. Even a trivial gaff can be given all sorts of connotations depending on where we stand and how we watch. The third question—of whether the laughing Cordelia makes a mockery of the history of reverence accorded to the Bard—raises the issue of canonicity that has been the subject of heated and, by now, prolonged debate. This last is the question I will explore in the present discussion, initially by discussing an international framework, and then by analyzing various Australian contexts—architecture, statues, a speech by the poet Oodgeroo, and an Australian editing project—that can respond to the debates provoked by challenges to Shakespeare's canonicity.

THE UNIVERSAL SHAKESPEARE

I have suggested above that the laughing Cordelia may evoke a decanonized Bard, a ludic and transgressive deconstruction for our times. Regardless of whether her laughter constitutes a "bad moment," however, Cordelia's very presence in this discussion assumes Shakespeare's "universal" interest and relevance. In itself, such a focus gives space to Shakespeare that other writers might just as usefully occupy. This effect reveals some unspoken assumptions that frame the multiple perspectives on the laughing Cordelia offered above. The "Shakespeare" who at first seems to have been freshly revivified in the disrupted tableau at the Theatre Royale reverberates in troubling ways as I walk through various streets of Sydney and Melbourne. Here can be seen scores of terrace houses, originally built by early settlers, lovingly and expensively remodeled by upper middle-income earners of the 1990s. While these houses are "restored" to their early state, they are not intended for anything like the living conditions of those who originally inhabited them. They become the historicized property of people who might not only be restoring homes that their forebears lived in, but who are also attempting to reconstruct an idealized state from which they "once" emerged.[3]

This fantasy defines their sense of alienation in a new land, justifying relationships that are both anxious and assertive.[4]

In wondering whether there is something of this sentiment in an attachment to "authentic" historical architecture, I think also of Shakespeare, a "universal genius" who has undergone both a transient nineteenth-century reconstruction in the performance of the laughing Cordelia and a twentieth-century reconstruction in my interpretation of the performative moment. While my discussion might appear to question the image of Shakespeare as a high cultural artifact, refreshing recontextualization may be uncomfortably close to tired (and tiresome) reification: enduring the constraints of time, geography, and climate, the indomitable Shakespeare reemerges in late-twentieth-century Australia with a protofeminist Cordelia whose laughter ushers in postmodern celebration.

This kind of concern provokes some critics to ask why Shakespeare is so often conceived of as a transhistorical, transatlantic genius, suggesting that his "universality" is a myth perpetuated in the interests of colonial appropriation of subordinated cultures.[5] Others challenge Shakespeare's place in the canon, critiquing liberal humanist "appeal[s] to the structures of feeling" that constitute "a 'backlash' against multiculturalism, race politics, canon expansion, feminisms, gay and lesbian studies, and other foregroundings of 'the political' in academic discourse."[6] In response to calls for Shakespeare's continued valency—for example, Brian Gibbons's affirmation that "[w]hile there are obvious differences between the formulations of the Renaissance and today, there is also a significant continuity, a shared interest in certain issues"[7]—we might usefully question the notion of "obvious differences" and "shared interests." Ideas of sameness and difference themselves pertain to specific cultural moments, so that criteria for their formulations reflect these moments while also resisting prescriptive analysis. Similarly, liberal humanist defenses of Shakespeare's universality ignore the fact that *anything* can be made universally relevant. There is universal relevance in the visual symbol of the apple that marks the system through which I generate this text. The apple is culturally resonant not for its intrinsic meaning (it is a graphic representation of an apple), but for what it has been made to signify in the iconography of recent technological information. So, "universality" is of interest not because of the thing it purports to be, but because of the social and historical ways in which it is constructed.

With this in mind we might consider Shirley Nelson Garner's

recollection of her first published essay: "What I wrote was informed by the women's movement, my own psychotherapy, and my experiences as a southern woman. Shakespeare was large enough to allow me to find myself in him, even if only in bits and pieces."[8] The idea of Shakespeare's ample girth, which "allowed" the supplicant to "find" herself "in him," suggests an uneven relationship between Shakespeare and a woman who reads his texts. While Nelson Garner asserts the value of her response, she also reduces her own presence in the dialogic relationship she discusses. In finding only "bits and pieces" of herself, she unwittingly (and somewhat parodically) takes on the guise of the conventional early modern subject of a love sonnet, the piecemeal representation of whose body parts—dazzling eyes, rosy cheeks, ruby lips, and so on—invokes the comparative breadth, depth, and wholeness of her masculine scribe. Attempts to define the cultural points that connect people in contemporary Australia or America or India to a sixteenth- or seventeenth-century English play, and thereby to explain the phenomenon of "Shakespeare's universality," can justifiably be read as a continuation of the homage paid to the master.

While for the sake of an argument it may be tempting to rebuke Nelson Garner's subjective identification, however, such rebukes have their own limitations. Of course, one might critique Nelson Garner for unashamed Bardic reverence—but as Cassius observes to Brutus, how else can the eye see itself "but by reflection"? This point is strongly brought home in Jean Trounstine's recent book *Shakespeare behind Bars*. Of the women in the prison where she taught Shakespeare for ten years, most "had toughed it out in a society that favors others—by gender, class or race. They are Desdemonas suffering because of jealous men, Lady Macbeths craving the power of their spouses, Portias disguised as men in order to get ahead, and Shylocks, who, being betrayed, take the law into their own hands."[9] Many of the inmates at first felt worlds apart from a Shakespeare who was "white man's theatre," and middle class to boot. Trounstine didn't try to reject this perspective but simply suggested to them that the plays can be more than this, leading them through the textual analysis and performance training that facilitated a vigorous and enthusiastically supported production of *The Merchant of Venice*. In the light of such uses for Shakespeare's plays, accusations of cultural subordination may seem precious and out-of-touch.

Kiernan Ryan approaches the question of Shakespeare's universality from a different perspective, that of textual analysis. He refers to "[t]he plays' roving impulse to displace the perspective across a spectrum of identities and attitudes," which "creates their structural identification with the common interests of our kind rather than with one sector of society at the expense of the rest."[10] Arguing that "[a] Shakespeare play does not roam free and innocent of history until it is pinned down and situated by an old or new historicist,"[11] Ryan alludes to "various verbal and theatrical devices" such as metatheater, dialogic discursive frames, and the reflexive opportunities offered by disguise and cross-dressing. He sees these devices as allowing for the plays' conditional and polyphonous range of meanings.[12] He goes on to criticize new historicism's yoking of contemporary subjectivity to early modern cultural formations. In his terms, new historicists unearth "primary documentation" that "squats ponderously alongside its literary pretext in embarrassed irrelevance."[13] He sees Shakespeare's relevance as residing rather in a delineation of "the inherent strategies of language and form which dictate how the plays conceive and judge their world."[14] I remain unconvinced by Ryan's own project of reaffirming Shakespeare's continued relevance through "a fully historical reading" and meanings "which are confirmable through close textual analysis."[15] Notwithstanding his claim to objectivity, Ryan's project is more likely to speak to his own codes than to Shakespeare's. Susan Bennett's study of Shakespeare in performance is helpful here. Calling on Lowenthall's critique of "a great and ennobling heritage," she refers to "nostalgia" for the "wholly ideal" past, which inspires reworkings of traditionally valued texts.[16] It is all very well to argue for the discovery of "encoded meanings," but Ryan's project (like Nelson Garner's) posits a Shakespeare who is both endlessly mutatory and endlessly flexible, always able to preempt one's own interpretive preoccupations.

Rethinking Shakespeare: Oodgeroo

It seems that Shakespeare can with equal vigor be portrayed as the encoder of meanings that will resonate through various critical endeavors in different ages, or as a liberal humanist bulwark resisting the vagaries of postmodern alienation. It is nonetheless true that however we construct Shakespeare, he remains a part of the way in which we read history, remaking it within our shifting experiences. And, as Jean Trounstine's experience has suggested, analyses of Shakespeare's imperial dominance have a narrow, specialized audience anyway.

Michael Bristol, in his broad-ranging study of the use of Shakespeare in cultural formations, notes that "Paradoxically it is the belief in Shakespeare's transcendent worth that underwrites his currency in popular culture and secures his commercial value."[17] As with the laughing Cordelia in the first part of this essay, here I again focus on a performative moment in which "Shakespeare's book" is rewritten. I have chosen the oral tradition represented by the late Australian Aboriginal writer Oodgeroo, who drew on Shakespeare's cultural prevalence in her speeches and writings, reshaping his image in her work. Oodgeroo said before her death in 1993: "I never did find out for a long time what 'home' was. I found out belatedly that it happened to be England, which shows I was definitely educated."[18] Though "educated" into a "whiteness" that recognizes its origins as English, she was sharply aware of the ambivalence that inscribed her as always already other-wise. In the lecture at the Sydney Opera House Oodgeroo declared her intention to do "a bit of mucking around with the Aboriginal language" in order to "jumpy" Shakespeare "up a bit."[19] From an awareness of being *outside* Australia's Anglophilic educational structures, she insinuated herself *inside* them by playing with them; and through this ludic involvement she changed her relationship to them.

Taking Shakespeare's line, "While greasy Joan doth keel the pot," Oodgeroo's speech changes "keel" to the Aboriginal word "geel." In the Aboriginal discourse she is referring to, "geel" is pronounced as "hiss," a rhyme for another well-known English word, "but what can I say to that—this is a hallowed place, this is the Opera House."[20] In alluding to the architectural significance of the Opera House as the "hallowed place" in which Australians and others pay homage to high culture, Oodgeroo pokes fun at the solidity of structures—physical, intellectual, emotional—to which Shakespeare belongs. The physical magnificence of the Opera House augments the physical solidity of "Shakespeare's book," the text that scholars have been at pains to determine once-and-for-all in definitive editions. Through Oodgeroo's wordplay, suddenly greasy Joan, a perfectly respectable representative of honest working-class labor, is pissing at her pot in a linguistic malapropism. Oodgeroo concludes, "So much for Shakespeare!"

By infusing her Aboriginal identity into her reading of Shakespeare, Oodgeroo resists the stern scholarly authority of the patriarchal "Bard" who has long helped to sustain Anglophilic educational structures. Viewing a Shakespeare text as a collection of words, she insists that its context can be transformed by altering just one word, and transformed again by playing with the aural connotations of that word. Even more important, in her ludic engagement with greasy Joan, Oodgeroo plays on the lowlife clowning that is such an engaging part of Shakespeare's works, yet all-too-often neglected in constructions of the authority of the English master. Ironically, then, her "mucking around" makes the text itself reverberate in ways that are not aberrant but resonant.

Oodgeroo's engagement with Shakespeare can also compare productively with the kinds of transformations that might be attributed to Shakespeare's heroines. Shakespearean characters such as Portia, Rosalind, and Viola effect their social roles by first transforming themselves (as cross-dressers) in order to transform the dramatic world around them. Cross-dressing one's garments is not unlike cross-dressing language: it plays with the connotations of representation. While many feminist critics have interpreted Shakespeare in terms of the notion that in order to effect social change women have to "be" men, this contention is also regularly reconsidered in the light of the "existence" of these female characters, in the Renaissance period, as male actors. Furthermore, I suggest that the capacity for cross-dressing itself implies a measure of control over identity because through cross-dressing, representations of subjectivity can be manipulated. This possibility illuminates Oodgeroo's capacity to manipulate her own subjectivity in playing with the interpretive possibilities of the Shakespeare text she reads. By highlighting her own language as well as the oral tradition in which it is expressed,[21] she effectively "dresses" the text in the garments of her Aboriginality. Oodgeroo's oral tradition transforms "geel" to *what it sounds like*, "hiss." And then in a twist she completes the transformation by turning the word, "hiss," again not to an Aboriginal connotation, but rather to the English word it aurally approximates, "piss."

Like a Shakespearean heroine who ends by taking back her "proper" role, Oodgeroo thus comes full circle to acknowledge the predominance of the linguistic system—that of the English language—within which she is forced to live and the boundaries of which she has playfully pushed out. Yet in this very acknowledgment is her alteration of the system as she sees it; once played with, this system can never be the same. Just as the fields of action in Shakespeare's plays are changed by the transformations realized by dramatic heroines, even though these characters slip back into place as "women" again, so too, despite Oodgeroo's conclusion with the English word "piss," is her Aboriginal incursion forever present. For those who have heard Oodgeroo's speech or read the transcript, "keel" will always have the connotation of pissing at a pot.

The flaw in this sanguine perspective is that I have somehow complied with the arguments of those critics who accord Shakespeare's texts some kind of universal value, a value that anticipates an attempt by Oodgeroo—or any other postcolonial writer—to assert the primacy of subjective identity over the text. In other words, one may conclude that Oodgeroo is mirroring the transformative powers of Shakespeare's heroines. This would be to assume that instead of really changing the text through her appropriation, Oodgeroo's incursion has in fact affirmed the supremacy of a Bard who, like David Williamson's evocation of his omniscient presence in *Dead White Males*,[22] can anticipate any kind of new-fangled selfhood. But it is important not to see Oodgeroo's strategy in a mimetic or paradigmatic relationship to Shakespeare or to the world. Instead, it should be read as engaging with texts in productive ways that fuel new ideas about Shakespeare's texts and the history of what they've been made to "mean." In Oodgeroo's hands, Shakespeare is not the staid occupant of shelves upon shelves in grand libraries: he is a ludic, festive construction. Rather than a unifying cultural emblem, Shakespeare—however we construct him—can be a focus of energetic intervention in the social, intellectual, and political structures in which we participate.

STATELY BODIES: SHAKESPEARE AND STATUES

One day in April 1995, my parents, who were visiting me in Canberra, Australia's capital, came home saying that they had seen a very funny statue by Lake Burley Griffin that they were sure represented Queen Elizabeth II and Prince Philip in the nude.[23] It turned out that this was indeed true, and that the statue (aptly named *Down by the Lake with Liz and Phil*) had been set in place only the day before. Within a fortnight the queen's head, and then that of her consort, had been lopped off amidst a public outcry. Ironically, as the statue lost its physical presence through the progressive removal of both heads, it took on a larger significance in the eyes of the public eagerly scanning the national newspapers for new light to be thrown on a burgeoning controversy.

The beheaded statue was intensely ambivalent in both subject and reception. In a loud radio interview, the sculptor Greg Taylor expressed puzzlement as to whether the heads had been removed in a gesture of allegiance to or repudiation of the monarchy. If it was a sign of allegiance, the disfigurement (or refiguring?) meant that the naked figures could no longer be seen as demeaning representations of the queen and her prince. On the other hand, the beheading of the figures could perhaps be seen as a metaphorical killing-off of authority in a prorepublican reenactment of the famous demise of King Charles I. From yet another standpoint the statue might signify both subjection to and rejection of the British Empire: with the heads on, its nakedness could demystify and ironize emblems of monarchical magnificence that have been seen by many to cow Australian culture for the past two hundred years; with the heads off, the statue could perhaps make fun of the dignified un-bodiedness that Australians have come to associate with a corseted queen and her militarily kitted-out husband. I call this type of dignity "unbodied" because among other things it decrees that the contours of high culture are acquired at some cost and are not meant to be comfortable or accessible.

In gesturing toward multiple meanings, the statue had the potential to challenge monolithic values, remapping their relationships to constructions of "reality." Shakespeare's status in contemporary Australia might be freed from the constraints of essentialist interpretations by relating it to these possible meanings. Like *Down by the Lake with Liz and Phil*, the reception of Shakespeare's plays in Australia highlights the ambivalent values associated with high culture and Anglophilia. If *Down by the Lake with Liz and Phil* can be read as a text, then, conversely it is possible that Shakespeare's drama is made to occupy the status—and the stasis—of a statue.

The statue's representational ambivalence connects with local readings of Shakespeare's plays in two specific aspects: appearance and location. By "appearance" I mean that in many current deployments Shakespeare has become an icon, connoting more the physical stasis of a statue than a body of words intended to be read and performed. Thus in the vigorous though ideologically driven 1993 collection of essays, *Shakespeare's Books*, the contributors evinced almost no interest in engaging with the texts of Shakespeare, whom they represented as a cultural monolith. (In terms of the anticanonical agenda set by *Shakespeare's Books*, manifest interest in the texts might well have betrayed an unseemly enjoyment of the very object of critical repudiation.) Shakespeare was caricatured as a crusty old symbol of empire-spawning, demonic, Oxbridge-educated professors and "heavy-footed Oberons" to be found wading through the "watery groves" of Sydney's academic pastures.[24]

A reading of Shakespeare or his works as statue strikes a further ironic connection with a well-known Australian physical emblem. A huge replica of Shakespeare stands outside the State Library of New South Wales in Sydney, where the traffic races past along the freeway. In order to get through the traffic to examine the statue, one has to endanger life and limb. Could one infer that Shakespeare, the icon of all that is tall and good, stands aloof from the mutabilities of modern life and will still stand supreme in another two hundred years? Alternatively, is Shakespeare—whose image one can barely recognize without crossing the median strip to stand directly beneath the statue—perhaps stuck out on his own, tired and alone, while modern life rushes obliviously by? Or does his position in the midst of the traffic suggest his universal standing, his openness to engagements not just with transcendent values but with the speeding currents of shifting times?

My second point—that of location—involves the existence of both *Down by the Lake with Liz and Phil* and the figure of Shakespeare within contemporary culture. Taylor's statue was situated in Canberra, the seat of governmental power (symbolized by Parliament House), the seat of intellectual power (the National Library), and the seat of cultural power (the National Gallery). The War Memorial, the National Portrait Gallery, the High Court, and the other monuments that dot Australia's capital city might no longer spell out the nation's subjection to imperial constraints. Yet as architectural houses of intellectual, social, and political governance clustered together, their geographical arrangement cannot help but invoke imperial associations. Nowhere is this more evident than in the design of Canberra's Parliament House: from the top of an incline, its huge claws reach out symbolically to clasp its subjects.

The meanings attached to *Down by the Lake with Liz and Phil* largely depended on its location amongst these symbols of governance. It suggested iconoclastic possibilities for public readings of artifacts of imperial power: do their solid structures inherit, and indeed generate, the strength of Australia's capital city? Or are they outmoded extrusions that stand in the way of its national growth? Shakespeare's uses for Australians today raise similar issues of imperial authority, dependence, and subjection. If readings and stagings of Shakespeare's plays shape the locations in which they are interpreted, readings of local issues and events also shape interpretations of Shakespeare's texts, determining their shifting cultural currency.

IN HIS FACE: PREPARING *KING LEAR* FOR AN AUSTRALIAN AUDIENCE

In the previous section I have addressed the shifting kinds of value that might be attached to artifacts in specific times and places. In exploring Shakespeare's local value in context with the controversy surrounding a particular statue, I have sought to highlight the contingency and negotiability of any such value, which depends on who is looking, on where they are doing the looking, and on the position(s) they are looking from. These shifting frames—in which both "Shakespeare" and contemporary contexts for reading and performance affect each other—can also be instanced by a project I have recently completed, the editing of *King Lear* for the Australia-based Bell Shakespeare Series.[25] The Bell Shakespeare Company is an independent Australian theater company, launched in 1990, "with a broad mandate to educate and entertain the public."[26] Linked to the theater company is the production of the Bell editions, geared largely toward a local public. Setting out to cover the international critical history of Shakespeare's plays, these editions also provide comprehensive Australian performance histories. I aimed to prepare an edition with a particularly feminist interest.

I decided to begin by exploring the kinds of assumptions with which editors underwrite textual editing—perhaps assumptions about "correct" ways of selecting and recording the texts, of interpreting them, or even of housing them for particular reading and theater audiences. These interpretations might close audiences off to more flexible perspectives, in particular to some kinds of feminist interventions. For instance, in the opening scene of *King Lear*, when Regan tells her father that she is "of that self mettle as my sister" (1.1.67), the customary gloss is to invoke the homonym, "metal," to suggest a hard nature. Regan's words are thus read as a proleptic sign of a future harshness that induces her to reject her father outright and later to demand the plucking-out of Gloucester's eyes. But to gloss the line this way is also to participate in a whole history of criticism that paints Regan and Goneril as villains and Cordelia as their angelic opposite.[27] Such stereotyping enables critics to push Cordelia to one end of a spectrum and Regan and Goneril to the other, turning their attention back to the two old men and their representation of "the human condition." I wrestled with this problem in my edition, trying in my gloss and introduction at least covertly to allude to this tendency, even if I also invoked its biases.

I discussed "gender" as society's way of fixing places for sexual bodies. Gender represents society's understanding of biology in terms of sexual codes of behavior that have no necessary relation to biological facts.[28] The mid-sixteenth-century poet Niccolo Grassi expressed a general view of love as "mingled with the bestial from the waist down, whereas in the other half formed by reason it becomes human, like us."[29] While writers such as Stephen Orgel have asked us to rethink gender roles and gender expectations in the early modern period,[30] it is a conventional understanding that in this period the lower impulses of love were seen as both carnal and gendered. When Lear says of Regan and Goneril, "Down from the waist / They're centaurs, though women all above' (4.5.118–19), he connotes their transgression of codes of chastity appropriate to their gender. Albany later agrees with him: "Proper deformity shows not in the fiend / So horrid as in woman" (4.2.36–37).

The constraints of womanhood were reinforced by well-known Biblical references that connected loose tongues with loose morality in women. The Book of Proverbs says:

> For the lips of an immoral woman drip honey, and
>   her mouth is smoother than oil;
> But in the end she is more bitter than wormwood,
>   Sharper than a two-edged sword.
>
> (5:3–4)[31]

Cordelia of course echoes this biblical passage in her reference to her sisters' "glib and oily art" (1.1.222). In alluding to their adultery to come, Cordelia seems to suggest that their honeyed words are to be taken as unequivocal evidence of their nascent immorality. By connecting with conventional attitudes to women, Cordelia's image could have prompted a seventeenth-century audience to make a division between herself as saint and Regan and Goneril as wicked adulteresses.

It was necessary to take account of these associations while also emphasizing the point that though tempting for conservative readers to position the three daughters according to their relation to femininity and associated conventions of chastity and silence, *King Lear* does not let any such division between them rest easily. The language used by Regan and Goneril should not be dismissed as "glib and oily" without the recognition that it is indeed elicited by Lear, who in the opening love-test still has the double authority of king and father. In demanding that his daughters verbalize their love publicly, Lear exacts the sort of stylized commitment that befits the rituals of his contemporary court. Two of his daughters (who are also his subjects) give him the material measures that he wants, and indeed formally demands, to hear: "Beyond what can be valued, rich or rare"; "I find she names my very deed of love" (1.1.55, 69). When Goneril says to Cordelia, "You have obedience scanted, / And well are worth the want that you have wanted" (1.1.276–77), is she not pointing out that in affirming her own love for Lear, she has simply done what her king and father has asked her to do?

In my keenness to address local and feminist issues in editing *King Lear*, I found it difficult to manage my desire to dispense with the things that every "good" introduction is expected to provide. I tested my own perspective along the way against those of my students, asking them, for example, to complete a small-group exercise in annotating the first scene of the play for an audience of their choosing. I struggled with the edition for three-and-one-half years. In the end I opted not for resolution but for a resting point, a feeling of having covered the conventional ground while maintaining sufficient feminist interest in the face of *King Lear*'s inheritance (for example, character parallels and contrasts, subplot and main plot, and various thematic readings). In thinking about my work on the play, Lear's own unwitting testament to the power of radical subjectivity, "Thou art the thing itself" (3.4.95), resonates ironically.[32] Perhaps an editor cannot get much closer than can the old, mad king to any definition of value. In preparing the play for other people's use, editors may ultimately have to stop seeking a definitive, all-inclusive, multipurpose version, acknowledging instead the ineluctable subjectivity that is both the strength and the limitation of each editorial perspective.

The questions of why and how Shakespeare can be the locus of "universal" value and what the point is of this continual reification can be addressed, as I have attempted here, by considering diverse responses offered by particular critical perspectives. Having initially explored the ambivalent image of the laughing Cordelia, I moved to examine some specific ways in which people have tried to rethink Shakespeare's value. While these efforts do not claim to clear the critical arena—an arena that, one could argue, writers other than Shakespeare might productively occupy—they can offer us the opportunity to question our own preoccupations and biases. Such questioning makes it possible to reshape our understandings of "critical heritage" and of our own capacity to intervene in it. Certain ideas and priorities may stand as given, but they need not remain pleasurably—or, indeed, unthinkingly—received.

NOTES

1. Reviews of this play in this period were predominantly conservative. Consider, for example, the production at Sydney's Prince of Wales Theatre, in which readers are assured of the properness of the superficially inordinate treatment meted out to Lear and Cordelia: both are sinners who have "tempted Providence by their imprudence" and have been aptly punished for their sins. The play "suggests to the unlearned the sadness of domestic wickedness." The critic goes on to praise G. V. Brooke's representation of "the thorough prostration of the monarch's intellect when Lear finds amusement in Mad Tom's straws, and is pleased to talk with that philosopher. . . . The scene, moreover, in which the intellect of Lear recovers, and he painfully and joyfully recognizes his Cordelia, was played by Mr. Brooke so truly, that tears started to the eyes of many, to whom it would be no shame to confess the weakness, or rather the tenderness of their nature." Cordelia was "rendered with much propriety and grace by Mrs. Poole," while Mr. Edwards played Edgar with "good taste and pleasing elocution"; the unsigned review is in *The Sydney Morning Herald*, 19 August 1858. Similarly, the anonymous reviewer of an 1867 production of *King Lear* in Sydney refers to "the stern, unyielding moral by which the whole composition is pervaded" and praises James Anderson for his restraint in playing Lear; rather than giving way to excesses of emotion, Lear was played "materially the same throughout": *Sydney Morning Herald*, 26 September 1867.

2. The first recorded performance of Shakespeare was in a penal production in the late eighteenth century. It has been recorded in Thomas Keneally's novel *The Playmaker* (Sydney: Hodder and Stoughton, 1987).

3. Homi K. Bhabha, "Signs Taken for Wonders: Questions of Ambivalence and Authority Under a Tree Outside Delhi, May 1817," *Critical Inquiry* 12, no. 1 (1985): 149.

4. For insights into the "imagined originary wholeness" that fuels this kind of nostalgia, see Homi K. Bhabha, "The Other Question," *Screen* 24, no. 6 (1983): 22.

5. See, for example, the essays in *Shakespeare's Books: Contemporary Cultural Politics and the Persistence of Empire*, ed. Marion Campbell and Philip Mead (Melbourne: Melbourne Univ. Press, 1993).

6. Linda Charnes, "What's Love Got to Do with It? Reading the Liberal Humanist Romance in *Antony and Cleopatra*," in *Shakespearean Tragedy and Gender*, ed. Shirley Nelson Garner and Madelon Sprengnether (Bloomington, Ind.: Indiana Univ. Press, 1996), 280.

7. Brian Gibbons, *Shakespeare and Multiplicity* (Cambridge: Cambridge Univ. Press, 1993), 9.

8. Shirley Nelson Garner, "Shakespeare in My Time and Place," in *Shakespearean Tragedy and Gender*, 296.

9. Jean Trounstine, *Shakespeare behind Bars: The Power of Drama in a Women's Prison* (New York: St. Martin's Press, 2001), 2.

10. Kiernan Ryan, *Shakespeare*, 2d ed. (London: Prentice Hall, 1995), 35.

11. Ibid., 25.

12. Ibid., 35–36.

13. Ibid., 26.

14. Ibid., 27.

15. Ibid., 18, 24.

16. Susan Bennett, *Performing Nostalgia: Shifting Shakespeare and the Contemporary Past* (London: Routledge, 1996), 10. The whole of chapter 1 is particularly useful to this point (1–38.)

17. Michael Bristol, *Big-Time Shakespeare* (London: Routledge, 1996), 90. See also Lawrence Levine, *Highbrow/Lowbrow: The Emergence of Cultural Hierarchy in America* (Cambridge: Harvard Univ. Press, 1988). Levine's study is more conservatively structured than Bristol's: an important premise for his argument is that a judgment can be shared about Shakespeare's qualitative superiority.

18. Oodgeroo, "Writers of Australia, 'I dips me lid'" (Goossens Lecture delivered at the Sydney Opera House, 9 June 1993), as cited in Kathleen J. Cochrane, *Oodgeroo/Kathie Cochrane* (Brisbane: Univ. of Queensland Press, 1994), 214.

19. Ibid., 214.

20. Ibid., 214

21. In *High Culture, Popular Culture: The Long Debate* (Sydney: Allen and Unwin, 1995), Peter Goodall has an interesting discussion of the relation of oral culture to conventional notions of literary "high culture" (162).

22. David Williamson, *Dead White Males* (Melbourne: Currency Press, 1995).

23. I first discussed this statue in an article published in Australia: "Talking with Statues: Shakespeare, Empire and Essentialism," *New Literatures Review: Postcolonial Elaborations* 32, no. 2 (1997): 49–56.

24. Stephen Knight, "In the Golden World: Shakespeare and the Pedagogy of Power," in *Shakespeare's Books*, 154.

25. Philippa Kelly, *King Lear*, Bell Shakespeare edition (Sydney: Halstead Press, forthcoming).

26. *The Bell Shakespeare Company*, 22 June 2001 <http://www.bellshakespeare.com.au/>.

27. James Calderwood gives a classic instance of this when he writes of Cordelia's "gentle conquest" in act 4: "Creative Uncreation in *King Lear*," *Shakespeare Quarterly* 37 (1986): 9. Calderwood places Goneril and Regan at an opposite extreme, mocking their actions in the first scene: "The ladies have become spacious in the possession of dirt" (6).

28. See Gayle Rubin, "The Traffic in Women: Notes on the 'Political Economy' of Sex," in *Toward an Anthropology of Women*, ed. Rayna Reiter (New York: Monthly Review Press, 1975), 157–220.

29. Quoted in Mary Pardo, "Artifice as Seduction in Titian," in *Sexuality and Gender in Early Modern Europe: Institutions, Texts, Images*, ed. James Grantham Turner (Cambridge: Cambridge Univ. Press, 1993), 84.

30. See Stephen Orgel, *Impersonations: The Performance of Gender in Shakespeare's England* (Cambridge: Cambridge Univ. Press, 1996).

31. I am indebted to Dosha Reichardt for alerting me to this connection.

32. In claiming specificity ("the thing itself"), Lear's words also acknowledge the fact that they can never be more specific than they are.

Materialist Shakespeare and Ideological Performance: Michael Bogdanov and Shakespeare in Production

Ian Maclennan

An audience member viewing a production of a Shakespear-ean play directed by the English director Michael Bogdanov might at first be shocked by the apparent disregard that Bogda-nov appears to have for convention. After all, the use of a red Alfa-Romeo by Tybalt in *Romeo and Juliet* (1986–87), or the abu-sive behavior in the audience of the actor playing Christopher Sly, culminating in the attempted destruction of the set by a drunken Sly as part of the Induction scene in *The Taming of the Shrew* (1979), is not what one expects to see or experience when participating in the ritual of attending a Shakespearean play. But Bogdanov purposely refuses to be hampered by the accretions of tradition, instead creating productions that are at once novel in design, yet faithful in content to the play. He does this because of his belief, as he says, that "the responsibility of [a] production is to remove the barriers between text and audience, strive for a new language of the stage in hopes of challenging a contemporary audience the way these plays challenged their audience in 1599."[1] It is this use of historical resonances and reverberations that indi-cates a concern with Marxist criticism. As Terry Eagleton states: "Marxist criticism is part of a larger body of theoretical analysis which aims to understand *ideologies*—the ideas, values and feel-ings by which men experience their societies at various times."[2] What appears to be happening in Bogdanov's productions is the creation of a kind of visual and aural Marxist semiotics around which the ideas, values, and feelings that the historical Shake-speare posited are transferred and transformed to make his plays relevant for today.

Bogdanov believes in the social responsibility of the artist and of production. He encodes this responsibility by making his productions more accessible to the average playgoer. In transforming Shakespearean plays into recognizable products of the twentieth century, Bogdanov has shown that Shakespeare is not the dreaded bore of so many classrooms but is vibrant, alive, and accessible four hundred years after first being written: "We are living . . . a watershed moment in the history of Shakespeare. Academics vastly outnumber practitioners, and classroom encounters with the canon often end up convincing students the Bard is an irrelevant bore . . . Shakespeare has suffered enormously from groups of people who perform these plays as if they had no relation with our society."[3] For Bogdanov it is important that the plays be accessible to the audience, that the production assist in the transfer of understanding between stage and audience, and that the performance be a vehicle for the transmission of the intent of the play as understood by the director and actors.

How does Bogdanov achieve all these goals? First, his productions are almost all modern dress. His *Romeo and Juliet* had the casualness of a hot Italian summer in Verona, and his *Measure for Measure* (1985) included a transvestite cabaret (with the obvious implication that appearances are deceptive). In *The Henrys* trilogy (1986–87) the French court was dressed Edwardian, with the English court Victorian for *1 and 2Henry IV*, and modern for *Henry V*, while the Boar's Head Tavern in Eastcheap was a punk hangout. As Bogdanov himself notes: "In an attempt to remove as many barriers as possible between the audience and the language, I had started, in 1976, to direct in modern dress. . . . I discovered that the language had a new meaning and character, and that young people, in particular, suddenly had an interest and a stake in the characters. They were able to understand immediately the complexities involved."[4]

For traditionalists, it is often sacrilege to tamper with the "historical" aspect of Shakespeare by appropriating modern dress to historical texts and visually transforming the past into the present. It spoils and desecrates the sacred text by supposedly "forcing" a modern visual interpretation upon the play. But Bogdanov's purpose, as he himself has said, is to remove the barriers between text and audience. One method of doing so is to present a visually modern production. The use of modern dress signals to a contemporary audience that these characters are in some ways like them. They can identify much more readily with a character dressed up as they might be than they can with characters in Renaissance dress. This simple means of accessing an audience creates a bond between stage and auditorium, not the barrier that the distancing inherent in historical production creates.

By making these plays more accessible visually, Bogdanov has created a space of representation that is accessible to all in the audience, not just to an initiated elite. In doing so, he creates the opening through which contemporary understanding of the text is possible. That is to say, the contemporizing of Shakespeare visually by Bogdanov indicates that the issues of the play may, therefore, have some contemporary relevance. An untutored audience is much more likely to feel less threatened and uneasy if the Shakespeare they see is presented to them in visual terms that they can recognize and for which they feel some affinity. This technique may, in some ways, also be seen as subversive, for it can lull its audience into a false sense of security through which the interpretative intentions of the director can then be imposed.

It is Bogdanov's view that "in all of Shakespeare's plays, a subversive view is clearly pitted against the theme of reconciliation. . . . Theater is an instrument of social change. When the chips are down, art is protest. It is the responsibility of artists to be part of the process of change."[5] Here the socially and politically motivated Bogdanov emerges. Born of avid trade-unionist parents, a person whose maternal side of the family were strong Welsh patriots, Bogdanov grew up in the class- and economic-conscious atmosphere of postwar Britain. His own pronouncements and productions strongly indicate his political and social beliefs. Bogdanov's productions relate to the social and political realities of 1980s Britain—Britain under Margaret Thatcher, with all its attendant social and economic problems. Successive Thatcher governments undermined the economic viability of the North, of Scotland, and of Wales, and created greater prosperity in the already prosperous Home Counties and Southeast.

In Bogdanov's Shakespeare, these contemporary realities are situated within the plays. *Romeo and Juliet*'s mise-en-scène is a "modern Verona of old-money Montagues, upstart Capulets and trendy idle youth."[6] This commentary on the upper echelons of society in present-day Britain, the legacy of Thatcherism and monetarism, gives "the sense of rich and pampered young people driven to decadence and feuding by boredom more than anything else."[7] This context produces the performative interpretation of the Britain where a small fortune was spent on the coming-of-age party for the then Viscount Althorp, heir to the Earl Spenser and brother of Diana, princess of Wales, while unemployment rates rose dramatically because of prevailing economic policies. The subtext, or subversive element (depending upon the viewer's political leanings), of Bogdanov's *Romeo and Juliet* is the exposure of the ancient and new aristocracies as selfish (Romeo's and Juliet's total lack of concern for anyone but themselves) and self-aggrandizing (Mercutio and Tybalt as leaders who are only concerned with maintaining their power over their coteries). These connections may seem a crude Marxist interpretation of class structure, but to British audiences familiar with the ramifications of a highly structured society, the Bogdanov vision of the present as seen onstage may run true.

In the Henry trilogy, Bogdanov appears to provide another critique of Britain under the Thatcher government. We see an end of concern for others, from a social democratic viewpoint, and the emergence of the cultural and political implications of "me first" inherent, according to opponents, in the prevailing policies. In the battle between Hotspur and Hal in *1Henry IV*, Bogdanov has the more experienced Hotspur gain the upper hand in the fight. Prince Hal loses his sword and the fair-minded Hotspur returns it to him, only to regret it soon after when Hal kills him. In this scene, Bogdanov had a spotlight face the audience, and when Hotspur died the light faded. This visual signal of light fading at the death of the chivalrous Hotspur may have several different meanings. Bogdanov may have intended simply to indicate the passing of an old age of light and the dawning of a new, darker age, where opportunism holds the upper hand and feeds upon the "misguided" notion of helping others by destroying the helping hand in order to advance. As one English critic notes: "Here, for the first time in my theater-going experience, we chart the changes in the national character, the way that society takes its cue from the man at the top. The raffish, disorderly England of the first part of *Henry IV*, with its stubborn codes of honor and obligation, gives way to a more plush and affluent world, self-centered, witty and devious, in the second part. By the time of *Henry V* the king has streamlined the ruthless ambition of his own autocracy, and he is a superb manipulator of the spotlight of power."[8] Thus it may also be read, in more specific contemporary terms, that this directorial signal may indicate a parallel between the extinction of light at Hotspur's death with the emergence of the "efficient" conservatism of Tory politics.

There are many other indications of contemporary British events in the trilogy, particularly in *Henry V*. The English soldiers at Agincourt are presented as the Paras at Goose Green in the Falklands. For many of her opponents, the implications of the

Falklands War confirmed their view of Thatcher as imperialist in the extreme, attempting to drag Britain kicking and screaming back into the nineteenth century—the period of British supremacy and hegemony. As Agincourt was to reinstate English claims in France, so the Falklands was a British attempt to retain or reinstate an imperialist outpost.

As well as a critique upon Thatcher's ambitions with regard to the Falklands, *Henry V* also can be viewed as a critique upon the attitudes of the British people during the incident. Given that there is a visual connection between Henry's soldiers and those of Mrs. Thatcher, it is of note that the crowds at Southampton who send the troops off to war resemble that scourge of British sport, the football hooligan. In Bogdanov's production, Eastcheap has migrated to Southampton for a glorious send-off of "our boys" who head off to France singing "'Ere we go, 'ere we go, 'ere we go!" There are also resonances of the jingoistic fervor of the tabloid press in Britain in 1982, emphasized by the banners that the crowd holds and waves. As the sinking of the Argentine cruiser Belgrano was announced to the British people by one tabloid newspaper as "Gotcha!" so Bogdanov's staging of Henry's patriotic send-off was highlighted by the Chorus waving a "Gotcha!" placard and by a bedsheet banner that trumpeted "Fuck the Frogs." French teenage audiences in the spring of 1987 understood only too clearly the implications of such a theatrical image, the 1980s being a time of strong anti-Europe sentiment in the Thatcher government.

While there was comedy in the embarkation scene, there were also frightening intimations of incipient fascism. The overpowering abundance of Union Jacks, reminiscent of an international football match, also appeared similar to visuals of marches of the National Front, the British neofascist movement. This juxtaposition of fascism and jingoism is a telling reference point in determining Bogdanov's understanding and critique of the political realities of Thatcher Britain. Bogdanov's productions indicate a fear of the growth of fascism under Thatcher, as national pride and mythology were used as the basis for her political success. The Prince Hal of the Henry trilogy in his impatient treatment of his father (visually represented by Hal's constant shifting about during the king's accusations to and about his son in *1Henry IV* 3.3) shows that "this Hal had no patience with anything that interfered with his own plans or seemed to make excessive demands upon him."[9] It is possible to read, through these signals, that Bogdanov's Prince Hal bears a striking resemblance in terms of personality to Magaret Thatcher. The parallel treatment of Falstaff by Prince Hal, when the prince rejects a mentor and friend, and Thatcher's treatment of Edward Heath and Michael Heseltine, one a former mentor and now opponent, the latter a member of Cabinet who stood up to her and was forced to resign, might be seen as a clue to Bogdanov's understanding and consequent directorial interpretation of Prince Hal. As a review in the *Melbourne Herald* observed during the 1988 tour: "This is no updating of a series of antique texts, but a reaching into the past in search of images of the present. . . . The great struggle between the forces of national unity and cultural autonomy that has characterized English history continues still, and is consistently and specifically touched on . . . an insight into the heart of Britain today, responding variously and violently as it does to the continuing urge to dominate in the South."[10]

One problem, of course, with this method of analogy is that audiences not familiar with the contemporary political situation will be unable to understand the directorial implications of the analogy. Audience perception of the interpretative relevance of the production is hindered. However, the audience base of these particular productions could be expected to be knowledgeable about the political situation as the trilogy toured England, Wales, Germany, France, and Canada.

It may be of concern to some literary scholars that a director would attempt to remove a Shakespearean play from its historical and literary setting and attempt to "modernize" it. Bogdanov, however, while visually adapting the play, does not desecrate the text. As Andrew Rissik states in his review of the trilogy in *Plays and Players*: "the exhortations to our contemporary historical sense are plain, but they take their meaning and justification from the text. . . . In the end, it is the visual logic of the production, the way it continually breaks the stranglehold of photographic representationalism, which ensures the supremacy of the text."[11] Bogdanov uses the text as the ground upon which the production is built. There is no attempt to adapt the text to fit the interpretation. Cuts do occur but they are for practical reasons, such as the elimination of references that would be unclear to modern audiences. There are no cuts in the text for interpretive purposes.

The aspect of historical past and historical present are extremely important aspects in a Marxist interpretation: "The question at issue is how the literature of the past is to relate to the future . . . the past significance of a literary work is indivisible from its present meaning."[12] What Bogdanov does is take the historical construct of a Shakespearean play and demonstrate its relevance to late-twentieth-century culture. By bringing history forward and taking history backward, he creates within his productions a world that is essentially relevant to both earlier and current contexts, although the visual aspects may date the physical mise-en-scène in more contemporary terms. It is this concern with past and present and the social critique inherent in his productions that indicate the social and political bent of the director.

Bogdanov is not shy about using the theater. Anyone conversant with the arts scene in Britain knows that "the chips were down" in the 1980s. Bogdanov's use of theater as the illuminator of parallels between past and present societies (remember that after the reign of Henry V came the Wars of the Roses—an England torn apart, as Bogdanov would argue it was under the economic policies that prevailed under Thatcher) and theater as protest (the portrayal of the historical icon, Henry V, as cold and calculating, parallelling a similar perception of Thatcher) was a warning about the state of British society under the Thatcher government and relates to his concern about theater as an instrument of social change. By presenting an analogy in the form of the Henry trilogy, Bogdanov is surreptitiously presenting a Marxist critique on the present (and by implication, past) social and political order in Britain. He does so by removing Shakespearean production from the theatrical accretions and conventions of the past and pointing out, visually and physically, the similarities of the past with the present in the hope of influencing the future.

NOTES

1. Quoted in Marianne Ackermann, "Mirvish, Marx and Shakespeare," *Canadian Theater Review* 50 (spring 1987): 63.

2. Terry Eagleton, *Marxism and Literary Criticism* (Berkeley and Los Angeles: Univ. of California Press, 1976), viii.

3. Quoted in Ackermann, "Mirvish," 63.

4. Michael Bogdanov and Michael Pennington, *The English Shakespeare Company: The Story of "The Wars of the Roses," 1986–1989* (London: Nick Hern Books, 1990), 242–43.

5. Quoted in Ackermann, "Mirvish," 63.

6. Gerald M. Berkowitz, "Shakespeare in London, January–July 1987," *Shakespeare Quarterly* 38 (1987): 497.

7. Ibid., 497.

8. Andrew Rissik, "The Henry Trilogy," *Plays and Players* 402 (March 1987): 11.

9. Roger Warren, "Shakespeare in England, 1986–87," *Shakespeare Quarterly* 38 (1987): 360.

10. Quoted in Bogdanov, *English Shakespeare Company*, 181.

11. Rissik, "The Henry Trilogy," 9, 10.

12. Gaylord C. Leroy and Ursula Bietz, eds. *Preserve and Create: Essays in Marxist Literary Criticism* (New York: Humanities Press, 1973), 8.

Epilogue

Travels on the Shakespeare Underground

R. S. White

The Shakespearean Underground

The map of the London underground railway system, the "tube," as it is familiarly known, is one of the most famous diagrams in the world. Although the system confuses millions of tourists visiting Britain ("Board the southbound Northern Line"), the map itself is a brilliant solution to the problem of representing an even more confusing geographical system, since the actual train lines do not follow the regular lines, arcs, and circles of the map. They run higgledy-piggledy in meandering and irregular paths that, if plotted on an overground map of London, would bear little resemblance to the map. Distances between stations are nowhere near so regular as the map implies. The diagram was invented by Harry Beck in 1933, in response to a competition to produce the most straightforward way of letting passengers know where they are going. The genius of the maker was rewarded with a disgracefully small sum of money and he lost all reproductive rights to the map. All other entrants mapped the literal path of the underground, ending up with what looks like spaghetti. The winner's conceptual breakthrough was to realize that the map did not need to look like the actual rail network, since it is only the stations that matter to passengers. They can descend onto one platform, change efficiently at others, and come up where they want to. Thus the map could be purely schematic, with a central oval and straight lines and with stations appearing to be at regular intervals. Travelers realize that London is not so much a homogeneous entity but a collection of villages, each with its own epicenter, ethos, and history. It is still being added to, as the metropolitan hinterland encompasses more and more towns and villages, old and new. In 1977 it linked up with Heathrow airport to the west and in the 1990s with the English Channel to Europe in the south. It is now being extended through the Thames Docklands, and farther out into the metropolitan area.

It may not be too fanciful to think of the history of Shakespearean criticism evolving as an underground system on the basis of the London train grid. It has a complex history of incorporating and linking old approaches, while developing new ones that are often untidily linked to the old. Shakespeare was also, like the underground stations, used as a point of patriotic shelter during World War II (for example, Laurence Olivier's 1944 film version of *Henry V*). Shakespeare had his most recent jubilee in 1965, and the underground jubilee line was opened in 1979. We should, then, be able to provide a map of the Shakespeare underground along the lines of the London tube map. It might have some usefulness in conceptualizing the network of Shakespeare criticism in the twentieth century, and in providing a working model of the relationship between the past and the present, raising theoretical questions on their links. As the following map is research in progress, I reserve the right of course to develop the links more closely in order to prove my ultimate hunch that in fact Shakespeare *is* the London underground, as well as the Statue of Liberty, the Sydney Opera House, and Moby Dick.

The roots of professional Shakespearean study were planted in the eighteenth century by scholars such as Edmond Malone and his friend and mentor Samuel Johnson. Their interests lay in writing the biography of William Shakespeare and in editing his texts. Both activities were informed by these scholars' saturation in classical literature, and so the search for sources became a general preoccupation of the serious Shakespeare scholar. At the same time, as ever, Shakespeare's works were being constantly staged, albeit in versions rewritten and revised by poets such as Dryden and Sheridan and canonized by Garrick. Theatrical adaptation can be seen as a legitimate, creative form of criticism, since it makes explicit the centers of attention or themes that the writers found in the "original" plays. The first stations in my fictional underground system, then, are biography, editing, source-finding, and theater, all of which have a critical dimension.

In the early nineteenth century, a group of disparate "Romantic" figures explored different aspects of Shakespearean texts, both as readers and as theatergoers. A. W. Schlegel, S. T. Coleridge, William Whiter, and Maurice Morgann fashioned a Shakespeare for readers, examining linguistic imagery and the construction of what they saw to be consistent characters, while Hazlitt combined a similarly literary approach with a respect for the stage, especially through the acting of the most famous actor of his time, Edmund Kean. By the time of Carlyle in mid-century, followed a little later by Matthew Arnold, the Bard as hero and as institution was reinforced by a powerful appeal to Shakespeare as a figure in history who reshaped not just literary history but history itself. By 1904, when A. C. Bradley published his *Shakespearean Tragedy*, which mainly explores characterization, a central "Circle Line" had been established: history, theater, biography, editing, sources, and character (with imagery being seen mainly as reflection of dramatic character). Right up to the 1970s, a thorough student of Shakespeare would be required to address the ways in which "meaning can be found" by alighting at each of these stations in turn, browsing there, and moving on. The circuit was a *central* line, with an inescapable quality.

Of course, changes were made to each station as time went on. Theater has always changed with popular opinion, in ways that revealed new potential in the text, from the celebration of empire in the Victorian proscenium arch to the "realistic" theater of Brecht and the pessimism of Beckett's and Pinter's influence. Nowadays "localization" is at the vanguard of theater history, a study of the ways in which regional identity issues into Shakespeare productions around the world, and a reflection of a new recognition of the inherent instability of dramatic texts. Shakespearean history became more politically defined by L. C. Knights in the 1930s, biography shrank in importance, and editing increasingly became a professionally exclusive site where fewer alighted. "Character" was modified by modernism to conform to a play's perceived symbolic unity, as in the criticism of G. Wilson Knight, who saw the plays as primarily poetic and metaphorical in essence, or to the anthropological archetypes in Northrop Frye's analysis. The stations became self-sufficient villages.

The Central Line became the dominant Anglo-American paradigm for the study of Shakespeare, and it was underpinned by certain assumptions about the subject. It assumed, for example, the universal significance of Shakespeare's works as if the dramatist had an innate understanding of "the essential human condition": just go round this line and you'll learn everything about human nature. And the ways in which "human" was defined were equally assumed: to be human meant to be male, Western European, middle class, and proudly individualistic. On my little map, then, I have constructed an airport transporting critics between North America and Britain, and a rail link called the Western Essentialist Line. Before about the mid 1960s the people who traveled this line were mainly men in suits, the odd Rhodes scholar from the colonies, and a handful of women. But as the

British Empire was perceived to be more and more anachronistic, so were these mandarins. After a decade of fierce fighting, conducted through the syllabus and precipitated by the socioeconomic expansion of higher education in developed countries and the development of mass youth culture, new travelers and even immigrants emerged, demanding equality and change.

Their radical perception was that the Central Line was not a natural geographical growth, immutable and unavoidable, but instead no more or less than a construction based ultimately on class, education, and property interests. It carried privileged people between palaces, stately homes, universities, and desirable residences, and excluded those not part of an elite. Like the London underground, passengers traveled in the dark between stops and were not encouraged to think about links between each. The idea that one needs to *know* so much to belong to the elitist club of Shakespearean scholars was challenged by a new generation. To them, no longer should "Shakespeare" be taken for granted as a cultural symbol of high art and of the effortless superiority of the British. His plays were from one side attacked and from the other side appropriated by disparate "single-issue" groups claiming a new stake in cultural life. In particular, women and Marxists began to travel on the underground. They were not content to sit back, slumber, and emerge blinking at the old buildings, but rather they interrogated, criticized, and analyzed the journey (and their fellow passengers) from specific stances, claiming that stations are not simply "given" but constructed, contextualized, and based on concealed assumptions and ideologies. The time-honored Circle Line was being seen as claustrophobic and, in a word, circular.

And so, due to mass popular demand, new branch lines were created. They may have started from some of the old stations, but they struck out in new directions, sometimes overland to take in the linking scenery, to cater to new intellectual communities. Underlying all these communities has been one assumption that ironically marked the point, some fifty-odd years after Einstein created the theory of relativity in science, of this theory's application to literature and, more broadly, social analysis. Whereas the old denizens of the Circle Line, as they endlessly went round and round the still center of London's turning world, are characterized as essentialists for whom truth is Truth, the new travelers believed that truth is at best relative to where one stands on fundamental issues such as gender, class, race, individualism, and community. In the new language, relativity becomes "contin-

gency" and "positionality," but despite the quasi-technical vocabulary, this concept is a rediscovery of the underpinning
strategy of More's *Utopia* and Shakespeare's drama of multiple
conversation. If these were the new travelers, then they are
reaching into often bizarre therapeutic applications of Shakespeare. Every year brings books onto the market claiming that
Shakespeare can enhance everything from our karma, our inner
child, and our wealth-creation to our sex lives, but so far these
have not been accepted into the serious Shakespeare Underground. Even Management Studies, a phenomenon of the 1990s
generated by a tribe of middle-managers made redundant by re-
cession, has got in on the act. Courses are being offered that
probe into the cases of Richard III, Henry V, and Macbeth as ex-
emplars of good management practice.

The first branch line of the Shakespeare underground began
with history and bravely headed north to Milton Keynes, under
the impetus of Arnold Kettle's vision for the Open University.
Kettle was a Marxist, and his embrace of social conscience, his
struggle against institutional vested interests, and his historical
determinism could amply cater to new readings of history: new
historicism, cultural materialism, and feminism, movements that
gathered momentum in the 1970s and 1980s. Meanwhile, quite
different kinds of travelers hopped on at history and off at either
theater or biography, but then headed north again, some of them
alighting at stations such as psychiatry, metacriticism, or film.
Some of them never got back on the train but others arrived eventually at cultural materialism, at first inhabited by a confluence
of Welsh scholars (Raymond Williams and Terry Hawkes) and
gritty northerners from places such as Sunderland Polytechnic
(as it was in the 1970s). Ever-expanding communities grew up
around each new station, and whole industries were generated.
Meanwhile, over on the east side in the 1980s a different line
again was constructed. Since the English do not without protest
move to embrace Europe, this line came as a hard-won incursion
from France, against great odds and lack of funding. "Wherefore
to Dover?" has always been the slightly outraged refrain from the
seat of empire in the West End of London—who on earth would
want to go that in that direction?[1] Anglo-Saxons have always had
trouble pronouncing names like Derrida, Foucault, and Lacan,
though they are more readily acceptable in North America and
Australia. A pincer movement from new American tourists in the
west and European intellectuals in the south created a need for
this branch line, although it has probably not been used as much

as was expected. Meanwhile, during the 1990s, yet another line was required, this time to the far south—what is called in Britain the far east—which was either entered by an express train from cultural materialism in the north, or joined from the airport bringing travelers from Asia, Africa, and Australia. With a barely disguised resentment of the old empire, it is named the Post-Colonial Line.

THE LONELINESS OF THE LONG DISTANCE REVIEWER

I have, by the kind of self-imposed masochism called reviewing, which I prefer more grandly to name metacriticism, traveled on all these lines from time to time. Like most scholars of my generation, the central line was my earliest experience of the journey, but also like most of my generation I came to realize that I may have been tricked into thinking it led somewhere when in fact it led back to the same increasingly familiar places. The new branch lines came as a refreshing change.

I am not sure why I was invited to write the review "The Year's Contribution in Critical Studies" for *Shakespeare Survey*, and even less do I know why I accepted the crippling task for five years. It is one of those coincidences that intrigues nobody but me that I am exactly as old as *Shakespeare Survey*, and always will be until one of us (surely it will be me first) falls and ceases. I don't exactly know what that means in terms of chaos theory, but it does lead me to reflect on the *Survey* from time to time. Looking back is like traveling backward from the newer extensions to the underground system to the original tracks. It may not look like it for such a respectable journal, but in fact the *Survey* has reflected new critical initiatives as they came along, mainly because it has been linked with biennial conferences that inevitably engage with current issues, and partly because its review articles of the year's work, while inevitably selective, incomplete, and opinionated, do bring to attention new developments. The *Survey* has always published a plural offering, ranging from the history of some theme in Shakespeare studies, through source studies, close analyses of plays, and Shakespearean films, to theory-driven articles. It has been open to genuinely international offerings, publishing articles from every country where Shakespeare is researched (which means every populated country). Inevitably, it has reflected the changes, even if there is a time lag of two or three years. There have been only four editors: Allardyce Nichol tended to let the *Survey* reflect his interests in the immediacy of theater and the distance of history. The socialist-inclining Kenneth Muir took over in the 1970s, the omnivorous Stanley Wells in the late 1980s, and Peter Holland in 2000. The consistency of the journal over its history must owe something to their influence, which has been benignly disposed to change. The American counterpart, *Shakespeare Quarterly*, in contrast, appears at least from the outside to be susceptible to periodical lurches in unexpected directions, as the personnel of collective editorial boards change.

Despite the onerous nature of the task, for five years I enjoyed reviewing the critical books for the *Survey*. I was always an apprehensive and somewhat reluctant writer for this exercise, since I have never been a great reader of criticism, except under duress. I was more comfortable with contemporary Renaissance sources than recent, but this has led me nowadays to preach to anybody willing to listen that recent theory is a revival of humanist rhetoric. In this sense I have not been uncomfortable with new theory because it feels familiar in its underlying concepts, such as the assumption that drama and literature are constructed rather than given, that they are made of nothing but language, based as much on issues as personalities, driven by ideological (didactic) concerns, and wittily playing off relative positions against each other, as in More's *Utopia* and almost by definition in Shakespeare's theater of dialogic conflict. From many books nowadays we see the political interventionism of Renaissance literature and a form of class analysis anticipating Marxism; from the avalanche of books by feminist critics we see that Shakespeare's plays can at least provide sites of contestation for gender theorists; and from the theories and practices of Bertolt Brecht we find the most radical theatrical developments in the twentieth century actually derived from the Elizabethan open, epic stage. From my own reading of *The Tempest* I would argue that this play, far from being an apology for colonization as many today argue, lays the groundwork for postcolonial theory by giving a range of attitudes to colonization, from Caliban, Gonzalo, and Antonio to Prospero. And if it is one of the tenets of postcolonialism as well as feminism and deconstructionism that margins become centers, the disenfranchised and silent become noisy presences, then we are all familiar with the moments in Shakespeare when the marginalized suddenly intervene: Barnardine's refusal to die for the convenience of a plot, the servant who stands up to Cornwall and attempts to stop the blinding of Gloucester, the disgruntled citizens in *Coriolanus*, Cinna the poet, and so on. These transgressions of narrativity can lead in interesting postmodern directions, including "gaps," deferrals, and differences—the announcement on at least one underground station today still has a mellifluous voice intoning constantly, "Mind the gap."

I referred in passing to chaos theory, and this gives a general model for contemplating the future of Shakespeare criticism. As I understand it, scientific chaos boils down to the phenomenon that predicting future events from the present is impossible because each event opens up an infinity of possible choices and lines for development; but that looking back from some vantage in the present and then the future we can see that everything was logical, if unexpected, and connected causally. Once again the train offers an image: we have free and unfettered choices (though nowadays we might dispute this) to board any train leaving from a particular platform and to depart at any other station; but once we have chosen we are inexorably committed to a certain journey until the next choice comes up. Bassanio's choice of caskets looks something like our choice of the future—counterlogical and yet in retrospect inevitable.

Nobody in 1960 could have predicted the current pluralism and diversity, the unpackaging of a canon, along with mesmeric returns to Shakespeare to test every new theory; and yet in retrospect it all had a certain inevitability. A more intriguing but analogous phenomenon is that, at least at universities I know, when Shakespeare ceased to be compulsory for students the numbers remained high: for example, at the University of Western Australia more students choose Shakespeare than almost any other area for study. All we can do now is hazard guesses about the growth points that will lead to the certainly unexpected future. The one thing that is certain is that there is no turning back the clock. Although the old Central Line will always be there, increasingly shabby-genteel, it will never again be exclusive or even essential traveling; and though some of the new branch lines might wither away through disuse, new ones will be built from them.

The other reasonably confident prediction one can make is that Shakespeare's plays will continue to be the testing ground for theory as it evolves and revolves. In the past, even movements that sought to dislodge Shakespeare altogether from his central position, not only in academia but in Britain's Royal Academy for Dramatic Art or Australia's National Institute of Dramatic Art, have ended up with an almost resigned fatalism reclaiming him.

Cultural studies and cultural materialism both tried to counter what seemed reactionary high art, only to discover in the cinema that Shakespeare is simultaneously a perennial bastion of popular culture, or at least a point where popular culture aims at legitimacy. Marxism tried to attack the absence of socialist realism and the prevalence of aristocratic and bourgeois attitudes in Shakespeare's plays, only to discover that these oppositional critiques had been found by Marx himself within the plays. Feminism at one of its stages took Shakespeare as abhorrently exemplary of a culture of patriarchy and male violence, only to discover once again that such attacks had been anticipated, addressed, and preempted. Whole books are written on Shakespeare by postcolonialists to show that whole books on Shakespeare should not be written.

In reading and thinking about changes in Shakespearean criticism over the last thirty or so years, I think it is possible to be afflicted with the traveler's melancholy of Jacques in *As You Like It*, one who has sold his own lands to see others'. And yet the opposite also has its dangers. Those who adopt a single-minded theoretical stance and claim the authority of a consistent perspective are rapidly dislodged by others. Among others, Derrida, Foucault, and Kristeva not so long ago seemed to hold such subtle and self-reflexive theoretical positions that all that seemed possible in the future was a steady application of their theories; but already the invocation of the names shows signs of losing its mantric qualities. Certainly each opened up a genuinely new way of looking at things that has been fruitfully absorbed into Shakespeare criticism—language as play and as freewheeling rhetoric, the contingency of history, the unnaturalness of gender divisions—but these were to be incorporated and superseded by the next. And while the figures themselves remain inescapable influences for radically questioning our assumptions, their followers, the Derrideans, Foucaultians, and all are already in danger of seeming as dated as Leavisites.

But in a sense this very pluralism, contradictoriness, and trickiness of the field—the inbuilt obsolescence of any theory, whether it depends on a totalizing ideology or rests content with fragmentation and disruption—suggest that to cope definitively with Shakespeare at least is a key to future developments. A paradigm text of the English Renaissance is, to my mind, More's *Utopia*, and its strategy informs a host of works in the sixteenth and seventeenth centuries, preeminently Shakespeare's. With rhetorical wit, More juxtaposes a set of incompatible worldviews—

idealistic and pragmatic, individualistic and communitarian, theory-driven and empiricist—and rather than providing or implying a master narrative to resolve the contradictions, he lets them stand unmediated, independently and interdependently. Critical attempts to mediate or resolve are baffled into holding at best half-truths, which implies that there is another truth available that is equally cogent. The same can be said of Shakespeare's plays, except that since in his drama there are not just two interlocutors but many, multiple linguistically coded worldviews jostle against each other. Perfect examples could be found by inspecting the fluctuating history of critical approaches to *Henry V* and *Hamlet*.

There have always been critics who embraced rather than struggled against this realization. Keats's favoring of the "negative capability" of Shakespeare's plays over the "egotistical sublime" of the epic narratives of Milton and Wordsworth sets the lead. A. P. Rossiter coined the phrase "radical ambivalence," while Norman Rabkin used "the complementary vision." William Empson's types of ambiguity and of pastoral and his exploration of "complex words" depend on the same tolerance of contradictions, and his work, as many critics currently acknowledge, is still surprisingly fertile. Placed beside the multidimensional pluralities of today's theorists, these writers seem quiet precursors.

One suburb that seems to me not yet fully developed, and one with the capacity to require an underground of its own in the future, is what we now call feminist or gender studies, along with its subgrouping, queer theory. It seems, of all the movements, the one that holds within itself a genuinely radical challenge toward a new conception of the field. Oddly enough, it may move away from its roots in gender construction and into virtually every other area of aesthetics and politics, because its underlying analysis has the political inclusiveness to enable a rethinking of all issues and to generate a new kind of literary history and criticism, reassessing received authority itself from the point of view of underclasses, the disenfranchised, and resistant readers. It holds the strengths of a scholarly historicization of issues and an adaptable, flexible, but emphatic point of view. Already I would say new historicism and some other new approaches are moving toward, or perhaps even assuming, this position. Cultural materialism, which laid foundations for such a movement, is also converging on it.

The other huge development that is already gathering swell and looks like being a potentially endless suburb or small city is the study of the reception and appropriation of Shakespeare in different countries, class contexts, and media. The huge success of films such as Baz Luhrmann's *Romeo + Juliet* and the very different Shakespeare films of Kenneth Branagh invite attention, at least in cultural materialist terms, to ascertain the markets that the films have reached in a global industry, and why. To link up feminism and reception, there has been surprisingly little work on the gendered reader in the Renaissance—the "fair ladies" addressed by Sidney in *Arcadia,* and the many who were undoubtedly in Shakespeare's audiences. A third tangent points to a different future again. Ficto-criticism openly admits the constructed and contextualized nature of all writing, to the extent that originary literary artifact merges with its interpretation, text is pretext as well as context for writing, and criticism is as creatively self-fashioning and as worthy of study as works that we call literary.

If forced to look forward, I would say that these three areas will predominate in years to come: rewriting literary history from a feminist or at least gendered point of view; rewriting literary history more generally from the point of view of receivers of texts rather than texts themselves; and rewriting literary history from a ficto-criticism (or what is sometimes called postcriticism) point of view. But history shames would-be prophets by twisting in all sorts of haphazard and unforeseeable ways, just as the London underground was expanded to cater for or even create new communities. I would certainly not "give and hazard all" on any of these hunches.[2]

CODA

At the end of that most artificial and bookish comedy *Love's Labor's Lost,* there is a sudden switch of tone and perspective, not only away from nuptials to harsh penance but also away from poetic drama to balladlike songs of spring and winter. Here is a similar switch. For all the intellectual games we may play with them, drama and literature are powerful forces. Poets have always been imprisoned and assassinated for alerting people to uncomfortable truths about their societies. Without reverting to some lost generation of Victorian critics, I think we can fairly acknowledge that in some way or another reading and attending plays has helped to fashion each of us individually—our worldviews, preoccupations, and most characteristic mental gestures. Plays have given us languages of reason and emotion, and language is feeling and thought, and as full of the body as the mind. Poetic language can invest with dignity experiences that might at best be chaotic and at worst humiliating or degrading. *Romeo and Juliet* gave us a specific way of thinking about and therefore experiencing love; the death of Cordelia perhaps once moved us to know exactly what despair feels like. We would not have devoted our professional lives to this particular pursuit if something like this is not—or was not at some stage of our lives—a trust. We cannot all be victims of false consciousness. It is relatively painless to argue that literature is as much a social construction as political parties or news broadcasts, but not so painless to rationalize away authenticated cases of suicides by teenagers obsessed by the latest film version of *Romeo and Juliet*. If we as critics and scholars cannot in some way convey that Shakespeare's plays are and have been agencies for change, that they *matter*, then it is not easy to justify why we are doing what we are doing.

NOTES

1. *King Lear* 3.7.52.
2. *Merchant of Venice* 2.7.9.

Notes on Contributors

LAURA RAIDONIS BATES is Assistant Professor of English at Indiana State University. She earned her Ph.D. in comparative literature at the University of Chicago, where her dissertation on the political appropriation of Shakespeare in the former Soviet Union was directed by David Bevington. She has taught Shakespeare to male and female inmates in correctional facilities, ranging from minimum to maximum to supermaximum security (solitary confinement), and has published related articles in *Shakespeare Magazine* and *Shakespeare Yearbook*.

RON BEDFORD is Reader in English at the University of New England in Australia. In addition to numerous articles on sixteenth- and seventeenth-century literature and drama, he is the author of *The Defence of Truth: Herbert of Cherbury and the Seventeenth Century* and *Dialogues with Convention: Readings in Renaissance Poetry*. He has recently completed a new study of irony in Milton's work.

SHARON A. BEEHLER is Associate Professor of English at Montana State University in Bozeman, Montana. She is the author of numerous articles on Shakespeare pedagogy and criticism, but has recently turned her investigations to the Renaissance use of *Kairos*. She is currently coediting volume 12 of *Shakespeare Yearbook* and is Editor of *Quidditas*, the journal of the Rocky Mountain Medieval and Renaissance Association. She is also coediting (with Linda Woodbridge) a book on women and violence in the early modern period.

ANN BLAKE is Honorary Associate of La Trobe University, Melbourne, and formerly a Senior Lecturer. She has published articles on Shakespeare and other dramatists, on crime fiction, and on Christina Stead. She is the author of *Christina Stead's Politics of Place* (1999) and coauthor of *England through Colonial Eyes in Twentieth-Century Fiction* (2001). Her current project is an in-

317

vestigation of the "Shakespearean" qualities of the novels of Jane Austen.

BARBARA BOWEN is Associate Professor of English at the Graduate Center and Queens College, City University of New York. She is the author and editor of essays and texts on Renaissance literature and is currently researching feminist rereadings of early modern discourses.

DEREK COHEN is Professor of English at York University in Toronto. He is the author of numerous articles on Shakespeare and has published three books, *Shakespearean Motives*, *The Politics of Shakespeare*, and *Shakespeare's Culture of Violence*, and co-edited (with Deborah Heller) *Jewish Presences in English Literature*.

LLOYD DAVIS teaches in the School of English at the University of Queensland in Brisbane. He is the author of essays and books on cultural studies, Victorian and early modern literature, as well as *Guise and Disguise: Rhetoric and Characterization in the English Renaissance*. He is the editor of *Sexuality and Gender in the English Renaissance: An Annotated Edition of Contemporary Documents* and also currently edits *AUMLA*, the journal of the Australasian Universities Languages and Literature Association.

GILLIAN M. DAY is Senior Lecturer in English Literature at the University of Central England in Birmingham. She studied at the University of London and earned her master's degree and doctorate at the Shakespeare Institute of the University of Birmingham. She has taught English and drama in secondary and higher education in Britain, North America, and Scandinavia, and has held visiting lectureships at the Universities of Helsinki and Duesseldorf. She is also a visiting academic at the Shakespeare Birthplace Trust in Stratford-upon-Avon, lecturing to university groups from Europe, Scandinavia, and North America on text and theater. Her study of *Richard III at Stratford* was published in 2001.

SIMON C. ESTOK is Assistant Professor at the Catholic University of Korea, where he teaches literature and theory. He has given conference papers in Canada, the United States, Jamaica, Korea, New Zealand, South Africa, and Australia and is the author of several articles, book reviews, and notes on Shakespeare and ecocriticism, which have appeared in *PMLA, Canadian Review of Comparative Literature, Shakespeare Review,* and *Journal of English Language and Literature.* He is currently finishing a book entitled *Ecocriticism and Shakespeare.*

JEAN E. HOWARD is Professor of English at Columbia University. In addition to numerous essays in early modern studies, her publications include *Shakespeare's Art of Orchestration, The Stage and Social Struggle in Early Modern England,* and, with Phyllis Rackin, *Engendering a Nation: A Feminist Account of Shakespeare's English Histories.* She is coeditor, with Marion O'Connor, of *Shakespeare Reproduced: The Text in History and Ideology* and, with Scott Shershow, of *Marxist Shakespeares,* and is also one of the four coeditors of *The Norton Shakespeare.* She is currently at work on a study of the development of dramatic genres from 1600 to 1642, entitled *Theater of a City: Social Change and Generic Innovation on the Early Modern Stage.*

PHILIPPA KELLY is a Senior Research Fellow in English at the University of New South Wales in Sydney. She has published numerous articles on critical theory, postcolonialism, Australian literature, and the cultural production of Shakespeare. She is the author of a monograph on *King Lear* and has also edited the play for the Bell Shakespeare series. She has recently edited a collection of essays on new historicism entitled, *The Touch of the Real: Communing with the Living and the Dead: Essays in Honour of Stephen Greenblatt.*

ADRIAN KIERNANDER is Professor of Theatre Studies at the University of New England in Australia. He has published extensively in many areas of theater and is the author of *Ariane Mnouchkine and the Théâtre du Soleil.* He has directed theater productions from many different periods, including numerous plays by Shakespeare and his contemporaries. He is currently editing an edition of *Richard III.*

ARTHUR LINDLEY is Associate Professor in the Department of English Language and Literature at the National University of Singapore, specializing in early modern English literature as well as film studies. He is the author of numerous articles on medieval and Renaissance literature and of *Hyperion and the Hobbyhorse.*

IAN MACLENNAN is Director of the Theatre Arts Programme at Laurentian University, Sudbury, Ontario, Canada, as well as

Registrar of Thorneloe College at the same university. As an actor and director, he has worked in Canada, Britain, and the United States. He teaches theater history and period-style acting, and his academic interests focus on performance of medieval and Renaissance theater, particularly the role of the boy player. He has published in *Theatre Studies* and *The Royal School of Church Music in America*.

RICHARD MADELAINE, Senior Lecturer in English at the University of New South Wales, is joint series editor of the Bell Shakespeare Series, author of *Antony and Cleopatra* in the Cambridge Shakespeare in Production series, joint editor of *O Brave New World: Two Centuries of Shakespeare on the Australian Stage*, and author of numerous papers on staging and iconographical issues in the plays of Shakespeare and his Jacobean contemporaries.

MICHAEL MULLIN, Professor Emeritus of English at the University of Illinois at Urbana-Champaign, is the author of *Macbeth Onstage*, *Theatre at Stratford-upon-Avon*, and *Design by Motley*, as well as many articles about Shakespeare on stage, film, and television. He also conceived, designed, and created *Our Shakespeares: Shakespeare across Cultures*, a prototype for an interactive multimedia CD-ROM. Since 1995 he has been founder and director of the Shakespeare Globe USA Website. He is currently Senior Research Scientist at the National Center for Supercomputing Applications (NCSA), a position stemming from his Cyber-Shakespeare project. He divides his time between Champaign, Illinois, and Melbourne, Australia.

SUSAN GUSHEE O'MALLEY is Professor of English at Kingsborough Community College, City University of New York and Professor of Liberal Studies at the City University of New York Graduate School and University Center. She also teaches at the City College Center for Worker Education sponsored by City University of New York. Currently she is finishing *"Custom Is an Idiot": Jacobean Pamphlet Literature on Women* (forthcoming). Her books include *Defences of Women: Jane Anger, Rachel Speght, Ester Sowernam and Constantia Munda* for Scolar Press in the Early Modern Englishwoman series, a scholarly edition of Thomas Goffe's *The Courageous Turk*, and *The Politics of Education*.

SARA JAYNE STEEN, Professor and Chair of English at Montana State University, is the author of numerous books and articles on

Shakespeare and on early modern women writers and theater. Her books include *The Letters of Lady Arbella Stuart* and *Ambrosia in an Earthern Vessel: Three Centuries of Audience and Reader Response to the Works of Thomas Middleton*. With Elizabeth H. Hageman, she coedited a special issue of *Shakespeare Quarterly*, entitled *Teaching Judith Shakespeare*. She has received her university's highest awards for scholarship and teaching.

KIM WALKER, who sadly passed away in 2002, earned her Ph.D. from the University of Edinburgh in 1985. Since then she had published on James Shirley and on the Anglo-Irish novelist Maria Edgeworth. Her most recent books include *Women Writers of the English Renaissance* and an edition, produced in collaboration with Heidi Thomson, of Edgeworth's *Absentee*, along with a couple of the shorter tales for the Pickering and Chatto *Collected Works*. She was Senior Lecturer in the School of English, Film and Theatre at Victoria University of Wellington, New Zealand.

R. S. WHITE is Professor of English at the University of Western Australia. He is a Fellow of the Australian Humanities Academy and Vice President of the Australian and New Zealand Shakespeare Association. In addition to many essays and reviews on Renaissance literature and Shakespeare, he is the author of *"Let wonder seem familiar": Endings in Shakespeare's Romance Vision; Innocent Victims: Poetic Injustice in Shakespearean Tragedy; Keats as a Reader of Shakespeare; Shakespeare's Macbeth;* and *Natural Law in English Renaissance Literature*. He is the editor of *Hazlitt's Criticism of Shakespeare* and three critical anthologies, most recently *Romeo and Juliet*. He is also the co-editor of the essay collections, *Constructing Gender: Feminism and Literary Studies* and *Shakespeare: Readers, Audiences, Players*.

Index